TEXTS IN COMPUTER SCIENCE

Editors
David Gries
Fred B. Schneider

An Integrated Approach to Software Engineering

Third Edition

Pankaj Jalote
Indian Institute of Technology Kanpur

 Springer

Pankaj Jalote
Department of Computer Science
    and Engineering
Indian Institute of Technology
Kanpur 208016
India

Series Editors
David Gries
Fred B. Schneider
Department of Computer Science
Cornell University
Upson Hall
Ithaca, NY 14853-7501

Pankaj Jalote
Indian Institute of Technology Kanpur

Library of Congress Cataloging-in-Publication Data

A C.I.P. Catalogue record for this book is available
From the Library of Congress

ISBN-10: 0-387-20881-X (HB) ISBN-10: 0-387-28132-0 (eBook)
ISBN-13: 978-0387-20881-7 (HB) ISBN-13: 978-0387-28132-2 (eBook)

Printed in the United States of America

9 8 7 6 5 4 3 2 1   SPIN 10949597

springeronline.com

Contents

Preface to the Third Edition

An introductory course in Software Engineering remains one of the hardest subjects to teach. Much of the difficulty stems from the fact that Software Engineering is a very wide field which includes a wide range of topics. Consequently, what should be the focus of an introductory course remains a challenge with many possible viewpoints.

This third edition of the book approaches the problem from the perspective of what skills a student should possess after the introductory course, particularly if it may be the only course on software engineering in the student's program. The goal of this third edition is to impart to the student knowledge and skills that are needed to successfully execute a project of a few person-months by employing proper practices and techniques. Incidently, a vast majority of the projects executed in the industry today are of this scope—executed by a small team over a few months. Another objective of the book is to lay the foundation for the student for advanced studies in Software Engineering.

Executing any software project requires skills in two key dimensions—engineering and project management. While engineering deals with issues of architecture, design, coding, testing, etc., project management deals with planning, monitoring, risk management, etc. Consequently, this book focuses on these two dimensions, and for key tasks in each, discusses concepts and techniques that can be applied effectively on projects.

The focus of the book remains as the first course in software engineering, and it retains its character of having a running case study with most of the outputs available. This edition draws upon my experience during my sabbaticals with two software companies—Infosys Technologies and Microsoft Corporation—and my practice-oriented book *Software Project Management in Practice* (Addison-Wesley, 2002) to bring, in addition to the concepts, more elements of how these concepts are actually applied in practice.

In this edition, new material has been added on current practices, outdated material has been removed, and discussion has been sharpened. The following key additions have been made:

- In "Software Process" a discussion on the timeboxing model for iterative development and on inspection process

- In "Requirements Analysis and Specification" a description of Use Cases

- A new chapter on "Software Architecture"

- In "Project Planning" some practical techniques for estimation, scheduling, tracking, risk management, etc.

- In "Object Oriented Design", discussion on UML and on concepts like cohesion, coupling, and open-closed principle

- In "Coding" many additions have been made. These include refactoring, test driven development, and pair programming, as well as a discussion on common coding defects, coding standards, and some useful coding practices.

- In "Testing" a discussion on pair-wise testing as an approach for functional testing, defect tracking, and defect analysis and prevention

In addition to the old case study, a new case study has been added. Various work products of the case studies, including the SRS, architecture document, project plan, design document, code, and test plan, have been made available through the Web site.

A Web site has been created for this edition. In addition to outputs of the case studies, implementations of some of some of the examples are also available from the site. The site will soon include presentation slides for teaching, as well as other instructional material like examples and illustrative studies. The URL of the website is:

http://www.cse.iitk.ac.in/JaloteSEbook

I would like to express my gratitude to many people who helped me in preparing the case study. These include Kapil Narula, Ragesh Jaiswal, Vivek Pandey, Nilesh Lunawat, and Rajneesh Malviya. My special thanks to Vipindeep Vangala and Raghu Lingampally whose help in manuscript and Web site preparation allowed me to focus on the contents.

Pankaj Jalote

1

Introduction

Ask any student who has had some programming experience the following question: You are given a problem for which you have to build a software system that most students feel will be approximately 10,000 lines of (say C or Java) code. If you are working full time on it, how long will it take you to build this system?

The answer of students is generally 1 to 3 months. And, given the programming expertise of the students, there is a good chance that they will be able to build a system and demo it to the Professor within 2 months. With 2 months as the completion time, the productivity of the student will be 5,000 lines of code (LOC) per person-month.

Now let us take an alternative scenario—we act as clients and pose the same problem to a company that is in the business of developing software for clients. Though there is no "standard" productivity figure and it varies a lot, it is fair to say a productivity figure of 1,000 LOC per person-month is quite respectable (though it can be as low as 100 LOC per person-month for embedded systems). With this productivity, a team of professionals in a software organization will take 10 person-months to build this software system.

Why this difference in productivity in the two scenarios? Why is it that the same students who can produce software at a productivity of a few thousand LOC per month while in college end up producing only about a thousand LOC per month when working in a company? Why is it that students seem to be more productive in their student days than when they become professionals?

The answer, of course, is that two different things are being built in the two scenarios. In the first, a *student system* is being built whose main purpose is to demo that it works. In the second scenario, a team of professionals in an organization is building the system for a client who is paying for it, and whose business may depend on proper working of the system. As should be evident, building the latter type of software is a different problem altogether. It is this problem in which software engineering is interested. The difference between the two types of software was recognized early and the term *software engineering* was coined at NATO sponsored conferences held in Europe in the 1960s to discuss the growing software crisis and the need to focus on software development.

In the rest of the chapter we further define our problem domain. Then we discuss some of the key factors that drive software engineering. This is followed by the basic approach followed by software engineering. In the rest of the book we discuss in more detail the various aspects of the software engineering approach.

1.1   The Problem Domain

In software engineering we are not dealing with programs that people build to illustrate something or for hobby (which we are referring to as student systems). Instead the problem domain is the software that solves some problem of some users where larger systems or businesses may depend on the software, and where problems in the software can lead to significant direct or indirect loss. We refer to this software as *industrial strength software*. Let us first discuss the key difference between the student software and the industrial strength software.

1.1.1   Industrial Strength Software

A student system is primarily meant for demonstration purposes; it is generally not used for solving any real problem of any organization. Consequently, nothing of significance or importance depends on proper functioning of the software. Because nothing of significance depends on the software, the presence of "bugs" (or defects or faults) is not a major concern. Hence the software is generally not designed with quality issues like portability, robustness, reliability, and usability in mind. Also, the student software system is generally used by the developer him- or herself, therefore the need for documentation is nonexistent, and again bugs are not critical issues as the user can fix them as and when they are found.

An *industrial strength software system*, on the other hand, is built to solve some problem of a client and is used by the clients organization for operating some part of business (we use the term "business" in a very broad sense—it may be to manage inventories, finances, monitor patients, air traffic control, etc.) In other words, important activities depend on the correct functioning of the system. And a malfunction of such a system can have huge impact in terms of financial or business loss, inconvenience to users, or loss of property and life. Consequently, the software system needs to be of high quality with respect to properties like dependability, reliability, user-friendliness, etc.

This requirement of high quality has many ramifications. First, it requires that the software be thoroughly tested before being used. The need for rigorous testing increases the cost considerably. In an industrial strength software project, 30% to 50% of the total effort may be spent in testing (while in a student software even 5% may be too high!)

Second, building high quality software requires that the development be broken into phases such that output of each phase is evaluated and reviewed so bugs can be removed. This desire to partition the overall problem into phases and identify defects early requires more documentation, standards, processes, etc. All these increase the effort required to build the software— hence the productivity of producing industrial strength software is generally much lower than for producing student software.

Industrial strength software also has other properties which do not exist in student software systems. Typically, for the same problem, the detailed requirements of what the software should do increase considerably. Besides quality requirements, there are requirements of backup and recovery, fault tolerance, following of standards, portability, etc. These generally have the effect of making the software system more complex and larger. The size of the industrial strength software system may be two times or more than the student system for the same problem.

Overall, if we assume one-fifth productivity, and an increase in size by a factor of two for the same problem, an industrial strength software system will take about 10 times as much effort to build as a student software system for the same problem. The rule of thumb Brooks gives also says that industrial strength software may cost about 10 times the student software[25]. The software industry is largely interested in developing industrial strength software, and the area of software engineering focuses on how to build such systems. In the rest of the book, when we use the term software, we mean industrial strength software.

IEEE defines *software* as the collection of computer programs, procedures, rules, and associated documentation and data [91]. This definition clearly states that software is not just programs, but includes all the associated documentation and data. This implies that the discipline dealing with the development of software should not deal only with developing programs, but with developing all the things that constitute software.

1.1.2 Software is Expensive

Industrial strength software is very expensive primarily due to the fact that software development is extremely labor-intensive. To get an idea of the costs involved, let us consider the current state of practice in the industry. Lines of code (LOC) or thousands of lines of code (KLOC) delivered is by far the most commonly used measure of software size in the industry.

As the main cost of producing software is the manpower employed, the cost of developing software is generally measured in terms of person-months of effort spent in development. And productivity is frequently measured in the industry in terms of LOC (or KLOC) per person-month.

The productivity in the software industry for writing fresh code generally ranges from 300 to 1,000 LOC per person-month. That is, for developing software, the average productivity per person, per month, over the entire development cycle is about 300 to 1,000 LOC. And software companies charge the client for whom they are developing the software upwards of $100,000 per person-year or more than $8,000 per person-month (which comes to about $50 per hour). With the current productivity figures of the industry, this translates into a cost per line of code of approximately $8 to $25. In other words, each line of delivered code costs between $8 and $25 at current costs and productivity levels! And even small projects can easily end up with software of 50,000 LOC. With this productivity, such a software project will cost between $ 0.5 million and $1.25 million!

Given the current compute power of machines, such software can easily be hosted on a workstation or a small server. This implies that software that can cost more than a million dollars can run on hardware that costs at most tens of thousands of dollars, clearly showing that the cost of hardware on which such an application can run is a fraction of the cost of the application software! This example clearly shows that not only is software very expensive, it indeed forms the major component of the total automated system, with the hardware forming a very small component. This is shown in the classic hardware-software cost reversal chart in Figure 1.1 [17].

As Figure 1.1 shows, in the early days, the cost of hardware used to

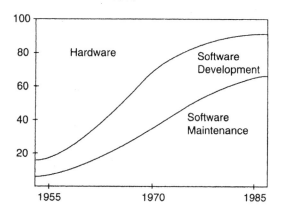

Figure 1.1: Hardware-software cost trend.

dominate the system cost. As the cost of hardware has lessened over the years and continues to decline, and as the power of hardware doubles every 2 years or so (the Moore's law) enabling larger software systems to be run on it, cost of software has now become the dominant factor in systems.

1.1.3 Late and Unreliable

Despite considerable progress in techniques for developing software, software development remains a weak area. In a survey of over 600 firms, more than 35% reported having some computer-related development project that they categorized as a *runaway*[131]. A runaway is not a project that is somewhat late or somewhat over budget—it is one where the budget and schedule are out of control. The problem has become so severe that it has spawned an industry of its own; there are consultancy companies that advise how to rein such projects, and one such company had more than $30 million in revenues from more than 20 clients [131].

Similarly, a large number of instances have been quoted regarding the unreliability of software; the software does not do what it is supposed to do or does something it is not supposed to do. In one defense survey, it was reported that more than 70% of all the equipment failures were due to software! And this is in systems that are loaded with electrical, hydraulic, and mechanical systems. This just indicates that all other engineering disciplines have advanced far more than software engineering, and a system comprising the products of various engineering disciplines finds that software is the

weakest component. Failure of an early Apollo flight was also attributed
to software. Similarly, failure of a test firing of a missile in India was attributed to software problems. Many banks have lost millions of dollars due
to inaccuracies and other problems in their software [122].

A note about the cause of unreliability in software: software failures are
different from failures of, say, mechanical or electrical systems. Products of
these other engineering disciplines fail because of the change in physical or
electrical properties of the system caused by aging. A software product, on
the other hand, never wears out due to age. In software, failures occur due
to bugs or errors that get introduced during the design and development
process. Hence, even though a software system may fail after operating
correctly for some time, the bug that causes that failure was there from the
start! It only got executed at the time of the failure. This is quite different
from other systems, where if a system fails, it generally means that sometime
before the failure the system developed some problem (due to aging) that
did not exist earlier.

1.1.4 Maintenance and Rework

Once the software is delivered and deployed, it enters the *maintenance* phase.
Why is maintenance needed for software, when software does not age? Software needs to be maintained not because some of its components wear out
and need to be replaced, but because there are often some residual errors
remaining in the system that must be removed as they are discovered. It
is commonly believed that the state of the art today is such that almost
all software that is developed has residual errors, or bugs, in it. Many of
these surface only after the system has been in operation, sometimes for a
long time. These errors, once discovered, need to be removed, leading to the
software being changed. This is sometimes called *corrective maintenance*.

Even without bugs, software frequently undergoes change. The main
reason is that software often must be upgraded and enhanced to include
more features and provide more services. This also requires modification of
the software. It has been argued that once a software system is deployed,
the environment in which it operates changes. Hence, the needs that initiated the software development also change to reflect the needs of the new
environment. Hence, the software must adapt to the needs of the changed
environment. The changed software then changes the environment, which in
turn requires further change. This phenomenon is sometimes called the *law
of software evolution*. Maintenance due to this phenomenon is sometimes

called *adaptive maintenance.*

Though maintenance is not considered a part of software development, it is an extremely important activity in the life of a software product. If we consider the total life of software, the cost of maintenance generally exceeds the cost of developing the software! The maintenance-to-development-cost ratio has been variously suggested as 80:20, 70:30, or 60:40. Figure 1.1 also shows how the maintenance costs are increasing.

Maintenance work is based on existing software, as compared to development work that creates new software. Consequently, maintenance revolves around understanding existing software and maintainers spend most of their time trying to understand the software they have to modify. Understanding the software involves understanding not only the code but also the related documents. During the modification of the software, the effects of the change have to be clearly understood by the maintainer because introducing undesired side effects in the system during modification is easy. To test whether those aspects of the system that are not supposed to be modified are operating as they were before modification, *regression testing* is done. Regression testing involves executing old test cases to test that no new errors have been introduced.

Thus, maintenance involves understanding the existing software (code and related documents), understanding the effects of change, making the changes—to both the code and the documents—testing the new parts, and retesting the old parts that were not changed. Because often during development, the needs of the maintainers are not kept in mind, few support documents are produced during development to help the maintainer. The complexity of the maintenance task, coupled with the neglect of maintenance concerns during development, makes maintenance the most costly activity in the life of software product.

Maintenance is one form of change that typically is done after the software development is completed and the software has been deployed. However, there are other forms of changes that lead to rework during the software development itself.

One of the biggest problems in software development, particularly for large and complex systems, is that what is desired from the software (i.e., the requirements) is not understood. To completely specify the requirements, *all* the functionality, interfaces, and constraints have to be specified before software development has commenced! In other words, for specifying the requirements, the clients and the developers have to *visualize* what the software behavior should be once it is developed. This is very hard to do, particularly for large and complex systems. So, what generally happens is that the development proceeds when it is believed that the requirements are generally in good shape. However, as time goes by and the understanding of the system improves, the clients frequently discover additional requirements they had not specified earlier. This leads to requirements getting changed. This change leads to *rework*; the requirements, the design, the code all have to be changed to accommodate the new or changed requirements.

Just uncovering requirements that were not understood earlier is not the only reason for this change and rework. Software development of large and complex systems can take a few years. And with the passage of time, the needs of the clients change. After all, the current needs, which initiate the software product, are a reflection of current times. As times change, so do the needs. And, obviously, the clients want the system deployed to satisfy their most current needs. This change of needs while the development is going on also leads to rework.

In fact, changing requirements and associated rework are a major problem of the software industry. It is estimated that rework costs are 30 to 40% of the development cost [22]. In other words, of the total development effort, rework due to various changes consume about 30 to 40% of the effort! No wonder change and rework is a major contributor to the software crisis. However, unlike the issues discussed earlier, the problem of rework and change is not just a reflection of the state of software development, as changes are frequently initiated by clients as their needs change.

1.2   The Software Engineering Challenges

Now we have a better understanding of the problem domain that software engineering deals with, let us orient our discussion to Software Engineering itself. *Software engineering* is defined as the systematic approach to the development, operation, maintenance, and retirement of software [91]. In this book we will primarily focus on development.

The use of the term *systematic approach* for the development of software implies that methodologies are used for developing software which are repeatable. That is, if the methodologies are applied by different groups of people, similar software will be produced. In essence, the goal of software engineering is to take software development closer to science and engineering and away from ad-hoc approaches for development whose outcomes are not predictable but which have been used heavily in the past and still continue

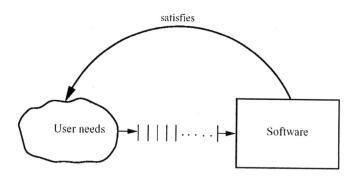

Figure 1.2: Basic problem.

to be used for developing software.

As mentioned, industrial strength software is meant to solve some problem of the client. (We use the term client in a very general sense meaning the people whose needs are to be satisfied by the software.) The problem therefore is to (systematically) develop software to satisfy the needs of some users or clients. This fundamental problem that software engineering deals with is shown in Figure 1.2.

Though the basic problem is to systematically develop software to satisfy the client, there are some factors which affect the approaches selected to solve the problem. These factors are the primary forces that drive the progress and development in the field of software engineering. We consider these as the primary challenges for software engineering and discuss some of the key ones here.

1.2.1 Scale

A fundamental factor that software engineering must deal with is the issue of scale; development of a very large system requires a very different set of methods compared to developing a small system. In other words, the methods that are used for developing small systems generally *do not scale up* to large systems. An example will illustrate this point. Consider the problem of counting people in a room versus taking a census of a country. Both are essentially counting problems. But the methods used for counting people in a room (probably just go row-wise or column-wise) will just not work when taking a census. Different set of methods will have to be used for

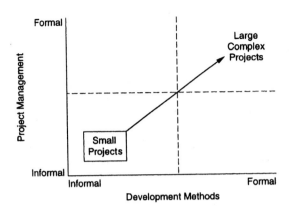

Figure 1.3: The problem of scale.

conducting a census, and the census problem will require considerably more management, organization, and validation, in addition to counting.

Similarly, methods that one can use to develop programs of a few hundred lines cannot be expected to work when software of a few hundred thousand lines needs to be developed. A different set of methods must be used for developing large software. Any large project involves the use of engineering and project management. For software projects, by engineering we mean the methods, procedures, and tools that are used. In small projects, informal methods for development and management can be used. However, for large projects, both have to be much more formal, as shown in Figure 1.3.

As shown in the figure, when dealing with a small software project, the engineering capability required is low (all you need to know is how to program and a bit of testing) and the project management requirement is also low. However, when the scale changes to large, to solve such problems properly, it is essential that we move in both directions—the engineering methods used for development need to be more formal, and the project management for the development project also needs to be more formal. For example, if we leave 50 bright programmers together (who know how to develop small programs well) without formal management and development procedures and ask them to develop an on-line inventory control system for an automotive manufacturer, it is highly unlikely that they will produce anything of use. To successfully execute the project, a proper method for engineering the system has to be used and the project has to be tightly managed to make sure that methods are indeed being followed and that cost, schedule, and quality are

Size (KLOC)	Software	Languages
980	gcc	ansic, cpp, yacc
320	perl	perl, ansic, sh
305	teTeX	ansic, perl
200	openssl	ansic, cpp, perl
200	Python	python, ansic
100	apache	ansic, sh
90	cvs	ansic, sh
65	sendmail	ansic
60	xfig	ansic
45	gnuplot	ansic, lisp
38	openssh	ansic
30,000	Red Hat Linux	ansic, cpp
40,000	Windows XP	ansic, cpp

Table 1.1: Size in KLOC of some well known products.

under control.

There is no universally acceptable definition of what is a "small" project and what is a "large" project, and the scales are clearly changing with time. However, informally, we can use the order of magnitudes and say that a project is *small* if its size is less than 10 KLOC, *medium* if the size is less than 100 KLOC (and more than 10), *large* if the size is less than one million LOC, and *very large* if the size is many million LOC. To get an idea of the sizes of some real software products, the approximate sizes of some well known products is given in Table 1.1.

1.2.2 Quality and Productivity

An engineering discipline, almost by definition, is driven by practical parameters of cost, schedule, and quality. A solution that takes enormous resources and many years may not be acceptable. Similarly, a poor-quality solution, even at low cost, may not be of much use. Like all engineering disciplines, software engineering is driven by the three major factors: cost, schedule, and quality.

The cost of developing a system is the cost of the resources used for the system, which, in the case of software, is dominated by the manpower cost, as development is largely labor-intensive. Hence, the cost of a software project

Figure 1.4: Software quality attributes.

is often measured in terms of person-months, i.e., the cost is considered to be the total number of person-months spent in the project. (Person-months can be converted into a dollar amount by multiplying it with the average dollar cost, including the cost of overheads like hardware and tools, of one person-month.)

Schedule is an important factor in many projects. Business trends are dictating that the time to market of a product should be reduced; that is, the cycle time from concept to delivery should be small. For software this means that it needs to be developed faster.

Productivity in terms of output (KLOC) per person-month can adequately capture both cost and schedule concerns. If productivity is higher, it should be clear that the cost in terms of person-months will be lower (the same work can now be done with fewer person-months.) Similarly, if productivity is higher, the potential of developing the software in shorter time improves—a team of higher productivity will finish a job in lesser time than a same-size team with lower productivity. (The actual time the project will take, of course, depends also on the number of people allocated to the project.) In other words, productivity is a key driving factor in all businesses and desire for high productivity dictates, to a large extent, how things are done.

The other major factor driving any production discipline is quality. Today, quality is a main mantra, and business strategies are designed around quality. Clearly, developing high-quality software is another fundamental goal of software engineering. However, while cost is generally well understood, the concept of quality in the context of software needs further discussion. We use the international standard on software product quality as the basis of our discussion here [94].

According to the quality model adopted by this standard, software quality comprises of six main attributes (called characteristics) as shown in Figure 1.4 [94]. These six attributes have detailed characteristics which are considered the basic ones and which can and should be measured using suitable metrics. At the top level, for a software product, these attributes can be defined as follows [94]:

- **Functionality.** The capability to provide functions which meet stated and implied needs when the software is used

- **Reliability.** The capability to maintain a specified level of performance

- **Usability.** The capability to be understood, learned, and used

- **Efficiency.** The capability to provide appropriate performance relative to the amount of resources used

- **Maintainability.** The capability to be modified for purposes of making corrections, improvements, or adaptation

- **Portability.** The capability to be adapted for different specified enviornments without applying actions or means other than those provided for this purpose in the product

The characteristics for the different attributes provide further details. Usability, for example, has characteristics of understandability, learnability, operability; maintainability has changeability, testability, stability, etc.; while portability has adaptability, installability, etc. Functionality includes suitability (whether appropriate set of functions are provided,) accuracy (the results are accurate,) and security. Note that in this classification, security is considered a characteristic of functionality, and is defined as "the capability to protect information and data so that unauthorized persons or systems cannot read or modify them, and authorized persons or systems are not denied access to them."

There are two important consequences of having multiple dimensions to quality. First, software quality cannot be reduced to a single number (or a single parameter). And second, the concept of quality is project-specific. For an ultra-sensitive project, reliability may be of utmost importance but not usability, while in a commercial package for playing games on a PC, usability may be of utmost importance and not reliability. Hence, for each software development project, a quality objective must be specified before the development starts, and the goal of the development process should be to satisfy that quality objective.

Despite the fact that there are many quality factors, reliability is generally accepted to be the main quality criterion. As unreliability of software comes due to presence of defects in the software, one measure of quality is the number of defects in the delivered software per unit size (generally taken to be thousands of lines of code, or KLOC). With this as the major quality criterion, the quality objective is to reduce the number of defects per KLOC as much as possible. Current best practices in software engineering have been able to reduce the defect density to less than 1 defect per KLOC.

It should be pointed out that to use this definition of quality, what a defect is must be clearly defined. A defect could be some problem in the software that causes the software to crash or a problem that causes an output to be not properly aligned or one that misspells some word, etc. The exact definition of what is considered a defect will clearly depend on the project or the standards the organization developing the project uses (typically it is the latter).

1.2.3 Consistency and Repeatability

There have been many instances of high quality software being developed with very high productivity. But, there have been many more instances of software with poor quality or productivity being developed. A key challenge that software engineering faces is how to ensure that successful results can be repeated, and there can be some degree of consistency in quality and productivity.

We can say that an organization that develops one system with high quality and reasonable productivity, but is not able to maintain the quality and productivity levels for other projects, does not know good software engineering. A goal of software engineering methods is that system after system can be produced with high quality and productivity. That is, the methods that are being used are repeatable across projects leading to consistency in the quality of software produced.

An organization involved in software development not only wants high quality and productivity, but it wants these consistently. In other words, a software development organization would like to produce consistent quality software with consistent productivity. Consistency of performance is an important factor for any organization; it allows an organization to predict the outcome of a project with reasonable accuracy, and to improve its processes to produce higher-quality products and to improve its productivity. Without consistency, even estimating cost for a project will become difficult.

Achieving consistency is an important problem that software engineering has to tackle. As can be imagined, this requirement of consistency will force some standardized procedures to be followed for developing software. There are no globally accepted methodologies and different organizations use different ones. However, within an organization, consistency is achieved by using its chosen methodologies in a consistent manner. Frameworks like ISO9001 and the Capability Maturity Model (CMM) encourage organizations to standardize methodologies, use them consistently, and improve them based on experience. We will discuss this issue a bit more in the next chapter.

1.2.4 Change

We have discussed above how maintenance and rework are very expensive and how they are an integral part of the problem domain that software engineering deals with. In todays world change in business is very rapid. As businesses change, they require that the software supporting to change. Overall, as the world changes faster, software has to change faster.

Rapid change has a special impact on software. As software is easy to change due to its lack of physical properties that may make changing harder, the expectation is much more from software for change.

Therefore, one challenge for software engineering is to accommodate and embrace change. As we will see, different approaches are used to handle change. But change is a major driver today for software engineering. Approaches that can produce high quality software at high productivity but cannot accept and accommodate change are of little use today—they can solve only very few problems that are change resistant.

1.3 The Software Engineering Approach

We now understand the problem domain and the basic factors that drive software engineering. We can view high quality and productivity (Q&P) as the basic objective which is to be achieved consistently for large scale problems and under the dynamics of changes. The Q&P achieved during a project will clearly depend on many factors, but the three main forces that govern Q&P are the people, processes, and technology, often called the Iron Triangle, as shown in Figure 1.5.

So, for high Q&P good technology has to be used, good processes or methods have to be used, and the people doing the job have to be properly

Figure 1.5: The iron triangle.

trained. In software engineering, the focus is primarily on processes, which were referred to as systematic approach in the definition given earlier. As processes form the heart of software engineering (with tools and technology providing support to efficiently execute the processes,) in this book we will focus primarily on processes. Process is what takes us from user needs to the software that satisfies the needs in Figure 1.2.

The basic approach of software engineering is to separate the process for developing software from the developed product (i.e., the software). The premise is that to a large degree the software process determines the quality of the product and productivity achieved. Hence to tackle the problem domain and successfully face the challenges that software engineering faces, one must focus on the software process. Design of proper software processes and their control then becomes a key goal of software engineering research. It is this focus on process that distinguishes Software Engineering from most other computing disciplines. Most other computing disciplines focus on some type of product—algorithms, operating systems, databases, etc.—while software engineering focuses on the process for producing the products. It is essentially the software equivalent of "manufacturing engineering." Though we will discuss more about processes in the next chapter, we briefly discuss two key aspects here—the development process and managing the development process.

1.3.1   Phased Development Process

A development process consists of various phases, each phase ending with a defined output. The phases are performed in an order specified by the process model being followed. The main reason for having a phased process is that it breaks the problem of developing software into successfully performing a set of phases, each handling a different concern of software development. This ensures that the cost of development is lower than what it would have been if the whole problem was tackled together. Furthermore, a phased process allows proper checking for quality and progress at some defined points during the development (end of phases). Without this, one would have to wait until the end to see what software has been produced. Clearly, this will not work for large systems. Hence, for managing the complexity, project tracking, and quality, all the development processes consist of a set of phases. A phased development process is central to the software engineering approach for solving the software crisis.

Various process models have been proposed for developing software. In fact, most organizations that follow a process have their own version. We will discuss some of the common models in the next chapter. In general, however, we can say that any problem solving in software must consist of requirement specification for understanding and clearly stating the problem, design for deciding a plan for a solution, coding for implementing the planned solution, and testing for verifying the programs.

For small problems, these activities may not be done explicitly, the start and end boundaries of these activities may not be clearly defined, and no written record of the activities may be kept. However, systematic approaches require that each of these four problem solving activities be done formally. In fact, for large systems, each activity can itself be extremely complex, and methodologies and procedures are needed to perform them efficiently and correctly. Though different process models will perform these phases in different manner, they exist in all processes. We will discuss different process models in the next chapter. Here we briefly discuss these basic phases; each one of them will be discussed in more detail during the course of the book (there is at least one chapter for each of these phases).

Requirements Analysis

Requirements analysis is done in order to understand the problem the software system is to solve. The emphasis in requirements analysis is on identifying what is needed from the system, not how the system will achieve its goals. For complex systems, even determining what is needed is a difficult task. The goal of the requirements activity is to document the requirements in a *software requirements specification* document.

There are two major activities in this phase: problem understanding or analysis and requirement specification. In problem analysis, the aim is to understand the problem and its context, and the requirements of the new system that is to be developed. Understanding the requirements of a system that does not exist is difficult and requires creative thinking. The problem becomes more complex because an automated system offers possibilities that do not exist otherwise. Consequently, even the users may not really know the needs of the system.

Once the problem is analyzed and the essentials understood, the requirements must be specified in the requirement specification document. The requirements document must specify all functional and performance requirements; the formats of inputs and outputs; and all design constraints that exist due to political, economic, environmental, and security reasons. In other words, besides the functionality required from the system, all the factors that may effect the design and proper functioning of the system should be specified in the requirements document. A preliminary user manual that describes all the major user interfaces frequently forms a part of the requirements document.

Software Design

The purpose of the design phase is to plan a solution of the problem specified by the requirements document. This phase is the first step in moving from the problem domain to the solution domain. In other words, starting with *what* is needed, design takes us toward *how* to satisfy the needs. The design of a system is perhaps the most critical factor affecting the quality of the software; it has a major impact on the later phases, particularly testing and maintenance.

The design activity often results in three separate outputs—*architecture design*, *high level design*, and *detailed design*. *Architecture* focuses on looking at a system as a combination of many different components, and how they interact with each other to produce the desired results. The *high level design* identifies the modules that should be built for developing the system and the specifications of these modules. At the end of system design all the major data structures, file formats, output formats, etc., are also fixed. In *detailed design*, the internal logic of each of the modules is specified.

In architecture the focus is on identifying components or subsystems and how they connect; in high level design the focus is on identifying the modules; and during detailed design the focus is on designing the logic for each of the modules. In other words, in architecture the focus is on what major components are needed, in high level design the attention is on *what* modules are needed, while in detailed design *how* the modules can be implemented in software is the issue. A *design methodology* is a systematic approach to creating a design by application of a set of techniques and guidelines. Most methodologies focus on high level design.

Coding

Once the design is complete, most of the major decisions about the system have been made. However, many of the details about coding the designs, which often depend on the programming language chosen, are not specified during design. The goal of the coding phase is to translate the design of the system into code in a given programming language. For a given design, the aim in this phase is to implement the design in the best possible manner.

The coding phase affects both testing and maintenance profoundly. Well-written code can reduce the testing and maintenance effort. Because the testing and maintenance costs of software are much higher than the coding cost, the goal of coding should be to reduce the testing and maintenance effort. Hence, during coding the focus should be on developing programs that are easy to read and understand, and not simply on developing programs that are easy to write. Simplicity and clarity should be strived for during the coding phase.

Testing

Testing is the major quality control measure used during software development. Its basic function is to detect defects in the software. During requirements analysis and design, the output is a document that is usually textual and nonexecutable. After coding, computer programs are available that can be executed for testing purposes. This implies that testing not only has to uncover errors introduced during coding, but also errors introduced during the previous phases. Thus, the goal of testing is to uncover requirement, design, and coding errors in the programs.

The starting point of testing is *unit testing*, where the different modules or components are tested individually. As modules are integrated into the system, *integration testing* is performed, which focuses on testing the interconnection between modules. After the system is put together, *system testing* is performed. Here the system is tested against the system requirements to see if all the requirements are met and if the system performs as specified by the requirements. Finally, *acceptance testing* is performed to demonstrate to the client, on the real-life data of the client, the operation of the system.

Testing is an extremely critical and time-consuming activity. It requires proper planning of the overall testing process. Frequently the testing process starts with a *test plan* that identifies all the testing-related activities that must be performed and specifies the schedule, allocates the resources, and specifies guidelines for testing. The test plan specifies conditions that should be tested, different units to be tested, and the manner in which the modules will be integrated. Then for different test units, a *test case specification document* is produced, which lists all the different test cases, together with the expected outputs. During the testing of the unit, the specified test cases are executed and the actual result compared with the expected output. The final output of the testing phase is the *test report* and the *error report*, or a set of such reports. Each test report contains the set of test cases and the result of executing the code with these test cases. The error report describes the errors encountered and the action taken to remove the errors.

1.3.2 Managing the Process

As stated earlier, a phased development process is central to the software engineering approach. However, a development process does not specify how to allocate resources to the different activities in the process. Nor does it specify things like schedule for the activities, how to divide work within a phase, how to ensure that each phase is being done properly, or what the risks for the project are and how to mitigate them. Without properly managing these issues relating to the process, it is unlikely that the cost and quality objectives can be met. These issues relating to managing the development process of a project are handled through project management.

The management activities typically revolve around a *plan*. A software plan forms the baseline that is heavily used for monitoring and controlling the development process of the project. This makes planning the most important project management activity in a project. It can be safely said that without proper project planning a software project is very unlikely to meet its objectives. We will devote a complete chapter to project planning.

Managing a process requires information upon which the management decisions are based. Otherwise, even the essential questions—is the schedule in a project is being met, what is the extent of cost overrun, are quality objectives being met,—cannot be answered. And information that is subjective is only marginally better than no information (e.g., Q: how close are you to finishing? A: We are almost there.) Hence, for effectively managing a process, objective data is needed. For this, software metrics are used.

Software metrics are quantifiable measures that could be used to measure different characteristics of a software system or the software development process. There are two types of metrics used for software development: *product metrics* and *process metrics*.

Product metrics are used to quantify characteristics of the product being developed, i.e., the software. *Process metrics* are used to quantify characteristics of the process being used to develop the software. Process metrics aim to measure such considerations as productivity, cost and resource requirements, effectiveness of quality assurance measures, and the effect of development techniques and tools

Metrics and measurement are necessary aspects of managing a software development project. For effective monitoring, the management needs to get information about the project: how far it has progressed, how much development has taken place, how far behind schedule it is, and the quality of the development so far. Based on this information, decisions can be made about the project. Without proper metrics to quantify the required information, subjective opinion would have to be used, which is often unreliable and goes against the fundamental goals of engineering. Hence, we can say that metrics-based management is also a key component in the software engineering strategy to achieve its objectives.

Though we have focused on managing the development process of a project, there are other aspects of managing a software process. Some of these will be discussed in the next chapter.

1.4 Summary

Software cost now forms the major component of a computer system's cost. Software is currently extremely expensive to develop and is often unreliable. In this chapter, we have discussed a few themes regarding software and software engineering:

1. The problem domain for software engineering is industrial strength software.

2. Software engineering!problem domain This software is not just a set of computer programs but comprises programs and associated data and documentation. Industrial strength software is expensive and difficult

to build, expensive to maintain due to changes and rework, and has high quality requirements.

3. Software engineering is the discipline that aims to provide methods and procedures for systematically developing industrial strength software. The main driving forces for software engineering are the problem of scale, quality and productivity (Q&P), consistency, and change. Achieving high Q&P consistently for problems whose scale may be large and where changes may happen continuously is the main challenge of software engineering.

4. The fundamental approach of software engineering to achieve the objectives is to separate the development process from the products. Software engineering focuses on process since the quality of products developed and the productivity achieved are heavily influenced by the process used. To meet the software engineering challenges, this development process is a phased process. Another key approach used in Software Engineering for achieving high Q&P is to manage the process effectively and proactively using metrics.

Exercises

1. Suppose a program for solving a problem costs C, and an industrial strength software for solving that problem costs 10C. Where do you think this extra 9C cost is spent? Suggest a possible breakdown of this extra cost.

2. If the primary goal is to make software maintainable, list some of the things you *will* do and some of the things you *will* *not* do during coding and testing.

3. List some problems that will come up if the methods you currently use for developing small software are used for developing large software systems.

4. Next time you do a programming project (in some course perhaps), determine the productivity you achieve. For this, you will have to record the effort you spent in the work. How does it compare with the illustrative productivity figures given in the Chapter.

5. Next time you do a programming project, try to predict the time you will take to do it in terms of hours as well as days. Then in the end, check how well your actual schedule matched the predicted one.

6. We have said that a commonly used measure for quality is defects per KLOC in delivered software. For a software product, how can its quality be measured? How can it be estimated before delivering the software?

7. If you are given extra time to improve the reliability of the final product developing a software product, where would you spend this extra time?

8. Suggest some ways to detect software errors in the early phases of the project when code is not yet available.

9. How does a phased process help in achieving high Q&P, when it seems that we are doing more tasks in a phased process as compared to an ad-hoc approach?

10. If absolutely no metrics are used, can you manage, or even define, a project? What is the bare minimum set of metrics that you must use for a development project?

2

Software Processes

As we saw in the previous chapter, the concept of process is at the heart of the software engineering approach. According to Webster, the term *process* means "a particular method of doing something, generally involving a number of steps or operations." In software engineering, the phrase *software process* refers to the methods of developing software.

A software process is a set of activities, together with ordering constraints among them, such that if the activities are performed properly and in accordance with the ordering constraints, the desired result is produced. The basic desired result is, as stated earlier, high quality and productivity. In this chapter, we will discuss the concept of software processes further, the component processes of a software process, and some models that have been proposed.

2.1   Software Process

In an organization whose major business is software development, there are typically many processes executing simultaneously. Many of these do not concern software engineering, though they do impact software development. These could be considered nonsoftware engineering process. Business processes, social processes, and training processes, are all examples of processes that come under this. These processes also affect the software development activity but are beyond the purview of software engineering.

The process that deals with the technical and management issues of software development is called a *software process*. Clearly, many different types of activities need to be performed to develop software. All these activities together comprise the software process. As different type of activities are being performed, which are frequently done by different people, it is better to view the software process as consisting of many component processes, each consisting of a certain type of activity. Each of these component processes typically has a different objective, though they obviously cooperate with each other to satisfy the overall software engineering objective. In this section, we will define the major component processes of a software process and what their objectives are.

2.1.1 Processes and Process Models

A successful project is the one that satisfies the expectations on all the three goals of cost, schedule, and quality (we are including functionality or features as part of quality.) Consequently, when planning and executing a software project, the decisions are mostly taken with a view to ultimately reduce the cost or the cycle time, or for improving the quality. Software projects utilize a process to organize the execution of tasks to achieve the goals on the cost, schedule, and quality fronts.

A project's process specification defines the tasks the project should perform, and the order in which they should be done. The actual process exists when the project is actually executed. Although process specification is distinct from the actual process, we will consider the process specification for a project and the actual process of the project as one and the same, and will use the term process to refer to both of them. It should, however, be mentioned that although we are assuming that there is no difficulty in a project following a specified process, in reality it is not as simple. Often the actual process being followed in the project may be very different from the project's process specification. Reasons for this divergence vary from laziness to lack of appreciation of importance of process to "old habits die hard." Ensuring that the project is following the process it planned for itself is an important issue for organizations in the business of executing projects, and there are different ways to deal with it—we will not discuss this issue in this book.

A process model specifies a general process, usually as a set of stages in which a project should be divided, the order in which the stages should be executed, and any other constraints and conditions on the execution of stages. The basic premise behind a process model is that, in the situations for which the model is applicable, using the process model as the projects process will lead to low cost, high quality, or reduced cycle time. In other words, a process is a means to reach the goals of high quality, low cost, and low cycle time, and a process model provides generic guidelines for developing a suitable process for a project.

A project's process may utilize some process model. That is, the project's process has a general resemblance to the process model with the actual tasks being specific to the project. However, using a process model is not simply translating the tasks in the process model to tasks in the project. Typically, to achieve the project's objectives, a project will require a process that is somewhat different from the process model. That is, the project's process is generally a tailored version of a general process model. How the process model has to be tailored for a particular project, of course, depends on the project characteristics. What we need to understand is that a project's process may be obtained from a process model, by tailoring the process model to suit the project needs. For organizations that use standard processes, tailoring is an important issue. We will not discuss it further—the reader can find more about tailoring in [96].

When a process is executed on a project, software products are produced, one of them being the final software. That is, a process specifies the steps, the project executes these steps, and during the course of execution products are produced. A process limits the degrees of freedom for a project by specifying what types of activities must be undertaken and in what order, such that the "shortest" (or the most efficient) path is obtained from the user needs to the software satisfying these needs. It should be clear that it is the process that drives a project and heavily influences the expected outcomes of a project. Due to this, the focus of software engineering lies heavily on the process.

2.1.2 Component Software Processes

We have mentioned that the development process is the central process which specifies the tasks to be done in a project. Planning and scheduling the tasks and monitoring their execution fall in the domain of project management process. Hence, there are clearly two major components in a software process—a development process and a project management process—corresponding to the two axes in Figure 1.3. The development process specifies the development and quality assurance activities that need to be performed, whereas the management process specifies how to plan and control these activities so that cost, schedule, quality, and other objectives are met.

During the project many products are produced which are typically composed of many items (for example, the final source code may be composed of many source files). These items keep evolving as the project proceeds, creating many versions on the way. To ensure that the software being produced uses the correct versions of these items requires suitable processes to control the evolution of these items. As development processes generally do not focus on evolution and changes, to handle them another process called *software configuration control process*, is often used. The objective of this component process is to primarily deal with managing change, so that the integrity of the products is not violated despite changes. Sometimes, changes in requirements may be handled separately by a *requirements change management process.*

These three constituent processes focus on the projects and the products and can be considered as comprising the *product engineering processes*, as their main objective is to produce the desired product. If the software process can be viewed as a static entity, then these three component processes will suffice. However, a software process itself is a dynamic entity, as it must change to adapt to our increased understanding about software development and availability of newer technologies and tools. Due to this, a process to manage the software process is needed.

The basic objective of the process management process is to improve the software process. By *improvement*, we mean that the capability of the process to produce quality goods at low cost is improved. For this, the current software process is studied, frequently by studying the projects that have been done using the process. The whole process of understanding the current process, analyzing its properties, determining how to improve, and then affecting the improvement is dealt with by the *process management process.*

The relationship between these major component processes is shown in Figure 2.1. These component processes are distinct not only in the type of activities performed in them, but typically also in the people who perform the activities specified by the process. In a typical project, development activities are performed by programmers, designers, testers, etc.; the project management process activities are performed by the project management; configuration control process activities are performed by a group generally called the *configuration controller*; and the process management process activities are performed by the *software engineering process group (SEPG).*

Later in the chapter we will briefly discuss each of these processes, as well as the inspection process which is used for quality control of various work products. In the rest of the book, however, we will focus primarily

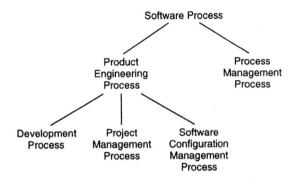

Figure 2.1: Software processes.

on processes relating to product engineering, as process management is an advanced topic beyond the scope of this book. Much of the book discusses the different phases of a development process and the processes or *methodologies* used for executing these phases. For the rest of the book, we will use the term *software process* to mean product engineering processes, unless specified otherwise.

2.1.3 ETVX Approach for Process Specification

A process has a set of phases (or steps), each phase performing a well-defined task which leads a project towards satisfaction of its goals. To reduce the cost, a process should aim to detect defects in the phase in which they are introduced. This requires that there be some verification at the end of each step, which in turn requires that there is a clearly defined output of a phase, which can be verified by some means. In other words, it is not acceptable to say that the output of a phase is an idea or a thought in the mind of someone; the output must be a formal and tangible entity. Such outputs of a development process, which are not the final output, are frequently called the *work products*. In software, a work product can be the requirements document, design document, code, prototype, and the like.

This restriction that the output of each step be some work product that can be verified suggests that the process should have a small number of steps. Having too many steps results in too many work products or documents. Due to this, at the top level, a process typically consists of a few steps, each satisfying a clear objective and producing a document which can be verified. How to perform the activity of the particular step or phase

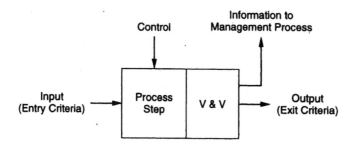

Figure 2.2: A step in a development process.

is generally addressed by *methodologies* for that activity. We will discuss various methodologies for different activities throughout the book.

As a process typically contains a sequence of steps, the next issue to address is when a phase should be initiated and terminated. This is frequently done by specifying the entry criteria and exit criteria for a phase. The *entry criteria* of a phase specifies the conditions that the input to the phase should satisfy to initiate the activities of that phase. The *exit criteria* specifies the conditions that the work product of this phase should satisfy to terminate the activities of the phase. The entry and exit criteria specify constraints of when to start and stop an activity. It should be clear that the entry criteria of a phase should be consistent with the exit criteria of the previous phase. In addition to the entry and exit criteria, the inputs and outputs of a step also need to be clearly specified. As errors can be introduced in every stage, a stage should end with some verification of its activities, and these should also be clearly stated. The specification of a step with its input, output, and entry and exit criteria is shown in Figure 2.2. This approach for process specification is called the ETVX (Entry criteria, Task, Verification, and eXit criteria) approach [128].

Besides the entry and exit criteria for the input and output, a step needs to produce some information to aid proper management of the process. This requires that a step produce some information that provides visibility into the state of the process. This information can then be used to take suitable actions, where necessary, to keep the process under control. The flow of information from a step and exercise of control is also shown in Figure 2.2.

2.2 Desired Characteristics of Software Process

We have not yet specified any process. Is any process suitable to use? Here we discuss some of the desirable characteristics of the software process. As a process may be used by many projects, it needs characteristics beyond satisfying the project goals. We will discuss some of the important ones in this section.

2.2.1 Predictability

Predictability of a process determines how accurately the outcome of following that process in a project can be predicted before the project is completed. Predictability can be considered a fundamental property of any process. In fact, if a process is not predictable, it is of limited use. Let us see why.

One way of estimating cost could be to say, "this project A is very similar to the project B that we did 2 years ago, hence A's cost will be very close to B's cost." However, even this simple method implies that the process that will be used to develop project A will be same as the process used for project B, *and* that following the process the second time will produce similar results as the first time. That is, this assumes that the process is *predictable*. If it was not predictable, then there is no guarantee that doing a similar project using the process will incur a similar cost.

The situation with quality is similar. The fundamental basis for quality prediction is that quality of the product is determined largely by the process used to develop it. Using this basis, quality of the product of a project can be estimated or predicted by seeing the quality of the products that have been produced in the past by the process being used in the current project. In fact, effective management of quality control activities largely depends on the predictability of the process. For example, for effective quality control, one method is to estimate what types and quantity of errors will be detected at what stage of the development, and then use them to determine if the quality assurance activities are being performed properly. This can only be done if the process is predictable; based on the past experience of such a process one can estimate the distribution of errors for the current project. Otherwise, how can anyone say whether detecting 10 errors per 100 lines of code (LOC) during testing in the current project is "acceptable"? With a predictable process, if the process is such that one expects around 10 errors per 100 LOC during testing, this means that the testing of this project was probably done properly. But, if past experience with the process shows that

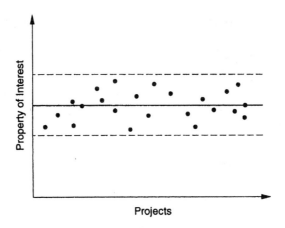

Figure 2.3: Process under statistical control.

about 2 errors per 100 LOC are detected during testing, then a careful look
at the testing of the current project is necessary.

It should be clear that if we want to use the past experience to control
costs and ensure quality, we must use a process that is predictable. With
low predictability, the experience gained through projects is of little value.
A predictable process is also said to be *under statistical control* [89, 101].
A process is under statistical control if following the same process produces
similar results—results will have some variation, but the variation is mostly
due to random causes and not due to process issues. This is shown in Figure
2.3; the y-axis represents some property of interest (quality, productivity,
etc.), and x-axis represents the projects. The dark line is the expected value
of the property for this process. Statistical control implies that most of the
times the property of interest will be within a bound around the expected
value. (Control charts provide a formal approach for defining these bounds.
For a discussion on control charts and how to define optimal bounds, the
reader is referred to [101].)

It should be clear that if one hopes to consistently develop software of
high quality at low cost, it is necessary to have a process that is under statistical control. A predictable process is an essential requirement for ensuring
good quality and low cost. Note that this does not mean that one can never
produce high-quality software at low cost without following such a process.
It is always possible that a set of bright people can do it. However, what
this means is that without such a process, such things cannot be repeated.

Hence, if one wants quality consistently across many projects, having a predictable process is essential. Because software engineering is interested in general methods that can be used to develop different software, a predictable process forms the backbone of the software engineering methods.

2.2.2 Support Testability and Maintainability

We have already seen that in the life of software the maintenance costs generally exceed the development costs. Clearly, if we want to reduce the overall cost of software or achieve "global" optimality in terms of cost rather than "local" optimality in terms of development cost only, the goal of development should be to reduce the maintenance effort. That is, one of the important objectives of the development project should be to produce software that is easy to maintain. And the process used should ensure this maintainability.

Even in development, coding is frequently given a great degree of importance. We have seen that a process consists of phases, and a process generally includes requirements, design, coding, and testing phases. Of the development cost, an example distribution of effort with the different phases could be:

Requirements	10%
Design	10%
Coding	30%
Testing	50%

The exact numbers will differ with organization and the nature of the process. However, there are some observations we can make. First is that coding consumes only about a third of the development effort. This is against the common naive notion that developing software is largely concerned with writing programs and that programming is the major activity.

Another way of determining the effort spent in programming is to study how programmers spend their time in a software organization. A study conducted in Bell Labs to determine how programmers spend their time, as reported in [60], found the distribution shown below:

Writing programs	13%
Reading programs and manuals	16%
Job communication	32%
Other (including personal)	39%

This data clearly shows that programming is not the major activity on which programmers spend their time. Even if we take away the time spent in "other" activities, the time spent by a programmer writing programs is still less than 25% of the remaining time. In the study reported by Boehm [20], it was found that programmers spend less than 20% of their time programming.

The second important observation from the data about effort distribution with phases is that testing consumes the most resources during development. This is, again, contrary to the common practice, which considers testing a side activity that is often not properly planned. Underestimating the testing effort often causes the planners to allocate insufficient resources for testing, which, in turn, results in unreliable software or schedule slippage.

Overall, we can say that the goal of the process should not be to reduce the effort of design and coding, but to reduce the cost of testing and maintenance. Both testing and maintenance depend heavily on the quality of design and code, and these costs can be considerably reduced if the software is designed and coded to make testing and maintenance easier. Hence, during the early phases of the development process the prime issues should be "can it be easily tested" and "can it be easily modified".

2.2.3 Support Change

Software changes for a variety of reasons. In Chapter 1, we emphasized the pervasiveness of change as a basic property of the problem domain. Here we focus on changes due to requirement changes. Though changes were always a part of life, change in today's world is much more and much faster. As organizations and businesses change, the software supporting the business has to change. Hence, any model that builds software and makes change very hard will not be suitable in many situations.

Besides changing an existing and working software, which one can argue is beyond the development process, change also takes place while development is going on. After all, the needs of the customer may change during the course of the project. And if the project is of any significant duration, considerable changes can be expected.

Besides the change driven by business need, changes may occur simply because people may change their minds as they think more about possibilities and alternatives. So, some part of a software system may be developed and shown to the users, and the users or customer is likely to use the feedback to find that what he had requested was not correct, or that he needs more, or that he needs something different. In other words, change is prevalent, and a process that can handle change easily is desirable.

2.2.4 Early Defect Removal

The notion that programming is the central activity during software development is largely due to programming being considered a difficult task and sometimes an "art." Another consequence of this kind of thinking is the belief that errors largely occur during programming, as it is the hardest activity in software development and offers many opportunities for committing errors. It is now clear that errors can occur at any stage during development. An example distribution of error occurrences by phase is:

Requirements	20%
Design	30%
Coding	50%

As we can see, errors occur throughout the development process. However, the cost of correcting errors of different phases is not the same and depends on when the error is detected and corrected. The relative cost of correcting requirement errors as a function of where they are detected is shown in Figure 2.4 [20].

As one would expect, the greater the delay in detecting an error after it occurs, the more expensive it is to correct it. As the figure shows, an error that occurs during the requirements phase, if corrected during acceptance testing, can cost up to 100 times more than correcting the error during the requirements phase itself.

The reason for this is fairly obvious. If there is an error in the requirements, then the design and the code will be affected by it. To correct the error after the coding is done would require both the design and the code to be changed, thereby increasing the cost of correction.

The main point of this discussion is that we should attempt to detect errors that occur in a phase during that phase itself and should not wait until testing to detect errors. Error detection and correction should be a continuous process that is done throughout software development. In terms of development phases, this means that we should try to verify the output of each phase before starting with the next (that is why the ETVX model has a V!) In other words, a process should have quality control activities spread through the process and in each phase. A quality control (QC) activity is one whose main purpose is to identify and remove defects.

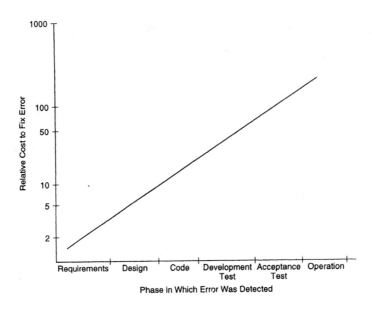

Figure 2.4: Cost of correcting errors.

Having QC tasks through the development is clearly an objective that should be supported by the process. However, it is even better to provide support for *defect prevention*. It is generally agreed that all the QC techniques that exist today are limited in their capability and cannot detect all the defects that are introduced. (Why else are there bugs in most software that is released that are then fixed in later versions?) Clearly, then, to reduce the total number of residual defects that exist in a system at the time of delivery and to reduce the cost of defect removal, an obvious approach is to prevent defects from being introduced. This requires that the process of performing the activities should be such that fewer defects are introduced. The method generally followed to support defect prevention is to use the development process to learn (from previous projects) so that the methods of performing activities can be improved. We will discuss this more in a later chapter.

2.2.5 Process Improvement and Feedback

As mentioned earlier, a process is not a static entity. Improving the quality and reducing the cost of products are fundamental goals of any engineering discipline. In the context of software, as the productivity (and hence the cost of a project) and quality are determined largely by the process, to satisfy the objectives of quality improvement and cost reduction, the software process must be improved.

Having process improvement as a fundamental objective requires that the software process be a closed-loop process. That is, the process must be improved based on previous experiences, and each project done using the existing process must feed information back to facilitate this improvement. As stated earlier, this activity of analyzing and improving the process is largely done in the process management component of the software process. However, to support this activity, information from various other processes will have to flow to the process management process. In other words, to support this activity, other processes will also have to take an active part.

Process improvement is also an objective in a large project where feedback from the early parts of the project can be used to improve the execution of the rest of the project. This type of feedback is eminently suited when the iterative development process model is used—feedback from one iteration is used to improve the execution of later iterations.

2.3   Software Development Process Models

In the software development process we focus on the activities directly related to production of the software, for example, design, coding, and testing. As the development process specifies the major development and quality control activities that need to be performed in the project, the development process really forms the core of the software process. The management process is decided based on the development process. Due to the importance of the development process, various models have been proposed. In this section we will discuss some of the major models.

2.3.1   Waterfall Model

The simplest process model is the *waterfall model*, which states that the phases are organized in a linear order. The model was originally proposed by Royce [132], though variations of the model have evolved depending on the nature of activities and the flow of control between them. In this model, a project begins with feasibility analysis. Upon successfully demonstrating the feasibility of a project, the requirements analysis and project planning begins. The design starts after the requirements analysis is complete, and coding begins after the design is complete. Once the programming is completed, the code is integrated and testing is done. Upon successful completion of testing, the system is installed. After this, the regular operation and maintenance of the system takes place. The model is shown in Figure 2.5.

The requirements analysis phase is mentioned as "analysis and planning." *Planning* is a critical activity in software development. A good plan is based on the requirements of the system and should be done before later phases begin. However, in practice, detailed requirements are not necessary for planning. Consequently, planning usually overlaps with the requirements analysis, and a plan is ready before the later phases begin. This plan is an additional input to all the later phases.

Linear ordering of activities has some important consequences. First, to clearly identify the end of a phase and the beginning of the next, some certification mechanism has to be employed at the end of each phase. This is usually done by some verification and validation means that will ensure that the output of a phase is consistent with its input (which is the output of the previous phase), and that the output of the phase is consistent with the overall requirements of the system.

The consequence of the need for certification is that each phase must have some defined output that can be evaluated and certified. That is, when the activities of a phase are completed, there should be some product that is produced by that phase. The outputs of the earlier phases are often called *work products* and are usually in the form of documents like the requirements document or design document. For the coding phase, the output is the code. Though the set of documents that should be produced in a project is dependent on how the process is implemented, the following documents generally form a reasonable set that should be produced in each project:

- Requirements document

- Project plan

- Design documents (architecture, system, detailed)

- Test plan and test reports

- Final code

- Software manuals (e.g., user, installation, etc.)

In addition to these work products, there are various other documents that are produced in a typical project. These include review reports, which are

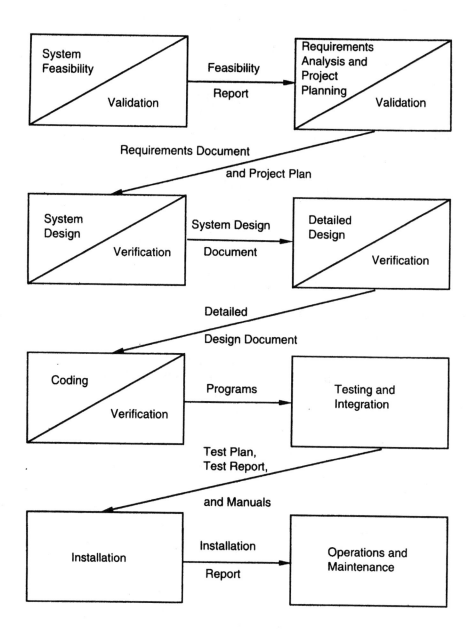

Figure 2.5: The waterfall model.

the outcome of reviews conducted for work products, as well as status reports that summarize the status of the project on a regular basis. Many other reports may be produced for improving the execution of the project or project reporting.

One of the main advantages of this model is its simplicity. It is conceptually straightforward and divides the large task of building a software system into a series of cleanly divided phases, each phase dealing with a separate logical concern. It is also easy to administer in a contractual setup—as each phase is completed and its work product produced, some amount of money is given by the customer to the developing organization.

The waterfall model, although widely used, has some strong limitations. Some of the key limitations are:

1. It assumes that the requirements of a system can be frozen (i.e., baselined) before the design begins. This is possible for systems designed to automate an existing manual system. But for new systems, determining the requirements is difficult as the user does not even know the requirements. Hence, having unchanging requirements is unrealistic for such projects.

2. Freezing the requirements usually requires choosing the hardware (because it forms a part of the requirements specification). A large project might take a few years to complete. If the hardware is selected early, then due to the speed at which hardware technology is changing, it is likely that the final software will use a hardware technology on the verge of becoming obsolete. This is clearly not desirable for such expensive software systems.

3. It follows the "big bang" approach—the entire software is delivered in one shot at the end. This entails heavy risks, as the user does not know until the very end what they are getting. Furthermore, if the project runs out of money in the middle, then there will be no software. That is, it has the "all or nothing" value proposition.

4. It is a document-driven process that requires formal documents at the end of each phase.

Despite these limitations, the waterfall model has been the most widely used process model. It is well suited for routine types of projects where the requirements are well understood. That is, if the developing organization is quite familiar with the problem domain and the requirements for the software are quite clear, the waterfall model works well.

2.3.2 Prototyping

The goal of a prototyping-based development process is to counter the first two limitations of the waterfall model. The basic idea here is that instead of freezing the requirements before any design or coding can proceed, a throwaway prototype is built to help understand the requirements. This prototype is developed based on the currently known requirements. Development of the prototype obviously undergoes design, coding, and testing, but each of these phases is not done very formally or thoroughly. By using this prototype, the client can get an actual feel of the system, because the interactions with the prototype can enable the client to better understand the requirements of the desired system. This results in more stable requirements that change less frequently.

Prototyping is an attractive idea for complicated and large systems for which there is no manual process or existing system to help determine the requirements. In such situations, letting the client "play" with the prototype provides invaluable and intangible inputs that help determine the requirements for the system. It is also an effective method of demonstrating the feasibility of a certain approach. This might be needed for novel systems, where it is not clear that constraints can be met or that algorithms can be developed to implement the requirements. In both situations, the risks associated with the projects are being reduced through the use of prototyping. The process model of the prototyping approach is shown in Figure 2.6.

A development process using throwaway prototyping typically proceeds as follows [72]. The development of the prototype typically starts when the preliminary version of the requirements specification document has been developed. At this stage, there is a reasonable understanding of the system and its needs and which needs are unclear or likely to change. After the prototype has been developed, the end users and clients are given an opportunity to use the prototype and play with it. Based on their experience, they provide feedback to the developers regarding the prototype: what is correct, what needs to be modified, what is missing, what is not needed, etc. Based on the feedback, the prototype is modified to incorporate some of the suggested changes that can be done easily, and then the users and the clients are again allowed to use the system. This cycle repeats until, in the judgment of the prototypers and analysts, the benefit from further changing the system and

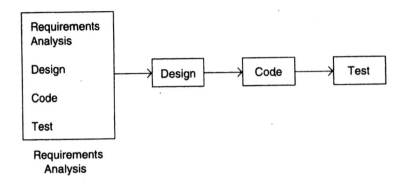

Figure 2.6: The prototyping model.

obtaining feedback is outweighed by the cost and time involved in making the changes and obtaining the feedback. Based on the feedback, the initial requirements are modified to produce the final requirements specification, which is then used to develop the production quality system.

For prototyping for the purposes of requirement analysis to be feasible, its cost must be kept low. Consequently, only those features are included in the prototype that will have a valuable return from the user experience. Exception handling, recovery, and conformance to some standards and formats are typically not included in prototypes. In prototyping, as the prototype is to be discarded, there is no point in implementing those parts of the requirements that are already well understood. Hence, the focus of the development is to include those features that are not properly understood. And the development approach is "quick and dirty" with the focus on quick development rather than quality. Because the prototype is to be thrown away, only minimal documentation needs to be produced during prototyping. For example, design documents, a test plan, and a test case specification are not needed during the development of the prototype. Another important cost-cutting measure is to reduce testing. Because testing consumes a major part of development expenditure during regular software development, this has a considerable impact in reducing costs. By using these type of cost-cutting methods, it is possible to keep the cost of the prototype less than a few percent of the total development cost.

Prototyping is often not used, as it is feared that development costs may become large. However, in some situations, the cost of software development without prototyping may be more than with prototyping. There are two major reasons for this. First, the experience of developing the prototype might reduce the cost of the later phases when the actual software development is done. Secondly, in many projects the requirements are constantly changing, particularly when development takes a long time. We saw earlier that changes in requirements at a late stage of development substantially increase the cost of the project. By elongating the requirements analysis phase (prototype development does take time), the requirements are "frozen" at a later time, by which time they are likely to be more developed and, consequently, more stable. In addition, because the client and users get experience with the system, it is more likely that the requirements specified after the prototype will be closer to the actual requirements. This again will lead to fewer changes in the requirements at a later time. Hence, the costs incurred due to changes in the requirements may be substantially reduced by prototyping. Hence, the cost of the development after the prototype can be substantially less than the cost without prototyping; we have already seen how the cost of developing the prototype itself can be reduced.

Prototyping is well suited for projects where requirements are hard to determine and the confidence in the stated requirements is low. In such projects, a waterfall model will have to freeze the requirements in order for the development to continue, even when the requirements are not stable. This leads to requirement changes and associated rework while the development is going on. Requirements frozen after experience with the prototype are likely to be more stable. Overall, in projects where requirements are not properly understood in the beginning, using the prototyping process model can be the most effective method for developing the software. It is an excellent technique for reducing some types of risks associated with a project. We will further discuss prototyping when we discuss requirements specification and risk management.

2.3.3 Iterative Development

The iterative development process model counters the third limitation of the waterfall model and tries to combine the benefits of both prototyping and the waterfall model. The basic idea is that the software should be developed in increments, each increment adding some functional capability to the system until the full system is implemented. At each step, extensions and design modifications can be made. An advantage of this approach is that it can result in better testing because testing each increment is likely to be easier than testing the entire system as in the waterfall model. Furthermore, as in

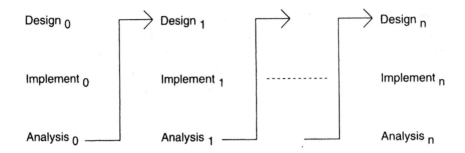

Figure 2.7: The iterative enhancement model.

prototyping, the increments provide feedback to the client that is useful for determining the final requirements of the system.

The iterative enhancement model [7] is an example of this approach. In the first step of this model, a simple initial implementation is done for a subset of the overall problem. This subset is one that contains some of the key aspects of the problem that are easy to understand and implement and which form a useful and usable system. A *project control list* is created that contains, in order, all the tasks that must be performed to obtain the final implementation. This project control list gives an idea of how far along the project is at any given step from the final system.

Each step consists of removing the next task from the list, designing the implementation for the selected task, coding and testing the implementation, performing an analysis of the partial system obtained after this step, and updating the list as a result of the analysis. These three phases are called *the design phase, implementation phase*, and *analysis phase*. The process is iterated until the project control list is empty, at which time the final implementation of the system will be available. The iterative enhancement model is shown in Figure 2.7.

The project control list guides the iteration steps and keeps track of all tasks that must be done. Based on the analysis, one of the tasks in the list can include redesign of defective components or redesign of the entire system. However, redesign of the system will generally occur only in the initial steps. In the later steps, the design would have stabilized and there is less chance of redesign. Each entry in the list is a task that should be performed in one step of the iterative enhancement process and should be simple enough to be completely understood. Selecting tasks in this manner will minimize the chances of error and reduce the redesign work. The design

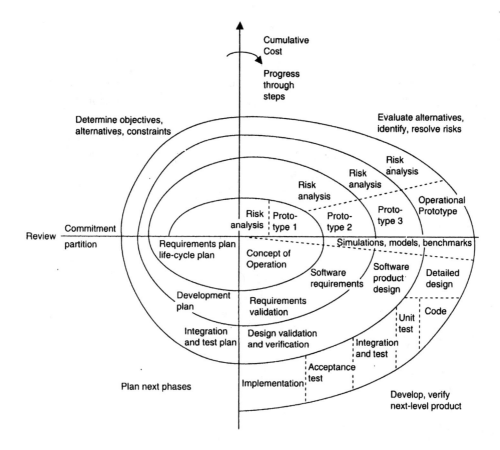

Figure 2.8: The spiral model.

and implementation phases of each step can be performed in a top-down manner or by using some other technique.

The spiral model is another iterative model that has been proposed [18]. As the name suggests, the activities in this model can be organized like a spiral that has many cycles as shown in Figure 2.8 [18].

Each cycle in the spiral begins with the identification of objectives for that cycle, the different alternatives that are possible for achieving the objectives, and the constraints that exist. The next step in the cycle is to evaluate these different alternatives based on the objectives and constraints. The focus of evaluation in this step is based on the risk perception for the project. The next step is to develop strategies that resolve the uncertainties and risks. This step may involve activities such as benchmarking, simulation, and prototyping. Next, the software is developed, keeping in mind the risks. Finally the next stage is planned.

One effective use of the iterative model is often seen in product development, in which the developers themselves provide the specifications and therefore have a lot of control on which specifications go in the system and which stay out. Generally, a version of the product is released that contains some capability. Based on the feedback from users and experience with this version, technology changes, business changes, etc., a list of additional desirable features and capabilities is generated. These features form the basis of enhancement of the software, and are included in the next version. In other words, the first version contains some core capability. And then more features are added to later versions.

In a customized software development, where the client has to provide and approve the specifications, this process model is becoming extremely popular, despite some difficulties in using it in this context. The main reason is the same—as businesses are changing very rapidly today, they never really know the "complete" requirements for the software, and there is a need to constantly add new capabilities to the software to adapt the business to changing situations. Furthermore, customers do not want to invest too much for a long time without seeing returns. In the current business scenario, it is preferable to see returns continuously of the investment made. The iterative model permits this—after each iteration some working software is delivered.

The iterative approach to software development is now widely used. Many contemporary development approaches like extreme programming [10] and Agile approaches [38] consider iterative development as a basic strategy for developing software for current times. Rational Unified Process (RUP) [108] also employs an iterative process.

2.3.4 Timeboxing Model

To speed up development, parallelism between the different iterations can be employed. That is, a new iteration commences before the system produced by the current iteration is released, and hence development of a new release happens in parallel with the development of the current release. By starting an iteration before the previous iteration has completed, it is possible to reduce the average delivery time for iterations. However, to support parallel execution, each iteration has to be structured properly and teams have to be organized suitably. The timeboxing model proposes an approach for these

[100, 99].

In the timeboxing model, the basic unit of development is a time box, which is of fixed duration. Since the duration is fixed, a key factor in selecting the requirements or features to be built in a time box is what can be fit into the time box. This is in contrast to regular iterative approaches where the functionality is selected and then the time to deliver is determined. Timeboxing changes the perspective of development and makes the schedule a non-negotiable and a high priority commitment.

Each time box is divided into a sequence of stages, like in the waterfall model. Each stage performs some clearly defined task for the iteration and produces a clearly defined output. The model also requires that the duration of each stage, that is, the time it takes to complete the task of that stage, is approximately the same. Furthermore, the model requires that there be a dedicated team for each stage. That is, the team for a stage performs only tasks of that stage—tasks for other stages are performed by their respective teams. This is quite different from other iterative models where the implicit assumption is that the same team performs all the different tasks of the project or the iteration.

Having time boxed iterations with stages of equal duration and having dedicated teams renders itself to pipelining of different iterations. (Pipelining is a concept from hardware in which different instructions are executed in parallel, with the execution of a new instruction starting once the first stage of the previous instruction is finished.) Let us consider a time box with duration T and consisting of n stages—S_1, S_2, ..., S_n, each stage S_i being executed by a dedicated team. The team of each stage has T/n time available to finish their task for a time box, that is, the duration of each stage is T/n. When the team of a stage i completes the tasks for that stage for a time box k, it then passes the output of the time box to the team executing the stage $i + 1$, and then starts executing its stage for the next time box $k + 1$. Using the output given by the team for S_i, the team for S_{i+1} starts its activity for this time box. By the time the first time box is nearing completion, there are $n - 1$ different time boxes in different stages of execution. And though the first output comes after time T, each subsequent delivery happens after T/n time interval, delivering software that has been developed in time T.

As an example, consider a time box consisting of three stages: requirement specification, build, and deployment. The requirement stage is executed by its team of analysts and ends with a prioritized list of requirements to be built in in this iteration along with a high level design. The build team

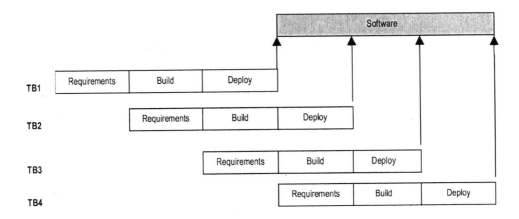

Figure 2.9: Executing the timeboxing process model.

develops the code for implementing the requirements, and performs the testing. The tested code is then handed over to the deployment team, which performs predeployment tests, and then installs the system for production use. These three stages are such that they can be done in approximately equal time in an iteration.

With a time box of three stages, the project proceeds as follows. When the requirement team has finished requirements for timebox-1, the requirements are given to the build team for building the software. The requirement team then goes on and starts preparing the requirements for timebox-2. When the build for the timebox-1 is completed, the code is handed over to the deployment team, and the build team moves on to build code for requirements for timebox-2, and the requirements team moves on to doing requirements for timebox-3. This pipelined execution of the timeboxing process is shown in Figure 2.9 [99].

With a three-stage time box, at most three iterations can be concurrently in progress. If the time box is of size T days, then the first software delivery will occur after T days. The subsequent deliveries, however, will take place after every T/3 days. For example, if the time box duration T is 9 weeks (and each stage duration is 3 weeks), the first delivery is made 9 weeks after the start of the project. The second delivery is made after 12 weeks, the third after 15 weeks, and so on. Contrast this with a linear execution of iterations, in which the first delivery will be made after 9 weeks, the second will be made after 18 weeks, the third after 27 weeks, and so on.

There are three teams working on the project—the requirements team,

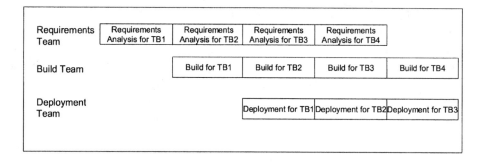

Figure 2.10: Tasks of different teams.

the build team, and the deployment team. The team-wise activity for the 3-stage pipeline discussed above is shown in Figure 2.10 [99].

It should be clear that the duration of each iteration has not been reduced. The total work done in a time box and the effort spent in it also remains the same—the same amount of software is delivered at the end of each iteration as the time box undergoes the same stages. If the same effort and time is spent in each iteration also remains the same, then what is the cost of reducing the delivery time? The real cost of this reduced time is in the resources used in this model. With timeboxing, there are dedicated teams for different stages and the total team size for the project is sum of teams of different stages. This is the main difference from the situation where there is a single team which performs all the stages and the entire team works on the same iteration.

For example, consider an iterative development with three stages, as discussed above. Suppose that it takes 2 people 2 weeks to do the requirements for an iteration, it takes 4 people 2 weeks to do the build for the iteration, and it takes 3 people 2 weeks to test and deploy. If the iterations are serially executed, then the team for the project will be 4 people (the maximum size needed for a stage)—in the first 2 weeks two people will primarily do the requirements, then all the 4 people will do the task of build, and then 3 people will do the deployment.

If this project is executed using the timeboxing process model, there will be 3 separate teams—the requirements team of size 2, the build team of size 4, and the deployment team of size 3. So, the total team size for the project is $(2+4+3) = 9$ persons. This is more than twice the peak team size if iterations are executed serially. It is due to this increase in team size that the throughput increases and the average delivery time decreases.

Hence, the timeboxing provides an approach for utilizing additional manpower to reduce the delivery time. It is well known that with standard methods of executing projects, we cannot compress the cycle time of a project substantially by adding more manpower. However, through the timeboxing model, we can use more manpower in a manner such that by parallel execution of different stages we are able to deliver software quicker. In other words, it provides a way of shortening delivery times through the use of additional manpower.

Timeboxing is well suited for projects that require a large number of features to be developed in a short time around a stable architecture using stable technologies. These features should be such that there is some flexibility in grouping them for building a meaningful system in an iteration that provides value to the users.

The model is not suitable for projects where it is difficult to partition the overall development into multiple iterations of approximately equal duration. It is also not suitable for projects where different iterations may require different stages, and for projects whose features are such that there is no flexibility to combine them into meaningful deliveries. We have only discussed the basic process model and have not discussed the impact of unequal stages, exceptions on the execution of this model, project management issues, etc. For further details about the model, as well as a detailed example of applying the model on a real commercial project, the reader is referred to [100, 99].

2.3.5   Comparision of Models

As discussed earlier, each process model is suitable for some context, and the main reason for studying different models is to develop the ability to choose the proper model for a given project. Using a model as the basis, the actual process for the project can be decided, which hopefully is the optimal process for the project. To help select a model, we summarize the strengths and weaknesses of the different models, along with the types of projects for which they are suitable, in Figure 2.11.

2.4   Other Software Processes

Though the development process is the central process in software processes, other processes are needed to properly execute the development process and

Strengths	Weaknesses	Types of projects
Waterfall Simple Easy to execute Intuitive and logical	All or nothing approach Requirements frozen early Disallows changes Cycle time too long May choose outdated hardware technology User feedback not allowed Encourages req. bloating	For well understood problems, short duration project, automation of existing manual systems
Prototyping Helps in requirements elicitation Reduces risk Leads to a better system	Front heavy process Possibly higher cost Disallows later changes	Systems with novice users When uncertainities in requirements When UI very important
Iterative Regular/quick deliveries Reduces risk Accommodates changes Allows user feedback Allows reasonable exit points Avoids req. bloating Prioritizes requirements	Each iteration can have planning overhead Cost may increase as work done in one iteration may have to be undone later System architecture and structure may suffer as frequent changes are made	For businesses where time is of essence Where risk of a long project cannot be taken Where requirements are not known and will be known only with time
Timeboxing All strengths of iterative Planning and negotiations somewhat easier Very short delivery cycle	Project management is complex Possibly increased cost Large team size	Where very short delivery times needed Flexibility in grouping features exists

Figure 2.11: Comparison of process models.

to achieve the desired characteristics of software processes. There are processes for each of the activities in the development process, e.g., design process, testing process, etc. These processes are often called methodologies and we will discuss them in their respective chapters. Here we discuss those processes that span the entire project and are not particular to any task in the development process. We discuss some of the important processes that are involved when developing software.

2.4.1   Project Management Process

Proper management is an integral part of software development. A large software development project involves many people working for a long period of time. We have seen that a development process typically partitions the problem of developing software into a set of phases. To meet the cost, quality, and schedule objectives, resources have to be properly allocated to each activity for the project, and progress of different activities has to be monitored and corrective actions taken, if needed. All these activities are part of the project management process.

The project management process specifies all activities that need to be done by the project management to ensure that cost and quality objectives are met. Its basic task is to ensure that, once a development process is chosen, it is implemented optimally. The focus is on issues like planning a project, estimating resource and schedule, and monitoring and controlling the project. In other words, the basic task is to plan the detailed implementation of the process for the particular project and then ensure that the plan is followed. For a large project, a proper management process is essential for success.

The activities in the management process for a project can be grouped broadly into three phases: planning, monitoring and control, and termination analysis. Project management begins with planning, which is perhaps the most critical project management activity. The goal of this phase is to develop a *plan* for software development following which the objectives of the project can be met successfully and efficiently. A software plan is usually produced before the development activity begins and is updated as development proceeds and data about progress of the project becomes available. During planning, the major activities are cost estimation, schedule and milestone determination, project staffing, quality control plans, and controlling and monitoring plans. Project planning is undoubtedly the single most important management activity, and it forms the basis for monitoring and control. We will devote one full chapter later in the book to project planning.

Project monitoring and control phase of the management process is the longest in terms of duration; it encompasses most of the development process. It includes all activities the project management has to perform while the development is going on to ensure that project objectives are met and the development proceeds according to the developed plan (and update the plan,

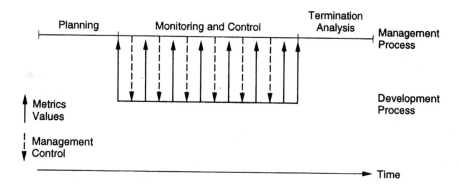

Figure 2.12: Temporal relationship between development and management process.

if needed). As cost, schedule, and quality are the major driving forces, most of the activity of this phase revolves around monitoring factors that affect these. Monitoring potential risks for the project, which might prevent the project from meeting its objectives, is another important activity during this phase. And if the information obtained by monitoring suggests that objectives may not be met, necessary actions are taken in this phase by exerting suitable control on the development activities.

Monitoring a development process requires proper information about the project. Such information is typically obtained by the management process from the development process. As shown earlier in Figure 2.2, the implementation of a development process model should be such that each step in the development process produces information that the management process needs for that step. That is, the development process provides the information the management process needs. However, interpretation of the information is part of monitoring and control.

Whereas monitoring and control last the entire duration of the project, the last phase of the management process—termination analysis—is performed when the development process is over. The basic reason for performing termination analysis is to provide information about the development process and learn from the project in order to improve the process. This phase is also often called *postmortem analysis*. In iterative development, this analysis can be done after each iteration to provide feedback to improve the execution of further iterations. We will not discuss it further in the book; for an example of a postmortem report the reader is referred to [96].

The temporal relationship between the management process and the development process is shown in Figure 2.12. This is an idealized relationship showing that planning is done before development begins, and termination analysis is done after development is over. As the figure shows, during the development, from the various phases of the development process, quantitative information flows to the monitoring and control phase of the management process, which uses the information to exert control on the development process.

2.4.2 The Inspection Process

The main goal of the inspection process is to detect defects in work products. Software inspections were first proposed by Fagan [58, 59]. Earlier inspections were focused on code, but over the years its use has spread to other work products too. In other words, the inspection process is used throughout the development process. Software inspections are now a recognized industry best practice with considerable data to support that they help in improving quality and also improve productivity (e.g., see reports given in [70, 77, 144]). There are books on the topic which describe in great detail how inspections should be conducted [70, 68].

An inspection is a review of a software work product by a group of peers following a clearly defined process. The basic goal of inspections is to improve the quality of the work product by finding defects. However, inspections also improve productivity by finding defects early and in a cost effective manner. Some of the characteristics of inspections are:

- An inspection is conducted by technical people for technical people

- It is a structured process with defined roles for the participants

- The focus is on identifying problems, not resolving them

- The review data is recorded and used for monitoring the effectiveness of the inspection process

As inspections are performed by a group of people, they can be applied to any work product, something that cannot be done with testing. The main advantage of this is that defects introduced in work products of the early parts of the life cycle, or in the work products produced by other processes like the project management process or the CM process, can be detected in that work product itself, thereby not incurring the much higher cost of detecting defects in later stages.

Inspections are performed by a team of reviewers (or inspectors) including the author, with one of them being the *moderator*. The moderator has the overall responsibility to ensure that the review is done in a proper manner and all steps in the review process are followed. Most methods for inspections are similar with minor variations. Here we discuss the inspection process employed by a commercial organization [97] The different stages in this process are: planning, preparation and overview, group review meeting, and rework and follow-up. These stages are generally executed in a linear order. We discuss each of these phases now.

Planning

The objective of the planning phase is to prepare for inspection. The author of the work product ensures that the work product is ready for inspection. The moderator checks that the entry criteria are satisfied by the work product. The entry criteria for different work products will be different. For example, for code an entry criteria is that the code compiles correctly and the available static analysis tools have been applied. The review (inspection) team is also formed in this phase.

The package that needs to be distributed to the review team is prepared. The package includes the work product to be reviewed, the specifications for that work product, relevant checklists and standards. The specifications for the work product are frequently the output of the previous phase and are needed to check the correctness of the current work product. For example, when a high level design has to be reviewed, then the package must include the requirement specification also, without which checking the correctness of design may not be possible.

Overview and Preparation

In this phase the package for review is given to the reviewers. The moderator may arrange an opening meeting, if needed, in which the author may provide a brief overview of the product and any special areas that need to be looked at carefully. The objective and overview of the inspection process might also be given in this meeting. The meeting is optional and can be omitted. In that case, the moderator provides a copy of the group review package to the reviewers.

| Project name and code :
Work product name and ID:
Reviewer name:
Effort spent for preparation (hrs):
Defect List: |

Sl	Location	Description	Criticality / Seriousness

Figure 2.13: Self review log.

The main task in this phase is for each reviewer to do a *self-review* of the work product. During the self-review, a reviewer goes through the entire work product and logs all the potential defects he or she finds in the self-preparation log. Often the reviewers will mark the defect on the work product itself. The reviewers also record the time they spent in the self-review. A standard form may be used for the self-preparation log; an example form is shown in Figure 2.13 [97].

Relevant checklists, guidelines, and standards may be used while reviewing. Checklists specifying the type of defects to look for are particularly useful. Ideally, the self review should be done in one continuous time span. The recommended time is less than two hours—that is, the work product is small enough that it can be fully examined in less than two hours. This phase of the review process ends when all reviewers have properly performed their self review and filled the self-review logs.

Group Review Meeting

The basic purpose of the group review meeting is to come up with the final defect list, based on the initial list of defects reported by the reviewers and the new ones found during the discussion in the meeting. The entry criterion for this step is that the moderator is satisfied that all the reviewers are ready for the meeting. The main outputs of this phase are the defect log and the defect summary report.

The moderator first checks to see if all the reviewers are prepared. This

Project	Xxxxxxxx
Work Product Type	Project Plan, V 1.0
Size of Product	14 pages
Review Team	P1, P2, P3, P4
Effort (Person Hours)	
Preparation	Total 10 person-hrs.
Group Review Meeting	10 person-hrs.
Total Effort	**20 person-hrs.**
Defects	
Number of Critical Defects	0
Number of Major Defects	3
Number of Minor Defects	16
Total Number of defects	**19**
Review Status	Accepted
Recommendations for next phase	
Comments	The plan has been well documented and presented

Figure 2.14: Summary report of an inspection.

is done by a brief examination of the effort and defect data in the self-review logs to confirm that sufficient time and attention has gone into the preparation. When preparation is not adequate, the group review is deferred until all participants are fully prepared.

If everything is ready, the group review meeting is held. The moderator is incharge of the meeting and has to make sure that the meeting stays focused on its basic purpose of defect identification and does not degenerate into a general brainstorming session or personal attacks on the author.

The meeting is conducted as follows. A team member (called the *reader*) goes over the work product line by line (or any other convenient small unit), and paraphrases each line to the team. Sometimes no paraphrasing is done and the team just goes over the work product line by line. At any line, if any reviewer has any issue from before, or finds any new issue in the meeting while listening to others, the reviewer raises the issue. There could be a discussion on the issue raised. The author accepts the issue as a defect or clarifies why it is not a defect. After discussion an agreement is reached and one member of the review team (called the *scribe*) records the identified defects in the defect log. At the end of the meeting, the scribe reads out the defects recorded in the defect log for a final review by the team members. Note that during the entire process of review, defects are only identified. It is not the purpose of the group to identify solutions—that is done later by the author.

The final defect log is the official record of the defects identified in the inspection and may also be used to track the defects to closure. For analyzing the effectiveness of a review, however, only summary level information is needed, for which a *summary report* is prepared. The summary report describes the work product, the total effort spent and its breakup in the different review process activities, total number of defects found for each category, and size. If types of defects were also recorded, then the number of defects in each category can also be recorded in the summary. A partially filled summary report of review of a project management plan is shown in Figure 2.14 [97].

The summary report is self-explanatory. Total number of minor defects found was 19, and the total number of major defects found was 3. That is, the defect density found is $16/14 = 1.2$ minor defects per page, and $3/14 = 0.2$ major defects per page. From experience, both of these rates are within the range seen in the past; hence it can be assumed that the review was conducted properly. The review team had 4 members, and each had spent 2.5 hours in individual review and the review meeting lasted 2.5 hours. This means that the coverage rate during preparation and review was $14/2.5 = 5.6$ pages per hour, which, from past experience, also seems acceptable.

If the modifications required for fixing the defects and addressing the issues are few, then the group review status is "accepted." If the modifications required are many, a follow up meeting by the moderator or a re-review might be necessary to verify whether the changes have been incorporated correctly. The moderator recommends what is to be done. In addition, recommendations regarding reviews in the next stages may also be made (e.g., in a detail design review it may be recommended code of which modules should undergo inspections.)

Rework and Follow Up

In this phase the author corrects all the defects raised during the inspection. The author may redo the work product, if that is what the moderator recommended. The author reviews the corrections with the moderator or in a re-review, depending on the decision of the group review meeting. The scribe ensures that the group review report and minutes of the meetings are communicated to the group review team.

Roles and Responsibilities

The inspection process is a structured process with different people having different responsibilities. The key roles in a group review are those of moderator, reader, scribe, author, and reviewer. These are logical roles and a person can be assigned multiple roles, with the restrictions that the author cannot be the moderator or the reader, and the moderator cannot be the reader. This implies that the minimum size of the group review team is three—the author, the moderator, and the reader. These three people are also reviewers and can assign the role of scribe to someone. The responsibilities of these roles should be clear from the inspection process. Here we briefly summarize the main activities of the moderator and the reviewers.

The moderator perhaps has the most important role during a group review. He has the overall responsibility of ensuring that the review goes well. The moderator should undergo formal training on how to conduct reviews, or should have experience of participating in a few reviews. The responsibilities of the moderator include:

- Schedule the group review meeting

- At the opening of group review meeting ensure that all participants are prepared and have submitted self-preparation log, or reschedule the group review

- Conduct the group review in an orderly and efficient manner

- Ensure that the meeting stays focused on the main task of defect identification

- Track each problem to resolution or ensure that it is tracked by someone else

- Ensure that group review reports are completed

During the meeting, the moderator has to make sure that all the participants contribute effectively, everyone is heard, there is an agreement on the findings of the review, and that the interest level does not drop. A key responsibility is to ensure that during the meeting the focus remains on problem identification and does not drift into problem resolution and that all reviewers remain focused on finding defects in the work product and do not get into finding faults with the author. Overall, orderly and amicable conduct of the meeting is largely the responsibility of the moderator. After the meeting, the moderator has to make sure that all participants are satisfied, the review reports have been filled and follow-up actions taken.

A reviewer is primarily responsible for finding defects. Generally, all members of the group review team are reviewers. The defects are found either through individual review or through the group review meeting. The main issues for a reviewer are:

- Be prepared for group review

- Be objective; focus on issues and not on people

- Concentrate on problems (offer solutions only after the group review)

- If something is not clear do not hesitate to stop progress until it is understood

- When proved wrong, move on

Guidelines for Work Products

All the work products in a project may not undergo group review as that may be prohibitively expensive and may not give commensurate returns. For each project it has to be decided which work products should be inspected, and the size of the inspection team. As the work products of the early part of the life cycle are very critical and defects in them have a multiplier effect in the later stages, it is recommended that early work products like the requirements document, architecture document, and project management plan, be inspected. Regarding team size, though a team size of three to five is often recommended, sometimes where the cost is not justified, an inspection team of just the author and another reviewer may be suitable [97]. This is also sometimes called one-person review.

Though the inspection process is same for any work product, the focus of the inspection is often different for different products. The constitution of the review team and the checklists used in review also depend on the nature of the work product. Some of the guidelines regarding the focus of the review and the composition of the inspection team are given in Table 2.1 [97].

Work product	Focus of Inspection	Participants
Requirement Specification	Requirements meet customer needs Requirements are implementable Omissions, inconsistencies and ambiguities in the requirements	Customer Designers Tester Developer
High Level Design	High-level design implements the requirements The design is implementable Omissions, and other defects in the design	Requirements author Detailed designer Developer
Code	Code implements the design Code is complete and correct Defects in code	Designer Tester Developer
System Test Cases	The set of test cases checks all conditions in the requirements Test cases are executable	Requirements author Tester Project leader
Project Management Plan	Plan is complete Project management plans is implementable Omissions and ambiguities	Project leader SEPG member Another project leader

Table 2.1: Guidelines for inspection of work products.

It is often hard to believe that a human-intensive process like the inspections can improve quality and productivity. Due to this and other reasons, inspections are often resisted. One way to find out the utility of inspections is to conduct some experiments and evaluate the benefits. Two simple experiments for this purpose are described in [98], along with the data of performing one in a commercial organization.

2.4.3 Software Configuration Management Process

Changes continuously take place in a software project—changes due to the evolution of work products as the project proceeds, changes due to defects

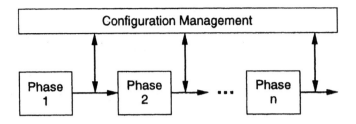

Figure 2.15: Configuration management and development process.

(bugs) being found and then fixed, and changes due to requirement changes. All these are reflected as changes in the files containing source, data, or documentation. Configuration management (CM) or *software configuration management (SCM)* is the discipline for systematically controlling the changes that take place during development [13, 12, 91]. The IEEE defines SCM as "the process of identifying and defining the items in the system, controlling the change of these items throughout their life cycle, recording and reporting the status of items and change requests, and verifying the completeness and correctness of items" [91]. Though all three are types of changes, changes due to product evolution and changes due to bug fixes can be, in some sense, treated as a natural part of the project itself which have to be dealt with even if the requirements do not change. Requirements changes, on the other hand, have a different dynamic. We will discuss the additional steps that need to be done for requirement changes as a separate process after discussing the CM process.

Software configuration management is a process independent of the development process largely because most development models look at the macro picture and not on changes to individual files. In a way, the development process is brought under the configuration control process, so that changes are allowed in a controlled manner, as shown in Figure 2.15 for a waterfall-type development process model [147]. Note that SCM directly controls only the products of a process and only indirectly influences the activities producing the product.

CM is essential to satisfy one of the basic objectives of a project—delivery of a high-quality software product to the client. What is this "software" that is delivered? At the least, it contains the various source or object files that make up the source or object code, scripts to build the working system from these files, and associated documentation. During the course of the project, the files change, leading to different versions. In this situation, how does a program manager ensure that the appropriate versions of sources are combined without missing any source, and the correct versions of the documents, which are consistent with the final source, are sent? This is ensured through proper CM.

CM Functionality

To better understand CM, let us consider some of the functionality that a project requires from the CM process. Though the requirements of a project from its CM process depends on the nature of the project, we discuss here a few functions that are generally needed.

- *Give latest version of a program.* Suppose that a program has to be modified. Clearly, the modification has to be carried out in the latest copy of that program; otherwise, changes made earlier may be lost. A proper CM process will ensure that latest version of a file can be obtained easily.

- *Undo a change or revert back to a specified version.* A change is made to a program, but later it becomes necessary to undo this change request. Similarly, a change might be made to many programs to implement some change request and later it may be decided that the entire change should be undone. The CM process must allow this to happen smoothly.

- *Prevent unauthorized changes or deletions.* A programmer may decide to change some programs, only to discover that the change has adverse side effects. The CM process ensures that unapproved changes are not permitted.

- *Gather all sources, documents, and other information for the current system.* All sources and related files are needed for releasing the product. The CM process must provide this functionality. All sources and related files of a working system are also sometimes needed for reinstallation.

These are some of the basic needs that a CM process must satisfy. There are other advanced requirements like handling concurrent updates or handle invariance [96].

CM Mechanisms

The main purpose of CM is to provide various mechanisms that can support the functionality needed by a project to handle the types of scenarios discussed above that arise due to changes. The mechanisms commonly used to provide the necessary functionality include the following

- Configuration identification and baselining

- Version control or version management

- Access control

As discussed above, the software being developed is not a monolith. A Software configuration item (SCI), or *item* is a document or an artifact that is explicitly placed under configuration control and that can be regarded as a basic unit for modification. As the project proceeds, hundreds of changes are made to these configuration items. Without periodically combining proper versions of these items into a state of the system, it will become very hard to get the system from the different versions of the many SCIs. For this reason, *baselines* are established. A baseline, once established, captures a logical state of the system, and forms the basis of change thereafter [14]. A baseline also forms a reference point in the development of a system.

A baseline essentially is an arrangement of a set of SCIs [14]. That is, a baseline is a set of SCIs and the relationship between them. For example, a requirements baseline may consist of many requirement SCIs (e.g., each requirement is an SCI) and how these SCIs are related in the requirements baseline (e.g., in which order they appear).

It should be noted that the SCIs being managed by SCM are not independent of one another and there are dependencies between various SCIs. An SCI X is said to *depend* on another SCI Y, if a change to Y might require a change to be made to X for X to remain correct or for the baselines to remain consistent [147]. A change request, though, might require changes be made to some SCIs; the dependency of other SCIs on the ones being changed might require that other SCIs also need to be changed. Clearly, the dependency between the SCIs needs to be properly understood and documented.

Version control is a key issue for CM [14, 12, 147], and many tools are available to help manage the various versions of programs. Without such a mechanism, many of the required CM functions cannot be supported. Version control helps preserve older versions of the programs whenever programs are changed. Commonly used CM systems like SCCS, CVS

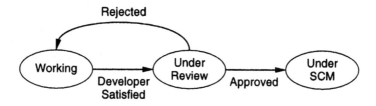

Figure 2.16: SCM life cycle of an item.

(www.cvshome.org), VSS (msdn.microsoft.com/vstudio/previous/ssafe), focus heavily on version control.

Most CM systems also provide means for access control. To understand the need for access control, let us understand the life cycle of an SCI. Typically, while an SCI is under development and is not visible to other SCIs, it is considered being in the *working* state. An SCI in the working state is not under SCM and can be changed freely. Once the developer is satisfied that the SCI is stable enough for it to be used by others, the SCI is given for review, and the item enters the state "under review." Once an item is in this state, it is considered as "frozen," and any changes made to a private copy that the developer may have made are not recognized. After a successful review the SCI is entered into a *library*, after which the item is formally under SCM. The basic purpose of this review is to make sure that the item is of satisfactory quality and is needed by others, though the exact nature of review will depend on the nature of the SCI and the actual practice of SCM. For example, the review might entail checking if the item meets its specifications or if it has been properly unit tested. If the item is not approved, the developer may be given the item back and the SCI enters the working state again. This "life cycle" of an item from the SCM perspective, is shown in Figure 2.16 [147].

Once an SCI is in the library, any modification should be controlled, as others may be using that item. Hence, access to items in the library is controlled. For making an approved change, the SCI is checked out of the library, the change is made, the modification is reviewed and then the SCI is checked back into the library. When a new version is checked in, the old version is not replaced and both old and new versions may exist in the library—often logically with one file being maintained along with information about changes to recreate the older version. This aspect of SCM is sometimes called *library management* and is done with the aid of tools.

CM Process

The CM process defines the set of activities that need to be performed to control change. As with most activities in project management, the first stage in the CM process is planning. Then the process has to be executed, generally by using some tools. Finally, as any CM plan requires some discipline from the project personnel in terms of storing items in proper locations, and making changes properly, monitoring the status of the configuration items and performing CM audits are therefore other activities in the CM process.

Planning for configuration management involves identifying the configuration items and specifying the procedures to be used for controlling and implementing changes to these configuration items. Identifying configuration items is a fundamental activity in any type of CM [12, 89, 147]. Typical examples of configuration items include requirements specifications, design documents, source code, test plans, test scripts, test procedures, test data, standards used in the project (such as coding standards and design standards), the acceptance plan, documents such as the CM plan and the project plan, user documentation such as the user manual, documents such as the training material, contract documents (including support tools such as a compiler or in-house tools), quality records (review records, test records), and CM records (release records, status tracking records). Any customer-supplied products or purchased items that will be part of the delivery (called "included software product") are also configuration items.

As there are typically a lot of items in a project, how they are to be organized is also decided in the planning phase. Typically, the directory structure that will be employed to store the different elements is decided in the plan. To facilitate proper naming of configuration items, the naming conventions for CM items are decided during the CM planning stages. In addition to naming standards, version numbering must be planned. When a configuration item is changed, the old item is not replaced with the new copy; instead, the old copy is maintained and a new one is created. This approach results in multiple versions of an item, so policies for version number assignment are needed. If a CM tool is being used, then sometimes the tool handles the version numbering. Otherwise, it has to be explicitly done in the project.

The configuration controller or the project manager do the CM planning. It is begun only when the project has been initiated and the operating environment and requirements specifications are clearly documented. The output of this phase is the CM plan.

The configuration controller (CC) is responsible for the implementation of the CM plan. Depending on the size of the system under development, his or her role may be a part-time or full-time job. In certain cases, where there are large teams or where two or more teams/groups are involved in the development of the same or different portions of the software or interfacing systems, it may be necessary to have a configuration control board (CCB). This board includes representatives from each of the teams. A CCB (or a CC) is considered essential for CM [89], and the CM plan must clearly define the roles and responsibilities of the CC/CCB. These duties will also depend on the type of file system and the nature of CM tools being used.

For a CM process to work well, the people in the project have to use it as per the CM plan and follow its policies and procedures. However, people make mistakes. And if by mistake an SCI is misplaced, or access control policies are violated, then the integrity of the product may be lost. To minimize mistakes and catch errors early, regular status checking of SCIs may be done. A configuration audit may also be performed periodically to ensure that the CM system integrity is not being violated. The audit may also check that the changes to SCIs due to change requests (discussed next) have been done properly and that the change requests have been implemented.

In addition to checking the status of the items, the status of change requests (discussed below) must be checked. To accomplish this goal, change requests that have been received since the last CM status monitoring operation are examined. For each change request, the state of the item as mentioned in the change request records is compared with the actual state. Checks may also be done to ensure that all modified items go through their full life cycle (that is, the state diagram) before they are incorporated in the baseline.

2.4.4 Requirements Change Management Process

Requirements change. And changes in requirements can come at any time during the life of a project (or even after that). The farther down in the life cycle the requirements change, the more severe the impact on the project. Instead of wishing that changes will not come, or hoping that somehow the initial requirements will be "so good" that no changes will be required, it is better that a project manager prepare to handle change requests as they come.

Uncontrolled changes to requirements can have a very adverse effect on the cost, schedule, and quality of the project. Requirement changes can account for as much as 40% of the total cost [22]. Due to the potentially large impact of requirement changes on the project, often a separate process is employed to deal with them.

The change management process defines the set of activities that are performed when there are some new requirements or changes to existing requirements (we will call both changes in the requirements). Though we are focusing on requirement changes, any major changes like design changes or major bug fixes to a system in deployment, this process can be used. Here we discuss a requirement change management process which is based on one used in a commercial organization [97]. The change management process has the following steps.

- Log the changes

- Perform impact analysis on the work products

- Estimate impact on effort and schedule

- Review impact with concerned stakeholders

- Rework work products

A change is initiated by a *change request*. A change request log is maintained to keep track of the change requests. Each entry in the log contains a change request number, a brief description of the change, the effect of the change, the status of the change request, and key dates.

The effect of a change request is assessed by performing impact analysis. Impact analysis involves identifying work products and configuration items that need to be changed and evaluating the quantum of change to each; reassessing the projects risks by revisiting the risk management plan; and evaluating the overall implications of the changes for the effort and schedule estimates.

Once a change is reviewed and approved, then it is implemented, i.e., changes to all the items are made. The actual tracking of implementation of a change request may be handled by the configuration management process, which has been discussed above.

One danger of requirement changes is that, even though each change is not large in itself, over the life of the project the cumulative impact of the changes is large. Hence, besides studying the impact of individual changes and tracking them, the cumulative impact of changes must also be monitored. For cumulative changes, the change log is used. To facilitate this analysis, the log is frequently maintained as a spreadsheet.

2.4.5 Process Management Process

A software process is not a static entity—it has to change to improve so that the products produced using the process are of higher quality and are less costly. As we have seen, improving quality and productivity are fundamental goals of engineering. To achieve these goals the software process must continually be improved, as quality and productivity are determined to a great extent by the process. As stated earlier, improving the quality and productivity of the process is the main objective of the process management process. It should be emphasized that process management is quite different from project management. In process management the focus is on improving the process which in turn improves the general quality and productivity for the products produced using the process. In project management the focus is on executing the current project and ensuring that the objectives of the project are met. The time duration of interest for project management is typically the duration of the project, while process management works on a much larger time scale as each project is viewed as providing a data point for the process.

Process management is an advanced topic beyond the scope of this book. Interested readers are referred to the book by Humphrey [89]. We will only briefly discuss some aspects here.

To improve its software process, an organization needs to first understand the status of the current status and then develop a plan to improve the process. It is generally agreed that changes to a process are best introduced in small increments and that it is not feasible to totally revolutionize a process. The reason is that it takes time to internalize and truly follow any new methods that may be introduced. And only when the new methods are properly implemented will their effects be visible. Introducing too many new methods for the software process will make the task of implementing the change very hard.

If we agree that changes to a process must be introduced in small increments, the next question is out of a large set of possible enhancements to a process, in what order should the improvement activities be undertaken? Or what small change should be introduced first? This depends on the current state of the process. For example, if the process is very primitive there is no point in suggesting sophisticated metrics-based project control as an improvement strategy; incorporating it in a primitive process is not easy. On the other hand, if the process is already using many basic models, such a step might be the right step to further improve the process. Hence, deciding what activities to undertake for process improvement is a function of the current state of the process. Once some process improvement takes place, the process state may change, and a new set of possibilities may emerge. This concept of introducing changes in small increments based on the current state of the process has been captured in the Capability Maturity Model (CMM) framework. The CMM framework provides a general roadmap for process improvement. We give a brief description of the CMM framework here; the reader is referred to [89, 134] for more details. An example of implementation of CMM in an organization can be found in [96].

Software process capability describes the range of expected results that can be achieved by following the process [134]. The process capability of an organization determines what can be expected from the organization in terms of quality and productivity. The goal of process improvement is to improve the process capability. A *maturity level* is a well-defined evolutionary plateau towards achieving a mature software process [134]. Based on the empirical evidence found by examining the processes of many organizations, the CMM suggests that there are five well-defined maturity levels for a software process. These are initial (level 1), repeatable, defined, managed, and optimizing (level 5). The CMM framework says that as process improvement is best incorporated in small increments, processes go from their current levels to the next higher level when they are improved. Hence, during the course of process improvement, a process moves from level to level until it reaches level 5. This is shown in Figure 2.17 [134].

The CMM provides characteristics of each level, which can be used to assess the current level of the process of an organization. As the movement from one level is to the next level, the characteristics of the levels also suggest the areas in which the process should be improved so that it can move to the next higher level. Essentially, for each level it specifies the areas in which improvement can be absorbed and will bring the maximum benefits. Overall, this provides a roadmap for continually improving the process.

The *initial process* (level 1) is essentially an ad hoc process that has no formalized method for any activity. Basic project controls for ensuring that activities are being done properly, and that the project plan is being adhered to, are missing. In crisis the project plans and development processes are abandoned in favor of a code-and-test type of approach. Success in such or-

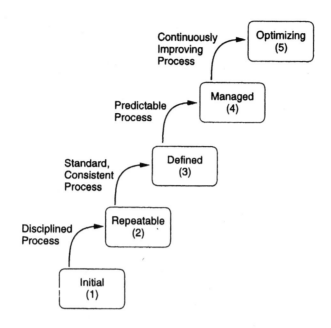

Figure 2.17: Capability Maturity Model.

ganizations depends solely on the quality and capability of individuals. The process capability is unpredictable as the process constantly changes. Organizations at this level can benefit most by improving project management, quality assurance, and change control.

In a *repeatable process* (level 2), policies for managing a software project and procedures to implement those policies exist. That is, project management is well developed in a process at this level. Some of the characteristics of a process at this level are: project commitments are realistic and based on past experience with similar projects, cost and schedule are tracked and problems resolved when they arise, formal configuration control mechanisms are in place, and software project standards are defined and followed. Essentially, results obtained by this process can be repeated as the project planning and tracking is formal.

At the *defined level* (level 3) the organization has standardized a software process, which is properly documented. A software process group exists in the organization that owns and manages the process. In the process each step is carefully defined with verifiable entry and exit criteria, methodologies for performing the step, and verification mechanisms for the output of the

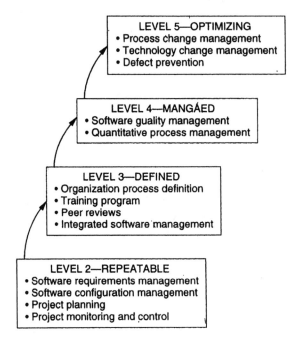

Figure 2.18: Some key process areas.

step. In this process both the development and management processes are formal.

At the *managed level* (level 4) quantitative goals exist for process and products. Data is collected from software processes, which is used to build models to characterize the process. Hence, measurement plays an important role in a process at this level. Due to the models built, the organization has a good insight of the process capability and its deficiencies. The results of using such a process can be predicted in quantitative terms.

At the *optimizing level* (level 5), the focus of the organization is on continuous process improvement. Data is collected and routinely analyzed to identify areas that can be strengthened to improve quality or productivity. New technologies and tools are introduced and their effects measured in an effort to improve the performance of the process. Best software engineering and management practices are used throughout the organization.

This CMM framework can be used to improve the process. Improvement requires first assessing the level of the current process. Based on the current level, the areas in which maximum benefits can be derived are known from the framework. For example, for improving a process at level 1 (or for going from level 1 to level 2), project management and the change control activities must be made more formal. The complete CMM framework provides more details about which particular areas need to be strengthened to move up the maturity framework. This is generally done by specifying the key process areas of each maturity level, which in turn, can be used to determine which areas to strengthen to move up. Some of the key process areas of the different levels are shown in Figure 2.18 [134].

Though the CMM framework specifies the process areas that should be improved to increase the maturity of the process, it does not specify how to bring about the improvement. That is, it is essentially a framework that does not suggest detailed prescriptions for improvement, but guides the process improvement activity along the maturity levels such that process improvement is introduced in increments and the improvement activity at any time is clearly focused. Many organizations have successfully used this framework to improve their processes. It is a major driving force for process improvement. A detailed example of how an organization that follows the CMM executes its project can be found in [96].

2.5 Summary

A software process is the set of activities, together with ordering constraints, such that if the activities are performed in accordance to the process, the desired results (of high quality and productivity) will be achieved. A software process consists of different component processes like the development process, the project management process, the configuration management process, and the process management process.

In order to satisfy the basic software engineering objectives, the software process must have some desirable properties. The process must be predictable, that is, following the same process produces more or less similar results. The process must also support testability and maintainability, as testing and maintenance are the activities that consume the most resources. The process should support defect removal and prevention throughout development, as the longer a defect stays, the more costly it is to remove it. And the process must be self-improving.

A process model is a general process specification which has been found useful in many circumstances. In this chapter, we discussed some process models for the development process. The waterfall model is conceptually the simplest model of software development, where the requirement, design, coding, and testing phases are performed in linear progression. There is a defined output after each phase, which is certified before the next phase begins. It has been very widely used, even though it has limitations. The major limitations of this model are that it follows the "all or nothing" approach, is document driven, and does not permit changes.

Another major model is the prototyping model, where a prototype is built before building the final system. The prototype is used to further develop the requirements leading to more stable requirements. Experience with the prototype also results in better design and development of the system.

In the iterative development model, software is developed in iterations, each iteration resulting in a working software system. Iterative development is now widely used as it allows software to be developed and delivered in parts, hence the risks are low. Furthermore, it does not require all requirements to be known in the start, which is usually not possible. The feedback from software of earlier iterations can also be used to improve the software in later iterations.

The timeboxing model is also an iterative model, but the different iterations are of equal time duration. Each iteration is also divided into equal length stages. There is a committed team for each stage of an iteration. The different iterations are then executed in a pipelined manner, with each dedicated team working on its stage but for different iterations. As multiple iterations are concurrently active, this model reduces the average completion time of each iteration and hence is useful in situations where short cycle time is highly desirable.

Besides the development process, there are other component processes of the software process. The project management process consists of three major phases—planning, monitoring and control, and termination analysis. Much of project management revolves around the project plan, which is produced during the planing phase. The monitoring and control phase requires accurate data about the project to reach project management, which uses this data to determine the state of the project and exercise any control it requires. For this purpose, metrics play an essential role in providing the project management quantified data about the state of development and of the products produced. In the end, a postmortem analysis is done to learn from the experience.

The inspection process is used for finding defects in a work product. In inspections, a work product is closely examined by a group of peer experts, who examine it for defects. There is a structured process, in which first the material to be inspected is examined individually by each of the reviewers. Once the reviewers have logged the defects they have found, a group review meeting is held in which the product is examined line by line. At any point, if a reviewer has an issue, it is discussed and, if needed, recorded as a defect. By the end of the process, all the defects found are recorded, and a summary of defects and effort spent prepared that can be used to judge if the review has been performed properly. Inspections are used heavily in practice and are recognized as an industry best practice.

The software configuration management (CM) process deals with managing the changes that take place during the project. The CM process typically focuses on controlling the changes to the individual CM items, such that latest copy of each item is easily available, and changes can be undone, if needed. Along with the CM process, there is a requirements change management process that focuses on handling changes in requirements. The purpose is to evaluate change requests for their impact, and then implement the changes of approved changes.

The process management process is frequently performed by the software engineering process group. The basic objective of this process is to improve the process such that the quality and productivity improves. A key aspect of this process is to understand the capability of the current process and characterize it so that the expected outcomes are known. The other major activity of this process is to improve the process so that the cost and quality of future products are improved. Frameworks like the CMM help in the process management process.

In the rest of the book we will focus on the important activities that are generally performed during a software development project, and discuss each one of them in more detail. The activities covered include project management as well as development process activities. A knowledge of these activities will enable a person to successfully execute a software project.

Exercises

1. What is the relationship between a process model, process specification, and process for a project?

2. What are the key outputs in a development project that follows the prototyping model? Write a ETVX specification for this process.

3. For the next project, the project manager wants to predict the number of defects she is likely to find in each of the quality control tasks in the process.

How will you do this? Assume that all the past data you need is available. Also make suitable assumptions on process predictability.

4. You have to design a process for a project using the iterative development model. If the main objective of this project is high quality, what are the quality control tasks you will have in the process?

5. It is reasonable to assume that if software is easy to test, it will be easy to maintain. Suppose that by putting extra effort in design and coding you increase the cost of these phases by 15%, but you reduce the cost of testing and maintenance by 5%. Will you put in the extra effort?

6. Which of the development process models discussed in this chapter would you follow for the following projects? Give justifications.

   (a) A simple data processing project.

   (b) A data entry system for office staff that has never used computers before. The user interface and user-friendliness are extremely important.

   (c) A new system for comparing fingerprints. It is not clear if the current algorithms can compare fingerprints in the given response time constraints.

   (d) A spreadsheet system that has some basic features and many other desirable features that use these basic features.

   (e) A new missile tracking system. It is not known if the current hardware/software technology is mature enough to achieve the goals.

   (f) An on-line inventory management system for an automobile industry.

   (g) A flight control system with extremely high reliability. There are many potential hazards with such a system.

   (h) A Web site for an on-line store which always has a list of desired features it wants to add and add them quickly.

7. Suppose that the stages in a time box in the timeboxing model are unequal. What will be the impact on delivery time and resource utilization?

8. A project uses the timeboxing process model with three stages in each time box (as discussed in the chapter), but with unequal length. Suppose the requirement specification stage takes 2 weeks with a team of 2 people, the build stage takes 3 weeks with a team of 4 people, and deployment takes 1 week with a team of 2 people. Design the process for this project that maximizes resource utilization. Assume that each resource can do any task. (Hint: Exploit the fact that the sum of durations of the first and the third stage is equal to the duration of the second stage.)

9. In the timeboxing process model, what will happen if one stage in an iteration takes longer or shorter than its allocated time?

10. Why is the CM process needed in addition to the development process?

11. What types of effect will the project monitoring activity of the project management process have on the development process? Explain with examples.

12. Suppose the SEPG undertakes some initiatives to improve the existing process. How will you verify that the initiatives are indeed improving the process?

3

Software Requirements Analysis and Specification

The complexity and size of software systems are continuously increasing. As the scale changes to more complex and larger software systems, new problems occur that did not exist in smaller systems (or were of minor significance), which leads to a redefining of priorities of the activities that go into developing software. Software requirements is one such area, to which little importance was attached in the early days of software development, as the emphasis was on coding and design. The tacit assumption was that the developers understood the problem clearly when it was explained to them, generally informally.

As systems grew more complex, it became evident that the goals of the entire system could not be easily comprehended. Hence the need for more rigorous requirements analysis arose. Now, for large software systems, requirements analysis is perhaps the most difficult and intractable activity; it is also very error-prone. Many believe that the software engineering discipline is weakest in this critical area.

Some of the difficulty is due to the scope of this activity. The software project is initiated by the client's needs. In the beginning, these needs are in the minds of various people in the client organization. The requirements analyst has to identify the requirements by talking to these people and understanding their needs. In situations where the software is to automate a currently manual process, many of the needs can be understood by observing the current practice. But no such methods exist for systems for which manual processes do not exist or for "new features," which are frequently added when automating an existing manual process. For such systems, the requirements problem is complicated by the fact that the needs and requirements of the system many not be known even to the user—they have to be visualized and created.

Hence, identifying requirements necessarily involves specifying what some people have in their minds (or what will come to their minds when they visualize it). As the information in their minds is, by nature, not formally stated or organized, the input to the software requirements specification phase is inherently informal and imprecise, and it is likely to be incomplete. When inputs from multiple people are to be gathered, these inputs are likely to be inconsistent as well.

The requirements phase translates the ideas in the minds of the clients (the input), into a formal document (the output of the requirements phase). Thus, the output of the phase is a set of precisely specified requirements, which hopefully are complete and consistent, while the input has none of these properties. Clearly, the process of specifying requirements cannot be totally formal; any formal translation process producing a formal output must have a precise and unambiguous input. This is why the software requirements activity cannot be fully automated, and any method for identifying requirements can be at best a set of guidelines.

In this chapter we will discuss what requirements are, why requirement specification is important, how requirements are analyzed and specified, how requirements are validated, and some metrics that can be applied to requirements. It ends with a discussion of the SRS of the case studies used in the book.

3.1 Software Requirements

IEEE defines a requirement as "(1) A condition of capability needed by a user to solve a problem or achieve an objective; (2) A condition or a capability that must be met or possessed by a system ... to satisfy a contract, standard, specification, or other formally imposed document." [91]. Note that in software requirements we are dealing with the requirements of the proposed system, that is, the capabilities that the system, which is yet to be developed, should have. It is because we are dealing with specifying a system that does not exist that the problem of requirements becomes complicated. The goal of the requirements activity is to produce the Software Requirements Specification (SRS), that describes *what* the proposed software should do without describing *how* the software will do it.

Producing the SRS is easier said than done. A basic limitation for this is that the user needs keep changing as the environment in which the system is to function changes with time. Even while accepting that some requirement change requests are inevitable, there are still pressing reasons why a thorough job should be done in the requirements phase to produce a high-quality and relatively stable SRS. Let us first look at some of these reasons.

3.1.1 Need for SRS

The origin of most software systems is in the needs of some clients. The software system itself is created by some developers. Finally, the completed system will be used by the end users. Thus, there are three major parties interested in a new system: the client, the developer, and the users. Somehow the requirements for the system that will satisfy the needs of the clients and the concerns of the users have to be communicated to the developer. The problem is that the client usually does not understand software or the software development process, and the developer often does not understand the client's problem and application area. This causes a communication gap between the parties involved in the development project. A basic purpose of software requirements specification is to bridge this communication gap. SRS is the medium through which the client and user needs are accurately specified to the developer. Hence one of the main advantages is:

- An SRS establishes the basis for agreement between the client and the supplier on what the software product will do.

This basis for agreement is frequently formalized into a legal contract between the client (or the customer) and the developer (the supplier). So, through SRS, the client clearly describes what it expects from the supplier, and the developer clearly understands what capabilities to build in the software. Without such an agreement, it is almost guaranteed that once the development is over, the project will have an unhappy. client, which almost always leads to unhappy developers. (The classic situation is, client: "Hey! there is a bug"; Developer: "No, it is a software feature.") Actually, the reality of the situation is that even with such an agreement, the client is frequently not satisfied! A related, but important, advantage is:

- An SRS provides a reference for validation of the final product.

That is, the SRS helps the client determine if the software meets the requirements. Without a proper SRS, there is no way a client can determine if the software being delivered is what was ordered, and there is no way the developer can convince the client that all the requirements have been fulfilled.

Providing the basis of agreement and validation should be strong enough reasons for both the client and the developer to do a thorough and rigorous job of requirement understanding and specification, but there are other very practical and pressing reasons for having a good SRS.

We have seen that the primary forces driving a project are cost, schedule, and quality. Consequently, anything that has a favorable effect on these factors should be considered desirable. Boehm found (as reported in [45]) that in some projects 54% of all the detected errors were detected after coding and unit testing was done and that 45% of these errors actually originated during requirement and early design stages. That is, a total of approximately 25% errors occur during requirement and early design stages. A report on errors in the A-7 project shows that about 80 errors were detected in the requirements document over a period of few months that resulted in change requests [8]. Another report indicates that more than 500 errors were found in an SRS that was earlier approved (as reported in [45]). Similarly, another project reported that more than 250 errors were found in a previously reviewed SRS by stating the requirements in a structured manner and using tools to analyze the document [47].

It is clear that many errors are made during the requirements phase. And an error in the SRS will most likely manifest itself as an error in the final system implementing the SRS; after all, if the SRS document specifies a wrong system (i.e., one that will not satisfy the client's objectives), then even a correct implementation of the SRS will lead to a system that will not satisfy the client. Clearly, if we want a high-quality end product that has few errors, we must begin with a high-quality SRS. In other words, we can conclude that:

- A high-quality SRS is a prerequisite to high-quality software.

Finally, we show that the quality of SRS has an impact on cost (and schedule) of the project. We have already seen that errors can exist in the SRS. We saw earlier that the cost of fixing an error increases almost exponentially as time progresses. That is, a requirement error, if detected and removed after the system has been developed, can cost up to 100 times more than

Phase	Cost (person-hours)
Requirements	2
Design	5
Coding	15
Acceptance test	50
Operation and maint.	150

Table 3.1: Cost of fixing requirement errors.

removing it during the requirements phase itself. Based on the data given in [8], which reported that on average it took about 2.4 person-hours to make a change to the requirements to correct an error (this average was without considering the outliers; with the outliers the average was about 5.0 person-hours), we assume that the average cost of fixing a requirement error in the requirement phase is about 2 person-hours. From this and the relative cost of fixing errors as reported in a multicompany study in [17, 20] (these costs were reflected graphically in Figure 1.1), the approximate average cost of fixing requirement errors (in person-hours) depending on the phase is shown in Table 3.1.

Clearly, we can have a tremendous reduction in the project cost by reducing the errors in the SRS. A simplified example will illustrate this point. Using the costs given earlier, by investing an additional 100 person-hours in the requirements phase, an average of about 50 new requirements errors will be detected and removed. (This oversimplification is likely to hold only for the errors detected early in the phase. As the number of remaining errors is reduced, the effort required to detect each error is likely to increase.) If these errors are not detected in the requirements phase, they will be detected in some later phase. In the A-7 project the following distribution was found [8]: of the requirements errors that remain after the requirements phase, about 65% are detected during design, 2% during coding, 30% during testing, and 3% during operation and maintenance. This type of distribution can be expected in general, as most of the requirements errors are likely to be caught in the design phases and the acceptance test phase, while the rest will be caught in other phases. Assume that these 50 requirement errors, if not removed, would have been detected (and fixed) in the later phases with the distribution given earlier. The total cost of fixing the errors in this case will be

$$32.5 * 5 + 1 * 15 + 15 * 50 + 1.5 * 150 = 1152 \text{ person} - \text{hours!}$$

In other words, by investing additional 100 person-hours in the requirements phase in this example, the development cost could be reduced by 1152 person-hours—a net reduction in cost of 1052 person-hours!

This can be viewed in another manner. An error that remains in the requirements will be detected in the later phases with the following probabilities: 0.4 in design, 0.1 in coding and unit testing, 0.4 in acceptance testing, 0.1 during operation and maintenance. The cost of fixing a requirement error in these phases was given earlier. Hence, the expected cost of fixing a requirement error that is not removed during the requirements phase is $0.4 * 5 + 0.1 * 15 + 0.4 * 50 + 0.1 * 150 = 38.5$ person-hours. Therefore, if the expected effort required to detect and remove an error during the requirements phase is less than this, it makes economic sense to spend the extra effort in the requirements phase and remove the error.

This is not the complete story. We know that requirements frequently change. As mentioned earlier, though some of the changes are inevitable due to the changing needs and perceptions, many changes come as the requirements were not properly analyzed and not enough effort was expended to validate the requirements. With a high-quality SRS, requirement changes that come about due to improperly analyzed requirements should be reduced considerably. And as changes tend to escalate the cost and throw the project schedule haywire, a reduction in the requirement change traffic will reduce the project cost, in addition to improving its chances of finishing on schedule.

Let us illustrate this with another simplified example. It is estimated that 20% to 40% of the total development effort in a software project is due to rework, much of which occurs due to change in requirements [22]. The cost of the requirement phase is typically about 6% of the total project cost, according to the COCOMO model [20] (the model is discussed in more detail in Chapter 4). Consider a project whose total effort requirement is estimated to be 50 person-months. For this project, the requirements phase consumes about 3 person-months. If by spending an additional 33% effort in the requirements phase we reduce the total requirement change requests by 33%, then the total effort due to rework (assuming all rework is due to requirement change requests) will reduce from 10 to 20 person-months to 6 to 12 person-months, resulting in a total saving of 5 to 11 person-months, i.e., a saving of 10% to 22% of the total cost! From these, we can conclude that

- A high quality SRS reduces the development cost.

Hence, the quality of the SRS impacts customer (and developer) satisfaction, system validation, quality of the final software, and the software development cost. The critical role the SRS plays in a software development project should be evident from these.

3.1.2 Requirement Process

The requirement process is the sequence of activities that need to be performed in the requirements phase and that culminate in producing a high-quality document containing the software requirements specification (SRS). The requirements process typically consists of three basic tasks: problem or requirement analysis, requirement specification, and requirements validation.

Problem analysis often starts with a high-level "problem statement."

During analysis the problem domain and the environment are modeled in an effort to understand the system behavior, constraints on the system, its inputs and outputs, etc. The basic purpose of this activity is to obtain a thorough understanding of what the software needs to provide. The understanding obtained by problem analysis forms the basis of *requirements specification*, in which the focus is on clearly specifying the requirements in a document. Issues such as representation, specification languages, and tools, are addressed during this activity. As analysis produces large amounts of information and knowledge with possible redundancies; properly organizing and describing the requirements is an important goal of this activity. *Requirements validation* focuses on ensuring that what has been specified in the SRS are indeed all the requirements of the software and making sure that the SRS is of good quality. The requirements process terminates with the production of the validated SRS.

Though it seems that the requirements process is a linear sequence of these three activities, in reality it is not so for anything other than trivial systems. In most real systems, there is considerable overlap and feedback between these activities. So, some parts of the system are analyzed and then specified while the analysis of the other parts is going on. Furthermore, if the validation activities reveal problems in the SRS, it is likely to lead to further analysis and specification. However, in general, for a part of the system, analysis precedes specification and specification precedes validation. This requirement process is shown in Figure 3.1.

As shown in the figure, from the specification activity we may go back to the analysis activity. This happens as frequently some parts of the problem

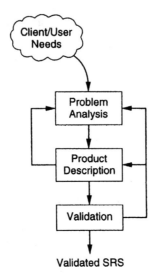

Figure 3.1: The requirement process.

are analyzed and then specified before other parts are analyzed and specified. Furthermore, the process of specification frequently shows shortcomings in the knowledge of the problem, thereby necessitating further analysis. Once the specification is "complete" it goes through the validation activity. This activity may reveal problems in the specifications itself, which requires going back to the specification step, or may reveal shortcomings in the understanding of the problem, which requires going back to the analysis activity.

During requirements analysis the focus is on understanding the system and its requirements. For a complex system, this is a hard task, and the time-tested method of "divide-and-conquer," i.e., decomposing the problem or system into smaller parts and then understanding the parts and their relationships, is inevitably applied to manage the complexity. Also, for managing the complexity and the large volume of information that becomes available during analysis, various structures are used during analysis to represent the information to help view the system as a series of abstractions. Examples of these structures are data flow diagrams and object diagrams (more about these in the next section). For a portion of the system, analysis typically precedes specification. Once the analysis is complete and the structures built, the system part has to be specified.

The transition from analysis to specification, though, seems as if it should be simple; this is not so. In fact, this transition can be quite hard. The reason for this transition being hard is the different objectives of the two activities. In specification, we have to specify only what the software is supposed to do, i.e., focus on the external behavior of the system. In order to identify all the external behaviors, the *structure* of the problem and its various components need to be clearly understood besides understanding its inputs and outputs. However, the structure itself may not be of much use in specification, as its focus is exclusively on the external behavior or the eventual system, not the internal structure of the problem domain. Due to this, one should not expect that once the analysis is done, specification will be straightforward. Furthermore, many "outputs" of the analysis are not used directly in the SRS. This does not mean that these outputs are not useful—they are essential in modeling the problem that leads to the proper understanding of the requirements, which is a prerequisite to specification. Hence, the use of the analysis activity and structures that it built may be indirect, aiding understanding rather than directly aiding specification.

It is worth noting that some similarities exist in the analysis activity and the design activity. As pointed out by Davis [45], the basic problem during software design is the same—managing the complexity. The approach used there is similar—decomposition and building structures to represent the system as a series of abstractions. Due to this similarity, the approaches used for problem analysis and design are frequently similar (e.g., data flow diagrams and object diagrams are used in analysis as well as design). However, although the approaches are similar, the objective of the two activities is completely different. Whereas analysis deals with the problem domain, with the basic objective of understanding the problem, design deals with the solution domain with the basic objective of optimizing the design [45]. Because to this, the application of similar approaches produces different structures during analysis and design. It is sometimes mistakenly believed that the structures produced during analysis will and should be carried through in design. This comes from a basic misunderstanding about the objectives of the two activities. Though some of the structures may eventually get used in design, this should be done only if the analysis structures are consistent with the design objective.

Finally, there is the issue of the level of detail that the requirement process should aim to uncover and specify. This is also an issue that cannot be easily resolved and that depends on the objective of the requirement specification phase. If the objective is to define the overall broad needs of the system, the requirements can be very abstractly stated. Generally, the purpose of such requirements is to perform some feasibility analysis or use the requirements for competitive bidding. At the lower level are the requirements where all the behavior and external interfaces of the software are clearly specified. Such requirements are clearly very detailed and are suitable for software development.

An example can illustrate this point. Suppose a car manufacturer wants to have an inventory control system. At an abstract level, the requirements of the inventory control system could be stated in terms of the number of parts it has to track, level of concurrency it has to support, whether it will be on-line or batch processing, what types of information and reports it will provide (e.g., status of each item on demand, purchase orders for items that are low in inventory, consumption patterns), etc. Requirements specification at this level of abstraction can be used to estimate the costs and perform a cost-benefit analysis. It can also be used to invite tenders from various developers. However, such a requirements specification is of little use for a developer given the contract to develop the software. That developer needs to know the exact format of the reports, all the queries that can be performed and their structure, total number of terminals the system has to support, the structure of the major databases that will exist, etc. These are all specifying the external behavior of the software, but when viewed from the higher level of abstraction they can be considered as specifying how the abstract requirements should be implemented (e.g., the details of a report can be viewed as defining how the basic objective of providing information is satisfied).

As should be clear, the abstract requirement level is not suitable for software development. Hence, we will focus mostly on the requirements at the lower level in which all the details about external behavior that are needed for the developer to build a software system are specified. That is, we view the SRS as providing all the detailed information needed by a software developer for properly developing the system. However, it is worth pointing out that even when obtaining the detailed requirements is the objective, abstract requirements can still play a useful role for complex systems. As the problem analysis starts with some initial description of the system's behavior or needs, the abstract requirements can play this role (besides being used for competitive bidding and/or feasibility analysis). In other words, specifying the requirements at an abstract level is likely to be useful in producing the SRS that contains the detailed requirements of the system.

The following sections will be devoted to providing a more detailed description of the activities in the three major activities in the requirements phase: analysis, specification, and verification.

3.2 Problem Analysis

The basic aim of problem analysis is to obtain a clear understanding of the needs of the clients and the users, what exactly is desired from the software, and what the constraints on the solution are [45]. Frequently the client and the users do not understand or know all their needs, because the potential of the new system is often not fully appreciated. The analysts have to ensure that the real needs of the clients and the users are uncovered, even if they don't know them clearly. That is, the analysts are not just collecting and organizing information about the client's organization and its processes, but they also act as *consultants* who play an *active* role of helping the clients and users identify their needs.

The basic principle used in analysis is the same as in any complex task: divide and conquer. That is, *partition* the problem into subproblems and then try to understand each subproblem and its relationship to other subproblems in an effort to understand the total problem.

The concepts of *state* and *projection* can sometimes also be used effectively in the partitioning process. A state of a system represents some conditions about the system. Frequently, when using state, a system is first viewed as operating in one of the several possible states, and then a detailed analysis is performed for each state. This approach is sometimes used in real-time software or process-control software.

In *projection*, a system is defined from multiple points of view [152]. While using projection, different viewpoints of the system are defined and the system is then analyzed from these different perspectives. The different "projections" obtained are combined to form the analysis for the complete system. Analyzing the system from the different perspectives is often easier, as it limits and focuses the scope of the study.

In the remainder of this section we will discuss a few methods for problem analysis. As the goal of analysis is to understand the problem domain, an analyst must be familiar with different methods of analysis and pick the approach that he feels is best suited to the problem at hand.

3.2.1 Informal Approach

The informal approach to analysis is one where no defined methodology is used. Like in any approach, the information about the system is obtained by interaction with the client, end users, questionnaires, study of existing documents, brainstorming, etc. However, with this approach no formal model is built of the system. The problem and the system model are essentially built in the minds of the analysts (or the analysts may use some informal notation for this purpose) and are directly translated from the minds of the analysts to the SRS.

Frequently, with such an approach, the analyst will have a series of meetings with the clients and end users. In the early meetings, the clients and end users will explain to the analyst about their work, their environment, and their needs as they perceive them. Any documents describing the work or the organization may be given, along with outputs of the existing methods of performing the tasks. In these early meetings, the analyst is basically the listener, absorbing the information provided. Once the analyst understands the system to some extent, he uses the next few meetings to seek clarifications of the parts he does not understand. He may document the information in some manner (he may even build a model if he wishes), and he may do some brainstorming or thinking about what the system should do. In the final few meetings, the analyst essentially explains to the client what he understands the system should do and uses the meetings as a means of verifying if what he proposes the system should do is indeed consistent with the objectives of the clients. An initial draft of the SRS may be used in the final meetings.

The informal approach to analysis is used widely and can be quite useful. The reason for its usefulness is that conceptual modeling-based approaches frequently do not model all aspects of the problem and are not always well suited for all the problems. Besides, as the SRS is to be validated and the feedback from the validation activity may require further analysis or specification (see Figure 3.1), choosing an informal approach to analysis is not very risky—the errors that may be introduced are not necessarily going to slip by the requirements phase. Hence such approaches may be the most practical approach to analysis in some situations.

3.2.2 Data Flow Modeling

Data-flow based modeling, often referred to as the structured analysis technique [48, 130], uses function-based decomposition while modeling the problem. It focuses on the functions performed in the problem domain and the data consumed and produced by these functions. It is a top-down refinement approach, which was originally called *structured analysis and specification*, and was proposed for producing the specifications. However, we will limit our attention to the analysis aspect of the approach. Before we describe the approach, let us the describe the data flow diagram and data dictionary on which the technique relies heavily.

Data Flow Diagrams and Data Dictionary

Data flow diagrams (also called *data flow graphs*) are commonly used during problem analysis. Data flow diagrams (DFDs) are quite general and are not limited to problem analysis for software requirements specification. They were in use long before the software engineering discipline began. DFDs are very useful in understanding a system and can be effectively used during analysis.

A DFD shows the flow of data through a system. It views a system as a function that transforms the inputs into desired outputs. Any complex system will not perform this transformation in a "single step," and a data will typically undergo a series of transformations before it becomes the output. The DFD aims to capture the transformations that take place within a system to the input data so that eventually the output data is produced. The agent that performs the transformation of data from one state to another is called a *process* (or a *bubble*). So, a DFD shows the movement of data through the different transformations or processes in the system. The processes are shown by named circles and data flows are represented by named arrows entering or leaving the bubbles. A rectangle represents a source or sink and is a net originator or consumer of data. A source or a sink is typically outside the main system of study. An example of a DFD for a system that pays workers is shown in Figure 3.2.

In this DFD there is one basic input data flow, the weekly timesheet, which originates from the source *worker*. The basic output is the paycheck, the sink for which is also the worker. In this system, first the employee's record is retrieved, using the employee ID, which is contained in the timesheet. From the employee record, the rate of payment and overtime are obtained. These rates and the regular and overtime hours (from the

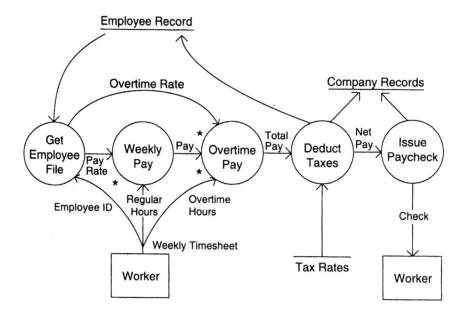

Figure 3.2: DFD of a system that pays workers.

timesheet) are used to compute the pay. After the total pay is determined, taxes are deducted. To compute the tax deduction, information from the tax-rate file is used. The amount of tax deducted is recorded in the employee and company records. Finally, the paycheck is issued for the net pay. The amount paid is also recorded in company records.

Some conventions used in drawing this DFD should be explained. All external files such as employee record, company record, and tax rates are shown as a labeled straight line. The need for multiple data flows by a process is represented by a '*' between the data flows. This symbol represents the AND relationship. For example, if there is a '*' between the two input data flows A and B for a process, it means that A AND B are needed for the process. In the DFD, for the process "weekly pay" the data flow "hours" and "pay rate" both are needed, as shown in the DFD. Similarly, the OR relationship is represented by a '+' between the data flows.

This DFD is an abstract description of the system for handling payment. It does not matter if the system is automated or manual. This diagram could very well be for a manual system where the computations are all done with calculators, and the records are physical folders and ledgers. The details and minor data paths are not represented in this DFD. For example, what happens if there are errors in the weekly timesheet is not shown in this DFD. This is done to avoid getting bogged down with details while constructing a DFD for the overall system. If more details are desired, the DFD can be further refined.

It should be pointed out that a DFD is *not* a flowchart. A DFD represents the flow of data, while a flowchart shows the flow of control. A DFD does not represent procedural information. So, while drawing a DFD, one *must not* get involved in procedural details, and procedural thinking must be consciously avoided. For example, considerations of loops and decisions must be ignored. In drawing the DFD, the designer has to specify the major transforms in the path of the data flowing from the input to output. *How* those transforms are performed is *not* an issue while drawing the data flow graph.

There are no detailed procedures that can be used to draw a DFD for a given problem. Only some directions can be provided. One way to construct a DFD is to start by identifying the major inputs and outputs. Minor inputs and outputs (like error messages) should be ignored at first. Then starting from the inputs, work toward the outputs, identifying the major transforms in the way. An alternative is to work down from the outputs toward the inputs. (Remember that it is important that procedural information like loops and decisions not be shown in the DFD, and the designer should not worry about such issues while drawing the DFD.) Following are some suggestions for constructing a data flow graph [154, 48]:

- Work your way consistently from the inputs to the outputs, or vice versa. If you get stuck, reverse direction. Start with a high-level data flow graph with few major transforms describing the entire transformation from the inputs to outputs and then refine each transform with more detailed transformations.

- Never try to show control logic. If you find yourself thinking in terms of loops and decisions, it is time to stop and start again.

- Label each arrow with proper data elements. Inputs and outputs of each transform should be carefully identified.

- Make use of * and + operations and show sufficient detail in the data flow graph.

- Try drawing alternate data flow graphs before settling on one.

Many systems are too large for a single DFD to describe the data processing clearly. It is necessary that some decomposition and abstraction mechanism be used for such systems. DFDs can be hierarchically organized, which helps in progressively partitioning and analyzing large systems. Such DFDs together are called a *leveled DFD set* [48].

A leveled DFD set has a starting DFD, which is a very abstract representation of the system, identifying the major inputs and outputs and the major processes in the system. Then each process is refined and a DFD is drawn for the process. In other words, a bubble in a DFD is expanded into a DFD during refinement. For the hierarchy to be consistent, it is important that the net inputs and outputs of a DFD for a process are the same as the inputs and outputs of the process in the higher-level DFD. This refinement stops if each bubble is considered to be "atomic," in that each bubble can be easily specified or understood. It should be pointed out that during refinement, though the net input and output are preserved, a refinement of the data might also occur. That is, a unit of data may be broken into its components for processing when the detailed DFD for a process is being drawn. So, as the processes are decomposed, data decomposition also occurs.

In a DFD, data flows are identified by unique names. These names are chosen so that they convey some meaning about what the data is. However, the precise structure of data flows is not specified in a DFD. The *data dictionary* is a repository of various data flows defined in a DFD. The associated data dictionary states precisely the structure of each data flow in the DFD. Components in the structure of a data flow may also be specified in the data dictionary, as well as the structure of files shown in the DFD. To define the data structure, different notations are used. These are similar to the notations for regular expressions (discussed later in this chapter). Essentially, besides sequence or composition (represented by '+') selection and iteration are included. Selection (represented by vertical bar '|') means one OR the other, and repetition (represented by '*') means one or more occurrences. In the DFD shown earlier, data flows for weekly timesheet are used. The data dictionary for this DFD is shown in Figure 3.3.

Most of the data flows in the DFD are specified here. Some of the more obvious ones are not shown here. The data dictionary entry for weekly timesheet specifies that this data flow is composed of three basic data entities—the employee name, employee ID, and many occurrences of the two-tuple consisting of regular hours and overtime hours. The last entity represents the daily working hours of the worker. The data dictionary also contains entries for specifying the different elements of a data flow.

```
weekly timesheet =
        Employee_name +
        Employee_Id +
        [Regular_hours + Overtime_hours] *

pay_rate =
        [Hourly | daily | weekly] +
        Dollar_amount

Employee_name =
        Last + First + Middle_initial

Employee_Id =
        digit + digit + digit + digit
```

Figure 3.3: Data dictionary.

Once we have constructed a DFD and its associated data dictionary, we have to somehow verify that they are "correct." There can be no formal verification of a DFD, because what the DFD is modeling is not formally specified anywhere against which verification can be done. Human processes and rules of thumb must be used for verification. In addition to the walk-through with the client, the analyst should look for common errors. Some common errors are [48]:

- Unlabeled data flows

- Missing data flows; information required by a process is not available

- Extraneous data flows; some information is not being used in the process

- Consistency not maintained during refinement

- Missing processes

- Contains some control information

Perhaps the most common error is unlabeled data flow. If an analyst cannot label the data flow, it is likely that he does not understand the purpose and structure of that data flow. A good test for this type of error is to see that the entries in the data dictionary are precise for all data flows.

To check if there are any missing data flows, for each process in the DFD the analyst should ask, "Can the process build the outputs shown from the given inputs?" Similarly, to check for redundant data flows, the following question should be asked: "Are all the input data flows required in the computation of the outputs?"

In a leveled set of DFDs it is important that consistency be maintained. Consistency can easily be lost if new data flows are added to the DFD during modification. If such changes are made, appropriate changes should be made in the parent or the child DFD. That is, if a new data flow is added in a lower-level DFD, it should also be reflected in the higher-level DFDs. Similarly, if a data flow is added in a higher-level DFD, the DFDs for the processes affected by the change should also be appropriately modified.

The DFDs should be carefully scrutinized to make sure that all the processes in the physical environment are shown in the DFD. None of the data flows should actually carry control information. A data flow without any structure or composition is a potential candidate for control information.

The Structured Analysis Method

Now let us return to the structured analysis method. The basic system view of this approach is that each system can be viewed as a transformation function operating within an environment that takes some inputs from the environment and produces some outputs for the environment. And as the overall transformation function of the entire system may be too complex to comprehend as a single function, the function should be partitioned into subfunctions that together form the overall function. The subfunctions can be further partitioned and the process repeated until we reach a stage where each function can be comprehended easily. And the basic approach used to uncover the functions being performed in the system (or the functions that are part of the overall system function) is to track the data as it flows through the system—from the input to the output. It is believed that in any complex system the data transformation from the input to the output will not occur in a single step; rather the data will be transformed from the input to the output in a series of transformations starting from the input and culminating in the desired output. By understanding the "states" the data is in as it goes through the transformation series, the functions in the system can be identified; each transformation of the data in the transformation series is performed by a transformation function. Hence, by tracking as the data flows through the system, the various functions being performed by a system can be identified. As this approach can be modeled easily by data flow diagrams, DFDs are used heavily in this method.

The first step in this method is to study the "physical environment." During this, a DFD of the current nonautomated (or partially automated) system is drawn, showing the input and output data flows of the system, how the data flows through the system, and what processes are operating on the data. This DFD might contain specific names for data flows and processes, as used in the physical environment. For example, names of departments, persons, local procedures, and organizational files can occur in the DFD for the physical environment. While drawing the DFD for the physical environment, an analyst has to interact with the users to determine the overall process from the point of view of the data. This step is considered complete when the entire physical data flow diagram has been described and the user has accepted it as a true representation of the operation of the current system. The step may start with a *context diagram* in which the entire system is treated as a single process and all its inputs, outputs, sinks, and sources are identified and shown.

The basic purpose of analyzing the current system is to obtain a logical DFD for the system, where each data flow and each process is a logical entity or operation, rather than an actual name. Drawing a DFD for the physical system is only to provide a reasonable starting point for drawing the logical DFD. Hence, the next step in the analysis is to draw the logical equivalents of the DFD for the physical system. During this step, the DFD of the physical environment is taken and all specific physical data flows are represented by their logical equivalents (for example, file 12.3.2 may be replaced by the employee salary file). Similarly, the bubbles for physical processes are replaced with logical processes. For example, a bubble named "To_John's_office" in the physical system might be replaced by "issue checks" in the logical equivalent. Bubbles that do not transform the data in any form are deleted from the DFD. This phase also ends when the DFD has been verified by the user.

In the first two steps, the current system is modeled. The next step is to develop a logical model of the new system after the changes have been incorporated, and a DFD is drawn to show how data will flow in the new system. During this step the analyst works in the logical mode, specifying only what needs to be done, not how it will be accomplished. No separation between the automated and nonautomated processes is made.

No general rules are provided for constructing the DFD for the new system. The new system still does not exist; it has to be invented. Consequently, what will be the data flows and major processes in this new system must be determined by the analyst, based on his experience and vision of the new system. No rules can be provided for this decision. However, before this can be done, the boundaries of change have to be identified in the logical DFD for the existing system. This DFD models the entire system, and only parts of it may be modified in the new system. Based on the goals of the clients and a clear concept about what the client wants to change, the boundaries of change have to be established in the logical DFD. The DFD for the new system will replace only that part of the existing DFD within this boundary. The inputs and outputs of the new DFD should be the same as the inputs and outputs for the DFD within the boundary.

The next step is to establish the man-machine boundary by specifying what will be automated and what will remain manual in the DFD for the new system. Note that even though some processes are not automated, they could be quite different from the processes in the original system, as even the manual operations may be performed differently in the new system. Often there is not just one option for the man-machine boundary. Different possibilities may exist depending on what is automated and the degree of automation. The analyst should explore and present the different possibilities.

The next two steps are evaluating the different options and then packaging or presenting the specifications.

For drawing a DFD, a top-down approach is suggested in the structured analysis method. In the structured analysis method, a DFD is constructed from scratch when the DFD for the physical system is being drawn and when the DFD for the new system is being drawn. The second step largely performs transformations on the physical DFD. Drawing a DFD starts with a top-level DFD called the context diagram, which lists all the major inputs and outputs for the system. This diagram is then refined into a description of the different parts of the DFD showing more details. This results in a leveled set of DFDs. As pointed out earlier, during this refinement, the analyst has to make sure consistency is maintained and that net input and output are preserved during refinement.

Clearly, the structured analysis provides methods for organizing and representing information about systems. It also provides guidelines for checking the accuracy of the information. Hence, for understanding and analyzing an existing system, this method provides useful tools. However, most of the guidelines given in the structured analysis are only applicable in the first two steps, when the DFD for a current system is to be constructed. For analyzing the target system and constructing the DFD or the data dictionary for the new system to be built (done in step three), this technique does not provide much guidance. Of course, the study and understanding of the existing system will help the analyst in this job, but there is no direct help from the method of structured analysis.

An Example

A restaurant owner feels that some amount of automation will help make her business more efficient. She also believes that an automated system might be an added attraction for the customers. So she wants to automate the operation of her restaurant as much as possible. Here we will perform the analysis for this problem. Details regarding interviews, questionnaires, or how the information was extracted are not described. First let us identify the different parties involved.

Client: The restaurant owner
Potential Users: Waiters, cash register operator

The context diagram for the restaurant is shown in Figure 3.4. The inputs and outputs of the restaurant are shown in this diagram. However, no details about the functioning of the restaurant are given here. Using this as a starting point, a logical DFD of the physical system is given in Figure 3.5 (the physical DFD was avoided for this, as the logical DFD is similar to the physical and there were no special names for the data or the processes in the physical system). Observing the operation of the restaurant and interviewing the owner were the basic means of collecting raw information for this DFD.

Now we must draw a DFD that models the new system to be built. After many meetings and discussions with the restaurant owner, the following goals for the new system were established:

- Automate much of the order processing and billing.

- Automate accounting.

- Make supply ordering more accurate so that leftovers at the end of the day are minimized and the orders that cannot be satisfied due to

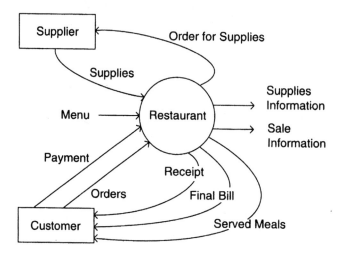

Figure 3.4: Context diagram for the restaurant.

nonavailability are also minimized. This was being done without a careful analysis of sales.

- The owner also suspects that the staff might be stealing/eating some food/supplies. She wants the new system to help detect and reduce this.

- The owner would also like to have statistics about sales of different items.

With these goals, we can define the boundaries for change in the DFD. It is clear that the new system will affect most aspects of the previous system, with the exception of making dishes. So, except for that process, the remaining parts of the old system all fall within our boundary of change. The DFD for the new system is shown in Figure 3.6. Note that although taking orders might remain manual in the new system, the process might change, because the waiter might need to fill in codes for menu items. That is why it is also within the boundary of change.

The DFD is largely self-explanatory. The major files in the system are: Supplies file, Accounting file, Orders file, and the Menu. Some new processes that did not have equivalents earlier have been included in the system. These

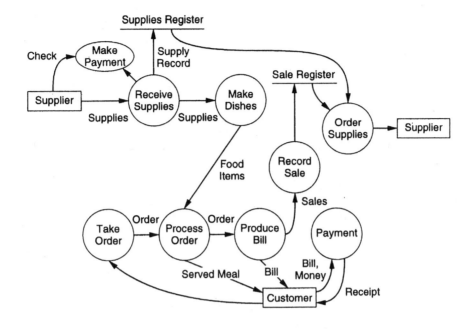

Figure 3.5: DFD for the existing restaurant system.

are "check for discrepancy," "accounting reports," and "statistics." Note that the processes are consistent in that the inputs given to them are sufficient to produce the outputs. For example, "checking for discrepancy" requires the following information to produce the report: total supplies received (obtained from the supplies file), supplies left at the end of the day, total orders placed by the customers (from the orders file), and the consumption rate for each menu item (from the menu). All these are shown as inputs to the process. Supplies required for the next day are assessed from the total orders placed in the day and the orders that could not be satisfied due to lack of supplies (both kept in the order file). To see clearly if the information is sufficient for the different processes, the structure and exact contents of each of the data flows has to be specified. The data dictionary for this is given in Figure 3.7.

The definitions of the different data flows and files are self-explanatory. Once this DFD and the data dictionary have been approved by the restaurant owner, the activity of understanding the problem is complete. After talking with the restaurant owner the man-machine boundary was also de-

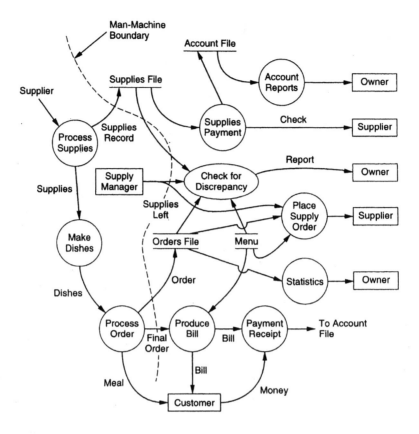

Figure 3.6: The DFD for the new restaurant system.

fined (it is shown in the DFD). Now, such tasks as determining the detailed requirements of each of the bubbles shown in the DFD, and determining the nonfunctional requirements, deciding codes for the items in the menu and in the supply list remain. Further refinement for some of the bubbles might be needed. For example, it has to be determined what sort of accounting reports or statistics are needed and what their formats should be. Once these are done, the analysis is complete and the requirements can then be compiled in a requirements specification document.

Supplies_file = [date + [item_no + quantity + cost]*]*
Orders_file = [date + [menu_item_no + quantity + status]*]*
status = satisfied | unsatisfied
order = [menu_item_no + quantity]*
menu = [menu_item_no + name + price + supplies_used]*
supplies_used = [supply_item_no + quantity]*
bill = [name + quantity + price]* +
      total_price + sales_tax + service_charge + grand_total
discrepancy_report = [supply_item_no +
      amt_ordered + amt_left + amt_consumed + descr]*

Figure 3.7: Data dictionary for the restaurant.

3.2.3 Object-Oriented Modeling

In object-oriented modeling, a system is viewed as a set of objects. The objects interact with each other through the services they provide. Some objects also interact with the users through their services such that the users get the desired services. Hence, the goal of modeling is to identify the objects (actually the object classes) that exist in the problem domain, define the classes by specifying what state information they encapsulate and what services they provide, and identify relationships that exist between objects of different classes, such that the overall model is such that it supports the desired user services.

Object-oriented modeling and systems have been getting a lot of attention in the recent past. The basic reason for this is the belief that object-oriented systems are going to be easier to build and maintain. It is also believed that transitioning from object-oriented analysis to object-oriented design (and implementation) will be easy, and that object-oriented analysis is more immune to change because objects are more stable than functions. That is, in a problem domain, objects are likely to stay the same even if the exact nature of the problem changes, while this is not the case with function-oriented modeling. Some approaches to object-oriented modeling and design were proposed early [36, 133, 23, 95]. Goals of many of these techniques regarding what to produce are quite similar, and their approaches and notations are also similar. Here, we briefly describe the approach proposed in [36]; the notation we use is UML ([24, 64] or www.uml.org), which is now the de-facto standard notation for OO modeling. We will discuss UML further in Chapter 7 when we discuss OO design; here we discuss some concepts needed to discuss analysis.

Basic Concepts and Notation

In understanding or modeling a system using an object-oriented modeling technique, the system is viewed as consisting of *objects*. Each object has certain *attributes*, which together define the object. Separation of an object from its attributes is a natural method that we use for understanding systems (a man is separate from his attributes of height, weight, etc.). In object-oriented systems, attributes hold the state (or define the state) of an object. An attribute is a pure data value (like integer, string, etc.), not an object.

Objects of similar type are grouped together to form an *object class* (or just *class*). A class is essentially a type definition, which defines the state space of objects of its type and the operations (and their semantics) that can be applied to objects of that type. Formation of classes is also a general technique used by humans for understanding systems and differentiating between classes (e.g., an apple tree is an instance of the class of trees, and the class of trees is different from the class of birds).

An object also provides some *services* or *operations*. These services are the only means by which the state of the object can be modified or viewed from outside. For operating a service, a *message* is sent to the object for that service. In general, these services are defined for a class and are provided for each object of that class. Encapsulating services and attributes together in an object is one of the main features that distinguishes an object-oriented modeling approach from data modeling approaches, like the ER diagrams.

Class diagrams represent a structure of the problem graphically using a precise notation. In a class diagram, a class is represented as a portrait-style rectangle divided into three parts. The top part contains the name of the class. The middle part lists the attributes that objects of this class possess. And the third part lists the services provided by objects of this class

To model relationship between classes, a few structures are used. The *generalization-specialization* structure can be used by a class to inherit all or some attributes and services of a general class and add more attributes and services. This structure is modeled in object-oriented modeling through inheritance. By using a general class and inheriting some of its attributes and services and adding more, one can create a class that is a specialized version of the general class. And many specialized classes can be created from

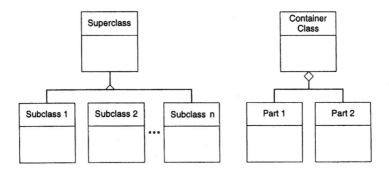

Figure 3.8: Class structures.

a general class, giving us class hierarchies. The *aggregation* structure models the whole-part relationship. An object may be composed of many objects; this is modeled through the aggregation structure. The representation of these in a class diagram is shown in Figure 3.8.

In addition to these, instances of a class may be related to objects of some other class. For example, an object of the class Employer may be related to many objects of the class Employee. This relationship between objects also has to be captured if a system is to be modeled properly. This is captured through *associations*. An association is shown in the class diagram by having a line between the two classes. The multiplicity of an association specifies how many instances of one class may relate to an instances of the other class through this association. An association between two classes can be one-to-one (i.e., one instance of one class is related to exactly one instance of the other class), one-to-many, or some other special cases. Multiplicity is specified by having a star (*) on the line adjacent to the class representing zero or more instances of the class may be related to an instance of the other class.

Let us illustrate the use of some of these relationships and their representation through the use of an example. Suppose a system is being contemplated for a drugstore that will compute the total sales of the drugstore along with the total sales of different chemists that man the drugstore. The drugs are of two major types—off-the-shelf and prescription drugs. The system is to provide help in procuring drugs when out of stock, removing them when expired, replenishing the off-the-shelf drugs when needed, etc. A model of the system is shown in Figure 3.9.

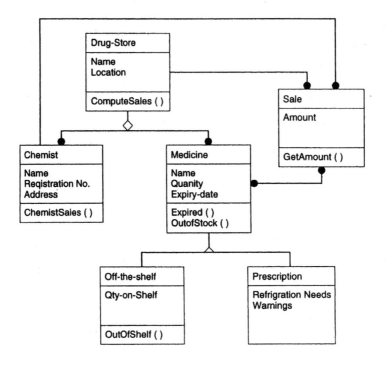

Figure 3.9: Model of a drugstore.

Let us briefly explain this class diagram. It has five classes of objects, each with a defined name, some attributes, and services. For example, an object of class Chemist has the attributes Name, Registration number, and Address. It has one service ChemistSales(), which computes the total sales by this chemist. The Drug-Store class is an aggregation of the class Medicine and the class Chemist (representing that a drugstore is composed of medicines and chemists). A Medicine may either be Off-the-shelf or Prescription. The class Medicine has some attributes like Name, Quantity in stock, and Expiry-date, and has services like Expired() (to list the expired medicines), OutOfStock() (to list medicines that are no longer in stock), etc. These attributes and services are inherited by the two specialized classes. In addition to these, the Off-the-shelf class has another attribute qty-on-shelf, representing how many have been put on the shelf and have services related to shelf stock. On the other hand, the Prescription class has Refrigeration-needs and Warnings as specialized attributes and services related to them. There are various associations in this model. For example, there is an association between `Sale` and `Medicine`. This association is one-to-many, that is, one sale could be of many medicines. Similarly, `Drug-Store` is associated to `Medicine` and `Chemist`, and `Chemist` is associated with `Sale`.

Performing Analysis

Now that we know what a model of a system consists of, the next question that arises is how to obtain the model for a system. In other words, how do we actually perform the analysis? As mentioned earlier, there can be no "algorithm" to perform the analysis or generate the SRS. Here we briefly discuss the set of guidelines given in [36], according to which the major steps in the analysis are:

- Identifying objects and classes

- Identifying structures

- Identifying attributes

- Identifying associations

- Defining services

Identifying Objects and Classes. An object during analysis is an encapsulation of attributes on which it provides some exclusive services [36]. It represents something in the problem space. It has been argued that though things like interfaces between components, functions, etc. are generally volatile and change with changing needs, objects are quite stable in a problem domain.

To identify analysis objects, start by looking at the problem space and its description. Obtain a brief summary of the problem space. In the summary and other descriptions of the problem space, consider the nouns. Frequently, nouns represent entities in the problem space which will be modeled as objects. Structures, devices, events remembered, roles played, locations, organizational units, etc. are good candidates to consider. A candidate should be included as an object if the system needs to remember something about the object, the system needs some services from the object to perform its own services, and the object has multiple attributes (i.e., it is a high-level object encapsulating some attributes). If the system does not need to keep information about some real-world entity or does not need any services from the entity, it should not be considered as an object for modeling. Similarly, carefully consider objects that have only one attribute; such objects can frequently be included as attributes in other objects. Though the analysis focuses on identifying objects, in modeling, classes for these objects are represented.

Identifying Structures. Structures represent the hierarchies that exist between object classes. All complex systems have hierarchies. In object-oriented modeling, the hierarchies are defined between classes that capture generalization-specialization and whole-part relationships. To identify the classification structure, consider the classes that have been identified as a generalization and see if there are other classes that can be considered as specializations of this. The specializations should be meaningful for the problem domain. For example, if the problem domain does not care about the material used to make some objects, there is no point in specializing the classes based on the material they are made of. Similarly, consider classes as specializations and see if there are other classes that have similar attributes. If so, see if a generalized class can be identified of which these are specializations. Once again, the structure obtained must naturally reflect the hierarchy in the problem domain; it should not be "extracted" simply because some classes have some attributes with the same names.

To identify assembly structure, a similar approach is taken. Consider each object of a class as an assembly and identify its parts or components. See if the system needs to keep track of the parts. If it does, then the parts must be reflected as objects; if not, then the parts should not be modeled as separate objects. Then, consider an object of a class as a part and see to which class's object it can be considered as belonging. Once again, this separation is maintained only if the system needs it. As before, the structures identified should naturally reflect the hierarchy in the problem domain and should not be "forced."

Identifying Attributes. Attributes add detail about the class and are the repositories of data for an object. For example, for an object of class Person, the attributes could be the name, sex, and address. The data stored in forms of values of attributes are hidden from outside the objects and are accessed and manipulated only by the service functions for that object. Which attributes should be used to define the class of an object depends on the problem and what needs to be done. For example, while modeling a hospital system, for the class Person attributes of height, weight, and date of birth may be needed, although these may not be needed for a database for a county that keeps track of populations in various neighborhoods.

To identify attributes, consider each class and see which attributes are needed by the problem domain. This is frequently a simple task. Then position each attribute properly using the structures; if the attribute is a common attribute, it should be placed in the superclass, while if it is specific to a specialized object it should be placed with the subclass. While identifying attributes, new classes may also get defined or old classes may disappear (e.g., if you find that a class really is an attribute of another).

Identifying Associations. Associations capture the relationship between instances of various classes. For example, an instance of the class Company may be related to an instance of the class Person by an "employs" relationship. This is similar to what is done in ER modeling. And like in ER modeling, an instance connection may be of 1:1 type representing that one instance of this type is related to exactly one instance of another class. Or it could be 1:M, indicating that one instance of this class may be related to many instances of the other class. There are M:M connections, and there are sometimes multi-way connections, but these are not very common. The associations between objects are derived from the problem domain directly once the objects have been identified. An association may have attributes of its own; these are typically attributes that do not naturally belong to either object. Although in many situations they can be "forced" to belong to one of the two objects without loosing any information, it should not be done unless the attribute naturally belongs to the object.

Defining Services. An object performs a set of predefined services. A service is performed when the object receives a message for it. Services really provide the active element in object-oriented modeling; they are the agent of state change or "processing." It is through the services that desired functional services can be provided by a system. To identify services, first identify the *occur* services, which are needed to create, destroy, and maintain the instances of the class. These services are generally not shown in the class diagrams. Other services depend on the type of services the system is providing. A method for identifying services is to define the system states and then in each state list the external events and required responses. For each of these, identify what services the different classes should possess.

All the classes and their relationships are shown in a class diagram. The class diagram, clearly, gets large and complex for large systems. To handle the complexity, a *subject layer* in which the class model is partitioned into various subjects, with each subject containing some part of the diagram is suggested. Typically, a subject will contain many related classes.

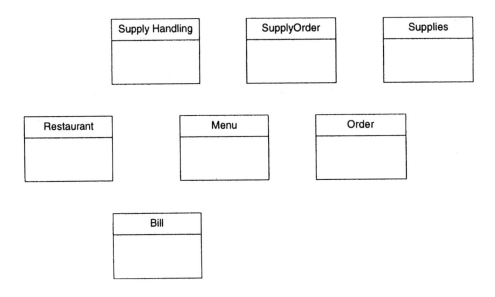

Figure 3.10: Initial classes in the restaurant example.

An Example

Let us consider the example of the restaurant, whose structured analysis was performed earlier. By stating the goals of the system (i.e., automate the bill generation for orders given by customers, obtain sale statistics, determine discrepancy between supplies taken and supplies consumed, automate ordering of supplies) and studying the problem domain (i.e., the restaurant with customer, supplier, menu, etc.), we can clearly see that there are at least the following classes of objects: Restaurant, Restaurant owner, Bill, Menu, CustomerOrder, Supplier, SupplyOrder, Supply Handling, and Dishes. Each of these entities plays an important role in the system. We consider this as the starting point and the initial classes. By looking at the objectives and scope of the system, we find that no information about the Supplier or the Operator needs to be maintained in the system. Hence, they need not be modeled in the system as objects. For the same reason, entities like Dishes and Restaurant owner are not modeled as objects. The initial classes are shown in Figure 3.10. Note that this model will further evolve and new classes may get added and some of these may eventually not be needed.

Now let us try to identify structure between these classes. Clearly, a

Restaurant is an aggregation of Menu and Supply handling. As dishes, operator, etc. are not considered objects, they do not show up as components of Restaurant. Further, a Menu is an aggregation of many MenuItems. This requires us to add MenuItem. Similarly, the SupplyOrder is an aggregation of (many) SupplyItems. This also requires us to add SupplyItem as a new class. Furthermore, the association between SupplyOrder and SupplyItem has an attribute quantity, reflecting the quantity ordered for a particular item by an order. There is no generalization-specialization hierarchy in this.

Many attributes of various items can be directly identified. A MenuItem has attributes of Number, Name, Price, Supplies used (i.e., which supplies it uses and quantity; this is needed to detect discrepancies in consumption and supplies used). Similarly, SupplyItem has Item name and Unit price as attributes.

With this, we are ready to identify relationships between objects. The Supply handling (unit) is related to (many) SupplyOrder. Similarly, an Order (by a customer) is related to many MenuItem. Furthermore, this association has an attribute of its own—quantity. The quantity of the particular MenuItem ordered in a particular Order is naturally a property of the association between the specific Order and the specific MenuItem.

Finally, we have to identify the services. Keeping our basic services of the system in mind (generate sales statistics, bill, discrepancy report, sale order), we define services of various classes. Supply handling object has the services CreditSupply() (used to record the receipt of supplies), DebitSupply() (used to record the supplies taken out), and PlaceOrder() (to place order of supplies). For SupplyOrder, one service is identified—ProduceCheck() to produce the check for the particular order. The object Order has one service—ProduceBill()—to produce the bill for the particular order. Handling the bill as essentially something generated for each order, we remove the object Bill from the object layer. The main object Restaurant has the services SaleStat() to generate the sale statistics for which it will require all order information (which it will obtain through its association with Order). It also has the service Discrepancy() to generate a discrepancy report. For this, it will need to find out what items have been consumed their quantity, and how much supply was debited. The former it can obtain from all the orders and the latter from Supply handling. The final class diagram is shown in Figure 3.11.

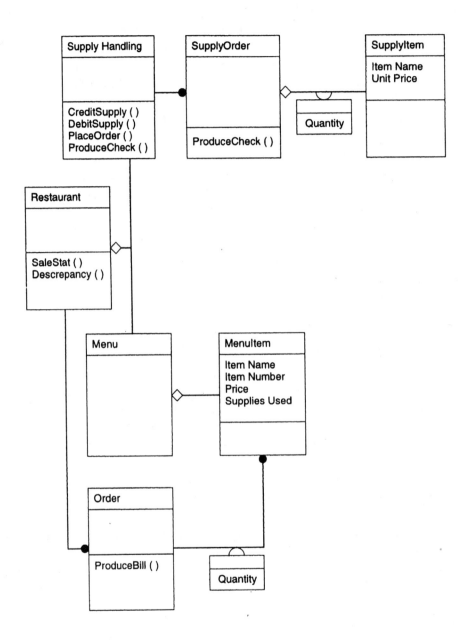

Figure 3.11: Class diagram for the restaurant.

3.2.4 Prototyping

Prototyping takes a different approach to problem analysis as compared to modeling-based approaches. In prototyping, a partial system is constructed, which is then used by the client, users, and developers to gain a better understanding of the problem and the needs. Hence, actual experience with a prototype that implements part of the eventual software system are used to analyze the problem and understand the requirements for the eventual software system. A software prototype can be defined as a partial implementation of a system whose purpose is to learn something about the problem being solved or the solution approach [46]. As stated in this definition, prototyping can also be used to evaluate or check a design alternative (such a prototype is called a *design prototype* [46]). Here we focus on prototyping used primarily for understanding the requirements.

The rationale behind using prototyping for problem understanding and analysis is that the client and the users often find it difficult to visualize how the eventual software system will work in their environment just by reading a specification document. Visualizing the operation of the software that is yet to be built and whether it will satisfy the ultimate objectives, merely by reading and discussing the paper requirements, is indeed difficult. This is particularly true if the system is a totally new system and many users and clients do not have a good idea of their needs. The idea behind prototyping is that clients and the users can assess their needs much better if they can see the working of a system, even if the system is only a partial system. Prototyping emphasizes that actual practical experience is the best aid for understanding needs. By actually experimenting with a system, people can say, "I don't want this feature" or "I wish it had this feature" or "This is wonderful."

There are two approaches to prototyping: throwaway and evolutionary [44, 46]. In the *throwaway* approach the prototype is constructed with the idea that it will be discarded after the analysis is complete, and the final system will be built from scratch. In the *evolutionary* approach, the prototype is built with the idea that it will eventually be converted into the final system. From the point of view of problem analysis and understanding, the throwaway prototypes are more suited. For the rest of the discussion we limit our attention to throwaway prototypes.

The first question that needs to be addressed is whether or not to prototype. In other words, it is important to clearly understand when prototyping should be done. The requirements of a system can be divided into

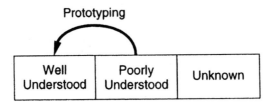

Figure 3.12: Throwaway prototyping.

three sets—those that are well understood, those that are poorly understood, and those that are not known [46]. In a throwaway prototype, the poorly understood requirements are the ones that should be incorporated. Based on the experience with the prototype, these requirements then become well understood, as shown in Figure 3.12.

It might be possible to divide the set of poorly understood requirements further into two sets—those critical to design, and those not critical to design [46]. The requirements that can be easily incorporated in the system later are considered noncritical to design. If which of the poorly understood requirements are critical and which are noncritical can be determined, then the throwaway prototype should focus mostly on the critical requirements. Overall, we can say that if the set of poorly understood requirements is substantial (in particular the subset of critical requirements), then a throwaway prototype should be built.

The development process using a throwaway prototype was discussed earlier in Chapter 2. The development activity starts with an SRS for the prototype. However, developing the SRS for the prototype requires identifying the functions that should be included in the prototype. This decision is typically application-dependent. As mentioned earlier, in general, those requirements that tend to be unclear and vague, or where the clients and users are unsure or keep changing their mind, are the ones that should be implemented in the prototype. User interface, new features to be added (beyond automating what is currently being done), and features that may be infeasible, are common candidates for prototyping. Based on what aspects of the system are included in the prototype, the prototyping can be considered *vertical* or *horizontal* [110]. In horizontal prototyping the system is viewed as being organized as a series of layers and some layer is the focus of prototyping. For example, the user interface layer is frequently a good candidate for such prototyping, where most of the user interface is included in the prototype. In vertical prototyping, a chosen part of the system, which is not well understood, is built completely. This approach is used to validate some functionality or capability of the system.

Development of a throwaway prototype is fundamentally different from developing final production-quality software. The basic focus during prototyping is to keep costs low and minimize the prototype production time. Due to this, many of the bookkeeping, documenting, and quality control activities that are usually performed during software product development are kept to a minimum during prototyping. Efficiency concerns also take a back seat, and often very high-level interpretive languages are used for prototyping. For these reasons, temptation to convert the prototype into the final system should be resisted.

Experience is gained by putting the system to use by the actual client and users. Constant interaction is needed with the client/users during this activity to understand their responses. Questionnaires and interviews might be used to gather user response.

The final SRS is developed in much the same way as any SRS is developed. The difference here is that the client and users will be able to answer questions and explain their needs much better because of their experience with the prototype. Some initial analysis is also available.

For prototyping for requirements analysis to be feasible, its cost must be kept low. Consequently, only those features that will have a valuable return from the user experience are included in the prototype. Exception handling, recovery, conformance to some standards and formats are typically not included in prototypes. Because the prototype is to be thrown away, only minimal development documents need to be produced during prototyping; for example, design documents, a test plan, and a test case specification are not needed during the development of the prototype. Another important cost-cutting measure is reduced testing. Testing consumes a major part of development expenditure during regular software development. By using cost-cutting methods, it is possible to keep the cost of the prototype to less than a few percent of the total development cost.

The cost of developing and running a prototype can be around 10% of the total development cost [72]. However, it should be pointed out that if the cost of prototyping is 10% of the total development cost, it does not mean that the cost of development has increased by this amount. The main reason is that the benefits obtained due to the use of prototype in terms of reduced requirement errors and reduced volume of requirement change requests are likely to be substantial (see the examples given earlier in this chapter), thereby reducing the cost of development itself.

An Example

Consider the example of the restaurant automation discussed earlier. An initial structured analysis of the problem was also shown earlier. During the analysis the restaurant owner was quite apprehensive about the ability and usefulness of the system. She felt that it was risky to automate, as an improper system might cause considerable confusion and lead to a loss of clientele. Due to the risks involved, it was decided to build a throwaway prototype. Note that the basic purpose of the prototype in this situation is not to uncover or clarify requirements but to ascertain the utility of the automated system. Of course, the experience with the prototype will also be used to ensure that the requirements are correct and complete.

The first step in developing a prototype is to prepare an SRS for the prototype. The SRS need not be formal but should identify the different system utilities to be included in the prototype. As mentioned earlier, these are typically the features that are most unclear or where the risk is high. It was decided that the prototype will demonstrate the following features:

1. Customer order processing and billing

2. Supply ordering and processing

The first was included, as that is where the maximum risk exists for the restaurant (after all, customer satisfaction is the basic objective of the restaurant, and if customers are unhappy the restaurant will lose business). The second was included, as maximum potential benefit can be derived from this feature. Accounting and statistics generation were not to be included in the prototype.

The prototype was developed using a database system, in which good facilities for data entry and form (bill) generation exist. The user interface for the waiters and the restaurant manager was included in the prototype. The system was used, in parallel with the existing system, for a few weeks, and informal surveys with the customers were conducted.

Customers were generally pleased with the accuracy of the bills and the details they provided. Some gave suggestions about the bill layout. Based on the experience of the waiters, the codes for the different menu items were modified to an alphanumeric code. They found that the numeric codes used in the prototype were hard to remember. The experience of the restaurant manager and feedback from the supplier were used to determine the final details about supply processing and handling.

3.3 Requirements Specification

The final output is the software requirements specification document (SRS). For smaller problems or problems that can easily be comprehended, the specification activity might come after the entire analysis is complete. However, it is more likely that problem analysis and specification are done concurrently. An analyst typically will analyze some parts of the problem and then write the requirements for that part. In practice, problem analysis and requirements specification activities overlap, with movement from both activities to the other, as shown in Figure 3.1. However, as all the information for specification comes from analysis, we can conceptually view the specification activity as following the analysis activity.

The first question that arises is: If formal modeling is done during analysis, why are the outputs of modeling—the structures that are built (e.g., DFD and DD, Object diagrams)—not treated as an SRS? The main reason is that modeling generally focuses on the problem structure, not its external behavior. Consequently, things like user interfaces are rarely modeled, whereas they frequently form a major component of the SRS. Similarly, for ease of modeling, frequently "minor issues" like erroneous situations (e.g., error in output) are rarely modeled properly, whereas in an SRS, behavior under such situations also has to be specified. Similarly, performance constraints, design constraints, standards compliance, recovery, etc., are not included in the model, but must be specified clearly in the SRS because the designer must know about these to properly design the system. It should therefore be clear that the outputs of a model cannot form a desirable SRS.

For these reasons, the transition from analysis to specification should also not be expected to be straightforward, even if some formal modeling is used during analysis. It is not the case that in specification the structures of modeling are just specified in a more formal manner. A good SRS needs to specify many things, some of which are not satisfactorily handled during modeling. Furthermore, sometimes the structures produced during modeling are not amenable for translation into external behavior specification (which is what is to be specified in an SRS). For example, the object diagram produced during an OO analysis is of limited use when specifying the external behavior of the desired system.

Essentially, what passes from requirements analysis activity to the specification activity is the knowledge acquired about the system. The modeling is essentially a tool to help obtain a thorough and complete knowledge about the proposed system. The SRS is written based on the knowledge acquired during analysis. As converting knowledge into a structured document is not straightforward, specification itself is a major task, which is relatively independent.

A consequence of this is that it is relatively less important to model "completely," compared to specifying completely. As the primary objective of analysis is problem understanding, while the basic objective of the requirements phase is to produce the SRS, the complete and detailed analysis structures are not critical. In fact, it is possible to develop the SRS without using formal modeling techniques. The basic aim of the structures used in modeling is to help in knowledge representation and problem partitioning, the structures are not an end in themselves.

With this in mind, let us start our discussion on requirements specification. We start by discussing the desirable characteristics of an SRS.

3.3.1   Characteristics of an SRS

To properly satisfy the basic goals, an SRS should have certain properties and should contain different types of requirements. In this section, we discuss some of the desirable characteristics of an SRS and components of an SRS. A good SRS is [91, 92]:

1. Correct

2. Complete

3. Unambiguous

4. Verifiable

5. Consistent

6. Ranked for importance and/or stability

7. Modifiable

8. Traceable

The discussion of these properties here is based on [91, 92]. An SRS is *correct* if every requirement included in the SRS represents something required in the final system. An SRS is *complete* if everything the software is supposed to do and the responses of the software to all classes of input data are specified in the SRS. Correctness and completeness go hand-in-hand; whereas correctness ensures that which is specified is done correctly, completeness ensures that everything is indeed specified. Correctness is an easier property to establish than completeness as it basically involves examining each requirement to make sure it represents the user requirement. Completeness, on the other hand, is the most difficult property to establish; to ensure completeness, one has to detect the absence of specifications, and absence is much harder to ascertain than determining that what is present has some property.

An SRS is *unambiguous* if and only if every requirement stated has one and only one interpretation. Requirements are often written in natural language, which are inherently ambiguous. If the requirements are specified in a natural language, the SRS writer has to be especially careful to ensure that there are no ambiguities. One way to avoid ambiguities is to use some formal requirements specification language. The major disadvantage of using formal languages is the large effort required to write an SRS, the high cost of doing so, and the increased difficulty reading and understanding formally stated requirements (particularly by the users and clients).

An SRS is *verifiable* if and only if every stated requirement is verifiable. A requirement is verifiable if there exists some cost-effective process that can check whether the final software meets that requirement. This implies that the requirements should have as little subjectivity as possible because subjective requirements are difficult to verify. Unambiguity is essential for verifiability. As verification of requirements is often done through reviews, it also implies that an SRS is understandable, at least by the developer, the client, and the users. Understandability is clearly extremely important, as one of the goals of the requirements phase is to produce a document on which the client, the users, and the developers can agree.

An SRS is *consistent* if there is no requirement that conflicts with another. Terminology can cause inconsistencies; for example, different requirements may use different terms to refer to the same object. There may be logical or temporal conflict between requirements that causes inconsistencies. This occurs if the SRS contains two or more requirements whose logical or temporal characteristics cannot be satisfied together by any software system. For example, suppose a requirement states that an event e is to occur before another event f. But then another set of requirements states (directly or indirectly by transitivity) that event f should occur before event e. Inconsistencies in an SRS can reflect of some major problems.

Generally, all the requirements for software are not of equal importance. Some are critical, others are important but not critical, and there are some which are desirable but not very important. Similarly, some requirements are "core" requirements which are not likely to change as time passes, while others are more dependent on time. An SRS is ranked for importance and/or stability if for each requirement the importance and the stability of the requirement are indicated. Stability of a requirement reflects the chances of it changing in future. It can be reflected in terms of the expected change volume.

Writing an SRS is an iterative process. Even when the requirements of a system are specified, they are later modified as the needs of the client change. Hence an SRS should be easy to modify. An SRS is *modifiable* if its structure and style are such that any necessary change can be made easily while preserving completeness and consistency. Presence of redundancy is a major hindrance to modifiability, as it can easily lead to errors. For example, assume that a requirement is stated in two places and that the requirement later needs to be changed. If only one occurrence of the requirement is modified, the resulting SRS will be inconsistent.

An SRS is traceable if the origin of each of its requirements is clear and if it facilitates the referencing of each requirement in future development [91]. Forward traceability means that each requirement should be traceable to some design and code elements. Backward traceability requires that it be possible to trace design and code elements to the requirements they support. Traceability aids verification and validation.

Of all these characteristics, completeness is perhaps the most important (and hardest to ensure). One of the most common problem in requirements specification is when some of the requirements of the client are not specified. This necessitates additions and modifications to the requirements later in the development cycle, which are often expensive to incorporate. Incompleteness is also a major source of disagreement between the client and the supplier. The importance of having complete requirements cannot be overemphasized.

3.3.2 Components of an SRS

Completeness of specifications is difficult to achieve and even more difficult to verify. Having guidelines about what different things an SRS should specify will help in completely specifying the requirements. Here we describe some of the system properties that an SRS should specify. The basic issues an SRS must address are:

- Functionality

- Performance

- Design constraints imposed on an implementation

- External interfaces

Conceptually, any SRS should have these components. If the traditional approach to requirement analysis is being followed, then the SRS might even have portions corresponding to these. However, functional requirements might be specified indirectly by specifying the services on the objects or by specifying the use cases.

Functional Requirements

Functional requirements specify which outputs should be produced from the given inputs. They describe the relationship between the input and output of the system. For each functional requirement, a detailed description of all the data inputs and their source, the units of measure, and the range of valid inputs must be specified.

All the operations to be performed on the input data to obtain the output should be specified. This includes specifying the validity checks on the input and output data, parameters affected by the operation, and equations or other logical operations that must be used to transform the inputs into corresponding outputs. For example, if there is a formula for computing the output, it should be specified. Care must be taken not to specify any algorithms that are not part of the system but that may be needed to implement the system. These decisions should be left for the designer.

An important part of the specification is the system behavior in abnormal situations, like invalid input (which can occur in many ways) or error during computation. The functional requirement must clearly state what the system should do if such situations occur. Specifically, it should specify the behavior of the system for invalid inputs and invalid outputs. Furthermore, behavior for situations where the input is valid but the normal operation cannot be performed should also be specified. An example of this situation is an airline reservation system, where a reservation cannot be made even for valid passengers if the airplane is fully booked. In short, the system behavior for all foreseen inputs and all foreseen system states should be specified. These special conditions are often likely to be overlooked, resulting in a system that is not robust.

Performance Requirements

This part of an SRS specifies the performance constraints on the software system. All the requirements relating to the performance characteristics of the system must be clearly specified. There are two types of performance requirements: static and dynamic.

Static requirements are those that do not impose constraint on the execution characteristics of the system. These include requirements like the number of terminals to be supported, the number of simultaneous users to be supported, and the number of files that the system has to process and their sizes. These are also called *capacity* requirements of the system.

Dynamic requirements specify constraints on the execution behavior of the system. These typically include response time and throughput constraints on the system. Response time is the expected time for the completion of an operation under specified circumstances. Throughput is the expected number of operations that can be performed in a unit time. For example, the SRS may specify the number of transactions that must be processed per unit time, or what the response time for a particular command should be. Acceptable ranges of the different performance parameters should be specified, as well as acceptable performance for both normal and peak workload conditions.

All of these requirements should be stated in measurable terms. Requirements such as "response time should be good" or the system must be able to "process all the transactions quickly" are not desirable because they are imprecise and not verifiable. Instead, statements like "the response time of command x should be less than one second 90% of the times" or "a transaction should be processed in less than one second 98% of the times" should be used to declare performance specifications.

Design Constraints

There are a number of factors in the client's environment that may restrict the choices of a designer. Such factors include standards that must be followed, resource limits, operating environment, reliability and security requirements, and policies that may have an impact on the design of the system. An SRS should identify and specify all such constraints.

Standards Compliance: This specifies the requirements for the standards the system must follow. The standards may include the report format and accounting procedures. There may be audit tracing requirements, which require certain kinds of changes, or operations that must be recorded in an audit file.

Hardware Limitations: The software may have to operate on some existing or predetermined hardware, thus imposing restrictions on the design. Hardware limitations can include the type of machines to be used, operating system available on the system, languages supported, and limits on primary and secondary storage.

Reliability and Fault Tolerance: Fault tolerance requirements can place a major constraint on how the system is to be designed. Fault tolerance requirements often make the system more complex and expensive. Requirements about system behavior in the face of certain kinds of faults is specified. Recovery requirements are often an integral part here, detailing what the system should do if some failure occurs to ensure certain properties. Reliability requirements are very important for critical applications.

Security: Security requirements are particularly significant in defense systems and many database systems. Security requirements place restrictions on the use of certain commands, control access to data, provide different kinds of access requirements for different people, require the use of passwords and cryptography techniques, and maintain a log of activities in the system. Given the current security needs even of common systems, they may also require proper assessment of security threats, proper programming techniques, and use of tools to detect flaws like buffer overflow.

External Interface Requirements

All the interactions of the software with people, hardware, and other software should be clearly specified. For the user interface, the characteristics of each user interface of the software product should be specified. User interface is becoming increasingly important and must be given proper attention. A preliminary user manual should be created with all user commands, screen formats, an explanation of how the system will appear to the user, and feedback and error messages. Like other specifications these requirements should be precise and verifiable. So, a statement like "the system should be user friendly" should be avoided and statements like "commands should be no longer than six characters" or "command names should reflect the function they perform" used.

For hardware interface requirements, the SRS should specify the logical characteristics of each interface between the software product and the hardware components. If the software is to execute on existing hardware or on predetermined hardware, all the characteristics of the hardware, including memory restrictions, should be specified. In addition, the current use and load characteristics of the hardware should be given.

The interface requirement should specify the interface with other software the system will use or that will use the system. This includes the interface with the operating system and other applications. The message content and format of each interface should be specified.

3.3.3   Specification Language

Requirements specification necessitates the use of some specification language. The language should support the desired qualities of the SRS—modifiability, understandability, unambiguous, and so forth. In addition, the language should be easy to learn and use. As one might expect, many of these characteristics conflict in the selection of a specification language. For example, to avoid ambiguity, it is best to use some formal language. But for ease of understanding a natural language might be preferable.

Though formal notations exist for specifying specific properties of the system, natural languages are now most often used for specifying requirements. If formal languages are to be used, they are often used to specify particular properties or for specific parts of the system, and these formal specifications are generally contained in the overall SRS, which is in a natural language. In other words, the overall SRS is generally in a natural language, and when feasible and desirable, some specifications in the SRS may use formal languages.

The major advantage of using a natural language is that both client and supplier understand the language. However, by the very nature of a natural language, it is imprecise and ambiguous. To reduce the drawbacks of natural languages, most often natural language is used in a structured fashion. In structured English (for example), requirements are broken into sections and paragraphs. Each paragraph is then broken into subparagraphs. Many organizations also specify strict uses of some words like "shall," "perhaps," and "should" and try to restrict the use of common phrases in order to improve the precision and reduce the verbosity and ambiguity. A general rule when using a natural language is to be precise, factual, and brief, and organize the requirements hierarchically where possible, giving unique numbers to each separate requirement.

In an SRS, as discussed, some parts can be specified better using some formal notation. For example, to specify formats of inputs or outputs, regular expressions can be very useful. Similarly, when discussing systems like communication protocols, finite state automata can be used. Decision tables are useful to formally specify the behavior of a system on different combinations of inputs or settings. Similarly, some aspects of the system may be specified or explained using the models that may have been built during problem analysis. Sometimes models may be included as supporting documents that help clarify the requirements and the motivation better.

3.3.4 Structure of a Requirements Document

All the requirements for the system have to be included in a document that is clear and concise. For this, it is necessary to organize the requirements document as sections and subsections. There can be many ways to structure a requirements document. Many methods and standards have been proposed for organizing an SRS. One of the main ideas of standardizing the structure of the document is that with an available standard, each SRS will fit a certain pattern, which will make it easier for others to understand (that is one of the roles of any standard). Another role these standards play is that by requiring various aspects to be specified, they help ensure that the analyst does not forget some major property. Here we discuss the organization proposed in the IEEE guide to software requirements specifications [92].

The IEEE standards recognize the fact that different projects may require their requirements to be organized differently, that is, there is no one method that is suitable for all projects. It provides different ways of structuring the SRS. The first two sections of the SRS are the same in all of them. The general structure of an SRS is given in Figure 3.13.

The introduction section contains the purpose, scope, overview, etc. of the requirements document. It also contains the references cited in the document and any definitions that are used. Section 2 describes the general factors that affect the product and its requirements. Specific requirements are not mentioned, but a general overview is presented to make the understanding of the specific requirements easier. Product perspective is essentially the relationship of the product to other products; defining if the product is independent or is a part of a larger product, and what the principal interfaces of

1. Introduction
    1.1 Purpose
    1.2 Scope
    1.3 Definitions, Acronyms, and Abbreviations
    1.4 References
    1.5 Overview
2. Overall Description
    2.1 Product Perspective
    2.2 Product Functions
    2.3 User Characteristics
    2.4 General Constraints
    2.5 Assumptions and Dependencies
3. Specific Requirements

Figure 3.13: General structure of an SRS.

the product are. A general abstract description of the functions to be performed by the product is given. Schematic diagrams showing a general view of different functions and their relationships with each other can often be useful. Similarly, typical characteristics of the eventual end user and general constraints are also specified.

The specific requirements section (section 3 of the SRS) describes all the details that the software developer needs to know for designing and developing the system. This is typically the largest and most important part of the document. For this section, different organizations have been suggested in the standard. These requirements can be organized by the modes of operation, user class, object, feature, stimulus, or functional hierarchy [92]. One method to organize the specific requirements is to first specify the external interfaces, followed by functional requirements, performance requirements, design constraints, and system attributes. This structure is shown in Figure 3.14 [92].

The external interface requirements section specifies all the interfaces of the software: to people, other softwares, hardware, and other systems. User interfaces are clearly a very important component; they specify each human interface the system plans to have, including screen formats, contents of menus, and command structure. In hardware interfaces, the logical charac-

3. Specific Requirements
    3.1 External Interface Requirements
        3.1.1 User Interfaces
        3.1.2 Hardware Interfaces
        3.1.3 Software Interfaces
        3.1.4 Communication Interfaces
    3.2. Functional Requirements
        3.2.1 Mode 1
            3.2.1.1 Functional Requirement 1.1
            $\vdots$
            $3.2.1.n$ Functional Requirement $1.n$
        $\vdots$
        3.2.m Mode m
            $3.2.m.1$ Functional Requirement $m.1$
            $\vdots$
            $3.2.m.n$ Functional Requirement $m.n$
    3.3 Performance Requirements
    3.4 Design Constraints
    3.5 Attributes
    3.6 Other Requirements

Figure 3.14: One organization for specific requirements.

teristics of each interface between the software and hardware on which the software can run are specified. Essentially, any assumptions the software is making about the hardware are listed here. In software interfaces, all other software that is needed for this software to run is specified, along with the interfaces. Communication interfaces need to be specified if the software communicates with other entities in other machines.

In the functional requirements section, the functional capabilities of the system are described. In this organization, the functional capabilities for all the modes of operation of the software are given. For each functional requirement, the required inputs, desired outputs, and processing requirements will have to be specified. For the inputs, the source of the inputs, the units of measure, valid ranges, accuracies, etc. have to be specified. For specifying the processing, all operations that need to be performed on the input data and any intermediate data produced should be specified. This includes validity checks on inputs, sequence of operations, responses to abnormal situations, and methods that must be used in processing to transform the inputs into corresponding outputs. Note that no algorithms are generally specified, only the relationship between the inputs and the outputs (which may be in the form of an equation or a formula) so that an algorithm can be designed to produce the outputs from the inputs. For outputs, the destination of outputs, units of measure, range of valid outputs, error messages, etc. all have to be specified.

The performance section should specify both static and dynamic performance requirements. All factors that constrain the system design are described in the performance constraints section. The attributes section specifies some of the overall attributes that the system should have. Any requirement not covered under these is listed under other requirements. Design constraints specify all the constraints imposed on design (e.g., security, fault tolerance, and standards compliance).

There are three other outlines proposed by the IEEE standard for organizing "specific requirements." However, these outlines are essentially guidelines. There are other ways a requirements document can be organized. The key concern is that after the requirements have been identified, the requirements document should be organized in such a manner that it aids validation and system design. For different projects many of these sections may not be needed and can be omitted. Especially for smaller projects, some of the sections and subsections may not be necessary to properly specify the requirements.

When use cases (discussed next) are employed, then the functional requirements section of the SRS is replaced by use case descriptions. (The format of a use case description is discussed later.) And the product perspective part of the SRS may provide an overview or summary of the use cases.

3.4 Functional Specification with Use Cases

Functional requirements often form the core of a requirements document. The traditional approach for specifying functionality is to specify each function that the system should provide. Use cases specify the functionality of a system by specifying the behavior of the system, captured as interactions of the users with the system. Use cases can be used to describe the business processes of the larger business or organization that deploys the software, or it could just describe the behavior of the software system. We will focus on describing the behavior of software systems that are to be built.

Though use cases are primarily for specifying behavior, they can also be used effectively during analysis. Later when we discuss how to develop use cases, we will see how they can help in eliciting requirements also.

Use cases drew attention after they were used as part of the object-oriented modeling approach proposed by Jacobson [95]. Due to this connection with an object-oriented approach, use cases are sometimes viewed as part of an object-oriented approach to software development. However, they are a general method for describing the interaction of a system (even non-IT systems.) The discussion of use cases here is based on the concepts and processes discussed in [39].

3.4.1 Basics

A software system (whose requirements are being uncovered) may be used by many users. However, in addition to users, the software system may also be used by other systems. In use case terminology, an *actor* is a person or a system which uses the system being built for achieving some goal. Note that actors need not be people only. Also, as an actor interacts for achieving some goal, it is a logical entity that represents a group of users (people or system) who behave in a similar manner. Different actors represent groups with different goals. So, it is better to have a "receiver" and a "sender" actor rather than having a generic "user" actor for a system in which some messages are sent by users and received by some other users.

A *primary actor* is the main actor that initiates a use case (UC) for achieving a goal, and whose goal satisfaction is the main objective of the use case. The primary actor is a logical concept and though we assume that the primary actor executes the use case, some agent may actually execute it on the behalf of the primary actor. For example, a VP may be the primary actor for *get sales growth report by region* use case, though it may actually be executed by an assistant. We consider the primary actor as the person who actually uses the outcome of the use case and who is the main consumer of the goal. Time driven trigger is another example of how a use case may be executed on behalf of the primary actor (in this situation the report is generated automatically at some time.)

Note, however, that although the goal of the primary actor is the driving force behind a use case, the use case must also fulfill any goals that other stakeholders might also have for this use case. That is, the main goal of a use case is to describe behavior of the system that results in satisfaction of the goals of all the stakeholders, although the use case may be driven by the goals of the primary actor. For example, a use case "withdraw money from the ATM" has a customer as its primary actor and will normally describe the entire interaction of the customer with the ATM. However, the bank is also a stakeholder of the ATM system and its interests may include that all steps are logged, money is given only if there are sufficient funds in the account, and no more than some amount is given at a time, etc. Satisfaction of these goals should also be shown by the use case "Withdraw money from the ATM."

For describing interaction, use cases use scenarios. A *scenario* describes a set of actions that are performed to achieve a goal under some specified conditions. The set of actions is generally specified as a sequence (as that is the most convenient way to express it in text), though in actual execution the actions specified may be executed in parallel or in some different order. Each step in a scenario is a logically complete action performed either by the actor or the system. Generally, a step is some action by the actor (e.g., enter information), some logical step that the system performs to progress towards achieving its goals (e.g., validate information, deliver information), or an internal state change by the system to satisfy some goals (e.g., log the transaction, update the record.)

A use case always has a *main success scenario*, which describes the interaction if nothing fails and all steps in the scenario succeed. There may be many success scenarios. Though the UC aims to achieve its goals, different situations can arise while the system and the actor are interacting which may not permit the system to achieve the goal fully. For these situations, a use case has *extension scenarios* which describe the system behavior if some of the steps in the main scenario do not complete successfully. Sometimes they are also called *exception scenarios*. A use case is a collection of all the success and extension scenarios related to the goal. The terminology of use cases is summarized in Table 3.4.1.

To achieve the desired goal, a system can divide it into sub-goals. Some of these sub-goals may be achieved by the system itself, but they may also be treated as separate use cases executed by supporting actors, which may be another system. For example, suppose for verifying a user in "Withdraw money from the ATM" an authentication service is used. The interaction with this service can be treated as a separate use case. A scenario in a use case may therefore employ another use case for performing some of the tasks. In other words, use cases permit a hierarchic organization.

It should be evident that the basic system model that use cases assume

Term	Definition
Actors	A person or a system which uses the system being built for achieving some goal.
Primary actor	The main actor for whom a use case is initiated and whose goal satisfaction is the main objective of the use case.
Scenario	A set of actions that are performed to achieve a goal under some specified conditions.
Main success scenario	Describes the interaction if nothing fails and all steps in the scenario succeed.
Extension scenario	Describe the system behavior if some of the steps in the main scenario do not complete successfully.

Table 3.2: Use Case terms.

is that a system primarily responds to requests from actors who use the system. By describing the interaction between actors and the system, the system behavior can be specified, and through the behavior its functionality is specified. A key advantage of this approach is that use cases focus on external behavior, thereby cleanly avoiding doing internal design during requirements, something that is desired but not easy to do with many modeling approaches.

Use cases are naturally textual descriptions, and represent the behavioral requirements of the system. This behavior specification can capture most of the functional requirements of the system. Therefore, use cases do not form the complete SRS, but can form a part of it. The complete SRS, as we have seen, will need to capture other requirements like performance and design constraints.

Though the detailed use cases are textual, diagrams can be used to supplement the textual description. For example, the use case diagram of UML provides an overview of the use cases and actors in the system and their dependency. A UML use case diagram generally shows each use case in the system as an ellipse, shows the primary actor for the use case as a stick figure connected to the use case with a line, and shows dependency between use cases by arcs between use cases. Some other relationships between use cases can also be represented. However, as use cases are basically textual in nature, diagrams play a limited role in either developing or specifying use cases. We will not discuss use case diagrams further.

3.4.2 Examples

Let us illustrate these concepts with a few use cases, which we will also use to explain other concepts related to use cases. Let us consider that a small on-line auction system is to be built, in which different persons can sell and buy goods. We will assume that there is a separate financial subsystem through which the payments are made and that each buyer and seller has an account in it.

In this system, though we have the same people who might be buying and selling, we dont have "users" as actors. Instead we have "buyers" and "sellers" as separate logical actors, as both have different goals to achieve. Besides these, the auction system itself is a stakeholder and an actor. The financial system is another. Let us first consider the main use cases of this system—"put some item for auction," "make a bid," and "complete an auction." These use cases are given in Fig 3.15.

The use cases are self-explanatory. This is the great value of use cases—they are natural and story-like which makes them easy to understand by both an analyst and a layman. This helps considerably in minimizing the communication gap between the developers and other stakeholders.

Some points about the use case are worth discussing. The use cases are generally numbered for reference purposes. The name of the use case specifies the goal of the primary actor (hence there is no separate line specifying the goal). The primary actor can be a person or a system—for UC1 and UC2 they are persons but for UC3, it is a system. The primary actor can also be another software which might request a service. The *precondition* of a use case specifies what the system will ensure before allowing the use case to be initiated. Common preconditions are "user is logged in," "input data exists in files or other data structures," etc. For an operation like delete it may be that "item exists," or for a tracking use case it may be that the "tracking number is valid."

It is worth noting that the use case description lists contains some actions that are not necessarily tied to the goals of the primary actor. For example, the last step in UC 2 is to update the bid price of other bidders. This action is clearly not needed by the current bidder for his goal. However, as the system and other bidders are also stakeholders for this use case, the use case has to ensure that their goals are also satisfied. Similar is the case with the last item of UC1.

The exception situations are also fairly clear. We have listed only the most obvious ones. There can be many more, depending on the goals of the

- *Use Case 1*: **Put an item up for auction**
  Primary Actor: Seller
  Precondition: Seller has logged in
  Main Success Scenario:

  1. Seller posts an item (its category, description, picture, etc.) for auction
  2. System shows past prices of similar items to seller
  3. Seller specifies the starting bid price and a date when auction will close
  4. System accepts the item and posts it

  Exception Scenarios:

  - 2 a) There are no past items of this category
    * System tells the seller this situation

- *Use Case 2*: **Make a bid**
  Primary Actor: Buyer
  Precondition: The buyer has logged in
  Main Success Scenario:

  1. Buyer searches or browses and selects some item
  2. System shows the rating of the seller, the starting bid, the current bids, and the highest bid; asks buyer to make a bid
  3. Buyer specifies a bid price, maximum bid price, and an increment
  4. System accepts the bid; Blocks funds in bidders account
  5. System updates the bid price of other bidders where needed, and updates the records for the item

  Exception Scenarios:

  - 3 a) The bid price is lower than the current highest
    * System informs the bidder and asks to rebid
  - 4 a) The bidder does not have enough funds in his account
    * System cancels the bid, asks the user to get more funds

Figure 3.15: Main use cases in an auction system.

- *Use Case 3*: **Complete auction of an item**
  Primary Actor: Auction System
  Precondition: The last date for bidding has been reached
  Main Success Scenario:

  1. Select highest bidder; send email to selected bidder and seller informing final bid price; send email to other bidders also.
  2. Debit bidder's account and credit seller's
  3. Transfer from seller's acct. commission amt. to organization's acct.
  4. Remove item from the site; update records

  Exception Scenarios: None

Figure 3.15: Main use cases in an auction system (contd.)

organization. For example, there could be one "user does not complete the transaction," which is a failure condition that can occur anywhere. What should be done in this case has to then be specified (e.g., all the records are cleaned).

A use cases can employ other use cases to perform some of its work. For example, in UC2 actions like "block the necessary funds" or "Debit bidder's account and credit seller's" are actions that need to be performed for the use case to succeed. However, they are not performed in this use case, but are treated as use cases themselves whose behavior has to be described elsewhere. If these use cases are also part of the system being built, then there must be descriptions of these in the requirements document. If they belong to some other system, then proper specifications about them will have to be obtained. The financial actions may easily be outside the scope of the auction system, so will not be described in the SRS. However, actions like "search" and "browse" are most likely part of this system and will have to be described in the SRS.

This allows use cases to be hierarchically organized and refinement approach can be used to define a higher level use case in terms of lower services and then defining the lower services. However, these lower-level use cases are proper use cases with a primary actor, main scenario, etc. The primary actor will often be the primary actor of the higher level use case. For example, the primary actor for the use case "find an item" is the buyer. It also implies that while listing the scenarios, new use cases and new actors might emerge. In the requirements document, all the use cases that are mentioned in this one will need to be specified if they are a part of the system being built.

3.4.3 Extensions

Besides specifying the primary actor, its goal, and the success and exceptional scenarios, a use case can also specify a scope. If the system being built has many subsystems, as is often the case, sometimes system use cases may actually be capturing the behavior of some subsystem. In such a situation it is better to specify the scope of that use case as the subsystem. For example, a use case for a system may be log in. Even though this is a part of the system, the interaction of the user with the system described in this use case is limited to the interaction with the "login and authentication" subsystem. If the architecture of the system has identified "login and authentication" as a subsystem or a component, then it is better to specify it as the scope. Generally, a business use case has the enterprise or the organization as the scope; a system use case has the system being built as the scope; and a component use case is where the scope is a subsystem.

UCs where the scope is the enterprise can often run over a long period of time (e.g., process an application of a prospective candidate.) These use cases may require many different systems to perform different tasks before the UC can be completed. (E.g., for processing an application the HR department has to do some things, the travel department has to arrange the travel and lodging, and the technical department has to conduct the interview.) The system and subsystem use cases are generally of the type that can be completed in one relatively short sitting. All the three use cases above are system use cases. As mentioned before, we will focus on describing the behavior of the software system we are interested in building. However, the enterprise level UCs provide the context in which the systems operate. Hence, sometimes it may be useful to describe some of the key business processes as *summary level* use cases to provide the context for the system being designed and built.

For example, let us describe the overall use case of performing an auction. A possible use case is given below in Fig 3.4.3. This use case is not a one-sitting use case and is really a business process, which provides the context for the earlier use cases. It is this use case that the earlier three use cases exist. Though this use case is also largely done by the system and is

---

- *Use Case 0*: **Auction an item**

  Primary Actor: Auction system

  Scope : Auction conducting organization

  Precondition: None

  Main Success Scenario:

  1. Seller performs *Put an item for auction*

  2. Various bidders perform *make a bid*

  3. On final date perform *Complete the auction of the item*

  4. Get feedback from seller; get feedback from buyer; update records

---

Figure 3.16: A summary level use case.

probably part of the system being built, frequently such use cases may not be completely part of the software system and may involve manual steps as well. For example, in the "auction an item" use case, if the delivery of the item being auctioned was to be ensured by the auctioning site, then that will be a step in this use case and it will be a manual step.

Use cases may also specify post conditions for the main success scenario, or some minimal guarantees they provide in all conditions. For example, in some use cases, atomicity may be a minimal guarantee. That is, no matter what exceptions occur either the entire transaction will be completed and the goal achieved, or the system state will be as if nothing was done. With atomicity, there will be no partial results and any partial changes will be rolled back.

3.4.4 Developing Use Cases

UCs not only document requirements, as their form is like story telling and uses text, both of which are easy and natural with different stakeholders, they also are a good medium for discussion and brainstorming. Hence, UCs can also be used for requirements elicitation and problem analysis. While developing use cases, informal or formal models may also be built, though they are not required.

UCs can be evolved in a stepwise refinement manner with each step adding more details. This approach allows UCs to be presented at different levels of abstraction. Though any number of levels of abstractions are possible, four natural levels emerge:

- **Actors and goals.** The actor-goal list enumerates the use cases and specifies the actors for each goal. (The name of the use case is generally the goal.) This table may be extended by giving a brief description of each of the use cases. At this level, the use cases specify the scope of the system and give an overall view of what it does. Completeness of functionality can be assessed fairly well by reviewing these.

- **Main success scenarios.** For each of the use cases, the main success scenarios are provided at this level. With the main scenarios, the system behavior for each use case is specified. This description can be reviewed to ensure that interests of all the stakeholders are met and that the use case is delivering the desired behavior.

- **Failure conditions.** Once the success scenario is listed, all the possible failure conditions can be identified. At this level, for each step in the main success scenario, the different ways in which a step can fail form the failure conditions. Before deciding what should be done in these failure conditions (which is done at the next level), it is better to enumerate the failure conditions and reviewed for completeness.

- **Failure handling.** This is perhaps the most tricky and difficult part of writing a use case. Often the focus is so much on the main functionality that people do not pay attention to how failures should be handled. Determining what should be the behavior under different failure conditions will often identify new business rules or new actors.

The different levels can be used for different purposes. For discussion on overall functionality or capabilities of the system, actors and goal level description is very useful. Failure conditions, on the other hand, are very useful for understanding and extracting detailed requirements and business rules under special cases.

The four levels can also guide the analysis activity. First just identify the actors and their goals and get an agreement with the concerned stakeholders on that. The actor-goal list will clearly define the scope of the system and will provide an overall view of what the system capabilities are. Then the main success scenario for each UC can be evolved, giving more details about the main functions of the system. Interaction and discussion are the primary means to uncover these scenarios though models may be built, if required. When the main success scenario for a use case is agreed upon and the main steps in its execution are specified, then the failure conditions can be examined. Enumerating failure conditions is an excellent method of uncovering special situations that can occur and which must be handled by the system. Finally, what should be done for these failure conditions should be examined and specified. As details of handling failure scenarios can require a lot of effort and discussion, it is better to first enumerate the different failure conditions and then get the details of these scenarios. Very often, when deciding the failure scenarios, many new business rules of how to deal with these scenarios get uncovered. Note that during this process an analyst may have to go back to earlier steps as during some detailed analysis new actors may emerge or new goals and new use cases may get uncovered. That is, using use cases for analysis is also an interactive task.

What should be the level of detail in a use case? There is no one answer to to a question like this; the actual answer always depends on the project and the situation. So it is with use cases. Generally it is good to have sufficient details which are not overwhelming but are sufficient to build the system and meet its quality goals. For example, if there is a small co-located team building the system, it is quite likely that use cases which list the main exception conditions and give a few key steps for the scenarios will suffice. On the other hand, for a project whose development is to be subcontracted to some other organization, it is better to have more detailed use cases.

For writing use cases, general technical writing rules apply. Use simple grammar, clearly specify who is performing the step, and keep the overall scenario as simple as possible. Also, when writing steps, for simplicity, it is better to combine some steps into one logical step, if it makes sense. For example steps "user enters his name," "user enter his SSN," and "user enters his address" can be easily combined into one step "user enters personal information."

3.5 Validation

The development of software starts with a requirements document, which is also used to determine eventually whether or not the delivered software system is acceptable. It is therefore important that the requirements specification contains no errors and specifies the client's requirements correctly. Furthermore, as we have seen, the longer an error remains undetected, the greater the cost of correcting it. Hence, it is extremely desirable to detect errors in the requirements before the design and development of the software begin.

Due to the nature of the requirement specification phase, there is a lot of room for misunderstanding and committing errors, and it is quite possible that the requirements specification does not accurately represent the client's needs. The basic objective of the requirements validation activity is to ensure that the SRS reflects the actual requirements accurately and clearly. A related objective is to check that the SRS document is itself of "good quality" (some desirable quality objectives are given later).

Before we discuss validation, let us consider the type of errors that typically occur in an SRS. Many different types of errors are possible, but the most common errors that occur can be classified in four types: omission, inconsistency, incorrect fact, and ambiguity. *Omission* is a common error in requirements. In this type of error, some user requirement is simply not included in the SRS; the omitted requirement may be related to the behavior of the system, its performance, constraints, or any other factor. Omission directly affects the external completeness of the SRS. Another common form of error in requirements is *inconsistency*. Inconsistency can be due to contradictions within the requirements themselves or to incompatibility of the stated requirements with the actual requirements of the client or with the environment in which the system will operate. The third common requirement error is *incorrect fact*. Errors of this type occur when some fact recorded in the SRS is not correct. The fourth common error type is *ambiguity*. Errors of this type occur when there are some requirements that have multiple meanings, that is, their interpretation is not unique.

Some projects have collected data about requirement errors. In [47] the effectiveness of different methods and tools in detecting requirement errors in specifications for a data processing application is reported. On an average, a total of more than 250 errors were detected, and the percentage of different types of errors was:

Omission	Incorrect Fact	Inconsistency	Ambiguity
26%	10%	38%	26%

In [8] the errors detected in the requirements specification of the A-7 project (which deals with a real-time flight control software) were reported. A total of about 80 errors were detected, out of which about 23% were clerical in nature. Of the remaining, the distribution with error type was:

Omission	Incorrect Fact	Inconsistency	Ambiguity
32%	49%	13%	5%

Though the distribution of errors is different in these two cases, reflecting the difference in application domains and the error detection methods used, they do suggest that the major problems (besides clerical errors) are omission, incorrect fact, inconsistency, and ambiguity. If we take the average of the two data tables, it shows that all four classes of errors are very significant, and a good fraction of errors belong to each of these types. This implies, that besides improving the quality of the SRS itself (e.g., no clerical errors), the validation should focus on uncovering these types of errors.

As requirements are generally textual documents that cannot be executed, inspections are eminently suitable for requirements validation. Consequently, inspections of the SRS, frequently called requirements review, are the most common method of validation. Because requirements specification formally specifies something that originally existed informally in people's minds, requirements validation must involve the clients and the users. Due to this, the requirements review team generally consists of client as well as user representatives. We have discussed the general procedure of inspections in an earlier chapter. Here we only discuss some aspects relevant to requirements reviews.

Requirements review is a review by a group of people to find errors and point out other matters of concern in the requirements specifications of a system. The review group should include the author of the requirements document, someone who understands the needs of the client, a person of the design team, and the person(s) responsible for maintaining the requirements document. It is also good practice to include some people not directly involved with product development, like a software quality engineer.

Although the primary goal of the review process is to reveal any errors in the requirements, such as those discussed earlier, the review process is also used to consider factors affecting quality, such as testability and readability. During the review, one of the jobs of the reviewers is to uncover the requirements that are too subjective and too difficult to define criteria for testing that requirement.

Checklists are frequently used in reviews to focus the review effort and ensure that no major source of errors is overlooked by the reviewers. A checklist for requirements review should include items like [52]:

- Are all hardware resources defined?

- Have the response times of functions been specified?

- Have all the hardware, external software, and data interfaces been defined?

- Have all the functions required by the client been specified?

- Is each requirement testable?

- Is the initial state of the system defined?

- Are the responses to exceptional conditions specified?

- Does the requirement contain restrictions that can be controlled by the designer?

- Are possible future modifications specified?

Requirements reviews are probably the most effective means for detecting requirement errors. The data in [8] about the A-7 project shows that about 33% of the total requirement errors detected were detected by review processes, and about 45% of the requirement errors were detected during the design phase when the requirement document is used as a reference for design. This clearly suggests that if requirements are reviewed then not only a substantial fraction of the errors are detected by them, but a vast majority of the remaining errors are detected soon afterwards in the design activity.

Though requirements reviews remain the most commonly used and viable means for requirement validation, other possibilities arise if some special purpose tools for modeling and analysis are used. For example, if the requirements are written in a formal specification language or a language specifically designed for machine processing, then it is possible to have tools to to verify some properties of requirements. These tools will focus on checks for internal consistency and completeness, which sometimes leads to checking of external completeness. However, these tools cannot directly check for external completeness (after all, how will a tool know that some requirement has been completely omitted?). For this reason, requirements reviews are needed even if the requirements are specified through a tool or are in a formal notation.

3.6 Metrics

As we stated earlier, the basic purpose of metrics at any point during a development project is to provide quantitative information to the management process so that the information can be used to effectively control the development process. Unless the metric is useful in some form to monitor or control the cost, schedule, or quality of the project, it is of little use for a project. There are very few metrics that have been defined for requirements, and little work has been done to study the relationship between the metric values and the project properties of interest. This says more about the state of the art of software metrics, rather than the usefulness of having such metrics. In this section, we will discuss some of the metrics and how they can be used.

3.6.1 Size—Function Points

A major problem after requirements are done is to estimate the effort and schedule for the project. For this, some metrics are needed that can be extracted from the requirements and used to estimate cost and schedule (through the use of some model). As the primary factor that determines the cost (and schedule) of a software project is its size, a metric that can help get an idea of the size of the project will be useful for estimating cost. This implies that during the requirement phase measuring the size of the requirement specification itself is pointless, unless the size of the SRS reflects the effort required for the project. This also requires that relationships of any proposed size measure with the ultimate effort of the project be established before making general use of the metric.

A commonly used size metric for requirements is the size of the text of the SRS. The size could be in *number of pages, number of paragraphs, number of functional requirements*, etc. As can be imagined, these measures are highly dependent on the authors of the document. A verbose analyst who likes to make heavy use of illustrations may produce an SRS that is many times the size of the SRS of a terse analyst. Similarly, how much an analyst refines the requirements has an impact on the size of the document. Generally, such metrics cannot be accurate indicators of the size of the project. They are used mostly to convey a general sense about the size of the project.

Function points [2] are one of the most widely used measures of software size. The basis of function points is that the "functionality" of a system, that is, what the system performs, is the measure of the system size. And as functionality is independent of how the requirements of the system are specified, or even how they are eventually implemented, such a measure has a nice property of being dependent solely on the system capabilities. In function points, the system functionality is calculated in terms of the number of functions it implements, the number of inputs, the number of outputs, etc.—parameters that can be obtained after requirements analysis and that are independent of the specification (and implementation) language.

The original formulation for computing the function points uses the count of five different parameters, namely, external input types, external output types, logical internal file types, external interface file types, and external inquiry types. According to the function point approach, these five parameters capture the entire functionality of a system. However, two elements of the same type may differ in their complexity and hence should not contribute the same amount to the "functionality" of the system. To account for complexity, each parameter in a type is classified as *simple*, *average*, or *complex*. The definition of each of these types and the interpretation of their complexity levels is given later [2].

Each unique input (data or control) type that is given as input to the application from outside is considered of *external input type* and is counted. An external input type is considered unique if the format is different from others or if the specifications require a different processing for this type from other inputs of the same format. The source of the external input can be the user, or some other application, files. An external input type is considered *simple* if it has a few data elements and affects only a few internal files of the application. It is considered *complex* if it has many data items and many internal logical files are needed for processing them. The complexity is *average* if it is in between. Note that files needed by the operating system or the hardware (e.g., configuration files) are not counted as external input files because they do not belong to the application but are needed due to the underlying technology.

Similarly, each unique output that leaves the system boundary is counted as an *external output type*. Again, an external output type is considered unique if its format or processing is different. Reports or messages to the users or other applications are counted as external input types. The complexity criteria are similar to those of the external input type. For a report, if it contains a few columns it is considered *simple*, if it has multiple columns it is considered *average*, and if it contains complex structure of data and references many files for production, it is considered *complex*.

Each application maintains information internally for performing its func-

Function type	Simple	Average	Complex
External input	3	4	6
External output	4	5	7
Logical internal file	7	10	15
External interface file	5	7	10
External inquiry	3	4	6

Table 3.3: Function point contribution of an element.

tions. Each logical group of data or control information that is generated, used, and maintained by the application is counted as a *logical internal file type*. A logical internal file is *simple* if it contains a few record types, *complex* if it has many record types, and *average* if it is in between.

Files that are passed or shared between applications are counted as *external interface file type*. Note that each such file is counted for all the applications sharing it. The complexity levels are defined as for logical internal file type.

A system may have queries also, where a query is defined as an input-output combination where the input causes the output to be generated almost immediately. Each unique input-output pair is counted as an *external inquiry type*. A query is unique if it differs from others in format of input or output or if it requires different processing. For classifying the query type, the input and output are classified as for external input type and external output type, respectively. The query complexity is the larger of the two.

Each element of the same type and complexity contributes a fixed and same amount to the overall function point count of the system (which is a measure of the functionality of the system), but the contribution is different for the different types, and for a type, it is different for different complexity levels. The amount of contribution of an element is shown in Table 3.3 [2, 113].

Once the counts for all five different types are known for all three different complexity classes, the raw or unadjusted function point (UFP) can be computed as a weighted sum as follows:

$$UFP = \sum_{i=1}^{i=5} \sum_{j=1}^{j=3} w_{ij} C_{ij},$$

where i reflects the row and j reflects the column in Table 3.3; w_{ij} is the entry in the ith row and jth column of the table (i.e., it represents the contribution of an element of the type i and complexity j); and C_{ij} is the count of the number of elements of type i that have been classified as having the complexity corresponding to column j.

Once the UFP is obtained, it is adjusted for the environment complexity. For this, 14 different characteristics of the system are given. These are data communications, distributed processing, performance objectives, operation configuration load, transaction rate, on-line data entry, end user efficiency, on-line update, complex processing logic, re-usability, installation ease, operational ease, multiple sites, and desire to facilitate change. The degree of influence of each of these factors is taken to be from 0 to 5, representing the six different levels: not present (0), insignificant influence (1), moderate influence (2), average influence (3), significant influence (4), and strong influence (5). The 14 degrees of influence for the system are then summed, giving a total N (N ranges from 0 to 14*5=70). This N is used to obtain a complexity adjustment factor (CAF) as follows:

$$CAF = 0.65 + 0.01N.$$

With this equation, the value of CAF ranges between 0.65 and 1.35. The delivered function points (DFP) are simply computed by multiplying the UFP by CAF. That is,

Delivered Function Points $= CAF *$ Unadjusted Function Points.

As we can see, by adjustment for environment complexity, the DFP can differ from the UFP by at most 35%. The final function point count for an application is the computed DFP.

Function points have been used as a size measure extensively and have been used for cost estimation. Studies have also been done to establish correlation between DFP and the final size of the software (measured in lines of code.) For example, according to one such conversion given in www.theadvisors.com/langcomparison.htm, one function point is approximately equal to about 125 lines of C code, and about 50 lines of C++ or Java code. By building models between function points and delivered lines of code (and existing results have shown that a reasonably strong correlation exists between DFP and KLOC so that such models can be built), one can estimate the size of the software in KLOC, if desired.

As can be seen from the manner in which the functionality of the system is defined, the function point approach has been designed for the data processing type of applications. For data processing applications, function points generally perform very well [106] and have now gained a widespread acceptance. For such applications, function points are used as an effective means of estimating cost and evaluating productivity. However, its utility as a size measure for nondata processing types of applications (e.g., real-time software, operating systems, and scientific applications) has not been well established, and it is generally believed that for such applications function points are not very well suited.

A major drawback of the function point approach is that the process of computing the function points involves subjective evaluation at various points and the final computed function point for a given SRS may not be unique and can depend on the analyst. Some of the places where subjectivity enters are: (1) different interpretations of the SRS (e.g., whether something should count as an external input type or an external interface type; whether or not something constitutes a logical internal file; if two reports differ in a very minor way should they be counted as two or one); (2) complexity estimation of a user function is totally subjective and depends entirely on the analyst (an analyst may classify something as complex while someone else may classify it as average) and complexity can have a substantial impact on the final count as the weighs for simple and complex frequently differ by a factor of 2; and (3) value judgments for the environment complexity. These factors make the process of function point counting somewhat subjective. Organizations that use function points try to specify a more precise set of counting rules in an effort to reduce this subjectivity. It has also been found that with experience this subjectivity is reduced [113]. Overall, despite this subjectivity, use of function points for data processing applications continues to grow.

The main advantage of function points over the size metric of KLOC, the other commonly used approach, is that the definition of DFP depends only on information available from the specifications, whereas the size in KLOC cannot be directly determined from specifications. Furthermore, the DFP count is independent of the language in which the project is implemented. Though these are major advantages, another drawback of the function point approach is that even when the project is finished, the DFP is not uniquely known and has subjectivity. This makes building of models for cost estimation hard, as these models are based on information about completed projects (cost models are discussed further in the next chapter). In addition, determining the DFP—from either the requirements or a completed project—cannot be automated. That is, considerable effort is required to obtain the size, even for a completed project. This is a drawback compared to KLOC measure, as KLOC can be determined uniquely by automated tools once the project is completed.

3.6.2 Quality Metrics

As we have seen, the quality of the SRS has direct impact on the cost of the project. Hence, it is important to ensure that the SRS is of good quality. For this, some quality metrics are needed that can be used to assess the quality of the SRS. Quality of an SRS can be assessed either directly by evaluating the quality of the document by estimating the value of one or more of the quality attributes of the SRS, or indirectly, by assessing the effectiveness of the quality control measures used in the development process during the requirements phase. Quality attributes of the SRS are generally hard to quantify, and little work has been done in quantifying these attributes and determining correlation with project parameters. Hence, the use of these metrics is still limited. However, process-based metrics are better understood and used more widely for monitoring and controlling the requirements phase of a project.

Number of errors found is a process metric that is useful for assessing the quality of requirement specifications. Once the number of errors of different categories found during the requirement review of the project is known, some assessment can be made about the SRS from the size of the project and historical data. This assessment is possible if the development process is under statistical control. In this situation, the error distribution during requirement reviews of a project will show a pattern similar to other projects executed following the same development process. From the pattern of errors to be expected for this process and the size of the current project (say, in function points), the volume and distribution of errors expected to be found during requirement reviews of this project can be estimated. These estimates can be used for evaluation.

For example, if much fewer than expected errors were detected, it means that either the SRS was of very high quality or the requirement reviews were not careful. Further analysis can reveal the true situation. If too many clerical errors were detected and too few omission type errors were detected, it might mean that the SRS was written poorly or that the requirements review meeting could not focus on "larger issues" and spent too much effort on "minor" issues. Again, further analysis will reveal the true situation. Similarly, a large number of errors that reflect ambiguities in the SRS can imply that the problem analysis has not been done properly and many more ambiguities may still exist in the SRS. Some project management decision to control this can then be taken (e.g., build a prototype or do further analysis).

Clearly, review data about the number of errors and their distribution can be used effectively by the project manager to control quality of the requirements. From the historical data, a rough estimate of the number of errors that remain in the SRS after the reviews can also be estimated. This can be useful in the rest of the development process as it gives some handle on how many requirement errors should be revealed by later quality assurance activities.

Requirements rarely stay unchanged. Change requests come from the clients (requesting added functionality, a new report, or a report in a different format, for example) or from the developers (infeasibility, difficulty in implementing, etc.). *Change request frequency* can be used as a metric to assess the stability of the requirements and how many changes in requirements to expect during the later stages.

Many organizations have formal methods for requesting and incorporating changes in requirements. We have earlier seen a requirements change management process. Change data can be easily extracted from these formal change approval procedures. The frequency of changes can also be plotted against time. For most projects, the frequency decreases with time. This is to be expected; most of the changes will occur early, when the requirements are being analyzed and understood. During the later phases, requests for changes should decrease.

For a project, if the change requests are not decreasing with time, it could mean that the requirements analysis has not been done properly. Frequency of change requests can also be used to "freeze" the requirements—when the frequency goes below an acceptable threshold, the requirements can be considered frozen and the design can proceed. The threshold has to be determined based on experience and historical data.

3.7 Summary

The main goal of the requirements phase is to produce the software requirements specification (SRS), which accurately captures the client's requirements and which forms the basis of software development and validation. The basic reason for the difficulty in specifying software requirements comes from the fact that there are three interested parties—the client, the end users, and the software developer. The requirements document has to be such that the client and users can understand it easily and the developers can use it as a basis for software development. Due to the diverse parties involved in software requirements specification, a communication gap exists. This makes the task of requirements specification difficult.

There are three basic activities in the requirements phase. The first is problem or requirement analysis. The goal of this activity is to understand such different aspects as the requirements of the problem, its context, and how it fits within the client's organization. The second activity is requirements specification, during which the understood problem is specified or written, producing the SRS. And the third activity is requirements validation, which is done to ensure that the requirements specified in the SRS are indeed what is desired.

There are three main approaches to analysis; unstructured approaches rely on interaction between the analyst, customer, and user to reveal all the requirements (which are then documented). The second is the modeling-oriented approach, in which a model of the problem is built based on the available information. The model is useful in determining if the understanding is correct and in ensuring that all the requirements have been determined. Modeling may be function-oriented or object-oriented. The third approach is the prototyping approach in which a prototype is built to validate the correctness and completeness of requirements.

To satisfy its goals, an SRS should possess characteristics like completeness, consistency, unambiguous, verifiable, modifiable, etc. A good SRS should specify all the functions the software needs to support, performance of the system, the design constraints that exist, and all the external interfaces.

One method for specifying the functional specifications that has become popular is the use case approach. With this approach the functionality of the system is specified through use cases, with each use case specifying the behavior of the system when a user interacts with it for achieving some goal. Each use case contains a normal scenario, as well as many exceptional scenarios, thereby providing the complete behavior of the system. Though use cases are meant for specification, as they are natural and story-like, by expressing them at different levels of abstraction they can also be used for problem analysis.

For validation, the most commonly used method is reviewing or inspecting the requirements. In requirements inspections, the team of reviewers also includes a representative of the client to ensure that all requirements are captured.

The main metric of interest for requirements is some quantification of system size, as it can be used to estimate the effort requirement of the project. The most commonly used size metric for requirements is the function points. The function point metric attempts to quantify the functionality of the system in terms of five parameters and their complexity levels which can be determined from the requirements of the system. Based on the count of these five parameters for different complexity levels, and the value of fourteen different environmental factors, the function point count for a system is obtained. The function point metric can be used for estimating the cost of the system.

Exercises

1. Is it possible to have a system that can automatically verify completeness of an SRS document? Explain your answer.

2. Construct an example of an inconsistent (incomplete) SRS.

3. How can you specify the "maintainability" and "user friendliness" of a software system in quantitative terms?

4. For a complete and unambiguous response time requirement, the environmental factors on which the response time depends must be specified. Which factors should be considered, and what units should be chosen to specify them?

5. The basic goal of the requirements activity is to get an SRS that has some desirable properties. What is the role of modeling in developing such an SRS? List three major benefits that modeling provides, along with justifications, for achieving the basic goal.

6. Make a friend of yours as the client. Perform structured analysis and object-oriented analysis for the following:

   (a) An electronic mail system.
   (b) A simple student registration system.
   (c) A system to analyze a person's diet.
   (d) A system to manage recipes for a household.
   (e) A system to fill tax forms for the current year tax laws.

7. Write the SRS for the restaurant example whose analysis is shown in the chapter.

8. Write the functional requirements for the restaurant example using use cases.

9. Develop a worksheet for calculating the function point for a given problem specification.

10. Compute the function points for the restaurant example (can use the worksheet).

Case Studies

We introduce our two running case studies here. We give the problem description and discuss the problem analysis of these case studies. The detailed SRS for both these case studies are available from the Web site.

Case Study 1—Course Scheduling

Problem Description

The computer science department in a university offers many courses every semester, which are taught by many instructors. These courses are scheduled based on some policy directions of the department. Currently the scheduling is done manually, but the department would like to automate it. We have to first understand the problem and then produce a requirements document based on our understanding of the problem.

Problem Analysis

We do the problem analysis here—the requirements specification document is available from the Web site of the book. For analysis, we first identify the parties involved.

Client: Chairman of the computer science department.
End Users: Department secretary and instructors.

Now we begin to study the current system. After speaking with the instructors, the department chairman, and the secretary, we find that the system operates as follows. Each instructor specifies, on a sheet of paper, the course he is teaching, expected enrollment, and his preferences for lecture times. These preferences must be valid lecture times, which are specified by the department. These sheets are given to the department secretary, who keeps them in the order they are received. After the deadline expires, the secretary does the scheduling. Copies of the final schedule are sent to the instructors. The overall DFD for the system is shown in Figure 3.17.

This DFD was discussed with the chairman and the department secretary and approved by them. We now focus on the scheduling process, which is our main interest. From the chairman we found that the two major policies regarding scheduling are: (1) the post-graduate (PG) courses are given preference over undergraduate (UG) courses, and (2) no two PG courses can be scheduled at the same time.

The department secretary was interviewed at length to find out the details of the scheduling activity. The schedule of the last few semesters, together with their respective inputs (i.e., the sheets) were also studied. It was found that the basic process is as follows. The sheets are separated into three piles—one for PG courses with preferences, one for UG courses with preferences, and one for courses with no preference. The order of the sheets in the three piles was maintained. First the courses in the PG pile were scheduled and then the courses in the UG pile were scheduled. The courses were scheduled in the order they appeared in the pile. During scheduling no backtracking was done, i.e., once a course is scheduled, the scheduling of later courses has no effect on its schedule. After all the PG and UG courses with preferences were processed, courses without any preferences were scheduled in the available slots. It was also found that information about classrooms and the department-approved lecture times was tacitly used during the scheduling. The DFD for the schedule process is shown in Figure 3.18.

The secretary was not able to explain the algorithm used for scheduling. It is likely that some hit-and-miss approach is being followed. However, while scheduling, the following was being checked:

1. Classroom capacity is sufficient for the course.
2. A slot for a room is never allotted to more than one course.

The two basic data flows are the sheets containing preferences and the final schedule. The data dictionary entry for these is:

collected_forms = [instructor_name +
    course_number + [preferences]*]
schedule = [course_number class_room lecture_time]*

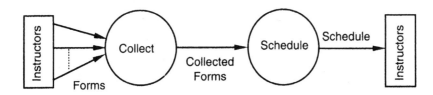

Figure 3.17: Top-level DFD for the current scheduling system.

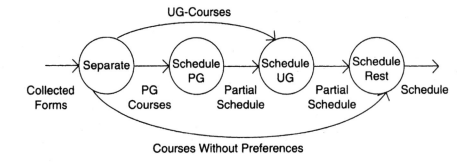

Figure 3.18: The DFD for the schedule process.

Now we have to define the DFD for the new or future automated system. Automating scheduling can affect the preference collection method, so boundaries of change include the entire system. After discussion with the chairman, the instructors, and the secretary, the following decisions were made regarding what the automated system should do and what the new environment should be:

1. The preferences will be electronically mailed to the secretary by the instructors. The secretary will put these preferences for different courses in a file in the order in which they are received. The secretary will also make entries for all courses for which no response has been given before the deadline. Entries for these courses will have no preferences.

2. The format for each course entry should be similar to the one currently being used.

3. Entries might have errors, so the system should be able to check for errors.

4. The current approach for scheduling should be followed. However, the system should make sure that scheduling of UG courses does not make a PG course without any preference unschedulable. This is not being done currently, but is desired.

5. A reason for unschedulability should be given for the preferences that are not satisfied or for courses that cannot be scheduled.

6. Information about department courses, classrooms, and valid lecture times will be kept in a file.

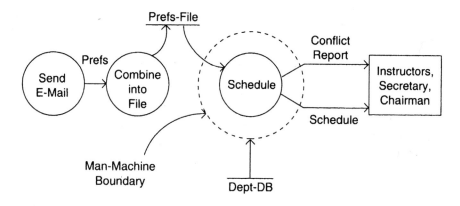

Figure 3.19: DFD for the new system.

The DFD for the new logical system (one with automation) is shown in Figure 3.19. The two important data entities are the two files in the DFD. The data dictionary entry for these is:

prefs_file = [pref]*
pref = course_number + enrollment + [preferences]*
dept_DB = [class_rooms]* + dept_course_list + [valid_lecture_time]*
class_rooms = room_no + capacity

It is decided that the scheduling process will be automated. The rest (such as combining preferences) will be done manually. Based on the format currently used in the sheets, a detailed format for the course entries was decided and approved by the instructors. A detailed format for the dept_DB file was also chosen and approved. The final formats and the requirements are given in the requirements document.

The complete SRS of this case study, which specifies the functional requirements by enumerating the functions of the system, is available from the Web site of the book.

Case Study 2—Personal Investment Management System

Problem Description

Many people invest their money in a number of securities (shares). Generally, an investor has multiple portfolios of investments, each portfolio having investments in many securities. From time to time an investor sells or buys some securities and gets dividends for the securities. There is a current value of each security—many sites give this current value. It is proposed to build a personal investment management system (PIMS) to help investors keep track of their investments, as well as determine the rate of returns he/she is getting on the individual investments as well as on the overall portfolio. The system should also allow an investor to determine the net-worth of the portfolios.

Problem Analysis

This project started with the above problem statement. During analysis, discussion with the clients were held to clarify various issues. After discussion, the following clarifications emerged.

- An investor can have multiple portfolios of investments. A portfolio can have many investments.

- In each investment, the investor invests some moneys from time to time, and withdraws some funds from time to time. The amount invested/withdrawn and the dates are provided by the investor. Any number of investments/withdrawls can be made.

- There is a current value of each investment. As a default, the previously given current value can be chosen. Provision should be made to get the current value from some recognized site on the Web. If for some reason the net is down, then the user should be able to specify the current value of the shares.

- An investor may also invest in instruments which have a maturity date and/or a fixed rate of return. Such investments should also be handled by the system. In addition, for such investments, the system should provide a provision of alerts (e.g., on maturity).

- The investor should be allowed to save information about his portfolio investments, etc.

- The investor should be allowed to edit entered data.

- An investor should be able to view any of his portfolios—in summary form or detailed form.

- Data being stored is very personal; even though the system is to work on a PC, it should provide some security.

- For each investment, the investor can determine the rate of return he is getting. Besides the rate of return on each investment, the investor should be given the overall rate of return for each portfolio as well as total investments. Information like how much money invested, how much has been earned, etc. can also be shown.

- Rates of return can be computed on a monthly basis. For example, month is the smallest unit for computing returns. The yearly return will be computed from this monthly return using monthly compounding (i.e., yearly return = (1+monthly return)**12 - 1.)

During the discussions, the scope of the project also got defined.

In Scope

- Managing investment of a single user, which would include maintaining bookkeeping information about entities like Portfolio, Security, and Transaction

- Computation of Net-Worth and Rate of Investment (ROI) of the Investor

- Giving alerts to the user, if it is requested

- Downloading the current prices of shares from the Web

- User authentication

Out of Scope

- Features for actual purchasing and selling of securities. That is, actually buying and selling of shares/securities is done outside PIMS.

- Tax computations for gains/losses

- Any market related prediction

Key Use Cases

For this project, a use-case-based requirement analysis and specification is done. That is, use cases are used for analysis as well as specification. The main actors for PIMS are the user and the system. During analysis, first the major use cases categories and key use cases in each category are identified. The broad categories and the use cases in each category are given in the table below.

Use Case Category	Use Cases
Installation	Installation
System authorization	Login, Change Password
Portfolio related	Create portfolio, Rename portfolio, Delete portfolio
Securities related	Create security, Rename security, Delete security
Transaction related	Add transaction, Edit transaction, Delete transaction
Information display	Display investment, Display portfolio, Display security
Computation	Compute net-worth, Compute ROI
Share prices	Get current share price, Edit share price
Alerts	Set alerts, Show alerts, Delete alerts

Once the main use cases were identified and agreed, details of the use cases were uncovered. As discussed earlier, first we defined the main success scenario for the use cases, and then we identified the exception scenarios.

The complete SRS for this case study is available from the book's Web site.

4

Software Architecture

A system is an entity that provides some behavior to its environment, where the environment can consist of people or other systems. In the previous chapter we saw that expected behavior of a proposed software system is defined through a software requirement specification (SRS) document. For building the specified software system, designing the software architecture is a key step, and is the topic of this chapter.

Any complex system is composed of sub systems that interact under the control of system design such that the system provides the expected behavior. While designing such a system, therefore, the logical approach is to identify the sub-systems that should compose the system, the interfaces of these subsystems, and the rules for interaction between the subsystems. This is what software architecture aims to do.

Software architecture is a relatively recent area. As the software systems increasingly become distributed and more complex, architecture becomes an important step in building the system. Due to a wide range of options now available for how a system may be configured and connected, carefully designing the architecture becomes very important. It is during the architecture design where choices like using some type of middleware, or some type of back end database, or some type of server, or some type of security component are made. It is not possible to design the details of the system and then try to accommodate these choices—the architecture must be created such that these decisions have been incorporated suitably in the system structure. Architecture is also the earliest place when properties like reliability and performance can be evaluated for the system, a capability that is increasingly becoming important.

In this chapter, we will focus primarily on architecture concepts and some notation for describing architecture. The issue of methodology, that is, how architecture should be created, is not discussed as architecture is a high-level creative activity for which methodologies do not really exist. However, we will discuss some architecture styles, which suggest some forms of architectures. A combination of some variation of these styles is likely to be useful for many systems. We also discuss some issues relating to software architectures like documentation, relationship to design, etc., and discuss one approach for analyzing architectures. We end the chapter with a dsicussion of architectures for the two case studies.

4.1   Role of Software Architecture

What is architecture? We must have a clear answer to this before we further discuss what its role is in building a software system and how we can go about creating and representing architecture.

At a top level, architecture is a design of a system which gives a very high level view of the parts of the system and how they are related to form the whole system. That is, architecture partitions the system in logical parts such that each part can be comprehended independently, and then describes the system in terms of these parts and the relationship between these parts.

Any complex system can be partitioned in many different ways, each providing an useful view and each having different types of logical parts. The same holds true for a software system—there is no unique structure of the system that can be described by its architecture; there are many possible structures.

Due to this possibility of having multiple structures, one of the most widely accepted definitions of software architecture is that *the software architecture of a system is the structure or structures of the system, which comprise software elements, the externally visible properties of those elements, and the relationships among them [9].* This definition implies that for elements in an architecture, we are only interested in those abstractions that specify those properties that other elements can assume to exist and that are needed to specify relationships. These properties could be about the functionality or services the component provides, or the performance and other quality properties it provides. Details on how these properties are supported are not needed for architecture. This is an important capability that allows architecture descriptions to represent a complex system in a succinct form that is easily comprehended. The definition also implies that the behavior of the elements is part of the architecture; hence any architecture documentation must clearly specify the behavior. Finally, as with most definitions, this definition does not say anything about whether an architecture is good or bad—this determination has to be done through some analysis.

An architecture description of a system will therefore describe the different structures of the system. The next natural question that arises is what are these structures in an architecture description good for? Why should a team building a software system for some customer be interested in creating and documenting the structures of the proposed system. Some of the important uses that software architecture descriptions play are [9, 35, 93].

1. *Understanding and communication*: An architecture description is primarily to communicate the architecture to its various stakeholders, which include the users who will use the system, the clients who commissioned the system, the builders who will build the system, and, of course, the architects. An architecture description is an important means of communication between these various stakeholders. Through this description the stakeholders gain an understanding of some macro properties of the system and how the system intends to fulfill the functional and quality requirements. As the description provides a common language between stakeholders, it also becomes the vehicle for negotiation and agreement amongst the stakeholders, who may have conflicting goals.

   Clearly, to facilitate communication, software architecture descriptions must facilitate the understanding of systems. An architecture description of the proposed system describes how the system will be composed, when it is built. By partitioning the system into parts, and presenting the system at a higher level of abstraction as composed of subsystems and their interactions, detailed level complexity is hidden. This facilitates the understanding of the system and its structure.

   Though we are focusing on new systems being created, it should be pointed out that architecture descriptions can also be used to understand an existing system—by specifying different high level views of the system structure, a system description is simplified with details about how parts are implemented hidden away. The reduction of system to a few parts and how they work together is a tremendous aid in understanding, as it reduces the complexity and allows a person to deal with a limited complexity at a given time.

2. *Reuse*: Architecture descriptions can help software reuse. Reuse is considered one of the main techniques by which productivity can be improved, thereby reducing the cost of software. The software engineering world has, for a long time, been working towards a discipline where software can be assembled from parts that are developed by different people and are available for others to use. If one wants to build a software product in which existing components may be reused, then architecture becomes the key point at which reuse at the highest level is decided. The architecture has to be chosen in a manner such that the components which have to be reused can fit properly and together with other components that may be developed, they provide the features that are needed.

   Architecture also facilitates reuse among products that are similar and building product families such that the common parts of these different but similar products can be reused. Architecture helps specify what is fixed and what is variable in these different products, and can help minimize the set of variable elements such that different products can share software parts to the maximum. Again, it is very hard to achieve this type of reuse at a detail level.

3. *Construction and Evolution.* As architecture partitions the system into parts, some architecture provided partitioning can naturally be used for constructing the system, which also requires that the system be broken into parts such that different teams (or individuals) can separately work on different parts. A suitable partitioning in the architecture can provide the project with the parts that need to be built to build the system. As, almost by definition, the parts specified in an architecture are relatively independent (the dependence between parts coming through their relationship), they can be built independently. Not only does an architecture guide the development, it also establishes the constraints—the system should be constructed in a manner that the structures chosen during the architecture creation are preserved. That is, the chosen parts are there in the final system and they interact in the specified manner.

   The construction of a software system usually does not end in delivery of the product—a software system also evolves with time. During evolution, often new features are added to the system. The architecture of the system can help in deciding where to add the new features with minimum complexity and effort, and what the impact on the rest of the system might be of adding the new features. Also, if some changes have to be made to the existing functionality, then architecture can help determine which are the parts of the system that will be affected by this change—an exercise that is extremely important in ensuring that the change is made properly without any unforeseen side effects.

4. *Analysis*. It is highly desirable if some important properties about the behavior of the system can be determined before the system is actually built. This will allow the designers to consider alternatives and select the one that will best suit the needs. Many engineering disciplines use models to analyze design of a product for its cost, reliability, performance, etc. Architecture opens such possibilities for software also. It is possible (thought the methods are not fully developed or standardized yet) to analyze or predict the properties of the system being built from its architecture. For example, the reliability or the performance of the system can be analyzed. Such an analysis can help determine whether the system will meet the quality and performance requirements, and if not, what needs to be done to meet the requirements. For example, while building a Web site for shopping, it is possible to analyze the response time or throughput for a proposed architecture, given some assumptions about the request load and hardware. It can then be decided whether the performance is satisfactory or not, and if not, what new capabilities should be added (for example, a different architecture or a faster server for the back end) to improve it to a satisfactory level.

One can easily think of other uses of architecture as well. However, not all of these uses may be significant in a project and which of these uses is pertinent to a project depends on the nature of the project. In some projects communication may be very important, but a detailed performance analysis may be unnecessary (because the system is too small or is meant for only a few users). In some other systems, performance analysis may be the primary use of architecture.

4.2 Architecture Views

There is a general view emerging that there is no unique architecture of a system. The definition that we have adopted (given above) also expresses this sentiment. Consequently, there is no one architecture drawing of the system. The situation is similar to that of civil construction a discipline that is the original user of the concept of architecture and from where the concept of software architecture has been borrowed. For a building, if you want to see the floor plan, you are shown one set of drawings. If you are an electrical engineer and want to see how the electricity distribution has been planned, you will be shown another set of drawings. And if you are interested in safety and firefighting, another set of drawings is used. These drawings are not independent of each other—they are all about the same building. However, each drawing provides a different view of the building, a view that focuses on explaining one aspect of the building and tries to a good job at that, while not divulging much about the other aspects. And no one drawing can express all the different aspects—such a drawing will be too complex for to be of any use.

Similar is the situation with software architecture. In software, the different drawings are called views. A view represents the system as composed of some types of *elements* and *relationships* between them. Which elements are used by a view, depends on what the view wants to highlight. Different views expose different properties and attributes, thereby allowing the stakeholders and analysts to properly evaluate those attributes for the system. By focusing only on some aspects of the system, a view reduces the complexity that a reader has to deal with at a time, thereby aiding system understanding and analysis.

A view describes a structure of the system. We will use these two concepts—views and structures—interchangeably. We will also use the term architectural view to refer to a view. Many types of views have been proposed. Most of the proposed views generally belong to one of these three types [35, 9]:

- Module

- Component and connector

- Allocation

In a module view, the system is viewed as a collection of code units, each implementing some part of the system functionality. That is, the main elements in this view are modules. These views are code-based and do not explicitly represent any runtime structure of the system. Examples of modules are packages, a class, a procedure, a method, a collection of functions, and a collection of classes. The relationships between these modules are also code-based and depend on how code of a module interacts with another module. Examples of relationships in this view are "is a part of" (i.e., module B is a part of module A), "uses or depends on" (a module A uses services of module B to perform its own functions and correctness of module A depends on correctness of module B,) and "generalization or specialization" (a module B is a generalization of a module A.)

In a component and connector (C&C) view, the system is viewed as a collection of runtime entities called components. That is, a component is a unit which has an identity in the executing system. Objects (not classes), a collection of objects, and a process are examples of components. While executing, components need to interact with others to support the system services. Connectors provide means for this interaction. Examples of connectors are pipes and sockets. Shared data can also act as a connector. If the components use some middleware to communicate and coordinate, then the middleware is a connector. Hence, the primary elements of this view are components and connectors.

An allocation view focuses on how the different software units are allocated to resources like the hardware, file systems, and people. That is, an allocation view specifies the relationship between software elements and elements of the environments in which the software system is executed. They expose structural properties like which processes run on which processor, and how the system files are organized on a file system.

An architecture description consists of views of different types, with each view exposing some structure of the system. Module views show how the software is structured as a set of implementation units, C&C views show how the software is structured as interacting runtime elements, and allocation views show how software relates to non-software structures. These three types of view of the same system form the architecture of the system, as represented in Figure 4.1.

Note that the different views are not unrelated. They all represent the same system. Hence, there are relationships between elements in one view and elements in another view. These relationships may be simple or may be complex. For example, the relationship between modules and components may be one to one in that one module implements one component. On the other hand, it may be quite complex with a module being used by multiple components, and a component using multiple modules. While creating the different views, the designers have to be aware of this relationship.

The next question is what are the standard views that should be expressed for describing the architecture of a system? For answering this question, the analogy with buildings may again help. If one is building a simple

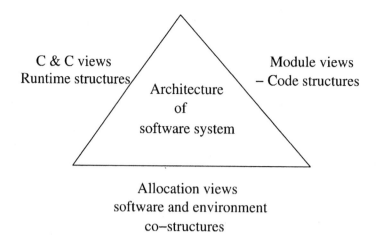

Figure 4.1: Views of Software Architecture.

small house, then perhaps there is no need to have a separate view describing the emergency and the fire system. Similarly, if there is no air conditioning in the building, there need not be any view for that. On the other hand, an office building will perhaps require both of these views, in addition to other views describing plumbing, space, wiring, etc.

The situation with software is similar which views are needed for a project depends on the project and the system being built. Depending on the needs of the project, it can be decided which views are needed. For example, if performance analysis is to be done, then the architecture must describe some component and connector view to capture the runtime structure of the system, as well as describe the allocation view to specify what hardware the different components run on. If it is to be used for planning the development, then a module view must be provided so that the different programmers or teams can be assigned different modules. In general, a large and complex project where a lot of money is at stake will require many different views so it can be analyzed from many different angles, and the risks of failures is reduced by doing so. On the other hand, for a smaller project, maybe a single view, or a couple of views, will suffice.

However, despite the fact that there are multiple drawings showing different views of a building, there is one view that predominates in construction—that of physical structure. This view forms the basis of other views in that other views cannot really be completed unless this view can be done. Other views may or may not be needed for constructing a building, depending on the nature of the project. Hence, in a sense, the view giving the building structure may be considered as the primary view in that it is almost always used, and other views rely on this view substantially. The view also captures perhaps the most important property to be analyzed in the early stages, namely, that of space organization.

The situation with software architecture is also somewhat similar. As we have said, depending on what properties are of interest, different views of the software architecture are needed. However, of these views, the component and connector (C&C) view has become the de-facto primary view, one which is almost always prepared when an architecture is designed (some definitions even view architecture only in terms of C&C views.) In this chapter, we will focus primarily on the C&C view, and will discuss the other two types only briefly. The module view will get discussed further in later chapters when discussing high level design, which focuses on identifying the different modules in the software.

4.3 Component and Connector View

Component and Connector (C&C) architecture view of a system has two main elements—components and connectors. Components are usually computational elements or data stores that have some presence during the system execution. Connectors define the means of interaction between these components. A C&C view of the system defines the components, and which component is connected to which and through what connector. A C&C view describes a runtime structure of the system—what components exist when the system is executing and how they interact during the execution. The C&C structure is essentially a graph, with components as nodes and connectors as edges.

C&C view is perhaps the most common view of architecture and most box-and-line drawings representing architecture attempt to capture this view. Most often when people talk about the architecture, they refer to the C&C view. Most architecture description languages also focus on the C&C view.

4.3.1 Components

Components are generally units of computation or data stores in the system. A component has a name, which is generally chosen to represent the role of the component or the function it performs. The name also provides a unique identity to the component, which is necessary for referencing details about

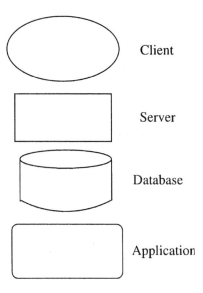

Figure 4.2: Component examples.

the component in the supporting documents, as a C&C drawing will only show the component names.

A component is of a component-type, where the type represents a generic component, defining the general computation and the interfaces a component of that type must have. Note that though a component has a type, in the C&C architecture view, we have components (i.e., actual instances) and not types. Examples of these types are clients, servers, filters, etc. Different domains may have other generic types like controllers, actuators, and sensors (for a control system domain.)

In a diagram representing a C&C architecture view of a system, it is highly desirable to have a different representation for different component types, so the different types can be identified visually. In a box-and-line diagram, often all components are represented as rectangular boxes. Such an approach will require that types of the components are described separately and the reader has to read the description to figure out the types of the components. It is much better to use a different symbol/notation for each different component type. If there are multiple components of the same type, then each of these components will be represented using the same symbol they will be distinguished from each other by their names.

Components use interfaces to communicate with other components. The interfaces are sometimes called ports. A component must clearly specify its ports. In a diagram, this is typically done by putting suitable marks on the edges of the symbol being used for the component.

It would be useful if there was a list of standard symbols that could be used to build an architecture diagram. However, as there is no standard list of component types, there is no such standard list. Some of the common symbols used for representing commonly found component types are shown in Figure 4.2.

As there are no standard notations for different component types and an architect can use his own symbols, the type information cannot be obtained by a reader from the symbols used. To make sure that the meanings of the different symbols is clear to the reader, it is therefore necessary to have a key of the different symbols to describe what type of component a symbol represents.

A component is essentially a system in its own right providing some behavior at defined interfaces (i.e., ports) to its environment. Like any system, a component may be complex and have a structure of its own, which can be determined by decomposing the component. In many situations, particularly for systems that are not too large, there may not be a need to decompose the components to determine their internal architecture. We will mostly work with atomic components, that is, components whose internal structure is not needed for describing or analyzing an architecture view.

4.3.2 Connectors

The different components of a system are likely to interact while the system is in operation to provide the services expected of the system. After all, components exist to provide parts of the services and features of the system, and these must be combined to deliver the overall system functionality. For composing a system from its components, information about the interaction between components is necessary.

Interaction between components may be through a simple means supported by the underlying process execution infrastructure of the operating system. For example, a component may interact with another using the procedure call mechanism (a connector,) which is provided by the runtime environment for the programming language. However, the interaction may involve more complex mechanisms as well. Examples of such mechanisms are remote procedure call, TCP/IP ports, and a protocol like HTTP. These mechanisms requires a fair amount of underlying runtime infrastructure, as well as special programming within the components to use the infras-

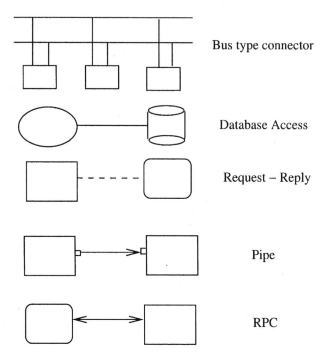

Figure 4.3: Connector examples.

tructure. Consequently, it is extremely important to identify and explicitly represent these connectors. Specification of connectors will help identify the suitable infrastructure needed to implement an architecture, as well as clarify the programming needs for components using them. Without a proper understanding of the connectors, a realization of the components using the connectors may not be possible.

Note that connectors need not be binary and a connector may provide a n-way communication between multiple components. For example, a broadcast bus may be used as a connector, which allows a component to broadcast its message to all the other components. (Of course, how such a connector will be implemented is another issue that must be resolved before the architecture can be implemented. Generally, while creating an architecture, it is wise for the architect to use the connectors which are available on the systems on which the software will be deployed. Otherwise, there must be plans to build those connectors, or buy them, if they are available.)

A connector also has a name that should describe the nature of interaction the connector supports. A connector also has a type, which is a generic description of the interaction, specifying properties like whether it is a binary or n-way, types of interfaces it supports, etc. Sometimes, the interaction supported by a connector is best represented as a protocol. A protocol implies that when two or more components use the connector using the protocol to communicate, they must follow some conventions about order of events or commands, order in which data is to be grouped for sending, error conditions etc. For example, if TCP ports are to be used to send information from one process to another (TCP ports are the connector between the two components of process type), the protocol requires that a connection must first be established and a port number obtained before sending the information, and that the connection should be closed in the end. A protocol description makes all these constraints explicit, and defines the error conditions and special scenarios. If a protocol is used by a connector type, it should be explicitly stated.

Just like with components, in a C&C architecture diagram of a system, it is best to use a different notation for the different connector type. It is a common mistake to use a simple line or an arrow to represent all types of connectors, forcing the reader to obtain the information about type from elsewhere. However, multiple instances of the same connector type need not be always distinguished through naming, as often the components being connected can provide the unique identification. As in components, as there are no commonly accepted notations, it is best to provide a key of the notations used. Some examples of connectors are shown in Figure 4.3.

It is worth pointing out that the implementation of a connector may be quite complex and may be distributed. For example, a middleware like CORBA provides connectors that may be used by objects for interaction. However, there is a lot of code in the form of ORB (object request broker) that is needed to support this connector. It is the ORB software that does the format translations between the sender and the receiver components and performs all the communication between them (using a protocol called IIOP), besides providing a host of other services that may be needed by the objects to cooperate. Hence, explicit representation of connectors is important, particularly in distributed systems where connectors play roles that cannot be easily changed to implicit language and OS mechanisms.

If the connector is provided by the underlying system, then the components just have to ensure that they use the connectors as per their specifications. If, however, the underlying system does not provide a connector used in an architecture, then as mentioned above, the connector will have to be implemented as part of the project to build the system. That is, during

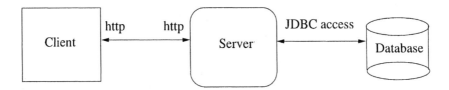

Figure 4.4: Architecture of the survey system.

the development, not only will the components need to be developed, but resources will have to be assigned to also develop the connector. (This situation might arise for a specialized system that requires connectors that are specific to the problem domain.)

4.3.3 An Example

We have now discussed the two key elements of a C&C architecture view of a software system, and how they work together. Let us now discuss an example, putting these concepts together.

Suppose we have to design and build a simple system for taking an on-line survey of students on a campus. There is a set of multiple choice questions, and the proposed system will provide the survey form to the student, who can fill and submit it on-line. We also want that when the user submits the form, he/she is also shown the current result of the survey, that is, what percentage of students so far have filled which options for the different questions.

The system is best built using the Web; this is the likely choice of any developer. For this simple system, a traditional 3-tier architecture is proposed. It consists of a client which will display the form that the student can fill and submit, and will also display the results. The second component is the server, which processes the data submitted by the student, and saves it on the database, which is the third component. The server also queries the database to get the outcome of the survey and sends the results in proper format (HTML) back to the client, which then displays the result. A figure giving the C&C view is shown in Figure 4.4.

Note that the client, server, and the database are all different types of components, and hence are shown using different symbols. Note also that the connectors between the components are also of different types. The diagram makes the different types clear, making the diagram stand alone and easy to comprehend.

Note that at the architecture level, a host of details are not discussed.

How is the URL of the survey set? What are the modules that go in building these components and what language they are written in? Questions like these are not the issues at this level.

Note also that the connector between the client and the server explicitly says that http is to be used. And the diagram also says that it is a Web client. This implies that it is assumed that there will be a Web browser running on the machines from which the student will take the survey. Having the http as the connector also implies that there is a proper http server running, and that the server of this system will be suitably attached to it to allow access by clients. In other words, the entire infrastructure of browser and the http server, for the purposes of this application, mainly provides the connector between the client and the server (and a virtual machine to run the client of the application).

There are some implications of choice of this connector on the components. The client will have to be written in a manner that it can send the request using http (this will imply using some type of scripting language or HTML forms). Similarly, it also implies that the server has to take its request from the http server in the format specified by the http protocol. Furthermore, the server has to send its results back to the client in the HTML format. These are all constraints on implementing this architecture. Hence, when discussing it and finally accepting it, the implications for the infrastructure as well as the implementation should be fully understood and actions should be taken to make sure that these assumptions are valid.

Extension I

The above architecture has no security and a student can take the survey as many times as he wishes. Furthermore, even a non-student can take the survey. Now the Dean of students wants that this system be open only to registered students, and that each student is allowed to take the survey at most once. To identify the students, it was explained that each student has an account, and their account information is available from the main proxy server of the institute.

Now the architecture will have to be quite different. The proposed architecture now has a separate login form for the user, and a separate server component which does the validation. For validation, it goes to the proxy for checking if the login and password provided are valid. If so, the server returns a cookie to the client (which stores it as per the cookie protocol). When the student fills the survey form, the cookie information validates the

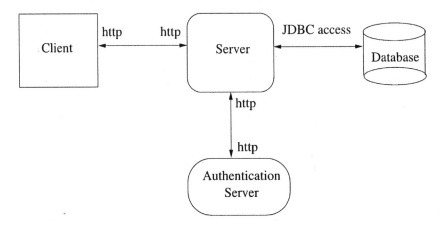

Figure 4.5: Architecture for the survey system with authentication.

user, and the server checks if this student has already filled the survey. The architecture for this system is shown in Figure 4.5.

Note that even though we are saying that the connection between the client and the server is that of http, it is somewhat different from the connection in the earlier architecture. In the first architecture, plain http is sufficient. In this one, as cookies are also needed, the connector is really http + cookies. So, if the user disables cookies, the required connector is not available and this architecture will not work.

Extension II

Now suppose, we want the system to be extended in a different way. It was found that the database server is somewhat unreliable, and is frequently down. It was also felt that when the student is given the result of the survey when he submits the form, a somewhat outdated result is acceptable, as the results are really statistical data and a little inaccuracy will not matter. We assume that the survey result can be outdated by about 5 data points (even if it does not include data of 5 surveys, it is OK). What the Dean wanted was to make the system more reliable, and provide some facility for filling the survey even when the database is down.

To make the system more reliable, the following strategy was thought. When the student submits the survey, the server interacts with the database as before. The results of the survey, however, are also stored in the cache by the server. If the database is down or unavailable, the survey data is stored locally in a cache component, and the result saved in the cache component

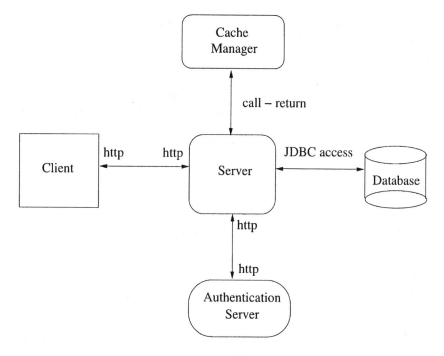

Figure 4.6: Architecture for the survey system with cache.

is used to provide the result to the student. (This can be done for up to 5 requests, after which the survey cannot be filled.) So, now we have another component in the server called the cache manager. And there is a connection between the server and this new component of the call/return type. This architecture is shown in Figure 4.6.

It should be clear that by using the cache, the availability of the system is improved. The cache will also have an impact on performance. These extensions shows how architecture affects both availability and performance, and how properly selecting or tuning the architecture can help meet the quality goals (or just improve the quality of the system). (Of course, detail level decisions like how a particular module is implemented also has implications on performance, but they are quite distinct and orthogonal to the architecture-level decisions.) We will later do a formal evaluation of these different architectures to see the impact of architectural decisions on some quality attributes.

4.4   Architecture Styles for C&C View

As mentioned above, an architecture view describes a structure of the system in terms of its elements and relationships among them. Clearly, different systems will have different structures, even for the same view. There are, however, some structures and related constraints that have been observed in many systems and that seem to represent general structures that are useful for architecture of a class of problems. These are called architectural styles. A style defines a family of architectures that satisfy the constraints of that style [35, 9, 135].

For example, for module views, some of the common styles are decomposition, uses, generalization, and layered. In decomposition style, a module is decomposed into sub-modules, and the system becomes a hierarchy of modules. In the uses style, modules are not parts of each other, but a module uses services of other modules (for example, a function call or a method invocation) to correctly do its own work. In the generalization style, modules are often classes, and a child class inherits the properties of the parent class and specializes it. This supports an is-a hierarchy, where a child module is also of the parent module type. In the layered style, the system is structured as a stack of layers, each layer representing some virtual machine that provides a clear set of services. In addition, a layer is allowed to use services only of its adjacent layers. Some of these will be discussed later in the design chapters.

In this section we discuss some common styles for the C&C view. Many styles have been proposed for C&C view, some for specific domains. Here we discuss only a few that are widely discussed in literature and which can be useful for a large set of problems [135, 35]. These styles can provide ideas for creating an architecture view for the problem at hand. Styles can be combined to form richer views. In fact, it is likely that for a problem, a combination of styles may provide the desired architecture. Many systems use multiple styles and different parts of a system may use different styles.

4.4.1   Pipe and Filter

Pipe and filter style of architecture is well suited for systems that primarily do data transformation some input data is received and the goal of the system is to produce some output data by suitably transforming the input data. A system using pipe-and-filter architecture achieves the desired transformation by applying a network of smaller transformations and composing them in a manner that together the overall desired transformation is achieved.

The pipe and filter style has only one component type called the filter. It also has only one connector type, called the pipe. A filter performs a data transformation, and sends the transformed data to other filters for further processing using the pipe connector. In other words, a filter receives the data it needs from some defined input pipes, performs the data transformation, and then sends the output data to other filters on the defined output pipes. A filter may have more than one inputs and more than one outputs. Filters can be independent and asynchronous entities, and as they are concerned only with the data arriving on the pipe, a filter need not know the identity of the filter that sent the input data or the identity of the filter that will consume the data they produce.

The pipe connector is a unidirectional channel which conveys streams of data received on one end to the other end. A pipe does not change the data in any manner but merely transports it to the filter on the receiver end in the order in which the data elements are received. As filters can be asynchronous and should work without the knowledge of the identity of the producer or the consumer, buffering and synchronization need to ensure smooth functioning of the producer-consumer relationship embodied in connecting two filters by a pipe is ensured by the pipe. The filters merely consume and produce data.

There are some constraints that this style imposes. First, as mentioned above, the filters should work without knowing the identity of the consumer or the producer; they should only require the data elements they need. Second, a pipe, which is a two-way connector, must connect an output port of a filter to an input port of another filter.

A pure pipe-and-filter structure will also generally have a constraint that a filter has independent thread of control which process the data as it comes. Implementing this will require suitable underlying infrastructure to support a pipe mechanism which buffers the data and does the synchronization needed (for example, blocking the producer when the buffer is full and blocking the consumer filter when the buffer is empty). For using this pipe, the filter builder must be fully aware of the properties of the pipe, particularly with regards to buffering and synchronization, input and output mechanisms, and the symbols for end of data.

However, there could be situations in which the constraint that a filter process the data as it comes may not be required. Without this constraint, pipe-and-filter style view may have filters that produce the data completely before passing it on, or which start their processing only after complete input is available. In such a system the filters cannot operate concurrently, and the system is like a batch-processing system. However, it can considerably

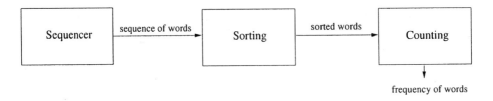

Figure 4.7: Pipe-and-Filter example.

simplify the pipes and easier mechanisms can be used for supporting them.

Lets consider an example of a system needed to count the frequency of different words in a file. An architecture using the pipes-and-filter style for a system to achieve this is given in Figure 4.7.

This architecture proposes that the input data be first split into a sequence of words by a component Sequencer. This sequence of words is then sorted by the component Sorting, which passes the output of sorted words to another filter (Counting) that counts the number of occurrences of the different words. This structure of sorting the words first has been chosen as it will make the task of determining the frequency more efficient, even though it involves a sort operation. It should be clear that this proposed architecture can implement the desired functionality. Later in the chapter we will further discuss some implementation issues related to this architecture.

As can be seen from this example, pipe and filter architectural style is well suited for data processing and transformation. Consequently, it is useful in text processing applications. Signal processing applications also find it useful as such applications typically perform encoding, error correction, and other transformations on the data.

The pipe and filter style, due to the constraints, allows a system's overall transformation to be composed of smaller transformations. Or viewing it in another manner, it allows a desired transformation to be factored into smaller transformations, and then filters built for the smaller transformations. That is, it allows the techniques of functional composition and decomposition to be utilized something that is mathematically appealing.

4.4.2   Shared-Data Style

In this style, there are two types of components—data repositories and data accessors. Components of data repository type are where the system stores shared data—these could be file systems or databases. These components provide a reliable and permanent storage, take care of any synchronization needs for concurrent access, and provide data access support. Components of data accessor type access data from the repositories, perform computation on the data obtained, and if they want to share the results with other components, put the results back in the depository. In other words, the accessors are computational elements that receive their data from the repository and save their data in the repository as well. These components do not directly communicate with each other—the data repository components are the means of communication and data transfer between them.

There are two variations of this style possible. In the blackboard style, if some data is posted on the data repository, all the accessor components that need to know about it are informed. In other words, the shared data source is an active agent as well which either informs the components about the arrival of interesting data, or starts the execution of the components that need to act upon this new data. In databases, this form of style is often supported through triggers. The other is the repository style, in which the data repository is just a passive repository which provides permanent storage and related controls for data accessing. The components access the repository as and when they want.

As can be imagined, many database applications use this architectural style. Databases, though originally more like repositories, now act both as repositories as well as blackboards as they provide triggers and can act as efficient data storage as well. Many Web systems frequently follow this style at the back end—in response to user requests, different scripts (data accessors) access and update some shared data. Many programming environments are also organized this way the common representation of the program artifacts is stored in the repository and the different tools access it to perform the desired translations or to obtain the desired information. (Some years back there was a standard defined for the common repository to facilitate integration of tools.)

As an example of a system using this style of architecture, let us consider a student registration system in a University. The system clearly has a central repository which contains information about courses, students, prerequisites, etc. It has an `Administrator` component that sets up the repository, rights to different people, etc. The `Registration` component allows students to register and update the information for students and courses. The `Approvals` component is for granting approvals for those courses that require instructor's consent. The `Reports` component produces the report regarding the students registered in different courses at the end of the registration. The component `Course Feedback` is used for taking feedback from

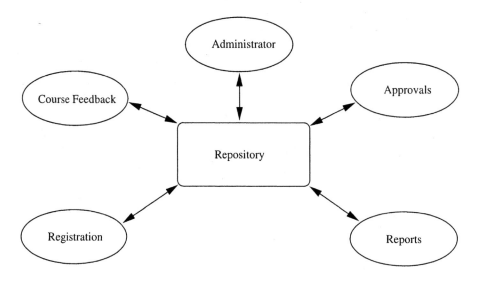

Figure 4.8: Shared data example.

students at the end of the course. This architecture is shown in Figure 4.8.

Note that the different computation components do not need to communicate with each other and do not even need to know about each others presence. For example, if later it is decided that the scheduling of courses can be automated based on data on registration (and other information about class rooms etc.), then another component called Scheduling can be simply added. No existing computation component needs to change or be informed about the new component being added. (This example is based on a system that is actually used in the author's University.)

There is really only one connector type in this style—read/write. Note, however, that this general connector style may take more precise form in particular architectures. For example, though a database can be viewed as supporting read and updates, for a program interacting with it, the database system may provide transaction services as well. Connectors using this transaction service allow complete transactions (which may involve multiple reads and writes and preserve atomicity) to be performed by an application.

Note also that as in many other cases, the connectors involve a considerable amount of underlying infrastructure. For example, read and writes to a file system involves a fair amount of file system software involving issues like directories, buffering, locking, and synchronization. Similarly, a considerable amount of software goes in databases to support the type of connections it provides for query, update, and transactions. We will see another use of this style later when we discuss the case studies.

4.4.3 Client-Server Style

Another very common style used to build systems today is the client server style. Client-server computing is one of the basic paradigms of distributed computing and this architecture style is built upon this paradigm.

In this style, there are two component types—clients and servers. A constraint of this style is that a client can only communicate with the server, and cannot communicate with other clients. The communication between a client component and a server component is initiated by the client the client sends a request for some service that the server supports. The server receives the request at its defined port, performs the service, and then returns the results of the computation to the client who requested the service.

There is one connector type in this style—the request/reply type. A connector connects a client to a server. This type of connector is asymmetric—the client end of the connector can only make requests (and receive the reply), while the server end can only send replies in response to the requests it gets through this connector. The communication is frequently synchronous—the client waits for the server to return the results before proceeding. That is, the client is blocked at the request, untill it gets the reply.

A general form of this style is a *n-tier* structure. In this style, a client sends a request to a server, but the server, in order to service the request, sends some request to another server. That is, the server also acts as a client for the next tier. This hierarchy can continue for some levels, providing a n-tier system. A common example of this is the 3-tier architecture. In this style, the clients that make requests and receive the final results reside in the client-tier. The middle tier, called the business-tier, contains the component that processes the data submitted by the clients and applies the necessary business rules. The third tier is the database tier in which the data resides. The business tier interacts with the database tier for all its data needs.

Most often, in a client server architecture, the client and the server component reside on different machines. Even if they reside on the same machine, they are designed in a manner that they can exist on different machines. Hence, the connector between the client and the server is expected to support the request/result type of connection across different machines. Consequently, these connectors are internally quite complex and involve a fair amount of networking to support. Many of the client-server systems today use TCP ports for their connectors. The Web uses the HTTP for supporting this connector.

Note that there is a distinction between a layered architecture and a tiered architecture. The tiered style is a component and connector architecture view in which each tier is a component, and these components communicate with the adjacent ones through a defined protocol. A layered architecture is a module view providing how modules are organized and used. In the layered organization, modules are organized in layers with modules in a layer allowed to invoke services only of the modules in the layer below. Hence, layered and tiered represent two different views. We can have a n-tiered architecture in which some tier(s) have a layered architecture. For example, in a client-server architecture, the server might have a layered architecture, that is, modules that compose the server are organized in the layered style.

4.4.4   Some Other Styles

Publish-Subscribe Style

In this style, there are two types of components. One type of component subscribes to a set of defined events. Other types of components generate or publish events. In response to these events, the components that have published their intent to process the event, are invoked. This type of style is most natural in user interface frameworks, where many events are defined (like mouse click) and components are assigned to these events. When that event occurs, the associated component is executed. As is the case with most connectors, it is the task of the runtime infrastructure to ensure that this type of connector (i.e., publish-subscribe) is supported. This style can be seen as a special case of the blackboard style, except that the repository aspect is not being used.

Peer-to-peer style, or object-oriented style

If we take a client server style, and generalize each component to be a client as well as a server, then we have this style. In this style, components are peers and any component can request a service from any other component. The object oriented computation model represents this style well. If we view components as objects, and connectors as method invocations, then we have this style. This model is the one that is primarily supported through middleware connectors like CORBA or .NET.

Communicating processes style

Perhaps the oldest model of distributed computing is that of communicating processes. This style tries to capture this model of computing. The components in this model are processes or threads, which communicate with each other either with message passing or through shared memory. This style is used in some form in many complex systems which use multiple threads or processes.

4.5 Discussion

Software architecture is an evolving area, and there are many issues that have not been fully resolved. In this section we discuss some issues in order to further clarify concepts relating to architecture and designing of architectures.

4.5.1 Architecture and Design

We have seen that while creating an architecture, the system may be partitioned in different ways, each providing a view that focuses on partitioning the system into parts to highlight some structure of the system. Views may highlight the runtime structure by showing the components that exist in the system and how the components interact, or the module structure which shows how the code modules are organized for the system, or the deployment structure which focuses on how the different units are assigned to resources.

As partitioning a system into smaller parts and composing the system from these parts is also a goal of design, a natural question is what is the difference between a design and architecture as both aim to achieve similar objectives and seem to fundamentally rely on the divide and conquer rule? First, it should be clear that architecture is a design in that it is in the solution domain and talks about the structure of the proposed system. Furthermore, an architecture view gives a high level view of the system, relying on abstraction to convey the meaning—something which design also does. So, architecture is design.

We can view architecture as a very high-level design, focusing only on main components, and the architecture activity as the first step in design. What we term as design is really about the modules that will eventually exist as code. That is, they are a more concrete representation of the implementation (though not yet an implementation). Consequently, during design lower level issues like the data structures, files, and sources of data, have to be addressed, while such issues are not generally significant at the architecture level. We also take the view that design can be considered as providing the module-view of the architecture of the system. As discussed before, we believe the third level of design (which we call the detailed design) is to design the logic of the various modules and their functions.

The boundaries between the first two levels of design—architecture and high-level design are not fully clear. The way the field has evolved, we can say that the line between architecture and design is really up to the designer or the architect. At the architecture level, one needs to show only those parts that are needed to perform the desired evaluation. The internal structure of these parts is not important. On the other hand, during design, designing the structure of the parts that can lead to constructing them is one of the key tasks. However, which parts of the structure should be examined and revealed during architecture and which parts during design is a matter of choice. Generally speaking, details that are not needed to perform the types of analysis we wish to do at the architecture time are unnecessary and should be left for design to uncover.

It should, however, be pointed out that having an architecture imposes constraints on choices that can be made during the design, and while creating the design of the system these constraints should be honored. We discuss this issue a bit more later in this section. Design might also have an influence on architecture—during design some shortcomings in the architecture from the design perspective might be revealed. This may require the architecture to be modified. This situation, however, is the same with any stage—a later stage may require output of an earlier stage to be modified.

4.5.2   Preserving the Integrity of an Architecture

What is the role of the architecture as the project moves forward and design and development is done? Many novice designers treat architectures as just pictures which help in understanding the system but which have no role to play while code is being developed. A mistake made by novices and professionals alike is that after the architecture is discussed and agreed, when the teams go to build the system, they build it the way they want to without regards to the architectural decisions. One informal study at an organization revealed that the architecture extracted from the code of a product (the actual architecture of the software) had little resemblance to the architecture that was planned and was supposed to be implemented. There are many reasons for this which we will not go into, but lack of communication and enforcement are important contributors.

For an architecture design to be meaningful, it should guide the design and development of the system. And if the integrity of the architecture is fully preserved, the architecture of the final system should be the same as the architecture designed and agreed to during the early stages of the project. That is, the implementation must have the components shown in the C&C view, and the components should interact in the manner prescribed in the view.

It is important that the architecture integrity is preserved as otherwise the value of the architecture is minimal. Furthermore, one of the key reasons for designing an architecture (rather than just letting some architecture evolve as the system is built) is to be able to analyze the system properties well before the system is built and evolve optimal strategies for the final system. This means that accepting an architecture is far more than just agreeing that the architecture is correct (in that it can implement the system). The process of acceptance will generally involve formal or informal analysis of the architecture, and final acceptance also means that the system having the proposed architecture will have the properties desired for the system. By deviating from the architecture, we may go in a direction in which the system does not have the desired properties. Hence, it is extremely important that the integrity of the architecture is preserved.

Let us understand the issue of architecture integrity preservation through an example. Earlier, we discussed the architecture of a system to determine the frequency of different words in a text file. The architecture designed and agreed is shown in Figure 4.7. The architecture says that the system, in its execution, will have a component to split the file in words, another component to sort the words, and the third component to count the frequency of different words. The data is passed between the components using pipes.

Now consider the following implementation of the system. Each of the components is written as a complete C program. The first program creates a pipe and writes to it. The second program reads from this pipe and writes to another pipe. The third program reads from this new pipe. The overall system is a small script that executes these programs in parallel.

This implementation is clearly consistent with the architecture view that was designed earlier. Each of the three components have a runtime presence (they will be executed as separate processes by UNIX,) and they pass data using the UNIX pipe, which has the same semantics as the pipe connector of the pipe-and-filter style, in that it provides a buffered, streaming, data

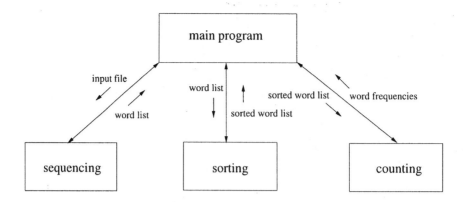

Figure 4.9: Another implementation of the system.

passing mechanism. Hence, it is easy to see that the C&C architecture view of this implementation is same as the architecture given earlier in Figure 4.7, and this implementation preservers the architectural integrity.

The above implementation clearly has huge performance overhead in that separate processes are created and the communication through UNIX pipes can be quite expensive. Now consider the following implementation, which avoids these performance problems by having the same functions in the system, but organizing them differently. The system, written in C, has three functions corresponding to the three components, and two functions for the two connectors. The connector function invokes one component function for getting the data, and then passes the data to the other component function. In the actual implementation, to further reduce the overhead, we let the main function perform the roles of both the connector functions. The structure is shown in Figure 4.9.

Does this implementation preserve the architecture integrity? The answer to this is not totally unambiguous. The three functions implement the same functionality as the components in the architecture design. But can they be treated as separate components, as they are really just functions? The answer is not obvious. The components satisfy some properties of the filters in that they do not need to know the identity of the components from which they get the data or send the data. The connector in this implementation is really the parameter passing mechanism. Though the data is being passed as an organized series of data items, it is really not streaming or buffered in that complete data is passed at once. Furthermore, this structure does not allow the three components to execute in parallel; they are executed strictly in sequence.

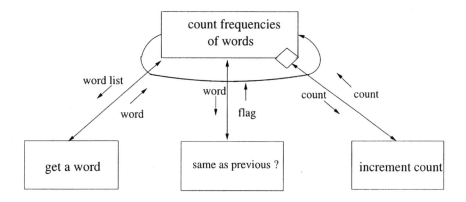

Figure 4.10: A third implementation.

Still, this implementation can be viewed as preserving the architectural integrity, particularly if no restrictions were explicitly placed on the components (in terms of parallel execution) and the connectors (in terms of buffering and data passing). Note that these restrictions could have been placed explicitly in the architecture description or implicitly during its analysis—for example, the analysis may have assumed that the components are executing in parallel and may have taken data transfer speeds to be such that they are consistent with a separate pipe.

Now consider a third implementation. A designer and a coder look at the problem statement (and do not look at the architecture designed) and decide that an easy way to implement the problem is to get a word at a time and then simply increment the count for the word, if it already exists in the frequency list, or add the word if it does not. In this, we have a main C program which has a word extractor and a frequency counter. When the data is finished, the frequency output program shows the frequencies of the different words. The structure of this implementation is shown in figure 4.10.

This implementation clearly is not consistent with the architecture designed above. It does not have the same components and the processing approach is different from the one envisaged in the architecture. It should be pointed out that this implementation is also correct for the problem statement (the system does implement the requirements). Note that this mismatch of architecture is largely due to the approach and not due to the fact that all components are combined in one program. Even if the implementation was done using separate programs which pass the data through pipes (an implementation that can be easily done for this approach), the mismatch between the architecture of the system and the designed architecture will remain.

It is this type of mismatch that frequently occurs. If the implementers of the system start from the requirements and do not consider the architecture that has been created, they can create a correct system that may provide the functionality, but the architecture integrity may not be preserved. This can have other consequences. For example, the performance of the final system may not be as was envisaged when the architecture was designed as the system may get engineered in a manner that it is unable to provide the performance. By preserving the architecture, if the architecture was designed and evaluated properly, the final engineered system is more likely to fulfill the other properties. Besides performance, an architecture may be evaluated for other properties like maintainability, suitability for use with the available resources, etc. By not preserving the integrity of the architecture, we risk not meeting requirements for these properties.

This example illustrates that it is easy to fall in the trap of ignoring the architecture and building the system from scratch. This is a pitfall that system designers and builders must avoid. The architecture design imposes some restrictions on how the system can be built and engineered, and these constraints and restrictions should be honored and the system should be built in a manner that the architecture of the final system is same as the architecture that was conceived (except, of course, the changes that were intentionally done after careful consideration and discussion).

4.5.3 Deployment View and Performance Analysis

As discussed earlier, there are different views through which software architectures can be represented and which views we use depends on the types of analysis we want to do at the architecture design time. We have focused on the C&C view as the primary view, and have discussed a few styles for this view as well.

If we want to analyze the performance of the architecture (to be exact, performance of the system that will have the proposed architecture,) then even though the C&C view represents the run-time structure, it is not enough. The reason is that though performance depends on the run-time structure of the software, it also depends on the hardware and other resources that will be used to execute the software. For example, the performance of a n-tier system will be very different if all the tiers reside on the same machine as compared to if they reside on different machines. In other words, the performance of a system whose architecture remains the same, can change depending on how the components of the architecture are allocated on the hardware. Hence, to do any meaningful performance analysis, we must specify the allocation as well. The same holds true if we want to do any reliability or availability analysis, as they also depend on the reliability of the hardware components involved in running the system.

To facilitate such an analysis, a deployment view needs to be provided. In a deployment view, the elements of a C&C style are allocated to execution resources like CPU and communication channels. Hence, the elements of this view are the software components and connectors from the C&C view, and the hardware elements like CPU, memory, and bandwidth. This view shows which software components are allocated to which hardware element. This allocation can be dynamic and this dynamism can also be represented.

Note that even the allocation view, which is necessary to do performance analysis, is not sufficient. To analyze the performance, besides the allocation, we will need to properly characterize the hardware elements in terms of their capacities, and the software elements in terms of their resource requirement and usage. Using the information, models can be built to determine bottlenecks, optimal allocation, etc. This is an active area of research and a survey of the area can be found in [4].

For doing any performance analysis, some models will have to be built, and these models will need information about the hardware and software components and how the software is allocated to software. The level of detail that can be obtained depends on the model used. At the basic level, some experience-based analysis can be done to see if there are any performance bottlenecks. The allocation of software can also be examined for optimality of performance, and if needed that allocation can be changed. For example, in a n-tier system, it may be found that the overhead of communication is too heavy between two tiers, and it may be better to allocate both of them to one machine. Or the analysis may reveal the reverse—allocating both the database and the business layer on the same machine might degrade the response time as concurrency will be lost, and it may be decided to add another machine to host the business layer and connect it to the machine hosting the database layer with a high speed connection.

Many such possibilities exist for performance analysis. Consequently, for C&C view of the architecture, it may be desirable to look at an allocation view at the time of creating the architecture. It may be added that not all

C&C views render themselves easily or fruitfully for allocation view. The n-tier style (or client-server style), or the process view clearly render itself to an allocation view. However, it is not clear if the allocation view of a publish-subscribe view will be very useful. For giving an allocation view, it is best to chose a C&C view that renders itself naturally to the allocation view. If the views obtained so far do not render themselves to an allocation view, but an allocation view is essential for the desired analysis, then a view should be created that can be used for such an allocation and analysis.

4.5.4 Documenting Architecture Design

So far we have focused on representing views through diagrams. While designing, diagrams are indeed a good way to explore options and encourage discussion and brainstorming between the architects. But when the designing is over, the architecture has to be properly communicated to all stakeholders for negotiation and agreement. This requires that architecture be precisely documented with enough information to perform the types of analysis the different stakeholders wish to make to satisfy themselves that their concerns have been adequately addressed. Without a properly documented description of the architecture, it is not possible to have a clear common understanding. Hence, properly documenting an architecture is as important as creating one. In this section, we discuss what an architecture document should contain. Our discussion is based on the recommendations in [93, 35, 9].

Just like different projects require different views, different projects will need different level of detail in their architecture documentation. In general, however, a document describing the architecture should contain the following:

- System and architecture context

- Description of architecture views

- Across views documentation

We know that an architecture for a system is driven by the system objectives and the needs of the stakeholders. Hence, the first aspect that an architecture document should contain is identification of stakeholders and their concerns. This portion should give an overview of the system, the different stakeholders, and the system properties for which the architecture will be evaluated. A context diagram that establishes the scope of the system, its boundaries, the key actors in that interact with the system, and sources and sinks of data can also be very useful. A context diagram is frequently represented by showing the system in the center, and showing its connections with people and systems, including sources and sinks of data.

With the context defined, the document can proceed with describing the different structures or views. As stated before, multiple views of different types may be needed, and which views are chosen depends on the needs of the project and its stakeholders. The description of views in the architecture documentation will almost always contain a pictorial representation of the view, which is often the *primary presentation of the view*. As discussed earlier, in any view diagram it is desirable to have different symbols for different element types and provide a key for the different types, such that the type of the different components (represented using the symbols) is clear to a reader. It is, of course, highly desirable to keep the diagram simple and uncluttered. If necessary, to keep the complexity of the view manageable, a hierarchical approach can be followed to make the main view simple (and provide further details as structure of the elements).

However, a pictorial representation is not a complete description of the view. It gives an intuitive idea of the design, but is not sufficient for providing the details. For example, what is the purpose and functionality of a module or a component is indicated only by its name which is not sufficient. Hence, supporting documentation is needed for the view diagrams. This supporting documentation should have some or all of the following:

- *Element Catalog.* Provides more information about the elements shown in the primary representation. Besides describing the purpose of the element, it should also describe the elements' interfaces (remember that all elements have interfaces through which they interact with other elements). All the different interfaces provided by the elements should be specified. Interfaces should have unique identity, and the specification should give both syntactic and semantic information. Syntactic information is often in terms of signatures, which describe all the data items involved in the interface and their types. Semantic information must describe what the interface does. The description should also clearly state the error conditions that the interface can return.

- *Architecture Rationale.* Though a view specifies the elements and and the relationship between them, it does not provide any insight into why the architect chose the particular structure. Architecture rationale gives the reasons for selecting the different elements and composing them in the way it was done. This section may also provide some discussion on the alternatives that were considered and why they were rejected. This discussion, besides explaining the choices, is also useful later when an analyst making a change wonders why the architecture should not be changed in some manner (that might make the change easy).

- *Behavior.* A view gives the structural information. It does not represent the actual behavior or execution. Consequently, in a structure, all possible interactions during an execution are shown. Sometimes, it is necessary to get some idea of the actual behavior of the system in some scenarios. Such a description is useful for arguing about properties like deadlock. Behavior description can be provided to help aid understanding of the system execution. Often diagrams like collaboration diagrams or sequence diagrams (we will discuss these further in the Chapter on OO design) are used.

- *Other Information.* This may include a description of all those decisions that have not been taken during architecture creation but have been deliberately left for future. For example, the choice of a server or protocol. If this is done, then it must be specified as fixing these will have impact on the architecture.

We know that the different views are related. In what we have discussed so far, the views have been described independently. The architecture document therefore, besides describing the views, should also describe the relationship between the different views. This is the primary purpose of the across view documentation. Essentially, this documentation describes the relationship between elements of the different views (for example, how modules in a module view relate to components in a component view, or how components in a C&C view relate to processes in a process view). This part of the document can also describe the rationale of the overall architecture, why the selected views were chosen, and any other information that cuts across views.

However, often the relationship between the different views is straightforward or very strong. In such situations, the different structures may look very similar and describing the views separately can lead to a repetition. In such situations, for practical reasons, it is better to combine different views into one. Besides eliminating the duplication, this approach can also help clearly show the strong relationship between the two views (and in the process also reduce the across view documentation). Combined views are also useful for some analysis which require multiple views, for example, performance analysis, which frequently requires both the C&C view as well as the allocation view. So, sometimes, it may be desirable to show some combined views.

Combining of views, however, should be done only if the relationship between the views is strong and straightforward. Otherwise, putting multiple views in one diagram will clutter the view and make it confusing. The objective of showing multiple views in one is not merely to reduce the number of views, but is to be done primarily to aid understanding and showing the relationships. An example of combining is when there are multiple modules in the module view that form the different layers in the layer view. In such a situation, it is probably more natural to show one view consisting of the layers, and overlaying the module structure on the layers. That is, showing the module structure within the layers. Many layered systems architectures actually use this approach. In such a situation, it is best to show them together, creating a hybrid style in which both a module view and a C&C view are captured. Overall, if the mapping can be shown easily and in a simple manner, then different views should be combined for the sake of simplicity and compactness. If, however, the relationship between the different views is complex (for example, a many-to-many relationship between elements of the different views), then it is best to keep them separate and specify the relationship separately.

The general structure discussed here can provide a guide for organizing the architecture document. However, the main purpose of the document is to clearly communicate the architecture to the stakeholders such that the desired analysis can be done. And if some of these sections are redundant for that purpose, they may not be included. Similarly, if more information needs to be provided, then it should be done.

Finally, a word on the language chosen for describing different parts of the architecture. Here the choice varies from the formal architecture description languages (ADLs) to informal notation. Many people now use UML to represent the architecture, which allows various possibilities to show the primary description of the view and also allows annotation capability for supporting document. We believe that any method can be used, as long as the objective is met. To allow flexibility, we suggest using a problem specific notation, but following the guidelines for good view representation, and using a combination of header definitions and text for the supporting documentation.

4.6   Evaluating Architectures

Architecture of a software system impacts some of the key nonfunctional quality attributes like modifiability, performance, reliability, portability, etc. The architecture has a much more significant impact on some of these properties than the design and coding choices. That is, even though choice of algorithms, data structures, etc., are important for many of these attributes, often they have less of an impact than the architectural choices. Clearly then evaluating a proposed architecture for these properties can have a beneficial impact on the project—any architectural changes that are required to meet the desired goals for these attributes can be done during the architecture design itself.

There are many nonfunctional quality attributes.   Not all of them are affected by architecture significantly. Some of the attributes on which architecture has a significant impact are performance, reliability and availability, security (some aspects of it), modifiability, reusability, and portability. Attributes like usability are only mildly affected by architecture.

How should a proposed architecture be evaluated for these attributes? For some attributes like performance and reliability, it is possible to build formal models using techniques like queuing networks and use them for assessing the value of the attribute. However, these models require information beyond the architecture description, generally in forms of execution times, and reliability of each component.

Another approach is procedural—a sequence of steps is followed to subjectively evaluate the impact of the architecture on some of the attributes. One such informal analysis approach that is often used is as follows. First identify the attributes of interest for which an architecture should be evaluated. These attributes are usually determined from stakeholder's interests— the attributes the different stakeholders are most interested in. These attributes are then listed in a table. Then for each attribute, an experience-based, subjective analysis is done (though quantitative analysis can also be done), to assess the level supported by the architecture. The analysis might mention the level for each attribute (e.g., good, average, poor), or might simply mention whether it is satisfactory or not. Based on the outcome of this analysis, the architecture is either accepted or rejected. If rejected, it may be enhanced to improve the performance for the attribute for which the proposed architecture was unsatisfactory.

Many techniques have been proposed for evaluation, and a survey of them is given in [51]. Here we briefly discuss some aspects of a more elaborate and formal technique called architectural tradeoff analysis method.

4.6.1 The ATAM Analysis Method

The architectural tradeoff analysis method (ATAM) [105, 35], besides analyzing the architecture for a set of properties, also helps in identifying dependencies between competing properties and perform a tradeoff analysis. We will, however, mostly focus on the analysis. The basic ATAM analysis has the following steps, which can be repeated, if needed:

1. *Collect Scenarios.* Scenarios describe an interaction of the system. For architecture analysis, scenarios list the situations the system could be in and for which we would like to evaluate the architecture for different attributes. Besides normal scenarios, exceptional scenarios of interest should also be mentioned.

2. *Collect Requirements or Constraints.* These specify what are the requirements for the system. That is, what is expected from the system in these scenarios. The scenarios together with requirements form the basis for evaluation—we want to ensure that the software will satisfy these requirements in these scenarios. These requirements essentially specify the desired levels (hopefully quantitatively) for the quality attributes of interest. So, for example, instead of saying performance is of interest in this system, a constraint or a requirement will be like "the average response time should be less than 1 ms."

3. *Describe Architectural Views.* The views of different proposed architectures are collected here. These are the architectures that will be evaluated. What views are needed to describe a proposed architecture depends on what analysis needs to be performed, which is driven by the requirements or constraints. We will limit our attention to component and connector view only.

4. *Attribute-Specific Analysis.* Now we have the proposed architectures, the different quality attributes of interest for the system, and the different scenarios under which these attributes should be evaluated. In

this step, each quality attribute is analyzed separately and individually. The analysis should result in what levels an architecture can support for the quality attribute. So, for example, an analysis can result in a statement like "the availability of this system is 0.95." Once the analysis for all the attributes is done, it can be seen to what degree the requirements identified earlier are met. The outcome of this analysis can become the basis for selecting one architecture over other. It can also form the basis of changing a proposed architecture in an attempt to meet the desired levels. If an architecture is changed, then the whole analysis needs to be repeated, making ATAM a spiral process.

5. *Indentify Sensitivities and Tradeoffs.* From the analysis, for each attribute, sensitivity of the different elements in the architecture view should be determined. That is, how much impact does an element have on the attribute value. From this we identify the *sensitivity points*, which are the elements that have the most significant impact on the attribute value. Sensitivity points are these elements whose change will have the maximum impact on the quality attribute. *Tradeoff points* are those elements that are sensitivity points for multiple attributes. Changing these elements will have a significant impact on multiple attributes. These elements are where tradeoffs decisions will have to be taken, particularly if changing it favorably affects one attribute but negatively affects the other. For example, in a n-tier architecture, a server will be the tradeoff point as it significantly affects performance as well as availability. Replicating the server and performing updates on each server (to keep each current) can improve the availability, but can have a detrimental effect on update performance.

4.6.2   An Example

Earlier in the chapter, we gave an example of the student-survey system. We will take that example for evaluation and consider the second and the third architectures proposed (we do not consider the first one as it does not have the same functionality as others). For analysis, we add another architecture, in which the cache component is between the server and the database component. That is, in this architecture, each request is directly sent to the cache, which then decides whether to respond using data from the cache or from the database. This architecture is shown in Figure 4.11. We assume that the cache component in this architectures updates the database

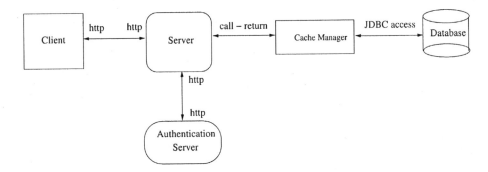

Figure 4.11: Another architecture for the student survey system.

as well as its own data after every 5th survey. (For analysis we add a requirement on data currency to allow this. The requirement is given below.) We focus only on survey-taking and ignore the feature of just getting the survey result.

Let us now analyze these architectures using ATAM. First we list the scenarios of interest. These are:

- *S1.* A student submits the survey form and gets current results of the survey (normal scenario; all servers are up, load normal.)

- *S2.* A student tries to take the survey many times.

- *S3.* The database server is temporarily down.

- *S4.* The network/system is highly loaded.

Some of the requirements or constraints for the system are:

- *Security.* A student should be allowed to take the survey at most once.

- *Response Time.* A student should get a response time of less than 2 sec on an average, 80% of the time.

- *Availability.* The system should at least have availability of 0.85 (that is, when a student comes, there is a 85% chance that he can successfully take the survey).

- *Data Currency.* The survey result given to a student should be reasonably current and should not be older than 5 submissions before.

Now let us evaluate the three architecture proposals for these attributes. For analysis, we will look at each of the attributes and then study the three architectures under the scenarios relevant for that attribute. For security and data currency, we will analyze based on our understanding of the architecture. For availability and response time, formal models are possible. We will use simple probability-based approach here.

For the availability analysis, we assume that the cache is on the same machine as the server, the database is on a different machine, and that availability of each of the machines is 0.9. We also assume that when the database goes down, during its repair time, on an average, 10 student survey requests come. For response time, we assume the following response times:

Component	Normal conditions	Heavily loaded
Server + security	300ms	600ms
Database	800ms	1600ms
Cache	50ms	50ms

We also assume that a timeout of about 2 seconds is used when the server tries to access the database, and that the network is heavily loaded 1% of the time.

We do not show all the computations here, but illustrate a few. The availability for the first architecture is the probability that both the server and database are up, as that is the only case in which a request can be serviced. This is 0.9 * 0.9 = 0.81. For the second and the third case, it is slightly more complex. When the database is down (on an average for 10 requests), up to 5 requests can still be serviced. Hence, even when the database is down, the system is up for half the time. This gives us an additional availability of 0.5 * 0.9 * 0.1 = 0.045 (half the probability that server is up and database is down). So, the availability of these architectures is 0.81 + 0.045 = 0.855.

Determining the average response time is slightly more involved, as we have to consider both the heavy load and normal load situations. In normal load, for first architecture, the average response time will be 300 + 800 = 1100 ms. When the database is down, then this architecture cannot service a request. For the second architecture, the response time is 300 + 800 + 50 = 1150 ms in the normal scenario. When the database is down, some requests can be serviced (probability computed above) by the cache but cache is used only after the database times out. That is, the response time in this scenario is 300 + 2000 + 50 = 2350 ms. For the third architecture, in the normal scenario, the average response time is 350 * 0.8 (for those requests serviced

Property (Scenario)	Architecture 1	Architecture 2	Architecture 3
Security (S1)	Yes	Yes	Yes
Security (S2)	Yes	Yes	Yes
Response time (S1)	1100	1150	550
Response time (S3)	N/A	2350	550
Response time (S4)	2200	2300	1100
Availability (S3)	0.81	0.855	0.855
Data Currency (S1)	Yes	Yes	Yes
Data Currency (S2)	N/A	Yes	Yes

Table 4.1: Analysis of the architecture options.

by cache) plus 1350 * 0.2 (for those that go to the database). That is, the average response time is 550 ms. When the database is down, the response time for the requests that can be serviced remains the same as they are serviced from the cache in a normal manner. Similar analysis can be done when the network is congested. For simplicity, we will double these times (as the response time when the system is congested is double that when it is not).

With these, we build a table for the different attributes for the scenarios of interest. This is given in Table 4.1.

From this table we can clearly see that security and data currency requirements are satisfied by all three architecture options. As the probability of normal scenario is over 0.8 for all architectures, and response time in normal scenario is less than the required for all, the response time requirement is also met by all the three architectures. However, the availability requirement is met by only the second and the third architectures. Of these two architectures, the third should be preferred as it provides a better response time.

4.7 Summary

Architecture of a software system is a design of the system that provides a very high level view of the system in terms of parts of the system and how they are related to form the whole system. Depending on how the system is partitioned, we get a different architectural view of the system. Consequently, the architecture of a software system is defined as the structures of the system which comprise software elements, their externally visible properties, and relationships among them. The macro level view that the architecture facilitates development of a high quality system. It also allows analysis of many of the system properties like performance that depend mostly on architecture to be done early in the software life cycle.

There are three main architectural views of a system—module, component and connector, and allocation. In a module view, the system is viewed as a structure of programming modules like packages, classes, functions, etc., which have to be later constructed. In a component and connector (C&C) view, the system is a collection of runtime entities called components. During execution, these components interact with each other through the connectors. An allocation view describes how the different software units are allocated to hardware resources in the system. These different views are related as they are of the same system, but this relationship may or may not be straightforward. If different views are created, then their relationship must be clearly identified and stated. In this chapter, we focus mostly on C&C view.

There are some common styles for a C&C view which have been found useful for creating this architecture view for a system. We have discussed pipe and filter, shared data, client server, publish-subscribe, peer to peer, and communicating processes styles. Each of these styles describe the types of components and connectors that exist and the constraints on how they are used. For example, the pipe and filter has one type of component (filter) and one type of connector (pipe) and components can be connected through the pipe. The client-server style has two types of components (client and server) and there is one connector (request/reply). A client can only communicate with the server, and an interaction is initiated by a client. In shared data style the two component types are repository and data accessors. Data accessors read/write the repository and share information among themselves through the repository.

Designing an architecture is the first step towards building a solution for the problem described in the SRS. The architecture forms the foundation for the system and rest of the design and development activities. Consequently, it should be properly documented. A proper architecture document should describe the context in which the architecture was designed, the different architectural views that were created, and how the different views relate to each other. In the context, it is important to identify the different stakeholders and their objectives, as that drives the architecture choices. Generally, one view is taken as the primary view and the architecture description revolves around that. Different views can be combined with the primary view, if this combination does not complicate the architecture diagram or description. The architecture description of a view, which often revolves around an architecture diagram, should clearly specify the different types of elements and their external behavior. The architecture rationale, or why the architecture choices were made, should also be documented.

As considerable analysis and thought can go into designing the architecture to ensure that the final selected architecture can support the desired system properties, it is essential that the architecture be preserved during the rest of the development. That is, the architecture, once selected and specified, constrains the design and development. It is essential that these constraints be respected and the design be consistent with the architecture. We have illustrated how these constraints can be violated while building a system that still provides the desired functionality. It is essential that such violations do not occur.

A considerable analysis of the system attributes like performance, security, reliability, and modifiability is possible when the architecture views are ready. There are many approaches for performing this analysis. We have briefly discussed the ATAM approach in which first the key scenarios are enumerated, along with the constraints for the attributes of interest for the system. Then the proposed architectures are evaluated to see how well they satisfy the constraints under the different scenarios. The result of this analysis can be used to compare different architecture choices. The analysis can also be extended to perform sensitivity and tradeoff analysis.

Exercises

1. Explain why architecture is not just one structure consisting of different parts and their relationship.

2. What do you think is the relationship between the component and connector view and the module view. In the situations where this relationship is simple, how will you express it in one diagram?

3. In the student-survey example, extend the architecture diagram to also show the module view. (If you want to look at the code for the architecture, it is available from the Web site.)

4. In the analysis done in Section 4.6.2 of the student-survey example, some allocation of software elements to hardware was chosen to perform the analysis. Draw an allocation view for this allocation.

5. For the example analyzed in Section 4.6.2 of the student-survey system, let us make the following changes: (1) Suppose the student can also ask for just

the survey result, and the response time requirement for this is different. (2) Assume that the availability of server is much higher (say 0.99) than the database server (0.9). Now do the analysis.

6. A closed-loop control system generally works as follows. A centralized controller gets values from the various sensors, does the computation to determine the various settings (often by solving some partial differential equations), and then issues necessary commands to the actuators in the system so that the system remains balanced and gives optimal performance. What would you chose as the primary view to describe the architecture of this control system—give reasons for your selection. Design and draw (the primary view) at least two architectures for this system, clearly defining the different elements in it.

7. For the above example, create some scenarios (including some for failures) and some requirements, and then analyze your architectures to see which one is the best.

8. Consider an interactive Web site which provides many different features to perform various tasks. Show that the architecture for this can be represented as a shared-data style as well as client-server style. Which one will you prefer and why?

9. Consider the instant messaging system that you use. Which of the views is best suited to describe its C&C view. Give a diagram to describe the architecture (C&C view) of such a system.

Case Studies

Here we briefly discuss the architecture for the two case studies. The complete architecture document is available from the Web site.

Case Study 1—Course Scheduling

This is a batch processing type system, where data is taken by the system in the start of the processing from the two input files, and the output is produced at the end. No data updates are done (that is, there is no need for a repository). For such a system, the pipe-and-filter style is eminently suited. Hence, we use this style for the architecture of this system. The proposed architecture is shown in Figure 4.12.

A bit more discussion and evaluation of the architecture is given in the architecture document for this case study, which is available from the Web site. It might be added that this case study was originally built without any architecture design in the process (architectures were not well established when this case study was done). However, this architecture, even though done retrospectively, is representative of the system and the actual system architecture closely resembles this architecture, as will be clear when we discuss the design of this case study in later chapters.

Case Study 2—PIMS

The main stakeholders for the PIMS system are the individual users who might use the system and the system designer/builder who will build PIMS. The main concerns of the two stakeholders are:

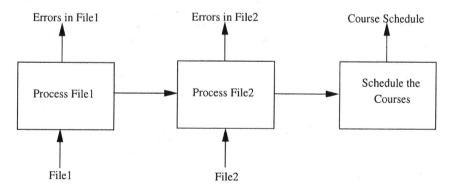

Figure 4.12: Architecture for course scheduling case study.

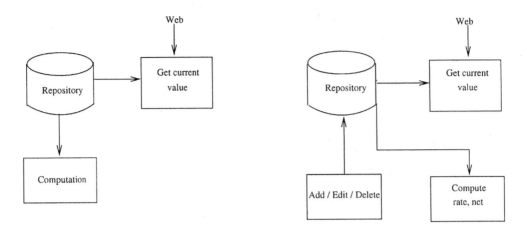

Figure 4.13: Initial architectures for PIMS.

- **For Users:** The usability of the system and providing rate or returns and the net-worth info. Reasonable response time is also a concern.

- **For designer/builder:** The system is easy to modify, particularly to handle future extensions mentioned in the SRS (that is, the system may become a multi-user system, which may require use of databases instead of files for keeping data). It should be easily portable.

Hence, the key property which the architecture should aim to satisfy (besides the functionality) is modifiability or extensibility of the system. Portability and response time are other factors which should drive the architecture decisions.

Due to the data-oriented nature of the system, it should be clear that a shared-data style would be the best. As the system is rather small, the first architecture proposal was to have two main components—a repository to keep the data on investments, and a processing component to do all the processing. And have another component to get the latest value of the shares from the Web into the repository.

We then realized that there are two independent aspects of processing, one dealing with data entry and edit, and the other which does the computation of rates of return and net worth. These two do not need to communicate with each other. Separating the two will make the system more modular and making modifications will be easier. For example, user interface changes will affect only the edit component, while any change in reporting or computations will affect the other only. The simplified view of these two architectures is shown in Figure 4.13.

Even though the second architecture is better than the first one as it has better modularity, the processing components are still very tightly coupled with the data repository. If the repository changes from one database to another, then besides making the changes to the repository, the code of both the computation components will have to be changed.

To separate the data access from the computation, a layer was added between the computation components and the repository. (By adding a layer, we are mixing module view and C&C view, but as it is clear and simple, we continue with it.) The complete description of this architecture, which includes the user interface component also, is given in the architecture document for this case study. The document also gives the complete picture of the previous architecture also, for which only a simplified view is given here.

The architecture document also gives a simple analysis of the different architecture, leading to the selection of one architecture as the proposed architecture for PIMS.

5

Planning a Software Project

For a successful project, both good project management and good engineering are essential. Lack of either one can cause a project to fail. We have seen that project management activities can be viewed as having three major phases: project planning, project monitoring and control, and project termination. Broadly speaking, planning entails all activities that must be performed before starting the development work. Once the project is started, project control begins. In other words, during planning all the activities that management needs to perform are planned, while during project control the plan is executed and updated.

Planning may be the most important management activity. Without a proper plan, no real monitoring or controlling of the project is possible. Often projects are rushed toward implementation with not enough time and effort spent on planning. No amount of technical effort later can compensate for lack of careful planning. Lack of proper planing is a sure ticket to failure for a large software project. For this reason, we treat project planning as an independent chapter.

The basic goal of planning is to look into the future, identify the activities that need to be done to complete the project successfully, and plan the scheduling and resources. The inputs to the planning activity are the requirements specification and the architecture description. A very detailed requirements document is not essential for planning, but for a good plan all the important requirements must be known, and it is highly desirable that architecture decisions have been taken. The major issues project planning addresses are:

Process planning

Effort estimation
Schedule and Resource Estimation
Quality plans
Configuration management plans
Risk management
Project monitoring plans

In the rest of this chapter we will discuss each of these issues and some techniques for handling them.

5.1   Process Planning

We have already discussed in detail the development process and the various process models. For a project, during planning, a key activity is to plan and specify the process that should be used in the project. This means specifying the various stages in the process, the entry criteria for each stage, the exit criteria, and the verification activities that will be done at the end of the stage. As discussed, some established process model may be used as a standard process and tailored to suit the needs of the project. In an organization, often standard processes are defined and a project can use any of these standard processes and tailor it to suit the specific needs of the project. Hence the process planning activity mostly entails selecting a standard process and tailoring it for the project.

Tailoring is an advanced topic which we will not discuss in any detail. Generally, however, based on the size, complexity and nature of the project, as well as the characteristics of the team, like the experience of the team members with the problem domain as well as the technology being used, the standard process is tailored. The common tailoring actions are modify a step, omit a step, add a step, or change the formality with which a step is done. After tailoring, the process specification for the project is available. This process guides rest of the planning, particularly detailed scheduling where detailed tasks to be done in the project are defined and assigned to people to execute them.

5.2   Effort Estimation

For a given set of requirements it is desirable to know how much it will cost to develop the software, and how much time the development will take.

These estimates are needed *before* development is initiated. The primary reason for cost and schedule estimation is cost-benefit analysis, and project monitoring and control. A more practical use of these estimates is in bidding for software projects, where cost estimates must be given to a potential client for the development contract.

The bulk of the cost of software development is due to the human resources needed, and therefore most cost estimation procedures focus on estimating effort in terms of person-months (PM). By properly including the "overheads" (i.e., the cost of hardware, software, office space, etc.) in the cost of a person-month, effort estimates can be converted into cost.

For a software development project, effort and schedule estimates are essential prerequisites for managing the project. Otherwise, even simple questions like "is the project late?" "are there cost overruns?" and "when is the project likely to complete?" cannot be answered. Effort and schedule estimates are also required to determine the staffing level for a project during different phases.

Estimates can be based on subjective opinion of some person or determined through the use of models. Though there are approaches to structure the opinions of persons for achieving a consensus on the effort estimate (e.g., the Delphi approach [20]), it is generally accepted that it is important to have a more scientific approach to estimation through the use of models. In this section we discuss only the model-based approach for effort estimation. Before we discuss the models, let us first understand the limitations of any effort estimation procedure.

5.2.1 Uncertainties in Effort Estimation

One can perform effort estimation at any point in the software life cycle. As the effort of the project depends on the nature and characteristics of the project, at any point, the accuracy of the estimate will depend on the amount of reliable information we have about the final product. Clearly, when the product is delivered, the effort can be accurately determined, as all the data about the project and the resources spent can be fully known by then. This is effort estimation with complete knowledge about the project. On the other extreme is the point when the project is being initiated or during the feasibility study. At this time, we have only some idea of the classes of data the system will get and produce and the major functionality of the system. There is a great deal of uncertainty about the actual specifications of the system. Specifications with uncertainty represent a range of possible final

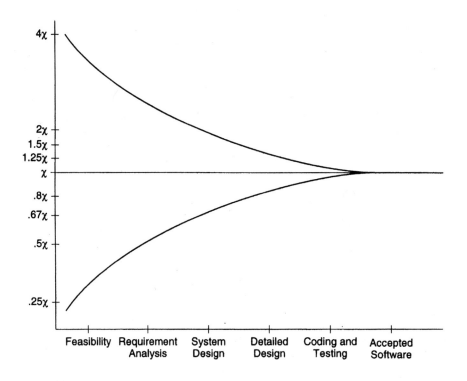

Figure 5.1: Accuracy of effort estimation.

products, not one precisely defined product. Hence, the effort estimation based on this type of information cannot be accurate. Estimates at this phase of the project can be off by as much as a factor of four from the actual final effort.

As we specify the system more fully and accurately, the uncertainties are reduced and more accurate effort estimates can be made. For example, once the requirements are completely specified, more accurate effort estimates can be made compared to the estimates after the feasibility study. Once the design is complete, the estimates can be made still more accurately. The obtainable accuracy of the estimates as it varies with the different phases is shown in Figure 5.1 [20, 21].

Note that this figure is simply specifying the limitations of effort estimating strategies—the best accuracy a effort estimating strategy can hope to achieve. It does not say anything about the existence of strategies that can provide the estimate with that accuracy. For actual effort estimation, estimation models or procedures have to be developed. The accuracy of the estimates will depend on the effectiveness and accuracy of the estimation procedures or models employed and the process (i.e., how predictable it is).

Despite the limitations, estimation models have matured considerably and generally give fairly accurate estimates. For example, when the CO-COMO model (discussed later) was checked with data from some projects, it was found that the estimates were within 20% of the actual effort 68% of the time.

It should also be mentioned that achieving an estimate after the requirements have been specified within 20% is actually quite good. With such an estimate, there need not even be any cost and schedule overruns, as there is generally enough slack or free time available (recall the study mentioned earlier that found a programmer spends more than 30% of his time in personal or miscellaneous tasks) that can be used to meet the targets set for the project based on the estimates. In other words, if the estimate is within 20% of the actual, the effect of this inaccuracy will not even be reflected in the final cost and schedule. Highly precise estimates are generally not needed. Reasonable estimates in a software project tend to become a self-fulfilling prophecy—people work to meet the schedules (which are derived from effort estimates).

5.2.2 Building Effort Estimation Models

An estimation model can be viewed as a "function" that outputs the effort estimate. clearly this estimation function will need inputs about the project, from which it can produce the estimate. The basic idea of having a model or procedure for estimation is that it reduces the problem of estimation to estimating or determining the value of the "key parameters" that characterize the project, based on which the effort can be estimated.

Note that an estimation model does not, and cannot, work in a vacuum; it needs inputs to produce the effort estimate as output. At the start of a project, when the details of the software itself are not known, the hope is that the estimation model will require values of parameters that can be measured at that stage.

Although the effort for a project is a function of many parameters, it is generally agreed that the primary factor that controls the effort is the size of the project, that is, the larger the project, the greater the effort requirement. One common approach therefore for estimating effort is to make it a function of *project size*, and the equation of effort is considered as

$$EFFORT = a * SIZE^b,$$

where a and b are constants [5], and project size is generally in KLOC or function points. Values for these constants for a particular process are determined through regression analysis, which is applied to data about the projects that has been performed in the past. For example, Watson and Felix [142] analyzed the data of more than 60 projects done at IBM Federal Systems Division, ranging from 4,000 to 467,000 lines of delivered source code, and found that if the SIZE estimate is in thousands of delivered lines of code (KLOC), the total effort, E, in person-months (PM) can be given by the equation $E = 5.2(SIZE)^{.91}$.

Often, however, simple productivity may be used to determine the overall estimate from the size. That is, if productivity is P KLOC/PM, then effort estimate for the project may be SIZE/P person-months. This approach will work if the size and type of the project are similar to the set of projects from which the productivity P was obtained.

This approach of determining total effort from the total size is what we refer to as the *top-down approach*, as overall effort is first determined and then from this the effort for different parts are obtained.

In a *top-down estimation* model by using size as the main input to the model, we have replaced the problem of effort estimation by size estimation. One may then ask, why not directly do effort estimation rather than size estimation? The answer is that size estimation is often easier than direct effort estimation. For estimating size, the system is generally partitioned into components it is likely to have. Once the components of the system are known, as estimating something about a small unit is generally much easier than estimating it for a larger system, sizes of components can be generally estimated quite accurately. Once size estimates for components are available, to get the overall size estimate for the system, the estimates of all the components can be added up. Similar property does not hold for effort estimation, as effort for developing a system is *not* the sum of effort for developing the components (as additional effort is needed for integration and other such activities when building a system from developed components). This key feature, that the system property is the sum of the properties of its parts, holds for size but not for effort, and is the main reason that size estimation is considered easier than effort estimation.

With top-down models, if the size estimate is inaccurate, the effort estimate produced by the models will also be inaccurate. Hence, it is important that good estimates for the size of the software be obtained. There is no known "simple" method for estimating the size accurately. When estimating software size, the best way may be to get as much detail as possible about the software to be developed and to be aware of our biases when estimating the size of the various components. By obtaining details and using them for size estimation, the estimates are likely to be closer to the actual size of the final software. In general, there is often a tendency by people to underestimate the size of software [20].

A somewhat different approach for effort estimation is the *bottom-up approach*. In this approach, the project is first divided into tasks and then estimates for the different tasks of the project are first obtained. From the estimates of the different tasks, the overall estimate is determined. That is, the overall estimate of the project is derived from the estimates of its parts. This type of approach is also called activity-based estimation. Essentially, in this approach the size and complexity of the project is captured in the set of tasks the project has to perform.

The bottom-up approach lends itself to direct estimation of effort; once the project is partitioned into smaller tasks, it is possible to directly estimate the effort required for them, specially if tasks are relatively small. A risk of bottom-up methods is that one may omit some important activities in the list of tasks. Also, directly estimating the effort for some overhead tasks, such as project management, that span the project can be difficult.

Both the top-down and the bottom-up approaches require information about the project: size (for top-down approaches) or a list of tasks (for bottom-up approaches). In many ways, these approaches are complementary, and often it may be desirable to determine the effort using both the approaches and then using these estimates to obtain the final estimate.

5.2.3 A Bottom-Up Estimation Approach

If architecture of the system to be built has been developed and if past information about how effort is distributed over different phases is known, then the bottom-up approach need not completely list all the tasks, and a less tedious approach is possible. Here we describe one such approach used in a commercial organization [97].

In this approach, the major programs (or units or modules) in the software being built are first determined. Each program unit is then classified as simple, medium, or complex based on certain criteria. For each classification unit, an average effort for coding (and unit testing) is decided. This standard coding effort can be based on past data from a similar project, from some guidelines, or some combination of these.

Once the number of units in the three categories of complexity is known and the estimated coding effort for each program is selected, the total coding effort for the project is known. From the coding effort, the effort required for the other phases and activities is determined as a percentage of coding effort. From information about the past performance of the process, the likely distribution of effort in different phases of this project is decided, and then used to determine the effort for other phases and activities. From these estimates, the total effort for the project is obtained.

This approach lends itself to a judicious mixture of experience and data. If suitable past data are not available (for example, if launching a new type of project), one can estimate the coding effort using experience once the nature of the different types of units is specified. With this estimate, we can obtain the estimate for other activities by working with some reasonable or standard effort distribution. This strategy can easily account for activities that are sometimes difficult to enumerate early but do consume effort by budgeting effort for "other" or "miscellaneous" category.

The procedure for estimation can be summarized as the following sequence of steps:

1. Identify modules in the system and classify them as simple, medium, or complex.

2. Determine the average coding effort for simple/medium/complex modules.

3. Get the total coding effort using the coding effort of different types of modules and the counts for them.

4. Using the effort distribution for similar projects, estimate the effort for other tasks and the total effort.

5. Refine the estimates based on project-specific factors.

This procedure uses a judicious mixture of past data (in the form of distribution of effort) and experience of the programmers. This approach is also simple and similar to how many of us plan any project. For this reason, for small projects, many people find this approach natural and comfortable.

Note that this method of classifying programs into a few categories and using an average coding effort for each category is used only for effort estimation. In detailed scheduling, when a project manager assigns each unit to a member of the team for coding and budgets time for the activity, characteristics of the unit are taken into account to give more or less time than the average.

5.2.4 COCOMO Model

A top-down model can depend on many different factors, instead of depending only on one variable, giving rise to multivariable models. One approach for building multivariable models is to start with an initial estimate determined by using the static single-variable model equations, which depend on size, and then adjusting the estimates based on other variables. This approach implies that size is the primary factor for cost; other factors have a lesser effect. Here we will discuss one such model called the COnstructive COst MOdel (COCOMO) developed by Boehm [20, 21]. This model also estimates the total effort in terms of person-months. The basic steps in this model are:

1. Obtain an initial estimate of the development effort from the estimate of thousands of delivered lines of source code (KLOC).

2. Determine a set of 15 multiplying factors from different attributes of the project.

3. Adjust the effort estimate by multiplying the initial estimate with all the multiplying factors.

The initial estimate (also called *nominal estimate*) is determined by an equation of the form used in the static single-variable models, using KLOC as the measure of size. To determine the initial effort E_i in person-months the equation used is of the type $E_i = a * (KLOC)^b$. The value of the constants a and b depend on the project type. In COCOMO, projects are categorized into three types—organic, semidetached, and embedded. These categories roughly characterize the complexity of the project with organic projects being those that are relatively straightforward and developed by a small team, and embedded are those that are ambitious and novel, with stringent constraints from the environment and high requirements for such aspects as interfacing and reliability. The constants a and b for different systems are:

System	a	b
Organic	3.2	1.05
Semidetached	3.0	1.12
Embedded	2.8	1.20

The value of the constants for a cost model depend on the process and have to be determined from past data. COCOMO has instead provided "global" constant values. These values should be considered as values to start with until data for some projects is available. With project data, the value of the constants can be determined through regression analysis.

There are 15 different attributes, called *cost driver attributes*, that determine the multiplying factors. These factors depend on product, computer, personnel, and technology attributes (called *project attributes*). Examples of the attributes are required software reliability (RELY), product complexity (CPLX), analyst capability (ACAP), application experience (AEXP), use of modern tools (TOOL), and required development schedule (SCHD). Each cost driver has a rating scale, and for each rating, a multiplying factor is provided. For example, for the product attribute RELY, the rating scale is very low, low, nominal, high, and very high (and in some cases extra high). The multiplying factors for these ratings are .75, .88, 1.00, 1.15, and 1.40, respectively. So, if the reliability requirement for the project is judged to be low then the multiplying factor is .75, while if it is judged to be very high the factor is 1.40. The attributes and their multiplying factors for different ratings are shown in Table 5.1 [20, 21]. The COCOMO approach also provides guidelines for assessing the rating for the different attributes [20].

The multiplying factors for all 15 cost drivers are multiplied to get the effort adjustment factor (EAF). The final effort estimate, E, is obtained by multiplying the initial estimate by the EAF. That is, $E = EAF * E_i$..

By this method, the overall cost of the project can be estimated. For planning and monitoring purposes, estimates of the effort required for the different phases is also desirable. In COCOMO, effort for a phase is a defined percentage of the overall effort. The percentage of total effort spent in a phase varies with the type and size of the project. The percentages for an organic software project are given in Table 5.2.

Using this table, the estimate of the effort required for each phase can be determined from the total effort estimate. For example, if the total effort estimate for an organic software system is 20 PM and the size estimate is 20KLOC, then the percentage effort for the coding and unit testing phase will be 40 + (38 - 40)/(32 - 8) * 20 = 39%. The estimate for the effort needed

Cost Drivers	Rating				
	Very Low	Low	Nom-inal	High	Very High
Product Attributes					
RELY, required reliability	.75	.88	1.00	1.15	1.40
DATA, database size		.94	1.00	1.08	1.16
CPLX, product complexity	.70	.85	1.00	1.15	1.30
Computer Attributes					
TIME, execution time constraint			1.00	1.11	1.30
STOR, main storage constraint			1.00	1.06	1.21
VITR, virtual machine volatility		.87	1.00	1.15	1.30
TURN, computer turnaround time		.87	1.00	1.07	1.15
Personnel Attributes					
ACAP, analyst capability	1.46	1.19	1.00	.86	.71
AEXP, application exp.	1.29	1.13	1.00	.91	.82
PCAP, programmer capability	1.42	1.17	1.00	.86	.70
VEXP, virtual machine exp.	1.21	1.10	1.00	.90	
LEXP, prog. language exp.	1.14	1.07	1.00	.95	
Project Attributes					
MODP, modern prog. practices	1.24	1.10	1.00	.91	.82
TOOL, use of SW tools	1.24	1.10	1.00	.91	.83
SCHED, development schedule	1.23	1.08	1.00	1.04	1.10

Table 5.1: Effort multipliers for different cost drivers.

Phase	Size			
	Small 2 KLOC	Intermediate 8 KLOC	Medium 32 KLOC	Large 128 KLOC
Product design	16	16	16	16
Detailed design	26	25	24	23
Code and unit test	42	40	38	36
Integration and test	16	19	22	25

Table 5.2: Phase-wise distribution of effort.

for this phase is 7.8 PM. This table does not list the cost of requirements as a percentage of the total cost estimate because the project plan (and cost estimation) is being done after the requirements are complete. In COCOMO the detailed design and code and unit testing are sometimes combined into one phase called the *programming phase*.

As an example, suppose a system for office automation has to be designed. From the requirements, it is clear that there will be four major modules in the system: data entry, data update, query, and report generator. It is also clear from the requirements that this project will fall in the organic category. The sizes for the different modules and the overall system are estimated to be:

Data Entry	0.6 KLOC
Data Update	0.6 KLOC
Query	0.8 KLOC
Reports	1.0 KLOC
TOTAL	3.0 KLOC

From the requirements, the ratings of the different cost driver attributes are assessed. These ratings, along with their multiplying factors, are:

Complexity	High	1.15
Storage	High	1.06
Experience	Low	1.13
Programmer Capability	Low	1.17

All other factors had a nominal rating. From these, the effort adjustment factor (EAF) is

$$EAF = 1.15*1.06*1.13*1.17 = 1.61.$$

The initial effort estimate for the project is obtained from the relevant equations. We have

$$E_i = 3.2 * 3^{1.05} = 10.14 PM.$$

Using the EAF, the adjusted effort estimate is

$$E = 1.61 * 10.14 = 16.3 PM.$$

Using the preceding table, we obtain the percentage of the total effort consumed in different phases. The office automation system's size estimate is 3 KLOC, so we will have to use interpolation to get the appropriate percentage (the two end values for interpolation will be the percentages for 2 KLOC and 8 KLOC). The percentages for the different phases are: design—16%, detailed design—25.83%, code and unit test—41.66%, and integration and testing—16.5%. With these, the effort estimates for the different phases are:

System Design   .16 * 16.3 = 2.6 PM
Detailed Design   .258 * 16.3 = 4.2 PM
Code and Unit Test .4166 * 16.3 = 6.8 PM
Integration   .165 * 16.3 = 2.7 PM.

5.3 Project Scheduling and Staffing

Once the effort is estimated, various schedules (or project duration) are possible, depending on the number of resources (people) put on the project. For example, for a project whose effort estimate is 56 person-months, a total schedule of 8 months is possible with 7 people. A schedule of 7 months with 8 people is also possible, as is a schedule of approximately 9 months with 6 people.

As is well known, however, manpower and months are not fully interchangeable in a software project. A schedule cannot be simply obtained from the overall effort estimate by deciding on average staff size and then determining the total time requirement by dividing the total effort by the average staff size. Brooks has pointed out that person and months (time) are not interchangeable. According to Brooks [25], "... man and months are interchangeable only for activities that require no communication among men, like sowing wheat or reaping cotton. This is not even approximately true of software...."

For instance, in the example here, a schedule of 1 month with 56 people is not possible even though the effort matches the requirement. Similarly, no one would execute the project in 28 months with 2 people. In other words, once the effort is fixed, there is some flexibility in setting the schedule by appropriately staffing the project, but this flexibility is not unlimited. Empirical data also suggests that no simple equation between effort and schedule fits well [127].

In a project, the scheduling activity can be broken into two subactivities: determining the overall schedule (the project duration) with major milestones, and developing the detailed schedule of the various tasks.

5.3.1 Overall Scheduling

One method to determine the normal (or nominal) overall schedule is to determine it as a function of effort. Any such function has to be determined from data from completed projects using statistical techniques like fitting a regression curve through the scatter plot obtained by plotting the effort and schedule of past projects. This curve is generally nonlinear because the schedule does not grow linearly with effort. Many models follow this approach [5, 20]. The IBM Federal Systems Division found that the total duration, M, in calendar months can be estimated by

$$M = 4.1E^{.36}.$$

In COCOMO, the equation for schedule for an organic type of software is

$$M = 2.5E^{.38}.$$

It should be clear that schedule is not a function solely of effort. Hence, the schedule determined in this manner is not really fixed. However, it can be used as a guideline or check of the schedules reasonableness, which might be decided based on other factors.

One rule of thumb, called the *square root check*, is sometimes used to check the schedule of medium-sized projects [97]. This check suggests that the proposed schedule can be around the square root of the total effort in person-months. This schedule can be met if suitable resources are assigned to the project. For example, if the effort estimate is 50 person-months, a schedule of about 7 to 8 months will be suitable.

From this macro estimate of schedule, we have to determine the schedule for the major milestones in the project. To determine the milestones, we must first understand the manpower ramp-up that usually takes place in a project. The number of people in a software project tends to follow the Rayleigh curve [126, 127]. That is, in the beginning and the end, few people work on the project; the peak team size (PTS) is reached somewhere near the middle of the project. This behavior occurs because only a few people are needed in the initial phases of requirements analysis and design. The human resources requirement peaks during coding and unit testing. Again, during system testing and integration, fewer people are required.

Often, the staffing level is not changed continuously in a project and approximations of the Rayleigh curve are used: assigning a few people at the start, having the peak team during the coding phase, and then leaving a few people for integration and system testing. If we consider design and analysis, build, and test as three major phases, the manpower ramp-up in projects typically resembles the function shown in Figure 5.2 [97].

For ease of scheduling, particularly for smaller projects, often the required people are assigned together around the start of the project. This approach can lead to some people being unoccupied at the start and toward

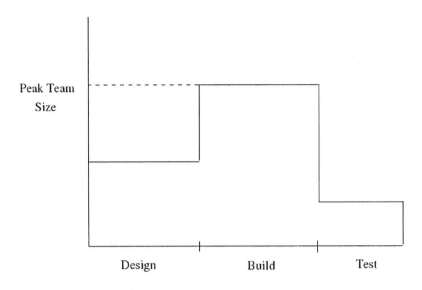

Figure 5.2: Manpower ramp-up in a typical project.

the end. This slack time is often used for supporting project activities like training and documentation.

Given the effort estimate for a phase, we can determine the duration of the phase if we know the manpower ramp-up. For these three major phases, the percentage of the schedule consumed in the build phase is smaller than the percentage of the effort consumed because this phase involves more people. Similarly, the percentage of the schedule consumed in the design and testing phases exceeds their effort percentages. The exact schedule depends on the planned manpower ramp-up, and how many resources can be used effectively in a phase on that project. Generally speaking, design requires about a quarter of the schedule, build consumes about half, and integration and system testing consume the remaining quarter. COCOMO gives 19% for design, 62% for programming, and 18% for integration.

5.3.2 Detailed Scheduling

Once the milestones and the resources are fixed, it is time to set the detailed scheduling. For detailed schedules, the major tasks fixed while planning the milestones are broken into small schedulable activities in a hierarchical manner. For example, the detailed design phase can be broken into tasks for developing the detailed design for each module, review of each detailed design, fixing of defects found, and so on. For each detailed task, the project manager estimates the time required to complete it and assigns a suitable resource so that the overall schedule is met.

At each level of refinement, the project manager determines the effort for the overall task from the detailed schedule and checks it against the effort estimates. If this detailed schedule is not consistent with the overall schedule and effort estimates, the detailed schedule must be changed. If it is found that the best detailed schedule cannot match the milestone effort and schedule, then the earlier estimates must be revised. Thus, scheduling is an iterative process.

Generally, the project manager refines the tasks to a level so that the lowest-level activity can be scheduled to occupy no more than a few days from a single resource. Activities related to tasks such as project management, coordination, database management, and configuration management may also be listed in the schedule, even though these activities have less direct effect on determining the schedule because they are ongoing tasks rather than schedulable activities. Nevertheless, they consume resources and hence are often included in the project schedule.

Rarely will a project manager complete the detailed schedule of the entire project all at once. Once the overall schedule is fixed, detailing for a phase may only be done at the start of that phase.

For detailed scheduling, tools like Microsoft Project or a spreadsheet can be very useful. For each lowest-level activity, the project manager specifies the effort, duration, start date, end date, and resources. Dependencies between activities, due either to an inherent dependency (for example, you can conduct a unit test plan for a program only after it has been coded) or to a resource-related dependency (the same resource is assigned two tasks) may also be specified. From these tools the overall effort and schedule of higher level tasks can be determined.

A detailed project schedule is never static. Changes may be needed because the actual progress in the project may be different from what was planned, because newer tasks are added in response to change requests, or because of other unforeseen situations. Changes are done as and when the need arises.

The final schedule, frequently maintained using some suitable tool, is often the most "live" project plan document. During the project, if plans must be changed and additional activities must be done, after the decision is made, the changes must be reflected in the detailed schedule, as this reflects the tasks actually planned to be performed. Hence, the detailed schedule becomes the main document that tracks the activities and schedule.

Task	Duration (days)	Work (person -days)	Start date	End date
Project initiation	33.78	24.2	5/4/00	6/23/00
Regular activities	87.11	35.13	6/5/00	10/16/00
Training	95.11	49.37	5/8/00	9/29/00
Knowledge sharing tasks	78.22	19.56	6/2/00	9/30/00
Inception phase	26.67	22.67	4/3/00	5/12/00
Elaboration Iteration 1	27.56	55.16	5/15/00	6/23/00
Elaboration Iteration 2	8.89	35.88	6/26/00	7/7/00
Construction Iteration 1	8.89	24.63	7/10/00	7/21/00
Construction Iteration 2	6.22	28.22	7/20/00	7/28/00
Construction Iteration 3	6.22	27.03	7/31/00	8/8/00
Transition phase	56	179.62	8/9/00	11/3/00
Back-end work	4.44	6.44	8/14/00	8/18/00

Table 5.3: High-level schedule for the project.

5.3.3 An Example

Consider the example of a project from [97]. The overall effort estimate for this project is 501 person-days, or about 24 person-months (this estimation was done using the bottom-up approach discussed earlier). The customer gave approximately 5.5 months to finish the project. Because this is more than the square root of effort in person-months, this schedule was accepted.

The milestones are determined by using the effort estimates for the phases and an estimate of the number of resources that can be fully occupied in this phase. Table 5.3 shows the high level schedule of the project. This project uses a process in which initial requirement and design is done in two iterations and the development is done in three iterations. The overall project duration with these milestones is 140 days.

This high-level schedule is not suitable for assigning resources and detailed planning. During detailed scheduling, these tasks are broken into schedulable activities. In this way, the schedule also becomes a checklist of tasks for the project. As mentioned before, this exploding of top-level activities is not done fully at the start but rather takes place many times during the project.

Table 5.4 shows part of the detailed schedule of the construction-iteration 1 phase of the project. For each activity, the table specifies the activity by a short name, the module to which the activity is contributing, and the duration and effort. For each task, how much is completed is given in the

Module	Task	Duration (days)	Effort (days)	Start date	End date	% done	Resource
-	Requirements	8.89	1.33	7/10	7/21	100	bb,bj
-	Design review	1	0.9	7/11	7/12	100	bb,bj,sb
-	Rework	1	0.8	7/12	7/13	100	bj, sb
History	coding	2.67	1.87	7/10	7/12	100	hp
History	Review UC17	0.89	0.27	7/14	7/14	100	bj,dd
History	Review UC19	0.89	0.27	7/14	7/14	100	bj,dd
History	Rework	0.89	2.49	7/17	7/17	100	dd,sb,hp
History	Test UC17	0.89	0.62	7/18	7/18	100	sb
History	Test UC19	0.89	0.62	7/18	7/18	100	hp
History	Rework	0.89	0.71	7/18	7/18	100	bj,sb,hp
Config.	Reconciliation	0.89	2.49	7/19	7/19	100	bj,sb,hp
Mgmt.	Tracking	7.11	2.13	7/10	7/19	100	bb
Quality	Analysis	0.89	0.62	7/19	7/19	100	bb

Table 5.4: Portion of the detailed schedule.

% Complete column. This information is used for activity tracking. The detailed schedule also specifies the resource to which the task is assigned (specified by initials of the person.) Sometimes, the predecessors of the activity (the activities upon which the task depends) are also specified. This information helps in determining the critical path and the critical resources. This project finally had a total of about 325 schedulable tasks.

5.3.4   Team Structure

We have seen that the number of resources is fixed when schedule is being planned. Detailed scheduling is done only after actual assignment of people has been done, as task assignment needs information about the capabilities of the team members. In our discussion above, we have implicitly assumed that the project's team is led by a project manager, who does the planning and task assignment. This form of hierarchical team organization is fairly common, and was earlier called the Chief Programmer Team.

In this hierarchical organization, the project manager is responsible for all major technical decisions of the project. He does most of the design and assigns coding of the different parts of the design to the programmers. The team typically consists of programmers, testers, a configuration controller, and possibly a librarian for documentation. There may be other roles like database manager, network manager, backup project manager, or a backup configuration controller. It should be noted that these are all logical roles and one person may do multiple such roles.

For a small project, a one-level hierarchy suffices. For larger projects, this organization can be extended easily by partitioning the project into modules, and having module leaders who are responsible for all tasks related to their module and have a team with them for performing these tasks.

A different team organization is the egoless team [114]: Egoless teams consist of ten or fewer programmers. The goals of the group are set by consensus, and input from every member is taken for major decisions. Group leadership rotates among the group members. Due to their nature, egoless teams are sometimes called *democratic teams*. This structure allows input from all members, which can lead to better decisions for difficult problems. This structure is well suited for long-term research-type projects that do not have time constraints. It is not suitable for regular tasks that have time constraints; for such tasks, the communication in democratic structure is unnecessary and results in inefficiency.

In recent times, for very large product developments, another structure has emerged. This structure recognizes that there are three main task categories in software development—management related, development related, and testing related. It also recognizes that it is often desirable to have the test and development team be relatively independent, and also not to have the developers or tests report to a nontechnical manager. In this structure, consequently, there is an overall unit manager, under whom there are three small hierarchic organizations—for program management, for development, and for testing. The primary job of developers is to write code and they work under a development manager. The responsibility of the testers is to test the code and they work under a test manager. The program managers provides the specifications for what is being built, and ensure that development and testing are properly coordinated. In a large product this structure may be replicated, one for each major unit. This type of team organization is used in corporations like Microsoft.

5.4 Software Configuration Management Plan

From the earlier discussions on software configuration management, it should be somewhat clear what the SCM plans should contain. The SCM plan, like other plans, has to identify the activities that must be performed, give guidelines for performing the activities, and allocate resources for them.

Planning for configuration management involves identifying the configuration items and specifying the procedures to be used for controlling and implementing changes to them. We have discussed CM planning while discussing the CM process in Chapter 2. To summarize, the configuration controller does the CM planning when the project has been initiated and the operating environment and requirements specifications are known. The activities in this stage include the following [97]:

- Identify configuration items, including customer-supplied and purchased items.

- Define a naming scheme for configuration items.

- Define the directory structure needed for CM.

- Define version management procedures, and methods for tracking changes to configuration items.

- Define access restrictions.

- Define change control procedures.

- Identify and define the responsibility of the CC.

- Identify points at which baselines will be created.

- Define a backup procedure and a reconciliation procedure, if needed.

- Define a release procedure.

The output of this phase is the CM plan. An example of a full CM plan for a project in a commercial organization is given in [96, 97].

5.5   Quality Plan

Earlier in Chapter 1, we discussed the notion of software quality. Even though there are different dimensions of quality, in practice, quality management often revolves around defects. Hence, we use "delivered defect density"—the number of defects per unit size in the delivered software—as the definition of quality. This definition is currently the de facto industry standard [41]. By defect we mean something in software that causes the software to behave in a manner that is inconsistent with the requirements or needs of the customer. Defect in software implies that its removal will result in some change being made to the software.

To ensure that the final product is of high quality, some quality control (QC) activities must be performed throughout the development. A QC task is one whose main purpose is to identify defects. The purpose of a quality plan in a project is to specify the activities that need to be performed for identifying and removing defects, and the tools and methods that may be used for that purpose.

In a project it is very unlikely that the intermediate work products are of poor quality, but the final product is of high quality. So, to ensure that the delivered software is of good quality, it is essential to ensure that all work products like the requirements specification, design, and test plan are also of good quality. For this reason, a quality plan should contain quality activities throughout the project.

The quality plan specifies the tasks that need to be undertaken at different times in the project to improve the software quality by removing defects, and how they are to be managed. Before we discuss these, let us first understand the defect injection and removal cycle.

5.5.1 Defect Injection and Removal Cycle

Software development is a highly people-oriented activity and hence it is error-prone. Defects can be injected in software at any stage during its evolution. That is, during the transformation from user needs to software to satisfy those needs, defects can be injected in all the transformation activities undertaken. These injection stages are primarily the requirements specification, the high-level design, the detailed design, and coding.

For high-quality software, the final product should have as few defects as possible. Hence, for delivery of high-quality software, active removal of defects through the quality control activities is necessary. The QC activities for defect removal include requirements reviews, design reviews, code reviews, unit testing, integration testing, system testing, and acceptance testing (we do not include reviews of plan documents, although such reviews also help in improving quality of the software). Figure 5.3 shows the process of defect injection and removal.

The task of quality management is to plan suitable quality control activities and then to properly execute and control them so the projects quality goals are achieved. With respect to quality control the terms *verification* and *validation* are often used. *Verification* is the process of determining whether or not the products of a given phase of software development fulfill the specifications established during the previous phase. *Validation* is the process of

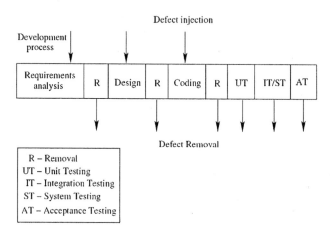

Figure 5.3: Defect injection and removal cycle.

evaluating software at the end of the software development to ensure compliance with the software requirements. Clearly, for high reliability we need to perform both activities. Together they are often called *V&V activities.*

The major V&V activities for software development are inspection and testing (both static and dynamic). The quality plan identifies the different V&V tasks for the different phases and specifies how these tasks contribute to the project V&V goals. The methods to be used for performing these V&V activities, the responsibilities and milestones for each of these activities, inputs and outputs for each V&V task, and criteria for evaluating the outputs are also specified.

5.5.2   Approaches to Quality Management

Reviews and testing are two most common QC activities. Whereas reviews are structured, human-oriented processes, testing is the process of executing software (or parts of it) in an attempt to identify defects. In the *procedural approach to quality management*, procedures and guidelines for the review and testing activities are planned. During project execution, they are carried out according to the defined procedures. In short, the procedural approach is the execution of certain processes at defined points to detect defects.

The procedural approach does not allow claims to be made about the percentage of defects removed or the quality of the software following the procedures completion. In other words, merely executing a set of defect removal procedures does not provide a basis for judging their effectiveness or assessing the quality of the final code. Furthermore, such an approach is highly dependent on the quality of the procedure and the quality of its execution. For example, if the test planning is done carefully and the plan is thoroughly reviewed, the quality of the software after testing will be better than if testing was done but using a test plan that was not carefully thought out or reviewed.

To better assess the effectiveness of the defect detection processes, metrics-based evaluation is necessary. Based on analysis of the data, we can decide whether more testing or reviews are needed. If controls are applied during the project based on quantitative data to achieve quantitative quality goals, then we say that a *quantitative quality management* approach is being applied. Quantitative quality management is an advanced concept, and we only briefly discuss it.

One approach to quantitative quality management is defect prediction. In this approach, the quality goal is set in terms of delivered defect density. Intermediate goals are set by estimating the number of defects that may be identified by various defect detection activities; then the actual number of defects are compared to the estimated defect levels. The effectiveness of this approach depends on how well you can predict the defect levels at various stages of the project. An approach like this requires past data for estimation—an example of this can be found in [97].

Another approach is to use statistical process control (SPC) for managing quality. In this approach, performance expectations of the various QC processes are set, such as testing and reviews, in terms of control limits. If the actual performance of the QC task is not within the limits, the situation is analyzed and suitable action taken. The control limits resemble prediction of defect levels based on past performance but can also be used for monitoring quality activities at a finer level, such as review or unit testing of a module.

5.5.3 Quality Plan

The quality plan for a project is what drives the quality activities in the project. The sophistication of the plan depends on the type of data or prediction models available. At the simplest, the quality plan specifies the quality control tasks that will be performed in the project. Typically, these will be schedulable tasks in the detailed schedule of the project. For example, it will specify what documents will be inspected, what parts of the code will be inspected, and what levels of testing will be performed. The plan will be considerably enhanced if some sense of defect levels that are expected to be found for the different quality control tasks are mentioned—these can then be used for monitoring the quality as the project proceeds.

Much of the quality plan revolves around testing and reviews. Testing will be discussed in detail in a later Chapter. Effectiveness of reviews depends on how they are conducted. One particular process of conducting reviews called inspections was discussed earlier in Chapter 2. This process can be applied to any work product like requirement specifications, design document, test plans, project plans, and code.

5.6   Risk Management

A software project is a complex undertaking. Unforeseen events may have an adverse impact on a projects cost, schedule, or quality. Risk management is an attempt to minimize the chances of failure caused by unplanned events. The aim of risk management is not to avoid getting into projects that have risks but to minimize the impact of risks in the projects that are undertaken.

A risk is a probabilistic event—it may or may not occur. For this reason, we frequently have an optimistic tendency to simply not see risks or to wish that they will not occur. Social and organizational factors also may stigmatize risks and discourage clear identification of them [30]. This kind of attitude gets the project in trouble if the risk events materialize, something that is likely to happen in a large project. Not surprisingly, then, risk management is considered first among the best practices for managing large software projects [26]. It first came to the forefront with Boehm's tutorial on risk management [19]. Since then, several books have targeted risk management for software [29, 78].

5.6.1   Risk Management Concepts

Risk is defined as an exposure to the chance of injury or loss. That is, risk implies that there is a possibility that something negative may happen. In the context of software projects, negative implies that there is an adverse effect on cost, quality, or schedule. *Risk management* is the area that tries to ensure that the impact of risks on cost, quality, and schedule is minimal.

Risk management can be considered as dealing with the possibility and actual occurrence of those events that are not "regular" or commonly expected, that is, they are probabilistic. The commonly expected events, such as people going on leave or some requirements changing, are handled by

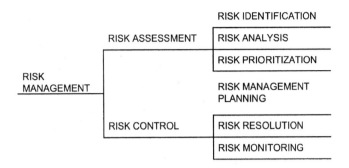

Figure 5.4: Risk management activities.

normal project management. So, in a sense, risk management begins where normal project management ends. It deals with events that are infrequent, somewhat out of the control of the project management, and which can have a major impact on the project.

Most projects have risk. The idea of risk management is to minimize the possibility of risks materializing, if possible, or to minimize the effects if risks actually materialize. For example, when constructing a building, there is a risk that the building may later collapse due to an earthquake. That is, the possibility of an earthquake is a risk. If the building is a large residential complex, then the potential cost in case the earthquake risk materializes can be enormous. This risk can be reduced by shifting to a zone that is not earthquake prone. Alternatively, if this is not acceptable, then the effects of this risk materializing are minimized by suitably constructing the building (the approach taken in Japan and California). At the same time, if a small dumping ground is to be constructed, no such approach might be followed, as the financial and other impact of an actual earthquake on such a building is so low that it does not warrant special measures.

It should be clear that risk management has to deal with identifying the undesirable events that can occur, the probability of their occurring, and the loss if an undesirable event does occur. Once this is known, strategies can be formulated for either reducing the probability of the risk materializing or reducing the effect of risk materializing. So the risk management revolves around *risk assessment* and *risk control*. For each of these major activities, some subactivities must be performed. A breakdown of these activities is given in Figure 5.4 [19].

5.6.2   Risk Assessment

Risk assessment is an activity that must be undertaken during project planning. This involves identifying the risks, analyzing them, and prioritizing them on the basis of the analysis. Due to the nature of a software project, uncertainties are highest near the beginning of the project (just as for cost estimation). Due to this, although risk assessment should be done throughout the project, it is most needed in the starting phases of the project.

The goal of risk assessment is to prioritize the risks so that attention and resources can be focused on the more risky items. *Risk identification* is the first step in risk assessment, which identifies all the different risks for a particular project. These risks are project-dependent and identifying them is an exercise in envisioning what can go wrong. Methods that can aid risk identification include checklists of possible risks, surveys, meetings and brainstorming, and reviews of plans, processes, and work products [78].

Checklists of frequently occurring risks are probably the most common tool for risk identification—most organizations prepare a list of commonly occurring risks for projects, prepared from a survey of previous projects. Such a list can form the starting point for identifying risks for the current project.

Based on surveys of experienced project managers, Boehm [19] has produced a list of the top 10 risk items likely to compromise the success of a software project. Though risks in a project are specific to the project, this list forms a good starting point for identifying such risks. Figure 5.5 shows these top 10 items along with the techniques preferred by management for managing these risks. Top risks in a commercial software organization can be found in [97].

The top-ranked risk item is personnel shortfalls. This involves just having fewer people than necessary or not having people with specific skills that a project might require. Some of the ways to manage this risk is to get the top talent possible and to match the needs of the project with the skills of the available personnel. Adequate training, along with having some key personnel for critical areas of the project, will also reduce this risk.

The second item, unrealistic schedules and budgets, happens very frequently due to business and other reasons. It is very common that high-level management imposes a schedule for a software project that is not based on the characteristics of the project and is unrealistic. Underestimation may also happen due to inexperience or optimism.

The next few items are related to requirements. Projects run the risk

	RISK ITEM	RISK MANAGEMENT TECHNIQUES
1	Personnel Shortfalls	Staffing with top talent; Job matching; Team building; Key personnel agreements; training; Prescheduling key people
2	Unrealistic Schedules and Budgets	Detailed multi source cost and schedule estimation; Design to cost; Incremental Development; Software reuse; Requirements scrubbing
3	Developing the Wrong Software Functions	Organization analysis; Machine analysis; Ops concept forumlation; User surveys; Prototyping; Early user's manuals
4	Developing the Wrong User Interface	Prototyping; Scenarios; Task analysis; User characterization
5	Gold Plating	Requirements scrubbing; Prototyping; Cost benefit analysis; Design to cost
6	Continuing Stream of Requirement Changes	High change threshold; Information hiding; Incremental development
7	Shortfalls in Externally Furnished Components	Benchmarking inspections; Reference checking; Compatibility analysis
8	Shortfalls in Externally Performed Tasks	Reference checking; Preaward audits; Award free contracts; Competetive design or prototyping; Team building
9	Real Time Performance Shortfalls	Simulation; Benchmarking; Modeling; Prototyping; Instrumentation; Tuning
10	Straining Computer Science Capabilities	Technical analysis; Cost benefit analysis; Prototyping; Reference checking

Figure 5.5: Top 10 risk items and techniques for managing them.

of developing the wrong software if the requirements analysis is not done properly and if development begins too early. Similarly, often improper user interface may be developed. This requires extensive rework of the user interface later or the software benefits are not obtained because users are reluctant to use it. Gold plating refers to adding features in the software that are only marginally useful. This adds unnecessary risk to the project because gold plating consumes resources and time with little return. Some requirement changes are to be expected in any project, but sometimes frequent changes are requested, which is often a reflection of the fact that the client has not yet understood or settled on its own requirements. The effect of requirement changes is substantial in terms of cost, especially if the changes occur when the project has progressed to later phases. Performance shortfalls are critical in real-time systems and poor performance can mean the failure of the project.

If a project depends on externally available components—either to be provided by the client or to be procured as an off-the-shelf component—the project runs some risks. The project might be delayed if the external component is not available on time. The project would also suffer if the quality of the external component is poor or if the component turns out to be incompatible with the other project components or with the environment in which the software is developed or is to operate. If a project relies on technology that is not well developed, it may fail. This is a risk due to straining the computer science capabilities.

Using the checklist of the top 10 risk items is one way to identify risks. This approach is likely to suffice in many projects. The other methods are decision driver analysis, assumption analysis, and decomposition [19]. Decision driver analysis involves questioning and analyzing all the major decisions taken for the project. If a decision has been driven by factors other than technical and management reasons, it is likely to be a source of risk in the project. Such decisions may be driven by politics, marketing, or the desire for short-term gain. Optimistic assumptions made about the project also are a source of risk. Some such optimistic assumptions are that nothing will go wrong in the project, no personnel will quit during the project, people will put in extra hours if required, and all external components (hardware or software) will be delivered on time. Identifying such assumptions will point out the source of risks. An effective method for identifying these hidden assumptions is comparing them with past experience. Decomposition implies breaking a large project into clearly defined parts and then analyzing them. Many software systems have the phenomenon that 20% of the modules cause 80% of the project problems. Decomposition will help identify these modules.

Risk identification merely identifies the undesirable events that might take place during the project, i.e., enumerates the "unforeseen" events that might occur. It does not specify the probabilities of these risks materializing nor the impact on the project if the risks indeed materialize. Hence the next tasks are *risk analysis* and *prioritization*.

In risk analysis, the probability of occurrence of a risk has to be estimated, along with the loss that will occur if the risk does materialize. This
is often done through discussion, using experience and understanding of the
situation. However, if cost models are used for cost and schedule estimation, then the same models can be used to assess the cost and schedule risk.
For example, in the COCOMO cost model, the cost estimate depends on
the ratings of the different cost drivers. One possible source of cost risk is
underestimating these cost drivers. The other is underestimating the size.
Risk analysis can be done by estimating the worst-case value of size and all
the cost drivers and then estimating the project cost from these values. This
will give us the worst-case analysis. Using the worst-case effort estimate, the
worst-case schedule can easily be obtained. A more detailed analysis can be
done by considering different cases or a distribution of these drivers.

The other approaches for risk analysis include studying the probability
and the outcome of possible decisions (decision analysis), understanding the
task dependencies to decide critical activities and the probability and cost
of their not being completed on time (network analysis), risks on the various
quality factors like reliability and usability (quality factor analysis), and
evaluating the performance early through simulation, etc., if there are strong
performance constraints on the system (performance analysis). The reader
is referred to [19] for further discussion of these topics.

Once the probabilities of risks materializing and losses due to material-
ization of different risks have been analyzed, they can be prioritized. One
approach for prioritization is through the concept of *risk exposure (RE)* [19],
which is sometimes called *risk impact*. RE is defined by the relationship

$$RE = Prob(UO) * Loss(UO),$$

where $Prob(UO)$ is the probability of the risk materializing (i.e., undesirable
outcome) and $Loss(UO)$ is the total loss incurred due to the unsatisfactory
outcome. The loss is not only the direct financial loss that might be incurred
but also any loss in terms of credibility, future business, and loss of property
or life. The RE is the expected value of the loss due to a particular risk.
For risk prioritization using RE, the higher the RE, the higher the priority
of the risk item.

It is not always possible to use models and prototypes to assess the
probabilities of occurrence and of loss associated with particular events. Due
to the nonavailability of models, assessing risk probabilities is frequently
subjective. A subjective assessment can be done by the estimate of one
person or by using a group consensus technique like the Delphi approach

[20]. In the Delphi method, a group of people discusses the problem of estimation and finally converges on a consensus estimate.

5.6.3 Risk Control

The main objective of risk management is to identify the top few risk items and then focus on them. Once a project manager has identified and prioritized the risks, the top risks can be easily identified. The question then becomes what to do about them. Knowing the risks is of value only if you can prepare a plan so that their consequences are minimal—that is the basic goal of risk management.

One obvious strategy is risk avoidance, which entails taking actions that will avoid the risk altogether, like the earlier example of shifting the building site to a zone that is not earthquake-prone. For some risks, avoidance might be possible.

For most risks, the strategy is to perform the actions that will either reduce the probability of the risk materializing or reduce the loss due to the risk materializing. These are called risk mitigation steps. To decide what mitigation steps to take, a list of commonly used risk mitigation steps for various risks is very useful here. Generally the compiled table of commonly occurring risks also contains the compilation of the methods used for mitigation in the projects in which the risks appeared.

Note that unlike risk assessment, which is largely an analytical exercise, risk mitigation comprises active measures that have to be performed to minimize the impact of risks. In other words, selecting a risk mitigation step is not just an intellectual exercise. The risk mitigation step must be executed (and monitored). To ensure that the needed actions are executed properly, they must be incorporated into the detailed project schedule.

Risk prioritization and consequent planning are based on the risk perception at the time the risk analysis is performed. Because risks are probabilistic events that frequently depend on external factors, the threat due to risks may change with time as factors change. Clearly, then, the risk perception may also change with time. Furthermore, the risk mitigation steps undertaken may affect the risk perception.

This dynamism implies that risks in a project should not be treated as static and must be monitored and reevaluated periodically. Hence, in addition to monitoring the progress of the planned risk mitigation steps, a project must periodically revisit the risk perception and modify the risk mitigation plans, if needed. *Risk monitoring* is the activity of monitoring the status of various risks and their control activities. One simple approach for risk monitoring is to analyze the risks afresh at each major milestone, and change the plans as needed.

5.6.4 A Practical Risk Management Approach

Though the concept of risk exposure is rich, a simple practical way of doing risk planning is to simply categorize risks and the impacts in a few levels and then use it for prioritization. This approach is used in many organizations. Here we discuss a simple approach used in an organization [97]. In this approach, the probability of a risk occurring is categorized as low, medium, or high. The risk impact can be also classified as low, medium, and high. With these ratings, the following simple method for risk prioritization can be specified:

1. For each risk, rate the probability of its happening as low, medium, or high.

2. For each risk, assess its impact on the project as low, medium, or high.

3. Rank the risks based on the probability and effects on the project; for example, a high-probability, high-impact item will have higher rank than a risk item with a medium probability and high impact. In case of conflict, use judgment.

4. Select the top few risk items for mitigation and tracking.

An example of this approach is given in Table 5.5, which shows the various ratings and the risk mitigation steps [97].

As we can see, the risk management part of the project management plan, which is essentially this table, can be very brief and focused. For monitoring the risks, one way is to redo risk management planning at milestones, giving more attention to the risks listed in the project plan. During risk monitoring at milestones, reprioritization may occur and mitigation plans for the remainder of the project may change, depending on the current situation and the impact of mitigation steps taken earlier.

5.7 Project Monitoring Plan

A project management plan is merely a document that can be used to guide the execution of a project. Even a good plan is useless unless it is properly

Seq Num	Risk	Prob.	Impact	Exp.	Mitigation Plan
1	Failure to meet the high performance	High	High	High	Study white papers and guidelines on perf. Train team on perf. tuning. Update review checklist to look for perf. pitfalls. Test application for perf. during system testing.
2	Lack of people with right skills	Med	Med	Med	Train resources. Review prototype with customer. Develop coding practices.
3	Complexity of application	Med	Med	Med	Ensure ongoing knowledge transfer. Deploy persons with prior experience with the domain.
4	Manpower attrition	Med	Med	Med	Train a core group of four people. Rotate assignments among people. Identify backups for key roles.
5	Unclear requirements	Med	Med	Med	Review a prototype. Conduct a midstage review.

Table 5.5: Risk management plan for a project.

executed. And execution cannot be properly driven by the plan unless it is monitored carefully and the actual performance is tracked against the plan.

Monitoring requires measurements to be made to assess the situation of a project. If measurements are to be taken during project execution, we must plan carefully regarding what to measure, when to measure, and how to measure. Hence, measurement planning is a key element in project planning. In addition, how the measurement data will be analyzed and reported must also be planned in advance to avoid the situation of collecting data but not knowing what to do with it. Without careful planning for data collection and its analysis, neither is likely to happen. In this section we discuss the issues of measurements and project tracking.

5.7.1 Measurements

The basic purpose of measurements in a project is to effectively monitor and control the project. For monitoring a project schedule, size, effort, and defects are the basic measurements that are needed [76, 134]. Schedule is one of the most important metrics because most projects are driven by schedules and deadlines. Only by monitoring the actual schedule can we properly assess if the project is on time or if there is a delay. It is, however, easy to measure because calendar time is usually used in all plans.

Effort is the main resource consumed in a software project. Consequently, tracking of effort is a key activity during monitoring; it is essential for evaluating whether the project is executing within budget. For effort data some type of timesheet system is needed where each person working on the project enters the amount of time spent on the project. For better monitoring, the effort spent on various tasks should be logged separately. Generally effort is recorded through some online system (like the weekly activity report system in [96]), which allows a person to record the amount of time spent on a particular activity. At any point, total effort on an activity can be aggregated.

Because defects have a direct relationship to software quality, tracking of defects is critical for ensuring quality. A large software project may include thousands of defects that are found by different people at different stages. Just to keep track of the defects found and their status, defects must be logged and their closure tracked. Once each defect found is logged (and later closed), analysis can focus on how many defects have been found so far, what percentage of defects are still open, and other issues. Defect tracking is considered one of the best practices for managing a project [26]. We will discuss it in Chapter 10.

Size is another fundamental metric because many data (for example, delivered defect density) are normalized with respect to size. The size of delivered software can be measured in terms of LOC (which can be determined through the use of regular editors and line counters) or function points. At a more gross level, just the number of modules or number of features might suffice.

5.7.2 Project Monitoring and Tracking

The main goal of monitoring is for project managers to get visibility into the project execution so that they can determine whether any action needs to be taken to ensure that the project goals are met. Different types of monitoring might be done for a project. The three main levels of monitoring are activity level, status reporting, and milestone analysis. Measurements taken on the project are employed for monitoring.

Activity-level monitoring ensures that each activity in the detailed schedule has been done properly and within time. This type of monitoring may be done daily in project team meetings or by the project manager checking the status of all the tasks scheduled to be completed on that day. A completed task is often marked as 100% complete in detailed schedule—this is used by tools like the Microsoft Project to track the percentage completion of the overall project or a higher level task.

Status reports are often prepared weekly to to take stock of what has happened and what needs to be done. Status reports typically contain a summary of the activities successfully completed since the last status report, any activities that have been delayed, any issues in the project that need attention, and if everything is in place for the next week.

The *milestone analysis* is done at each milestone or every few weeks, if milestones are too far apart. Analysis of actual versus estimated for effort and schedule is often included in the milestone analysis. If the deviation is significant, it may imply that the project may run into trouble and might not meet its objectives. This situation calls for project managers to understand the reasons for the variation and to apply corrective and preventive actions if necessary.

A graphical method of capturing the basic progress of a project as compared to its plans is the cost-schedule-milestone [20] graph. The graph shows the planned schedule and cost of different milestones, along with shows the actual cost and schedule of achieving the milestones achieved so far. By having both the planned cost versus milestones and the actual cost versus milestones on the same graph, the progress of the project can be grasped easily.

The x-axis of this graph is time, where the months in the project schedule are marked. The y-axis represents the cost, in dollars or PMs. Two curves are drawn. One curve is the planned cost and planned schedule, in which each important milestone of the project is marked. This curve can be completed after the project plan is made. The second curve represents the actual cost and actual schedule, and the actual achievement of the milestones is marked. Thus, for each milestone the point representing the time when the milestone is actually achieved and the actual cost of achieving it are marked. A cost-schedule-milestone graph for the example is shown in

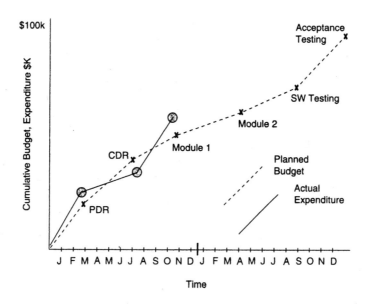

Figure 5.6: A cost-schedule-milestone graph.

Figure 5.6.

The chart shown in Figure 5.6 is for a hypothetical project whose cost is estimated to be $100K. Different milestones have been identified and a curve is drawn with these milestones. The milestones in this project are PDR (preliminary design review), CDR (critical design review), Module 1 completion, Module 2 completion, integration testing, and acceptance testing. For each of these milestones some budget has been allocated based on the estimates. The planned budget is shown by a dotted line. The actual expenditure is shown with a bold line. This chart shows that only two milestones have been achieved, PDR and CDR, and though the project was within budget when PDR was complete, it is now slightly over budget.

5.8 Summary

A proper project plan is an important ingredient for a successful project. Without proper planning, a software development project is unlikely to succeed. Good planning can be done after the requirements and architecture for the project are available. The important planning activities are: process planning, effort estimation, scheduling and staffing planning, quality planning, configuration management planning, project monitoring planning, and risk management.

Process planning generally involves selecting a proper process model and tailoring it to suit the project needs. In effort estimation overall effort requirement for the project and the breakup of the effort for different phases is estimated. In a top-down approach, total effort is first estimated, frequently from the estimate of the size, and then effort for different phases or tasks is determined. In a bottom-up approach, the main tasks in the project are identified, and effort for them is estimated first. From the effort estimates of the tasks, the overall estimate is obtained.

The overall schedule and the major milestones of a project depend on the effort estimate and the staffing level in the project and simple models can be used to get a rough estimate of schedule from effort. Often, an overall schedule is determined using a model, and then adjusted to meet the project needs and constraints. The detailed schedule is one in which the tasks are broken into smaller, schedulable tasks, and then assigned to specific team members, while preserving the overall schedule and effort estimates. The detailed schedule is the most live document of project planning as it lists the tasks that have to be done; any changes in the project plan must be reflected suitably in the detailed schedule.

Quality plans are important for ensuring that the final product is of high quality. The project quality plan identifies all the V&V activities that have to be performed at different stages in the development, and how they are to be performed.

The goal of configuration management is to control the changes that take place during the project. The configuration management plan identifies the configuration items which will be controlled, and specifies the procedures to accomplish this and how access is to be controlled.

Risks are those events which may or may not occur, but if they do occur, they have a negative impact on the project. To meet project goals even under the presence of risks requires proper risk management. Risk management requires that risks be identified, analyzed, and prioritized. Then risk mitigation plans are made and performed to minimize the effect of the highest priority risks.

For a plan to be successfully implemented it is essential that the project be monitored carefully. Activity level monitoring, status reports, and milestone analysis are the mechanisms that are often used. For analysis and reports, the actual effort, schedule, defects, and size should be measured.

With these measurements, it is possible to monitor the performance of a project with respect to its plan. And based on this monitoring, actions can be taken to correct the course of execution, if the need arises.

Overall, project planning lays out the path the project should follow in order to achieve the project objectives. It specifies all the tasks that the project members should perform, and specifies who will do what, in how much time, and when in order to execute this plan. With a detailed plan, what remains to be done is to execute the plan, which is done through the rest of the project. Of course, plans never remain unchanged, as things do not always work as planned. With proper monitoring in place, these situations can be identified and plans changed accordingly. Basic project planning principles and techniques can be used for plan modification also.

Exercises

1. Suppose that the requirements specification phase is divided into two parts: the initial requirements and feasibility study and the detailed requirements specification. Suppose that first part costs about 25% of the total requirement cost. Based on the cost distribution data given earlier, develop a cost estimation model that can be used to predict the cost *after* (a) the feasibility study and (b) the detailed requirements. What are the basic parameters for this cost model? How accurate is this cost model?

2. For the above, if effort is estimated after the feasibility study, some clear risks emerge. What are these and what will be your mitigation plan?

3. Consider a project to develop a full-screen editor. The major components identified are (1) screen edit, (2) command language interpreter, (3) file input and output, (4) cursor movement, and (5) screen movement. The sizes for these are estimated to be 4K, 2K, 1K, 2K, and 3K delivered source code lines. Use the COCOMO model to determine overall effort and schedule estimates (assume values for different cost drivers, with at least three of them being different from 1.0) and effort and schedule estimates for different phases. (b) Use the bottom-up approach given in the chapter to estimate the effort.

4. For the preceding example, assuming that you have a team of 3 people, develop a high level schedule, and a detailed schedule.

5. What are the limitations of the cost estimation models?

6. Assume that testing (and bug fixing) effort is proportional to the number of errors detected (regardless of the nature of error). Suppose that testing detects 90% of the total errors (10% remain undetected). By adding design and code reviews, suppose the cost of the design and coding phases increases

by 10% each (from the base distribution given earlier), and 10% of the errors are detected in design reviews and 10% in code reviews. (So, testing now detects only 70% of errors.) What is the impact on the overall cost of reviews?

7. You want to monitor the effort spent on different phases in the project and the time spent on different components. Design a time sheet or form to be filled in by the programmers that can be used to get this data. The design should be such that automated processing is possible.

8. For a student project being done in a semester course, list the major risks and risk mitigation strategy for them.

9. For a group student project in the software engineering course, device a suitable monitoring plan, and plans for data collection for this monitoring.

10. For a project to manage enrollment and activities in a hobby club, design a suitable quality plan.

11. Suppose a customer gives a project to build parts of a larger system to your group, and other parts to some other groups. Your group has to use an internal tool of the customer, whose new version is to come out soon. Prepare a risk management plan for your project.

12. In the defect injection and removal cycle, suppose the defect injection rates in requirements, design, and coding are 5 defects per KLOC, 10 defects per KLOC, and 60 defects per KLOC respectively. Develop a quality plan and give some removal rates for the different QC tasks in your plan such that the final quality is less than 2 defects per KLOC.

13. For the injection rates given above, suppose the defect removal efficiency of requirement review, design review, unit testing, and system testing are 80% each. What would be the final delivered quality, assuming that these are the only QC tasks performed in the project.

14. In the example above, suppose there are different effort for removing defects in different QC tasks, and that the effort increases as the removal efficiency of the task increases. On what basis would you allocate effort to different QC tasks? (An approach for a general form of this problem can be found in [102].)

Case Studies

Case Study 1—Course Scheduling

Here we present some aspects of developing the project plan. The complete plan is available from the book's Web site. The project has three main modules. The size estimates for these in lines of code are:

$$
\begin{array}{ll}
\text{Input} & 650 \\
\text{Schedule} & 650 \\
\text{Output} & 150 \\
\text{TOTAL} & 1450 = 1.45 \text{ KLOC}
\end{array}
$$

Because this project is somewhat small and straightforward, a waterfall type of process will be used. We use the simple method of determining the total effort from the size based on average productivity. Based on experience and capability of programmers (though no data has been formally collected for this), it is felt that for a project of this size the productivity will be of the order of 600 LOC per PM. From this, we get the effort estimate:

$$ E = 1.45/.6 = 2.4 PM. $$

To get the phase-wise breakup of cost we use the distribution of costs given earlier for COCOMO. The phase-wise cost breakup for the project is

$$
\begin{array}{lll}
\text{Design} & 2.4 * 0.16 & = 0.38 \text{ PM} \\
\text{Detailed Design} & .26 * 2.4 & = 0.62 \text{ PM} \\
\text{Coding and Testing} & .42 * 2.4 & = 1.0 \text{ PM} \\
\text{Integration} & 0.16 * 2.4 & = 0.38 \text{ PM}
\end{array}
$$

The total coding and unit testing effort is one PM, in which the different modules will be coded and tested. We approximate the effort for the different modules in this phase by dividing one PM in the ratio of the sizes of the modules. From this we get the estimate for coding and unit testing of different modules.

The team consists of three persons, all of whom are students who will devote about one-third to one-fourth of their time to the project. A relatively flat team structure will be used with a leader who will allocate tasks to team members. During system design, only the two members will be involved. During detailed design, coding and unit testing, all three will work. There will be no librarian or configuration controller in the project, as it is a small project, and the programmers themselves will do the documentation and configuration management tasks.

The project will produce the following documents (besides the SRS): System design, code, system test plan, and system test report. No unit testing report is needed. Similarly, detailed design is treated as an activity to help the programmer but its output need not be submitted or reviewed. The quality plan will be fixed accordingly.

The final project plan for the project is available from the Web site.

Case Study 2—PIMS

In this case study, as it was felt that the requirements are not fully clear and may evolve, an interactive development process was chosen, with two iterations. What will be done in the two iterations was decided, as given below.

Iteration 1. Basic functionality of PIMS without authentication and without getting current value data from the Web. That is, all modules related to data access and main control, and modules for key computations.

Iteration 2. Enhance to get current data from the Web, build security, installation module, and the alert system.

A bottom-up estimation was done for these two iterations. The effort and schedule estimates for the two iterations were.

- Iteration 1: 192 person days; 27 days.

- Iteration 2: 88 person-days; 10 days.

The assignment to team members was straightforward. The risk management plan was also simple. The complete project management plan is available from the Web site—it is self explanatory.

6

Function-Oriented Design

The design activity begins when the requirements document for the software to be developed is available and the architecture has been designed. During design we further refine the architecture. Generally, design focuses on the what we have called the *module view* in Chapter 4. That is, during design we determine what modules should the system have and which have to be developed. Sometimes, the module view may effectively be a module structure of each component in the architecture. That is, the design exercise determines the module structure of the components. However, this simple mapping of components and modules may not always hold. In that case we have to ensure that the module view created in design is consistent with the architecture.

The design of a system is essentially a blueprint or a plan for a solution for the system. Here we consider a system to be a set of modules with clearly defined behavior which interact with each other in a defined manner to produce some behavior or services for its environment. A module of a system can be considered a system, with its own modules.

The design process for software systems often has two levels. At the first level the focus is on deciding which modules are needed for the system, the specifications of these modules, and how the modules should be interconnected. This is what is called the *system design* or *top-level design*. In the second level, the internal design of the modules, or how the specifications of the module can be satisfied, is decided. This design level is often called *detailed design* or *logic design*. Detailed design essentially expands the system design to contain a more detailed description of the processing logic and data structures so that the design is sufficiently complete for coding.

A *design methodology* is a systematic approach to creating a design by applying of a set of techniques and guidelines. Most design methodologies focus on the system design, and do not reduce the design activity to a sequence of steps that can be blindly followed by the designer.

In this chapter we discuss the function-oriented methods for design and describe one particular methodology—the structured design methodology—in some detail. In a function-oriented design approach, a system is viewed as a transformation function, transforming the inputs to the desired outputs. The purpose of the design phase is to specify the components for this transformation function, so that each component is also a transformation function. That is, each module in design supports a functional abstraction. The basic output of the system design phase, when a function oriented design approach is being followed, is the definition of all the major data structures in the system, all the major modules of the system, and how the modules interact with each other.

In this chapter, we first discuss some general design principles. Then we discuss a notation for expressing function-oriented designs and describe the structured design methodology for developing a design. Then we discuss some verification methods for design and some metrics that are applicable to function-oriented designs. As in most chapters, we will end with the case studies.

6.1   Design Principles

The design of a system is *correct* if a system built precisely according to the design satisfies the requirements of that system.   Clearly, the goal during the design phase is to produce correct designs. However, correctness is not the sole criterion during the design phase, as there can be many correct designs. The goal of the design process is not simply to produce *a* design for the system. Instead, the goal is to find the *best* possible design within the limitations imposed by the requirements and the physical and social environment in which the system will operate.

To evaluate a design, we have to specify some properties and criteria that can be used for evaluation. Ideally, these properties should be as quantitative as possible. In that situation we can precisely evaluate the "goodness" of a design and determine the best design. However, criteria for quality of software design is often subjective or non-quantifiable. In such a situation, criteria are essentially thumb rules that aid design evaluation.

A design should clearly be verifiable, complete (implements all the specifications), and traceable (all design elements can be traced to some requirements). However, the two most important properties that concern designers are efficiency and simplicity. *Efficiency* of any system is concerned with the proper use of scarce resources by the system. The need for efficiency arises due to cost considerations. If some resources are scarce and expensive, it is desirable that those resources be used efficiently. In computer systems, the resources that are most often considered for efficiency are processor time and memory. An efficient system is one that consumes less processor time and requires less memory. In earlier days, the efficient use of CPU and memory was important due to the high cost of hardware. Now that the hardware costs are low compared to the software costs, for many software systems traditional efficiency concerns now take a back seat compared to other considerations. One of the exceptions is real-time systems, for which there are strict execution time constraints.

Simplicity is perhaps the most important quality criteria for software systems. We have seen that maintenance of software is usually quite expensive. Maintainability of software is one of the goals we have established. The design of a system is one of the most important factors affecting the maintainability of a system. During maintenance, the first step a maintainer has to undertake is to understand the system to be maintained. Only after a maintainer has a thorough understanding of the different modules of the system, how they are interconnected, and how modifying one will affect the others should the modification be undertaken. A simple and understandable design will go a long way in making the job of the maintainer easier.

These criteria are not independent, and increasing one may have an unfavorable effect on another. For example, often the "tricks" used to increase efficiency of a system result in making the system more complex. Therefore, design decisions frequently involve trade-offs. It is the designers' job to recognize the trade-offs and achieve the best balance. For our purposes, simplicity is the primary property of interest, and therefore the objective of the design process is to produce designs that are simple to understand.

Creating a simple (and efficient) design of a large system can be an extremely complex task that requires good engineering judgment. As designing is fundamentally a creative activity, it cannot be reduced to a series of steps that can be simply followed, though guidelines can be provided. In this section we will examine some basic guiding principles that can be used to produce the design of a system. Some of these design principles are concerned with providing means to effectively handle the complexity of the design process. Effectively handling the complexity will not only reduce the effort needed for design (i.e., reduce the design cost), but can also reduce the scope of introducing errors during design. The principles discussed here form the basis for most of the design methodologies.

It should be noted that the principles that can be used in design are the same as those used in problem analysis. In fact, the methods are also similar because in both analysis and design we are essentially constructing models. However, there are some fundamental differences. First, in problem analysis, we are constructing a model of the problem domain, while in design we are constructing a model for the solution domain. Second, in problem analysis, the analyst has limited degrees of freedom in selecting the models as the problem is given, and modeling has to represent it. In design, the designer has a great deal of freedom in deciding the models, as the system the designer is modeling does not exist; in fact the designer is creating a model for the system that will be the basis of building the system. That is, in design, the system depends on the model, while in problem analysis the model depends on the system. Finally, as pointed out earlier, the basic aim of modeling in problem analysis is to understand, while the basic aim of modeling in design is to optimize (in our case, simplicity and performance). In other words, though the basic principles and techniques might look similar, the activities of analysis and design are very different.

6.1.1   Problem Partitioning and Hierarchy

When solving a small problem, the entire problem can be tackled at once. The complexity of large problems and the limitations of human minds do not allow large problems to be treated as huge monoliths. For solving larger problems, the basic principle is the time-tested principle of "divide and conquer." Clearly, dividing in such a manner that all the divisions have to be conquered together is not the intent of this wisdom. This principle, if elaborated, would mean "divide into smaller pieces, so that each piece can be conquered separately."

For software design, therefore, the goal is to divide the problem into manageably small pieces that can be solved separately. It is this restriction of being able to solve each part separately that makes dividing into pieces a complex task and that many methodologies for system design aim to address. The basic rationale behind this strategy is the belief that if the pieces of a problem are solvable separately, the cost of solving the entire problem is more than the sum of the cost of solving all the pieces.

However, the different pieces cannot be entirely independent of each other, as they together form the system. The different pieces have to cooperate and communicate to solve the larger problem. This communication adds complexity, which arises due to partitioning and may not have existed in the original problem. As the number of components increases, the cost of partitioning, together with the cost of this added complexity, may become more than the savings achieved by partitioning. It is at this point that no further partitioning needs to be done. The designer has to make the judgment about when to stop partitioning.

As discussed earlier, two of the most important quality criteria for software design are simplicity and understandability. It can be argued that maintenance is minimized if each part in the system can be easily related to the application and each piece can be modified separately. If a piece can be modified separately, we call it *independent* of other pieces. If module A is independent of module B, then we can modify A without introducing any unanticipated side effects in B. Total independence of modules of one system is not possible, but the design process should support as much independence as possible between modules. Dependence between modules in a software system is one of the reasons for high maintenance costs. Clearly, proper partitioning will make the system easier to maintain by making the design easier to understand. Problem partitioning also aids design verification.

Problem partitioning, which is essential for solving a complex problem, leads to hierarchies in the design. That is, the design produced by using problem partitioning can be represented as a hierarchy of components. The relationship between the elements in this hierarchy can vary depending on the method used. For example, the most common is the "whole–part of" relationship. In this, the system consists of some parts, each part consists of subparts, and so on. This relationship can be naturally represented as a hierarchical structure between various system parts. In general, hierarchical structure makes it much easier to comprehend a complex system. Due to this, all design methodologies aim to produce a design that employs hierarchical structures.

6.1.2 Abstraction

Abstraction is a very powerful concept that is used in all engineering disciplines. It is a tool that permits a designer to consider a component at an abstract level without worrying about the details of the implementation of the component. Any component or system provides some services to its environment. An abstraction of a component describes the external behavior of that component without bothering with the internal details that produce the behavior. Presumably, the abstract definition of a component is much simpler than the component itself.

Abstraction is an indispensable part of the design process and is essential for problem partitioning. Partitioning essentially is the exercise in determining the components of a system. However, these components are not isolated from each other; they interact with each other, and the designer has to specify how a component interacts with other components. To decide how a component interacts with other components, the designer has to know, at the very least, the external behavior of other components. If the designer has to understand the details of the other components to determine their external behavior, we have defeated the purpose of partitioning—isolating a component from others. To allow the designer to concentrate on one component at a time, abstraction of other components is used.

Abstraction is used for existing components as well as components that are being designed. Abstraction of existing components plays an important role in the maintenance phase. To modify a system, the first step is understanding what the system does and how. The process of comprehending an existing system involves identifying the abstractions of subsystems and components from the details of their implementations. Using these abstractions, the behavior of the entire system can be understood. This also helps determine how modifying a component affects the system.

During the design process, abstractions are used in the reverse manner than in the process of understanding a system. During design, the components do not exist, and in the design the designer specifies only the abstract specifications of the different components. The basic goal of system design is to specify the modules in a system and their abstractions. Once the different modules are specified, during the detailed design the designer can concentrate on one module at a time. The task in detailed design and implementation is essentially to implement the modules so that the abstract specifications of each module are satisfied.

There are two common abstraction mechanisms for software systems: *functional abstraction* and *data abstraction*. In *functional abstraction*, a module is specified by the function it performs. For example, a module to compute the log of a value can be abstractly represented by the function log. Similarly, a module to sort an input array can be represented by the specification of sorting. Functional abstraction is the basis of partitioning in function-oriented approaches. That is, when the problem is being partitioned, the overall transformation function for the system is partitioned into smaller functions that comprise the system function. The decomposition of the system is in terms of functional modules.

The second unit for abstraction is *data abstraction*. Any entity in the real world provides some services to the environment to which it belongs. Often the entities provide some fixed predefined services. The case of data entities is similar. Certain operations are required from a data object, depending on the object and the environment in which it is used. Data abstraction supports this view. Data is not treated simply as objects, but is treated as objects with some predefined operations on them. The operations defined on a data object are the only operations that can be performed on those objects. From outside an object, the internals of the object are hidden; only the operations on the object are visible. Data abstraction forms the basis for *object-oriented design*, which is discussed in the next chapter. In using this abstraction, a system is viewed as a set of objects providing some services. Hence, the decomposition of the system is done with respect to the objects the system contains.

6.1.3 Modularity

As mentioned earlier, the real power of partitioning comes if a system is partitioned into modules so that the modules are solvable and modifiable separately. It will be even better if the modules are also separately compilable (then changes in a module will not require recompilation of the whole system). A system is considered *modular* if it consists of discreet components so that each component can be implemented separately, and a change to one component has minimal impact on other components.

Modularity is a clearly a desirable property in a system. Modularity helps in system debugging—isolating the system problem to a component is easier if the system is modular; in system repair—changing a part of the system is easy as it affects few other parts; and in system building—a modular system can be easily built by "putting its modules together."

A software system cannot be made modular by simply chopping it into a set of modules. For modularity, each module needs to support a well-defined abstraction and have a clear interface through which it can interact with other modules. Modularity is where abstraction and partitioning come together. For easily understandable and maintainable systems, modularity is clearly the basic objective; partitioning and abstraction can be viewed as concepts that help achieve modularity.

6.1.4   Top-Down and Bottom-Up Strategies

A system consists of components, which have components of their own; indeed a system is a hierarchy of components. The highest-level component correspond to the total system. To design such a hierarchy there are two possible approaches: top-down and bottom-up. The top-down approach starts from the highest-level component of the hierarchy and proceeds through to lower levels. By contrast, a bottom-up approach starts with the lowest-level component of the hierarchy and proceeds through progressively higher levels to the top-level component.

A top-down design approach starts by identifying the major components of the system, decomposing them into their lower-level components and iterating until the desired level of detail is achieved. Top-down design methods often result in some form of *stepwise refinement*. Starting from an abstract design, in each step the design is refined to a more concrete level, until we reach a level where no more refinement is needed and the design can be implemented directly. The top-down approach has been promulgated by many researchers and has been found to be extremely useful for design. Most design methodologies are based on the top-down approach.

A bottom-up design approach starts with designing the most basic or primitive components and proceeds to higher-level components that use these lower-level components. Bottom-up methods work with *layers of abstraction*. Starting from the very bottom, operations that provide a layer of abstraction are implemented. The operations of this layer are then used to implement more powerful operations and a still higher layer of abstraction, until the stage is reached where the operations supported by the layer are those desired by the system.

A top-down approach is suitable only if the specifications of the system are clearly known and the system development is from scratch. However, if a system is to be built from an existing system, a bottom-up approach is more suitable, as it starts from some existing components. So, for example, if an iterative enhancement type of process is being followed, in later iterations, the bottom-up approach could be more suitable (in the first iteration a top-down approach can be used).

Pure top-down or pure bottom-up approaches are often not practical. For a bottom-up approach to be successful, we must have a good notion of the top to which the design should be heading. Without a good idea about the operations needed at the higher layers, it is difficult to determine what operations the current layer should support. Top-down approaches require some idea about the feasibility of the components specified during design. The components specified during design should be implementable, which requires some idea about the feasibility of the lower-level parts of a component. A common approach to combine the two approaches is to provide a layer of abstraction for the application domain of interest through libraries of functions, which contains the functions of interest to the application domain. Then use a top-down approach to determine the modules in the system, assuming that the abstract machine available for implementing the system provides the operations supported by the abstraction layer. This approach is frequently used for developing systems. It can even be claimed that it is almost universally used these days, as most developments now make use of the layer of abstraction supported in a system consisting of the library functions provided by operating systems, programming languages, and special-purpose tools.

6.2 Module-Level Concepts

In the previous section we discussed some general design principles. Now we turn our attention to some concepts specific to function-oriented design. Before we discuss these, let us define what we mean by a module. A *module* is a logically separable part of a program. It is a program unit that is discreet and identifiable with respect to compiling and loading. In terms of common programming language constructs, a module can be a macro, a function, a procedure (or subroutine), a process, or a package. In systems using functional abstraction, a module is usually a procedure of function or a collection of these.

To produce modular designs, some criteria must be used to select modules so that the modules support well-defined abstractions and are solvable and modifiable separately. In a system using functional abstraction, coupling and cohesion are two modularization criteria, which are often used together.

6.2.1 Coupling

Two modules are considered independent if one can function completely without the presence of other. Obviously, if two modules are independent, they are solvable and modifiable separately. However, all the modules in a system cannot be independent of each other, as they must interact so that together they produce the desired external behavior of the system. The more connections between modules, the more dependent they are in the sense that more knowledge about one module is required to understand or solve the other module. Hence, the fewer and simpler the connections between modules, the easier it is to understand one without understanding the other. The notion of coupling [138, 154] attempts to capture this concept of "how strongly" different modules are interconnected.

Coupling between modules is the strength of interconnections between modules or a measure of interdependence among modules. In general, the more we must know about module A in order to understand module B, the more closely connected A is to B. "Highly coupled" modules are joined by strong interconnections, while "loosely coupled" modules have weak interconnections. Independent modules have no interconnections. To solve and modify a module separately, we would like the module to be loosely coupled with other modules. The choice of modules decides the coupling between modules. Because the modules of the software system are created during system design, the coupling between modules is largely decided during system design and cannot be reduced during implementation.

Coupling increases with the complexity and obscurity of the interface between modules. To keep coupling low we would like to minimize the number of interfaces per module and the complexity of each interface. An interface of a module is used to pass information to and from other modules. Coupling is reduced if only the defined entry interface of a module is used by other modules (for example, passing information to and from a module exclusively through parameters). Coupling would increase if a module is used by other modules via an indirect and obscure interface, like directly using the internals of a module or using shared variables.

Complexity of the interface is another factor affecting coupling. The more complex each interface is, the higher will be the degree of coupling. For example, complexity of the entry interface of a procedure depends on the number of items being passed as parameters and on the complexity of the items. Some level of complexity of interfaces is required to support the communication needed between modules. However, often more than this minimum is used. For example, if a field of a record is needed by a procedure, often the entire record is passed, rather than just passing that field of the record. By passing the record we are increasing the coupling unnecessarily. Essentially, we should keep the interface of a module as simple and small as possible.

The type of information flow along the interfaces is the third major factor affecting coupling. There are two kinds of information that can flow along an interface: data or control. Passing or receiving control information means

	Interface Complexity	Type of Connection	Type of Communication
Low	Simple obvious	To module by name	Data
			Control
High	Complicated obscure	To internal elements	Hybrid

Table 6.1: Factors affecting coupling.

that the action of the module will depend on this control information, which makes it more difficult to understand the module and provide its abstraction. Transfer of data information means that a module passes as input some data to another module and gets in return some data as output. This allows a module to be treated as a simple input-output function that performs some transformation on the input data to produce the output data. In general, interfaces with only data communication result in the lowest degree of coupling, followed by interfaces that only transfer control data. Coupling is considered highest if the data is hybrid, that is, some data items and some control items are passed between modules. The effect of these three factors on coupling is summarized in Table 6.1 [138].

6.2.2 Cohesion

We have seen that coupling is reduced when the relationships among elements in different modules are minimized. That is, coupling is reduced when elements in different modules have little or no bonds between them. Another way of achieving this effect is to strengthen the bond between elements of the same module by maximizing the relationship between elements of the same module. Cohesion is the concept that tries to capture this intramodule [138, 154]. With cohesion, we are interested in determining how closely the elements of a module are related to each other.

Cohesion of a module represents how tightly bound the internal elements of the module are to one another. Cohesion of a module gives the designer an idea about whether the different elements of a module belong together in the same module. Cohesion and coupling are clearly related. Usually, the greater the cohesion of each module in the system, the lower the coupling between modules is. This correlation is not perfect, but it has been observed in practice. There are several levels of cohesion:

- Coincidental

- Logical

- Temporal

- Procedural

- Communicational

- Sequential

- Functional

Coincidental is the lowest level, and functional is the highest. These levels do not form a linear scale. Functional binding is much stronger than the rest, while the first two are considered much weaker than others. Often, many levels can be applicable when considering cohesion between two elements of a module. In such situations, the highest level is considered. Cohesion of a module is considered the highest level of cohesion applicable to all elements in the module.

Coincidental cohesion occurs when there is no meaningful relationship among the elements of a module. Coincidental cohesion can occur if an existing program is "modularized" by chopping it into pieces and making different pieces modules. If a module is created to save duplicate code by combining some part of code that occurs at many different places, that module is likely to have coincidental cohesion. In this situation, the statements in the module have no relationship with each other, and if one of the modules using the code needs to be modified and this modification includes the common code, it is likely that other modules using the code do not want the code modified. Consequently, the modification of this "common module" may cause other modules to behave incorrectly. The modules using these modules are therefore not modifiable separately and have strong interconnection between them. We can say that, generally speaking, it is poor practice to create a module merely to avoid duplicate code (unless the common code happens to perform some identifiable function, in which case the statements will have some relationship between them) or to chop a module into smaller modules to reduce the module size.

A module has logical cohesion if there is some logical relationship between the elements of a module, and the elements perform functions that fall in the same logical class. A typical example of this kind of cohesion is a module that performs all the inputs or all the outputs. In such a situation, if we want to input or output a particular record, we have to somehow convey this to the module. Often, this will be done by passing some kind of special status flag, which will be used to determine what statements to execute in the module. Besides resulting in hybrid information flow between modules, which is generally the worst form of coupling between modules, such a module will usually have tricky and clumsy code. In general, logically cohesive modules should be avoided, if possible.

Temporal cohesion is the same as logical cohesion, except that the elements are also related in time and are executed together. Modules that perform activities like "initialization," "clean-up," and "termination" are usually temporally bound. Even though the elements in a temporally bound module are logically related, temporal cohesion is higher than logical cohesion, because the elements are all executed together. This avoids the problem of passing the flag, and the code is usually simpler.

A procedurally cohesive module contains elements that belong to a common procedural unit. For example, a loop or a sequence of decision statements in a module may be combined to form a separate module. Procedurally cohesive modules often occur when modular structure is determined from some form of flowchart. Procedural cohesion often cuts across functional lines. A module with only procedural cohesion may contain only part of a complete function or parts of several functions.

A module with communicational cohesion has elements that are related by a reference to the same input or output data. That is, in a communicationally bound module, the elements are together because they operate on the same input or output data. An example of this could be a module to "print and punch record." Communicationally cohesive modules may perform more than one function. However, communicational cohesion is sufficiently high as to be generally acceptable if alternative structures with higher cohesion cannot be easily identified.

When the elements are together in a module because the output of one forms the input to another, we get sequential cohesion. If we have a sequence of elements in which the output of one forms the input to another, sequential cohesion does not provide any guidelines on how to combine them into modules. Different possibilities exist: combine all in one module, put the first half in one and the second half in another, the first third in one and the rest in the other, and so forth. Consequently, a sequentially bound module may contain several functions or parts of different functions. Sequentially cohesive modules bear a close resemblance to the problem structure. However, they are considered to be far from the ideal, which is functional cohesion.

Functional cohesion is the strongest cohesion. In a functionally bound module, all the elements of the module are related to performing a single function. By function, we do not mean simply mathematical functions; modules accomplishing a single goal are also included. Functions like "compute square root" and "sort the array" are clear examples of functionally cohesive modules.

How does one determine the cohesion level of a module? There is no mathematical formula that can be used. We have to use our judgment for this. A useful technique for determining if a module has functional cohesion is to write a sentence that describes, fully and accurately, the function or purpose of the module. The following tests can then be made [138]:

1. If the sentence must be a compound sentence, if it contains a comma, or it has has more than one verb, the module is probably performing more than one function, and it probably has sequential or communicational cohesion.

2. If the sentence contains words relating to time, like "first," "next," "when," and "after" the module probably has sequential or temporal cohesion.

3. If the predicate of the sentence does not contain a single specific object following the verb (such as "edit all data") the module probably has logical cohesion.

4. Words like "initialize" and "cleanup" imply temporal cohesion.

Modules with functional cohesion can always be described by a simple sentence. However, if a description is a compound sentence, it does not mean that the module does not have functional cohesion. Functionally cohesive modules can also be described by compound sentences. If we cannot describe it using a simple sentence, the module is not likely to have functional cohesion.

6.3   Design Notation and Specification

During the design phase there are two things of interest: the design of the system, the producing of which is the basic objective of this phase, and the process of designing itself. It is for the latter that principles and methods are needed. In addition, while designing, a designer needs to record his thoughts and decisions and to represent the design so that he can view it and play with it. For this, design notations are used.

Design notations are largely meant to be used during the process of design and are used to represent design or design decisions. They are meant largely for the designer so that he can quickly represent his decisions in a compact manner that he can evaluate and modify. These notations are frequently graphical.

Once the designer is satisfied with the design he has produced, the design is to be precisely specified in the form of a document. Whereas a design represented using the design notation is largely to be used by the designer, a design specification has to be so precise and complete that it can be used as a basis of further development by other programmers. Often, design specification uses textual structures, with design notation helping understanding.

6.3.1 Structure Charts

For a function-oriented design, the design can be represented graphically by structure charts. The structure of a program is made up of the modules of that program together with the interconnections between modules. Every computer program has a structure, and given a program its structure can be determined. The structure chart of a program is a graphic representation of its structure. In a structure chart a module is represented by a box with the module name written in the box. An arrow from module A to module B represents that module A invokes module B. B is called the *subordinate* of A, and A is called the *superordinate* of B. The arrow is labeled by the parameters received by B as input and the parameters returned by B as output, with the direction of flow of the input and output parameters represented by small arrows. The parameters can be shown to be data (unfilled circle at the tail of the label) or control (filled circle at the tail). As an example consider the structure of the following program, whose structure is shown in Figure 6.1.

```
main()
{
    int sum, n, N, a[MAX];
    readnums(a, &N); sort(a, N); scanf(&n);
    sum = add_n(a, n); printf(sum);
}

readnums(a, N)
```

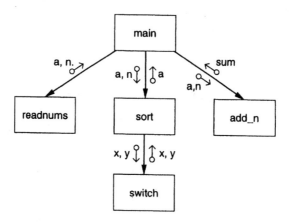

Figure 6.1: The structure chart of the sort program.

```
int a[], *N;
{
    :
}

sort(a, N)
int a[], N;
{
    :
    if (a[i] > a[t]) switch(a[i], a[t]);
    :
}

/* Add the first n numbers of a */
add_n(a, n)
int a[], n;
{
    :
}
```

In general, procedural information is not represented in a structure chart, and the focus is on representing the hierarchy of modules. However, there are situations where the designer may wish to communicate certain procedural information explicitly, like major loops and decisions. Such information can

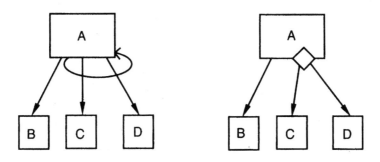

Figure 6.2: Iteration and decision representation.

also be represented in a structure chart. For example, let us consider a situation where module A has subordinates B, C, and D, and A repeatedly calls the modules C and D. This can be represented by a looping arrow around the arrows joining the subordinates C and D to A, as shown in Figure 6.2. All the subordinate modules activated within a common loop are enclosed in the same looping arrow.

Major decisions can be represented similarly. For example, if the invocation of modules C and D in module A depends on the outcome of some decision, that is represented by a small diamond in the box for A, with the arrows joining C and D coming out of this diamond, as shown in Figure 6.2.

Modules in a system can be categorized into few classes. There are some modules that obtain information from their subordinates and then pass it to their superordinate. This kind of module is an *input module*. Similarly, there are *output modules.* that take information from their superordinate and pass it on to its subordinates. As the name suggests, the input and output modules are typically used for input and output of data from and to the environment. The input modules get the data from the sources and get it ready to be processed, and the output modules take the output produced and prepare it for proper presentation to the environment. Then there are modules that exist solely for the sake of transforming data into some other form. Such a module is called a *transform module*. Most of the computational modules typically fall in this category. Finally, there are modules whose primary concern is managing the flow of data to and from different subordinates. Such modules are called *coordinate modules*. The structure chart representation of the different types of modules is shown in Figure 6.3.

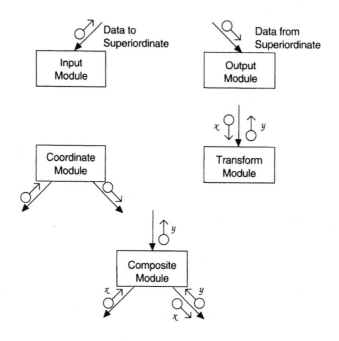

Figure 6.3: Different types of modules.

A module can perform functions of more than one type of module. For example, the composite module in Figure 6.3 is an input module from the point of view of its superordinate, as it feeds the data Y to the superordinate. Internally, A is a coordinate module and views its job as getting data X from one subordinate and passing it to another subordinate, which converts it to Y. Modules in actual systems are often composite modules.

A structure chart is a nice representation mechanism for a design that uses functional abstraction. It shows the modules and their call hierarchy, the interfaces between the modules, and what information passes between modules. It is a convenient and compact notation that is very useful while creating the design. That is, a designer can make effective use of structure charts to represent the model he is creating while he is designing. However, it is not sufficient for representing the final design, as it does not give all the information needed about the design. For example, it does not specify the scope, structure of data, specifications of each module, etc. Hence, it is generally supplemented with textual specifications to convey design to the implementer.

We have seen how to determine the structure of an existing program. But once the program is written, its structure is fixed and little can be done about altering the structure. However, for a given set of requirements many different programs can be written to satisfy the requirements, and each program can have a different structure. That is, although the structure of a given program is fixed, for a given set of requirements, programs with different structures can be obtained. The objective of the design phase using function-oriented method is to control the eventual structure of the system by fixing the structure during design.

6.3.2 Specification

Using some design rules or methodology, a conceptual design of the system can be produced in terms of a structure chart. As seen earlier, in a structure chart each module is represented by a box with a name. The functionality of the module is essentially communicated by the name of the box, and the interface is communicated by the data items labeling the arrows This is alright while the designer is designing but inadequate when the design is to be communicated. To avoid these problems, a design specification should define the major data structures, modules and their specifications, and design decisions.

During system design, the major data structures for the software are identified; without these, the system modules cannot be meaningfully defined during design. In the design specification, a formal definition of these data structures should be given.

Module specification is the major part of system design specification. All modules in the system should be identified when the system design is complete, and these modules should be specified in the document. During system design only the module specification is obtained, because the internal details of the modules are defined later. To specify a module, the design document must specify (a) the *interface of the module* (all data items, their types, and whether they are for input and/or output), (b) the *abstract behavior* of the module (*what* the module does) by specifying the module's functionality or its input/output behavior, and (c) all other modules used by the module being specified—this information is quite useful in maintaining and understanding the design.

Hence, a design specification will necessarily contain specification of the major data structures and modules in the system. After a design is approved (using some verification mechanism), the modules will have to be implemented in the target language. This requires that the module "headers" for the target language first be created from the design. This translation of the design for the target language can introduce errors if it's done manually. To eliminate these translation errors, if the target language is known (as is generally the case after the requirements have been specified), it is better to have a design specification language whose module specifications can be used almost directly in programming. This not only minimizes the translation errors that may occur, but also reduces the effort required for translating the design to programs. It also adds incentive for designers to properly specify their design, as the design is no longer a "mere" document that will be thrown away after review—it will now be used directly in coding. In the case study, a design specification language close to C has been used. From the design, the module headers for C can easily be created with some simple editing.

To aid the comprehensibility of the design, all major *design decisions* made by the designers during the design process should be explained explicitly. The choices that were available and the reasons for making a particular choice should be explained. This makes a design more *visible* and will help in understanding the design.

6.4   Structured Design Methodology

Creating the software system design is the major concern of the design phase. Many design techniques have been proposed over the years to provide some discipline in handling the complexity of designing large systems. The aim of design methodologies is not to reduce the process of design to a sequence of mechanical steps but to provide guidelines to aid the designer during the design process. Here we describe the structured design methodology [138, 154] for developing system designs.

Structured design methodology (SDM) views every software system as having some inputs that are converted into the desired outputs by the software system. The software is viewed as a transformation function that transforms the given inputs into the desired outputs, and the central problem of designing software systems is considered to be properly designing this transformation function. Due to this view of software, the structured design methodology is primarily function-oriented and relies heavily on functional abstraction and functional decomposition.

The concept of the structure of a program lies at the heart of the structured design method. During design, structured design methodology aims to control and influence the structure of the final program. The aim is to design a system so that programs implementing the design would have a hierarchical structure, with functionally cohesive modules and as few interconnections between modules as possible.

In properly designed systems it is often the case that a module with subordinates does not actually perform much computation. The bulk of actual computation is performed by its subordinates, and the module itself largely coordinates the data flow between the subordinates to get the computation done. The subordinates in turn can get the bulk of their work done by their subordinates until the "atomic" modules, which have no subordinates, are reached. *Factoring* is the process of decomposing a module so that the bulk of its work is done by its subordinates. A system is said to be completely factored if all the actual processing is accomplished by bottom-level atomic modules and if non-atomic modules largely perform the jobs of control and coordination. SDM attempts to achieve a structure that is close to being completely factored.

The overall strategy is to identify the input and output streams and the primary transformations that have to be performed to produce the output. High-level modules are then created to perform these major activities, which are later refined. There are four major steps in this strategy:

1. Restate the problem as a data flow diagram

2. Identify the input and output data elements

3. First-level factoring

4. Factoring of input, output, and transform branches

We will now discuss each of these steps in more detail. The design of the case study using structured design will be given later. For illustrating each step of the methodology as we discuss them, we consider the following problem: there is a text file containing words separated by blanks or new lines. We have to design a software system to determine the number of unique words in the file.

6.4.1 Restate the Problem as a Data Flow Diagram

To use the SD methodology, the first step is to construct the data flow diagram for the problem. We studied data flow diagrams in Chapter 3.

However, there is a fundamental difference between the DFDs drawn during requirements analysis and those drawn during structured design. In the requirements analysis, a DFD is drawn to model the problem domain. The analyst has little control over the problem, and hence his task is to extract from the problem all the information and then represent it as a DFD.

During design activity, we are no longer modeling the problem domain, but rather are dealing with the solution domain and developing a model for the *eventual system*. That is, the DFD during design represents how the data will flow in the system when it is built. In this modeling, the major transforms or functions in the software are decided, and the DFD shows the major transforms that the software will have and how the data will flow through different transforms. So, drawing a DFD for design is a very creative activity in which the designer visualizes the eventual system and its processes and data flows. As the system does not yet exist, the designer has complete freedom in creating a DFD that will solve the problem stated in the SRS. The general rules of drawing a DFD remain the same; we show what transforms are needed in the software and are not concerned with the logic for implementing them. Consider the example of the simple automated teller machine that allows customers to withdraw money. A DFD for this ATM is shown in Figure 6.4.

There are two major streams of input data in this diagram. The first is the account number and the code, and the second is the amount to be debited. The DFD is self-explanatory. Notice the use of * at different places in the DFD. For example, the transform "validate," which verifies if the account number and code are valid, needs not only the account number and code, but also information from the system database to do the validation. And the transform debit account has two outputs, one used for recording the transaction and the other to update the account.

As another example, consider the problem of determining the number of different words in an input file. The data flow diagram for this problem is shown in Figure 6.5.

This problem has only one input data stream, the input file, while the desired output is the count of different words in the file. To transform the input to the desired output, the first thing we do is form a list of all the words in the file. It is best to then sort the list, as this will make identifying different words easier. This sorted list is then used to count the number of different words, and the output of this transform is the desired count, which is then printed. This sequence of data transformation is what we have in the data flow diagram.

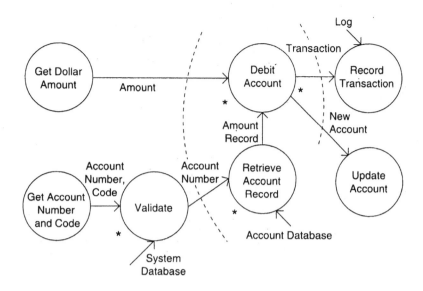

Figure 6.4: Data flow diagram of an ATM.

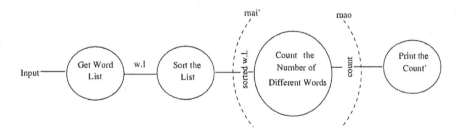

Figure 6.5: DFD for the word-counting problem.

6.4.2 Identify the Most Abstract Input and Output Data Elements

Most systems have some basic transformations that perform the required operations. However, in most cases the transformation cannot be easily applied to the actual physical input and produce the desired physical output. Instead, the input is first converted into a form on which the transformation can be applied with ease. Similarly, the main transformation modules often produce outputs that have to be converted into the desired physical output. The goal of this second step is to separate the transforms in the data flow diagram that convert the input or output to the desired format from the ones that perform the actual transformations.

For this separation, once the data flow diagram is ready, the next step is to identify the highest abstract level of input and output. *The most abstract input data elements* are those data elements in the data flow diagram that are farthest removed from the physical inputs but can still be considered inputs to the system. The most abstract input data elements often have little resemblance to the actual physical data. These are often the data elements obtained after operations like error checking, data validation, proper formatting, and conversion are complete.

Most abstract input (MAI) data elements are recognized by starting from the physical inputs and traveling toward the outputs in the data flow diagram, until the data elements are reached that can no longer be considered incoming. The aim is to go as far as possible from the physical inputs, without losing the incoming nature of the data element. This process is performed for each input stream. Identifying the most abstract data items represents a value judgment on the part of the designer, but often the choice is obvious.

Similarly, we identify the *most abstract output data elements* (MAO) by starting from the outputs in the data flow diagram and traveling toward the inputs. These are the data elements that are most removed from the actual outputs but can still be considered outgoing. The MAO data elements may also be considered the logical output data items, and the transforms in the data flow diagram after these data items are basically to convert the logical output into a form in which the system is required to produce the output.

There will usually be some transforms left between the most abstract input and output data items. These *central transforms* perform the basic transformation for the system, taking the most abstract input and transforming it into the most abstract output. The purpose of having central transforms deal with the most abstract data items is that the modules implementing these transforms can concentrate on performing the transformation without being concerned with converting the data into proper format, validating the data, and so forth. It is worth noting that if a central transform has two outputs with a + between them, it often indicates the presence of a major decision in the transform (which can be shown in the structure chart).

Consider the data flow diagram shown in Figure 6.5. The arcs in the data flow diagram are the most abstract input and most abstract output.

The choice of the most abstract input is obvious. We start following the input. First, the input file is converted into a word list, which is essentially the input in a different form. The sorted word list is still basically the input, as it is still the same list, in a different order. This appears to be the most abstract input because the next data (i.e., count) is not just another form of the input data. The choice of the most abstract output is even more obvious; count is the natural choice (a data that is a form of input will not usually be a candidate for the most abstract output). Thus we have one central transform, count-number-of-different-words, which has one input and one output data item.

Consider now the data flow diagram of the automated teller shown in Figure 6.4. The two most abstract inputs are the dollar amount and the validated account number. The validated account number is the most abstract input, rather than the account number read in, as it is still the input—but with a guarantee that the account number is valid. The two abstract outputs are obvious. The abstract inputs and outputs are marked in the data flow diagram.

6.4.3 First-Level Factoring

Having identified the central transforms and the most abstract input and output data items, we are ready to identify some modules for the system. We first specify a main module, whose purpose is to invoke the subordinates. The main module is therefore a coordinate module. For each of the most abstract input data items, an immediate subordinate module to the main module is specified. Each of these modules is an input module, whose purpose is to deliver to the main module the most abstract data item for which it is created.

Similarly, for each most abstract output data item, a subordinate module that is an output module that accepts data from the main module is specified. Each of the arrows connecting these input and output subordinate modules are labeled with the respective abstract data item flowing in the proper direction.

Finally, for each central transform, a module subordinate to the main one is specified. These modules will be transform modules, whose purpose is to accept data from the main module, and then return the appropriate data back to the main module. The data items coming to a transform module from the main module are on the incoming arcs of the corresponding transform in the data flow diagram. The data items returned are on the outgoing arcs

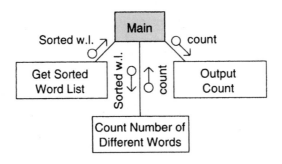

Figure 6.6: First-level factoring.

of that transform. Note that here a module is created for a transform, while input/output modules are created for data items. The structure after the first-level factoring of the word-counting problem (its data flow diagram was given earlier) is shown in Figure 6.6.

In this example, there is one input module, which returns the sorted word list to the main module. The output module takes from the main module the value of the count. There is only one central transform in this example, and a module is drawn for that. Note that the data items traveling to and from this transformation module are the same as the data items going in and out of the central transform.

Let us examine the data flow diagram of the ATM. We have already seen that this has two most abstract inputs, two most abstract outputs, and two central transforms. Drawing a module for each of these, we get the structure chart shown in Figure 6.7.

As we can see, the first-level factoring is straightforward, after the most abstract input and output data items are identified in the data flow diagram. The main module is the overall control module, which will form the main program or procedure in the implementation of the design. It is a coordinate module that invokes the input modules to get the most abstract data items, passes these to the appropriate transform modules, and delivers the results of the transform modules to other transform modules until the most abstract data items are obtained. These are then passed to the output modules.

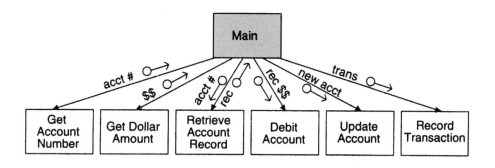

Figure 6.7: First-level factoring for ATM.

6.4.4 Factoring the Input, Output, and Transform Branches

The first-level factoring results in a very high-level structure, where each subordinate module has a lot of processing to do. To simplify these modules, they must be factored into subordinate modules that will distribute the work of a module. Each of the input, output, and transformation modules must be considered for factoring. Let us start with the input modules.

The purpose of an input module, as viewed by the main program, is to produce some data. To factor an input module, the transform in the data flow diagram that produced the data item is now treated as a central transform. The process performed for the first-level factoring is repeated here with this new central transform, with the input module being considered the main module. A subordinate input module is created for each input data stream coming into this new central transform, and a subordinate transform module is created for the new central transform. The new input modules now created can then be factored again, until the physical inputs are reached. Factoring of input modules will usually not yield any output subordinate modules.

The factoring of the input module get-sorted-list in the first-level structure is shown in Figure 6.8. The transform producing the input returned by this module (i.e., the sort transform) is treated as a central transform. Its input is the word list. Thus, in the first factoring we have an input module to get the list and a transform module to sort the list. The input module can be factored further, as the module needs to perform two functions, getting a word and then adding it to the list. Note that the looping arrow is used

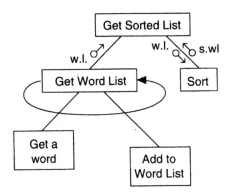

Figure 6.8: Factoring the input module.

to show the iteration.

The factoring of the output modules is symmetrical to the factoring of the input modules. For an output module we look at the next transform to be applied to the output to bring it closer to the ultimate desired output. This now becomes the central transform, and an output module is created for each data stream going out of this transform. During the factoring of output modules, there will usually be no input modules. In our example, there is only one transform after the most abstract output, so this factoring need not be done.

If the data flow diagram of the problem is sufficiently detailed, factoring of the input and output modules is straightforward. However, there are no such rules for factoring the central transforms. The goal is to determine subtransforms that will together compose the overall transform and then repeat the process for the newly found transforms, until we reach the atomic modules. Factoring the central transform is essentially an exercise in functional decomposition and will depend on the designers' experience and judgment.

One way to factor a transform module is to treat it as a problem in its own right and start with a data flow diagram for it. The inputs to the data flow diagram are the data coming into the module and the outputs are the data being returned by the module. Each transform in this data flow diagram represents a subtransform of this transform. The central transform can be factored by creating a subordinate transform module for each of the transforms in this data flow diagram. This process can be repeated for the

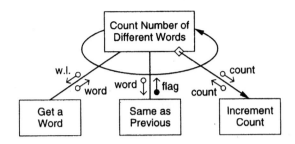

Figure 6.9: Factoring the central transform.

new transform modules that are created, until we reach atomic modules. The factoring of the central transform count-the-number-of-different-words is shown in Figure 6.9.

This was a relatively simple transform, and we did not need to draw the data flow diagram. To determine the number of words, we have to get a word repeatedly, determine if it is the same as the previous word (for a sorted list, this checking is sufficient to determine if the word is different from other words), and then count the word if it is different. For each of the three different functions, we have a subordinate module, and we get the structure shown in Figure 6.9.

It should be clear that the structure that is obtained depends a good deal on what are the most abstract inputs and most abstract outputs. And as mentioned earlier, determining the most abstract inputs and outputs requires making a judgment. However, if the judgment is different, though the structure changes, it is not affected dramatically. The net effect is that a bubble that appears as a transform module at one level may appear as a transform module at another level. For example, suppose in the word-counting problem we make a judgment that word-list is another form of the basic input but sorted-word-list is not. If we use word-list as the most abstract input, the net result is that the transform module corresponding to the sort bubble shows up as a transform module one level above. That is, now it is a central transform (i.e., subordinate to the main module) rather than a subordinate to the input module "get-sorted-word-list." So, the SDM has the desired property that it is not very sensitive to some variations in the identification of the most abstract input and most abstract output.

6.4.5   Design Heuristics

The design steps mentioned earlier do not reduce the design process to a series of steps that can be followed blindly. The strategy requires the designer to exercise sound judgment and common sense. The basic objective is to make the program structure reflect the problem as closely as possible. With this in mind the structure obtained by the methodology described earlier should be treated as an initial structure, which may need to be modified. Here we mention some heuristics that can be used to modify the structure, if necessary. Keep in mind that these are merely pointers to help the designer decide how the structure can be modified. The designer is still the final judge of whether a particular heuristic is useful for a particular application or not.

Module size is often considered an indication of module complexity. In terms of the structure of the system, modules that are very large may not be implementing a single function and can therefore be broken into many modules, each implementing a different function. On the other hand, modules that are too small may not require any additional identity and can be combined with other modules.

However, the decision to split a module or combine different modules should not be based on size alone. Cohesion and coupling of modules should be the primary guiding factors. A module should be split into separate modules only if the cohesion of the original module was low, the resulting modules have a higher degree of cohesion, and the coupling between modules does not increase. Similarly, two or more modules should be combined only if the resulting module has a high degree of cohesion and the coupling of the resulting module is not greater than the coupling of the submodules. Furthermore, a module usually should not be split or combined with another module if it is subordinate to many different modules. As a rule of thumb, the designer should take a hard look at modules that will be larger than about 100 lines of source code or will be less than a couple of lines.

Another parameter that can be considered while "fine-tuning" the structure is the fan-in and fan-out of modules. *Fan-in* of a module is the number of arrows coming in the module, indicating the number of superordinates of a module. *Fan-out* of a module is the number of arrows going out of that module, indicating the number of subordinates of the module. A very high fan-out is not very desirable, as it means that the module has to control and coordinate too many modules and may therefore be too complex. Fan-out can be reduced by creating a subordinate and making many of the current subordinates subordinate to the newly created module. In general the fan-out should not be increased above five or six.

Whenever possible, the fan-in should be maximized. Of course, this should not be obtained at the cost of increasing the coupling or decreasing the cohesion of modules. For example, implementing different functions into a single module, simply to increase the fan-in, is not a good idea. Fan-in can often be increased by separating out common functions from different modules and creating a module to implement that function.

Another important factor that should be considered is the correlation of the scope of effect and scope of control. The scope of effect of a decision (in a module) is the collection of all the modules that contain any processing that is conditional on that decision or whose invocation is dependent on the outcome of the decision. The scope of control of a module is the module itself and all its subordinates (not just the immediate subordinates). The system is usually simpler when the scope of effect of a decision is a subset of the scope of control of the module in which the decision is located. Ideally, the scope of effect should be limited to the modules that are immediate subordinates of the module in which the decision is located. Violation of this rule of thumb often results in more coupling between modules.

There are some methods that a designer can use to ensure that the scope of effect of a decision is within the scope of control of the module. The decision can be removed from the module and "moved up" in the structure. Alternatively, modules that are in the scope of effect but are not in the scope of control can be moved down the hierarchy so that they fall within the scope of control.

6.4.6 Transaction Analysis

The structured design technique discussed earlier is called *transform analysis*, where most of the transforms in the data flow diagram have a few inputs and a few outputs. There are situations where a transform splits an input stream into many different substreams, with a different sequence of transforms specified for the different substreams. For example, this is the case with systems where there are many different sets of possible actions and the actions to be performed depend on the input command specified. In such situations the transform analysis can be supplemented by *transaction analysis.* and the detailed data flow diagram of the transform splitting the input may look like the DFD shown in Figure 6.10.

The module splitting the input is called the *transaction center;* it need

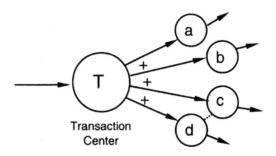

Figure 6.10: DFD for transaction analysis.

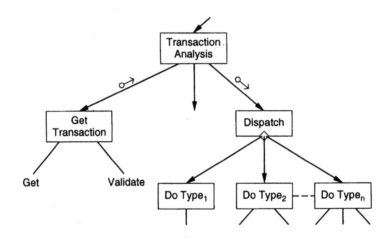

Figure 6.11: Factored transaction center.

not be a central transform and may occur on either the input branch or the output branch of the data flow diagram of the system. One of the standard ways to convert a data flow diagram of the form shown in Figure 6.10 into a structure chart is to have an input module that gets the analyzed transaction and a dispatch module that invokes the modules for the different transactions. This structure is shown in Figure 6.11.

For smaller systems the analysis and the dispatching can be done in the transaction center module itself, giving rise to a flatter structure. For designing systems that require transaction analysis, start with a data flow diagram, as in transform analysis, and identify the transform centers. Factor the data flow diagram, as is done in transform analysis. For the modules corresponding to the transform centers, draw the detailed data flow diagram, which will be of the form shown in Figure 6.11. Choose one of the transaction-centered organizations, either one with a separate dispatch and input module or one with all combined in one module. Specify one subordinate module for each transaction. Temptations to combine many similar transactions into one module should be avoided, as it would result in a logically cohesive module. Then each transaction module should be factored, as is done in transform analysis. There are usually many distinct actions that need to be performed for a transaction; they are often specified in the requirements for each transaction. In such cases one subordinate module to the transaction module should be created for each action. Further factoring of action modules into many detailed action modules may be needed. In many transaction-oriented systems, there is a lot of commonality of actions among the different transactions. This commonality should be exploited by sharing the modules at either the action level or the detailed action level.

6.4.7 Discussion

No design methodology reduces design to a series of steps that can be mechanically executed. All design methodologies are, at best, a set of guidelines that, if applied, will most likely give a design that will satisfy the design objectives. The basic objective is to produce a design that is modular and simple. One way to achieve modularity is to have a design that has highly cohesive modules with low coupling between different modules. In other words, the basic objective of the design activity using a function-oriented approach is to create an architecture, that, if implemented, will satisfy the SRS, and that contains cohesive modules that have low coupling with others. Structured design methodology is an approach for creating a design that is likely to satisfy this objective. Now that we have studied the methodology, let us see how it actually achieves this goal.

The basic principle behind the SDM, as with most other methodologies, is problem partitioning, in which the problem is partitioned into subproblems that can be solved separately. In SDM, at the very basic level, this is done by partitioning the system into subsystems that deal with input, subsystems that deal with output, and subsystems that deal with data transformation.

The rationale behind this partitioning is that in many systems, particularly data processing systems, a good part of the system code deals with managing the inputs and outputs. The components dealing with inputs have to deal with issues of screens, reading data, formats, errors, exceptions, completeness of information, structure of the information, etc. Similarly, the modules dealing with output have to prepare the output in presentation formats, make charts, produce reports, etc. Hence, for many systems, it is indeed the case that a good part of the software has to deal with inputs and outputs. The actual transformation in the system is frequently not very complex—it is dealing with data and getting it in proper form for performing the transformation or producing the output in the desired form that requires considerable processing.

Structured design methodology clearly separates the system at the very top level into various subsystems, one for managing each major input, one for managing each major output, and one for each major transformation. The modules performing the transformation deal with data at an abstract level, that is, in the form that is most convenient for processing. Due to this, these modules can focus on the conceptual problem of how to perform the transformation without bothering with how to obtain "clean" inputs or how to "present" the output. And these subsystems are quite independent of each other, interacting only through the main module. Hence, this partitioning leads to independent subsystems that do not interact directly, and hence can be designed and developed separately.

This partitioning is at the heart of SDM. In the SDM itself, this partitioning is obtained by starting with a data flow diagram. However, the basic idea of the SDM can be effectively used even if one wants to go directly to the first structure (without going through a DFD).

Besides this central idea, another basic idea behind the SDM is that processing of an input subsystem should be done in a progressive manner, starting from the raw input and progressively applying transformations to eventually reach the most abstract input level (what this input subsystem has to produce). Similar is the case with the structure for the subsystems dealing with outputs. The basic idea here is to separate the different transformations performed on the input before it is in a form ready to be "consumed." And if the SDM is followed carefully, this leads to a "thin and tall" tree as a structure for the input or output subsystem. For example, if an input goes through a series of bubbles in the DFD before it is considered most abstract, the structure for this will be a tree with each node having two subordinates—one obtaining the input data at its level of abstraction and the other a transform module that is used to transform the data to the next abstract level (which is passed to the superordinate). Similar effect can also be obtained by the main input module having one input module and then a series of transform modules, each performing one transform. In other words, the basic idea in SDM for processing an input is to partition the processing of an input into a series of transforms. As long as this approach is followed, it is not terribly important how the structure for the input subsystem is obtained.

These ideas that the methodology uses to partition the problem into smaller modules lead to a structure in which different modules can be solved separately and the connections between modules are minimized (i.e., the coupling is reduced)—most connections between modules go through some coordinate modules. These ideas of structuring are sound and lead to a modular structure. It is important that these fundamental ideas behind the SDM be kept in mind when using this approach. It may not be so important to follow SDM down to the smallest detail. This is how experienced designers use most methodologies; the detailed steps of the methodology are not necessarily followed, but the philosophy is. Many experienced designers do not start with a detailed DFD when using the SDM; they prefer to work directly with the structure or with a very high-level DFD. But they do use these principles when creating the structure. Such an approach is recommended only when one has some experience with the SDM.

6.5 Verification

The output of the system design phase, like the output of other phases in the development process, should be verified before proceeding with the activities of the next phase. If the design is expressed in some formal notation for which analysis tools are available, then through tools it can be checked for internal consistency (e.g., those modules used by another are defined, the interface of a module is consistent with the way others use it, data usage is consistent with declaration, etc.) If the design is not specified in a formal, executable language, it cannot be processed through tools, and other means for verification have to be used. The most common approach for verification is design review or inspections. We discuss this approach here.

The purpose of design reviews is to ensure that the design satisfies the requirements and is of "good quality." If errors are made during the design process, they will ultimately reflect themselves in the code and the final system. As the cost of removing faults caused by errors that occur during design increases with the delay in detecting the errors, it is best if design errors are detected early, before they manifest themselves in the system. Detecting errors in design is the purpose of design reviews.

The system design review process is similar to the inspection process, in that a group of people get together to discuss the design with the aim of revealing design errors or undesirable properties. The review group must include a member of both the system design team and the detailed design team, the author of the requirements document, the author responsible for maintaining the design document, and an independent software quality engineer. As with any review, it should be kept in mind that the aim of the meeting is to uncover design errors not to try to fix them; fixing is done later.

The number of ways in which errors can come in a design is limited only by the creativity of the designer. However, there are some forms of errors that are more often observed. Here we mention some of these [52]. Perhaps the most significant design error is omission or misinterpretation of specified requirements. Clearly, if the system designer has misinterpreted or not accounted for some requirement it will be reflected later as a fault in the system. Sometimes, this design error is caused by ambiguities in the requirements.

There are some other quality factors that are not strictly design errors but that have implications on the reliability and maintainability of the system. An example of this is weak modularity (that is, weak cohesion and/or strong coupling). During reviews, elements of design that are not conducive to modification and expansion or elements that fail to conform to design standards should also be considered "errors."

A Sample Checklist: The use of checklists can be extremely useful for any review. The checklist can be used by each member during private study of the design and during the review meeting. For best results the checklist should be tailored to the project at hand, to uncover problem-specific errors. Here we list a few general items that can be used to construct a checklist for a design review [52]:

- Is each of the functional requirements taken into account?

- Are there analyses to demonstrate that performance requirements can be met?

- Are all assumptions explicitly stated, and are they acceptable?

- Are there any limitations or constraints on the design beyond those in the requirements?

- Are external specifications of each module completely specified?

- Have exceptional conditions been handled?

- Are all the data formats consistent with the requirements?

- Are the operator and user interfaces properly addressed?

- Is the design modular, and does it conform to local standards?

- Are the sizes of data structures estimated? Are provisions made to guard against overflow?

6.6 Metrics

We have already seen that the basic purpose of metrics is to provide quantitative data to help monitor the project. Here we discuss some of the metrics that can be extracted from a design and that could be useful for evaluating the design. We do not discuss the standard metrics of effort or defect that are collected (as per the project plan) for project monitoring.

Size is always a product metric of interest, as size is the single most influential factor deciding the cost of the project. As the actual size of the project is known only when the project ends, at early stages the project size is only an estimate. As we saw in Figure 5.1, our ability to estimate size becomes more accurate as development proceeds. Hence, after design, size (and cost) re-estimation are typically done by project management. After design, as all the modules in the system and major data structures are known, the size of the final system can be estimated quite accurately.

For estimating the size, the *total number of modules* is an important metric. This can be easily obtained from the design. By using an average size of a module, from this metric the final size in LOC can be estimated. Alternatively, the size of each module can be estimated, and then the total size of the system will be estimated as the sum of all the estimates. As a module is a small, clearly specified programming unit, estimating the size of a module is relatively easy.

Another metric of interest is complexity, as one of our goals is to strive for simplicity and ease of understanding. A possible use of complexity metrics at design time is to improve the design by reducing the complexity of the modules that have been found to be most complex. This will directly improve the testability and maintainability. If the complexity cannot be reduced because it is inherent in the problem, complexity metrics can be used to highlight the more complex modules. As complex modules are often more error-prone, this feedback can be used by project management to ensure that strict quality assurance is performed on these modules as they evolve. Overall, complexity metrics are of great interest at design time and they can be used to evaluate the quality of design, improve the design, and improve quality assurance of the project. We will describe some of the metrics that have been proposed to quantify the complexity of design.

6.6.1   Network Metrics

Network metrics for design focus on the structure chart (mostly the call graph component of the structure chart) and define some metrics of how "good" the structure or network is in an effort to quantify the complexity of the call graph. As coupling of a module increases if it is called by more modules, a good structure is considered one that has exactly one caller. That is, the call graph structure is simplest if it is a pure tree. The more the structure chart deviates from a tree, the more complex the system. Deviation of the tree is then defined as the *graph impurity* of the design [153]. Graph impurity can be defined as

$$Graph\ impurity = n - e - 1$$

where n is the number of nodes in the structure chart and e is the number of edges. As in a pure tree the total number of nodes is one more than the number of edges, the graph impurity for a tree is 0. Each time a module has a fan-in of more than one, the graph impurity increases. The major drawback of this approach is that it ignores the common use of some routines like library or support routines. An approach to handle this is not to consider the lowest-level nodes for graph impurity because most often the lowest-level modules are the ones that are used by many different modules, particularly if the structure chart was factored. Library routines are also at the lowest level of the structure chart (even if they have a structure of their own, it does not show in the structure chart of the application using the routine).

Other network metrics have also been defined. For most of these metrics, significant correlations with properties of interest have not been established. Hence, their use is limited to getting some idea about the structure of the design.

6.6.2 Stability Metrics

We know that maintainability of software is a highly desired quality attribute. Maintenance activity is hard and error-prone as changes in one module require changes in other modules to maintain consistency, which require further changes, and so on. It is clearly desirable to minimize this ripple effect of performing a change, which is largely determined by the structure of the software. *Stability* of a design is a metric that tries to quantify the resistance of a design to the potential ripple effects that are caused by changes in modules [151]. The higher the stability of a program design, the better the maintainability of the program. Here we define the stability metric as defined in [151].

At the lowest level, stability is defined for a module. From this, the stability of the whole system design can be obtained. The aim is to define a measure so that the higher the measure the less the ripple effect on other modules that in some way are related to this module. The modules that can be affected by change in a module are the modules that invoke the module or share global data (or files) with the module. Any other module will clearly not be affected by change in a module. The potential ripple effect is defined as the total number of assumptions made by other modules regarding the module being changed. Hence, counting the number of assumptions made by other modules is central to determining the stability of a module.

As at design time only the interfaces of modules are known and not their internals, for calculating design stability only the assumptions made about the interfaces need be considered. The interface of a module consists of all elements through which this module can be affected by other modules, i.e., through which this module can be coupled with other modules. Hence, it consists of the parameters of the modules and the global data the module uses. Once the interface is identified, the structure of each element of the interface is examined to determine all the *minimal* entities in this element for which assumptions can be made. The minimal entities generally are the constituents of the interface element. For example, a record is broken into its respective fields as a calling module can make assumptions about a particular field.

For each minimal entity at least two categories of assumptions can be made—about the type of the entity and about the value of the entity. (The assumption about the type is typically checked by a compiler if the programming language supports strong typing.) Each minimal entity in the interface is considered as contributing one assumption in each category. A structured type is considered as contributing one more assumption about its structure in addition to the assumptions its minimal elements contribute. The procedure for determining the stability of a module x and the stability of the program can be broken into a series of steps [151]:

Step 1: From the design, analyze the module x and all the modules that call x or share some file or data structure with x, and obtain the following sets.

$J_x = \{$modules that invoke $x\}$

$J'_x = \{$modules invoked by $x\}$

$R_{xy} = \{$passed parameters returned from x to y, $y \in J_x\}$

$R'_{xy} = \{$parameters passed from x to y, $y \in J'_x\}$

$GR_x = \{$Global data referenced in $x\}$

$GD_x = \{$Global data defined in $x\}$

Note that determining GR_x and GD_x is not always possible when pointers and indirect referencing are used. In that case, a conservative estimate is to be used. From these, for each global data item i, define the set G_i as

$$G_i = \{x | i \in GR_x \cup GD_x\}.$$

The set G_i represents the set of modules where the global data i is either referenced or defined. Where it is not possible to compute G accurately, the worst case should be taken.

Step 2: For each module x, determine the number of assumptions made by a caller module y about elements in R_{xy} (parameters returned from module x to y) through these steps:

1. Initialize assumption count to 0.

2. If i is a structured data element, decompose it into base types, and increment the assumption count by 1; else consider i minimal.

3. Decompose base types, and if they are structured, increment the count by 1.

4. For each minimal entity i, if module y makes some assumption about the value of i, increment the count by 2; else increment by 1.

Let TP_{xy} represent the total number of assumptions made by a module y about parameters in R_{xy}.

Step 3: Determine TP'_{xy}, the total number of assumptions made by a module y called by the module x about elements in R'_{xy} (parameters passed from module x to y). The method for computation is the same as in the previous step.

Step 4: For each data element $i \in GD_x$ (i.e., the global data elements modified by the module x), determine the total number of assumptions made by other modules about i. These will be the modules other than x that use or modify i, i.e., the set of modules to be considered is $\{G_i - \{x\}\}$. The counting method of step 2 is used. Let TG_x be the total number of assumptions made by other modules about the elements in GD_x.

Step 5: For a module x, the design logical ripple effect (DLRE) is defined as:

$$DLRE_x = TG_x + \sum_{y \in J_x} TP_{xy} + \sum_{y \in J'_x} TP'_{xy}.$$

$DLRE_x$ is the total number of assumptions made by other modules that interact with x through either parameters or global data. The design stability (DS) of a module x is then defined as

$$DS_x = 1/(1 + DLRE_x).$$

Step 6: The program design stability (PDS) is computed as

$$PDS = 1/(1 + \sum_x DLRE_x).$$

By following this sequence of steps, the design stability of each module and the overall program can be computed. The stability metric, in a sense, is trying to capture the notion of coupling of a module with other modules. The stability metrics can be used to compare alternative designs—the larger the stability, the more maintainable the program. It can also be used to identify modules that are not very stable and that are highly coupled with other modules with a potential of high ripple effect. Changes to these modules will not be easy, hence a redesign can be considered to enhance the stability. Only a limited validation has been done for this metric. Some validation has been given in [151], showing that if programming practices are followed which are generally recognized as enhancing maintainability, then higher program stability results.

Another stability metric was described in [121]. In this formulation, the effect of a change in a module i on another module j is represented as a probability. For the entire system, the effect of change is captured by the probability of change metrics C. An element $C[i, j]$ of the matrix represents the probability that a change in module i will result in a change in module j. With this matrix the ripple effect of a change in a module can also be easily computed. This can then be used to model the stability of the system. The main problem with this metric is to estimate the elements of the matrix.

6.6.3   Information Flow Metrics

The network metrics of graph impurity had the basis that as the graph impurity increases, the coupling increases. However, it is not a very good approximation for coupling, as coupling of a module increases with the complexity of the interface and the total number of modules a module is coupled with, whether it is the caller or the callee. So, if we want a metric that is better at quantifying coupling between modules, it should handle these. The information flow metrics attempt to define the complexity in terms of the total information flowing through a module.

In one of the earliest work on information flow metrics [84, 85], the complexity of a module is considered as depending on the intramodule complexity and the intermodule complexity. The intramodule complexity is approximated by the size of the module in lines of code (which is actually the estimated size at design time). The intermodule complexity of a module depends on the total information flowing in the module (*inflow*) and the total information flowing out of the module (*outflow*). The inflow of a module is the total number of abstract data elements flowing in the module (i.e., whose values are used by the module), and the outflow is the total number of abstract data elements that are flowing out of the module (i.e., whose values are defined by this module and used by other modules). The module design complexity, D_c, is defined as

$$D_c = size * (inflow * outflow)^2.$$

The term ($inflow * outflow$) refers to the total number of combinations of input source and output destination. This term is squared, as the interconnection between the modules is considered a more important factor (compared to the internal complexity) determining the complexity of a module. This is based on the common experience that the modules with more interconnections are harder to test or modify compared to other similar-size modules with fewer interconnections.

The metric defined earlier defines the complexity of a module purely in terms of the total amount of data flowing in and out of the module and the module size. A variant of this was proposed based on the hypothesis that the module complexity depends not only on the information flowing in and out, but also on the number of modules to or from which it is flowing. The module size is considered an insignificant factor, and complexity D_c for a module is defined as [155]:

$$D_c = fan\_in * fan\_out + inflow * outflow$$

where fan_in represents the number of modules that call this module and fan_out is the number of modules this module calls.

The main question that arises is how good these metrics are. For "good," we will have to define their purpose, or how we want to use them. Just having a number signifying the complexity is, in itself, of little use, unless it can be used to make some judgment about cost or quality. One way to use the information about complexity could be to identify the complex modules, as these modules are likely to be more error prone and form "hot spots" later, if they are left as is. Once these modules are identified, the design can be evaluated to see if the complexity is inherent in the problem or if the design can be changed to reduce the complexity.

To identify modules that are "extra complex," we will have to define what complexity number is normal. Having a threshold complexity above which a module is considered complex assumes the existence of a globally accepted threshold value. This may not be possible, as designs in different problem domains produce different types of modules. Another alternative is to consider a module against other modules in the current design only, instead of comparing the modules against a prespecified standard. That is, evaluate the complexity of the modules in the design and highlight modules that are, relatively speaking, more complex. In this approach, the criteria for marking a module complex is also determined from the current design.

One such method for highlighting the modules was suggested in [155]. Let *avg_complexity* be the average complexity of the modules in the design being evaluated, and let *std_deviation* be the standard deviation in the design complexity of the modules of the system. The proposed method classifies the modules in three categories: error-prone, complex, and normal. If D_c is the complexity of a module, it can be classified as follows:

Error-prone   If $D_c > avg\_complexity + std\_deviation$
Complex   If $avg\_complexity < D_c < avg\_complexity$
                                               $+ std\_deviation$
Normal   Otherwise

Note that this definition of error-prone and complex is independent of the metric definition used to compute the complexity of modules. With this approach, a design can be evaluated by itself, not for overall design quality, but to draw attention to the error-prone and complex modules. This information can then be used to redesign the system to reduce the complexity of these modules (which also results in overall complexity reduction). This approach has been found to be very effective in identifying error-prone modules [155]. In evaluations of some completed projects, it has been shown that error-prone and complex modules together highlight the modules in which most errors occurred [155]. This suggests that for a project, modules thus highlighted during design time point to modules that will be "hot spots" if the design is not improved by reducing their complexity. Another use of this is that even if the complexity of these modules is not reduced (perhaps because the complexity is intrinsic in the problem), identification of error-prone modules can help in quality assurance later; these modules can be required to undergo more rigorous quality assurance.

6.7 Summary

The design of a system is a plan for a solution such that if the plan is implemented, the implemented system will satisfy the requirements of the system and will preserve its architecture. The design activity is a two-level process. The first level produces the *system design* which defines the modules needed for the system, and how the components interact with each other. The *detailed design* refines the system design, by providing more description of the processing logic of components and data structures. A design methodology is a systematic approach to creating a design. Most design methodologies concentrate on system design. During system design a module view of the system is developed, which should be consistent with the component view created during architecture design.

The design process uses the time tested strategy of problem partitioning, through which the complexity of designing large systems is broken into smaller problems that can be solved separately. Effective partitioning depends on the use of abstraction, which permits a designer to concentrate on one module or component at a time by using the abstraction of other modules or components.

Modularity is a means of problem partitioning in software design. A system is considered modular if each component has a well-defined abstraction and if change in one component has minimal impact on other components. Two criteria used for deciding the modules during design are *coupling* and *cohesion*. Coupling is a measure of interdependence between modules, while cohesion is a measure of the strength with which the different elements of a module are related. There are different levels of cohesion, functional and type cohesion being the highest levels and incidental being the lowest. In general, other properties being equal, coupling should be minimized and cohesion maximized.

The structured design method is one of the best known methods for developing the design of a software system. This method creates a structure chart that can be used to implement the system. The goal is to produce a structure where the modules have minimum dependence on each other (low coupling) and a high level of cohesion. The basic methodology has four steps: (1) restate the problem as a data flow graph; (2) identify the most abstract input and output data elements; (3) perform first-level factoring, which is done by specifying an input module for each of the most abstract inputs, an output module for each of the most abstract outputs, and a transform module for each of the central transforms; and (4) factor each of the input, output, and transform modules.

The methodology does not reduce the problem of design to a series of steps that can be followed blindly. The essential goal is to get a clear hierarchical structure. A number of design heuristics can be used to improve the structure resulting from the application of the basic methodology. The basic guiding principles are simplicity, high cohesion, and low coupling.

The most common method for verifying a design is design reviews or inspection, in which a team of people reviews the design for the purpose of finding defects. If the design is expressed in some formal notation, then some amount of consistency checking can be done automatically through the aid of tools.

There are a number of metrics that can be used to evaluate function-oriented designs. Network metrics evaluate the structure chart and consider deviation from the tree as the metric signifying the quality of design. The stability metric we discussed tries to quantify how resistant the design is to the ripple effects caused by changes by explicitly counting the number of assumptions modules make about each other. The information flow complexity metrics define design complexity based on the internal complexity of the module and the number of connections between modules.

Exercises

1. What is the relationship between an architecture and system-level design?

2. Consider a program containing many modules. If a global variable x must be used to share data between two modules A and B, how would you design the modules to minimize coupling?

3. List a set of poor programming practices, based on the criteria of coupling and cohesion.

4. What is the cohesion of the following module? How would you change the module to increase cohesion?

> procedure file (file_ptr, file_name, op_name);
> begin
>   case op_name of
>   "open": perform activities for opening the file.
>   "close": perform activities for opening the file.
>   "print": print the file
>   end case
> end

5. If some existing modules are to be re-used in building a new system, will you use a top-down or bottom-up approach? Why?

6. If a module has logical cohesion, what kind of coupling is this module likely to have with others?

7. What is the difference between a flow chart and a structure chart?

8. Draw the structure chart for the following program:

```
main();
{    int x, y;
     x = 0; y = 0;
     a(); b(); }
a()
{    x = x+y; y = y+5; }
b()
{    x = x+5; y = y+x; a(); }
```

How would you modify this program to improve the modularity?

9. If a '+' or a '*' is present between two output streams from a transform in a data flow graph, state some specific property about the module for that transform.

10. Use the structured design methodology to produce a design for the following:

   (a) A system to convert ASCII to EBSDIC.

   (b) A system to analyze your diet when given your daily intake (and some data files about different types of food and recommended intakes).

   (c) A system to do student registration in the manner it is done at your college.

   (d) A system to manage the inventory at a hardware store.

   (e) A system for a drug store that will manage inventory, keep track of expiration dates, and track allergy records of patients to avoid issuing medicines that might be harmful.

   (f) A system that acts as a calculator with only basic arithmetic functions.

11. Is this statement true: "If we follow the structured design methodology (without applying any heuristics), the resulting structure will always have one transform module for each bubble in the data flow graph"? Explain your answer.

12. Given a structure with high fan-out, how would you convert it to a structure with a low fan-out?

13. Discuss some approaches on how you can use metrics to guide you in design to produce a design that is easy to modify.

14. Design an experiment to study whether the information flow metrics and stability metrics are correlated.

15. If you have all the metrics data available for design, how will you use this data? Specify your objectives, the metrics you will use, how you will interpret the value, and what possible actions you will take based on the interpretation.

Case Studies

Here we discuss how we went about creating the design for Case Study 1 using the structured design methodology. Here we discuss only the process of creating the design; the design document giving the final design is available from the Web site.

The function-oriented design for the case study 2 was not done and hence is not discussed here.

Structured Design

We first discuss creating the design for Case Study 1 (course scheduling) using structured design methodology. We describe how the design was obtained; the details of the design are available from the Web site.

Data Flow Diagram: This is the first step in the structured design method. In our case study, there are two inputs: file1 and file2. Three outputs are required: the timetable, the conflict table, and the explanations for the schedule. A high-level data flow diagram of this problem is given in Figure 6.12.

The diagram is fairly clear. First we get from file1 the information about classrooms, lecture times, and courses, and we validate their format. The validated input from file1 is used for cross-validating information in file2. After validating the file2 input, we get an array of valid course records (with preferences, etc.) that must be scheduled. Because PG courses have to be scheduled before UG courses, these course records are separated into different groups: PG courses with preferences, UG courses with preferences, PG courses with no preference, and UG courses with no preference. This separated course list is the input to the schedule transform, the output of which is the three desired outputs.

The most abstract input and most abstract output are fairly obvious here. The "separated course schedule" is the most abstract input and the three outputs of the schedule transform are the most abstract outputs. There is only one central transform: schedule.

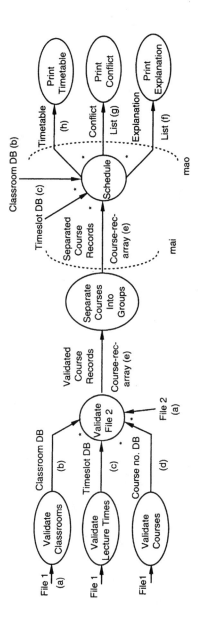

Figure 6.12: Data flow diagram for the case study.

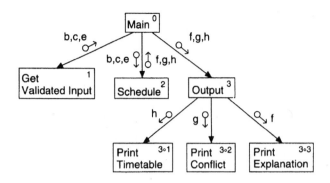

Figure 6.13: First level factoring.

First-Level Factoring: The first-level structure chart can easily be obtained and is shown in Figure 6.13. In the structure chart, instead of having one output module for each of the three outputs, as is shown in the data flow diagram, we have only one output module, which then invokes three output modules for the different outputs.

Factoring the Input and Output Modules: The output module does not need any factoring. According to the design methodology, the input module get_validated_input will have one input module to get the array of validated course records and one transform module to separate into course groups. This input module can then be further factored into three input modules to get different validated inputs from file1, one input module to get data from file2, and one module for validating the file2 data. Because the data from file1 is also needed for the central transform, we modify the structure of the input branch. The structure chart for the input branch is shown in Figure 6.14.

Factoring the Central Transform: Now the central transform has to be factored. According to the requirements, PG courses have to be given preference over UG courses, and the highest priority of each course must be satisfied. This means that the courses with no priority should be scheduled after the courses with priority. Hence, we have four major subordinate modules to the central transform: schedule PG courses with preferences, schedule UG courses with preferences, schedule PG courses with no preferences, and schedule UG courses with no preferences. The structure of the central transform is shown in Figure 6.15.

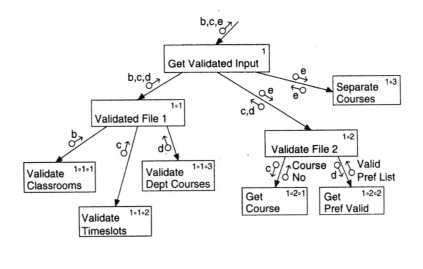

Figure 6.14: Factoring of the input branch.

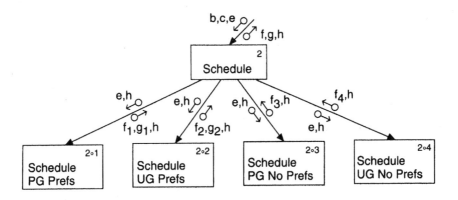

Figure 6.15: Factoring the central transform.

These can then be combined into a structure chart for the system. The overall structure chart is shown in Figure 6.16. This structure chart gives an overall view of the strategy for structuring the programs. Further details about each module will evolve during detailed design and coding.

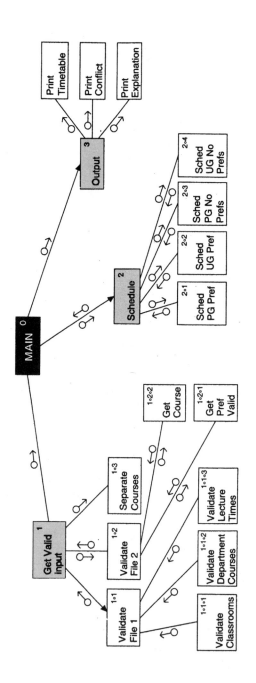

Figure 6.16: Structure chart for the system.

Analysis Using Information Flow Metrics

Based on the structure chart, the design of the system was first specified completely: this required formally specifying the data structures and all the modules. For each module, we specified the purpose of the module, its interface, the modules it invokes, and the estimated size of the module (in LOC). This formed the first version of the design document.

The first thing that could be noted was that when specifying a complete design from the structure chart, the design usually expands. For example, we found that for supporting the module for scheduling the UG courses with preferences (SchedUgPrefs) a lot more needs to be done. The reason is as follows. The UG courses with preferences are scheduled before PG courses with no preferences. However, PG courses are to be given preferences and no two PG courses can be scheduled in the same time slot. Hence, a UG course should not be allotted a slot that makes a PG course "unschedulable." This requires that "safety" of a room and time for a UG course should be checked before allocation.

For this, another data structure was specified. Essentially, a three-dimensional linked list was defined, which contained for each PG course the list of time slots for which it could be allotted, and for each time slot a list of all rooms where it could be allotted was maintained. This structure can be used for checking the safety—an allocation should not make a PG course unschedulable. In addition to this, a lot of utility routines needed to be defined to support the other functions, e.g., sort_rooms(), get_index(), and chk_fmt_course_no().

The complete first version design was then analyzed using information flow metrics described earlier in the chapter. We followed the approach of comparing modules of the design among themselves and then highlight the "error-prone" and "complex modules" (as described earlier). In the case study we used the metric where complexity of a module is defined as $D_c = fan\_in * fan\_out + inflow * outflow$. The definition of error-prone and complex is as given earlier, except that we also use size for classification; the size of the module must also be above average or above (average + standard deviation) for it to be classified as complex or error prone. A locally developed tool called dmetric was used to extract the information flow metrics. The overall metrics and results of the analysis are given here.

```
-----------------------------------------------------------------
OVERALL METRICS
-----------------------------------------------------------------
```

```
#modules: 35  Total size: 1330      Avg. size: 38   Std.Deviation: 27
Total complexity: 595           Avg. complexity: 17   Std.Deviation: 33

Deviation of the structure chart from a tree  = 0
(without considering leaves)


-----------------------------------------------------------------
ERROR-PRONE MODULES
-----------------------------------------------------------------
8) sched_ug_pref
      call_in: 1  call_out: 4   inflow: 5   outflow:13   size:100
      design complexity:   69


-----------------------------------------------------------------
COMPLEX  MODULES
-----------------------------------------------------------------
5) validate_file2
      call_in: 1  call_out: 4   inflow: 4   outflow: 8   size:100
      design complexity:   36

7) sched_pg_pref
      call_in: 1  call_out: 1   inflow: 1   outflow: 6   size:75
      design complexity:    7

13) is_safe_allotment
      call_in: 1   call_out: 0   inflow: 3   outflow: 1   size:80
      design complexity:    3

15) validate_classrooms
      call_in: 1   call_out: 5   inflow: 3   outflow: 7   size:80
      design complexity:   26

16) validate_dept_courses
      call_in: 1   call_out: 3   inflow: 2   outflow: 5   size:75
      design complexity:   13

17) validate_lec_times
      call_in: 1   call_out: 3   inflow: 2   outflow: 5   size:70
      design complexity:   13
-----------------------------------------------------------------
```

This data flow analysis clearly points out that the module to schedule UG courses with preferences is the most complex, with a complexity considerably higher than the average. It also shows that the overall structure is a tree (with a 0 deviation). Hence, we considered the structure to be alright. Based on this analysis, parts of the design dealing with scheduling of UG courses was re-examined in an effort to reduce complexity.

During analysis we observed that much of the complexity was due to the 3-D linked data structure being used for determining safety. Through discussions, we then developed a different approach for determining safety. The idea was that instead of using a separate data structure, before allocating a UG course, we would "simulate" the scheduling of the PgNoPref courses, using the regular function for scheduling these courses. If the number of courses the function sched_pg_no_prefs() returns is the same before and after the planned UG course scheduling, then the current allocation is safe. For this approach, we just have to make sure that is_safe_allotment() invokes sched_pg_no_prefs() with temporary data structures such that the actual timetable is not affected during this "simulation." The design was then modified to incorporate this approach. On analyzing the complexity again, we found that this approach reduced the complexity of the sched_ug_pref() module significantly and the complexity of this module was now similar to complexity of other modules. Overall, we considered the modified design satisfactory.

This demonstrates how highlighting of "hot spots" can be used to focus the attention of the designer or analysts and to improve the quality of the design. Note that this is done before the coding has started, which makes it very efficient from the point of view of cost. For example, if the same decision of changing the method of determining safety was taken after the code was developed, it would require that some parts of the old code be discarded, new code developed, and the design document changed to reflect the new design. All this will require considerably more effort than what was spent to change the design. Metrics-based analysis can also be used for monitoring by the project management; a quick look at the results of complexity and structure analysis will reveal if the structure and complexity are "acceptable" or if the design needs improvement.

The specification of the final design is available from the book's Web site.

7

Object-Oriented Design

Object-oriented (OO) approaches for software development have become extremely popular in recent years. Much of the new development is now being done using OO techniques and languages. There are many advantages that OO systems offer. An OO model closely represents the problem domain, which makes it easier to produce and understand designs. As requirements change, the objects in a system are less immune to these changes, thereby permitting changes more easily. Inheritance and close association of objects in design to problem domain entities encourage more reuse, that is, new applications can use existing modules more effectively, thereby reducing development cost and cycle time. Object-oriented approaches are believed to be more natural and provide richer structures for thinking and abstraction. Common design patterns have also been uncovered that allow reusability at a higher level. (Design patterns is an advanced topic which we will not discuss further; interested readers are referred to [69].)

The object-oriented design approach is fundamentally different from the function-oriented design approaches primarily due to the different abstraction that is used. It requires a different way of thinking and partitioning. It can be said that thinking in object-oriented terms is most important for producing truly object-oriented designs.

During design, as mentioned in the previous chapter, our focus is on what is called the module view in architecture. That is, the goal is to identify the modules that the system should have, and their interfaces and relationships. In OOD, we are therefore identifying the classes that should exist in the software and the relationship between these classes. During architecture design, the component and connector view is typically fixed. A goal of

design is to ensure that the architecture is preserved, and the relationship
between the components and modules is clear.

In this chapter, we will discuss some important concepts that form the
basis of object-orientation. Then we will discuss some concepts that influence
a designer in creating a an object-oriented design (OOD). We'll then describe
the UML notation that can be used while doing an object-oriented design,
followed by an OOD methodology. Then we'll discuss some metrics that
are applicable on OOD and that can be used to evaluate the quality of
design. We do not discuss verification methods, as the design verification
methods discussed in the previous chapter are general methods that can be
used regardless of the approach used for producing the design. Finally, as
with other chapters, we'll end by doing the OO design of the case studies.
Before we proceed, let us understand the relationship between OO analysis
and OO design.

7.1   OO Analysis and OO Design

Pure object-oriented development requires that object-oriented techniques
be used during the analysis, design, and implementation of the system. However, much of the focus of the object-oriented approach to software development has been on analysis and design. Various methods have been proposed
for analysis and design, many of which propose a combined analysis and
design technique. We will refer to a combined method as object-oriented
analysis and design (OOAD). In OOAD the boundary between analysis and
design is blurred. One reason for this blurring is the similarity of basic
constructs (i.e., objects and classes) that are used in analysis and design.
Though there is no agreement about what parts of the object-oriented development process belong to analysis and what parts to design, there is some
general agreement about the domains of the two activities.

The fundamental difference between object-oriented analysis (OOA) and
object-oriented design (OOD) is that the former models the problem domain,
leading to an understanding and specification of the problem, while the latter
models the solution to the problem. That is, analysis deals with the problem
domain, while design deals with the solution domain. However, in OOAD
it is believed that the problem domain representation created by OOA is
generally subsumed in the solution domain representation. That is, the
solution domain representation, created by OOD, generally contains much
of the representation created by OOA, and more. This is shown in Figure

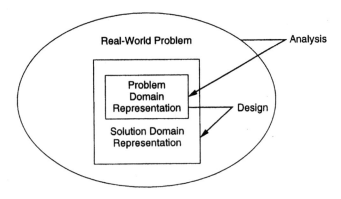

Figure 7.1: Relationship between OOA and OOD.

7.1 [118].

As the objective of both OOA and OOD is to model some domain, frequently the OOA and OOD processes (i.e., the methodologies) and the representations look quite similar. This contributes to the blurring of the boundaries between analysis and design. It is often not clear where analysis ends and design begins. The separating line is a matter of perception. The lack of clear separation between analysis and design can also be considered one of the strong points of the object-oriented approach—the transition from analysis to design is "seamless." This is also the main reason OOAD methods—where analysis and design are both performed—have been proposed.

Despite the difference in perceptions on the boundary between OOA and OOD, one thing is clear. The main difference between OOA and OOD, due to the different domains of modeling, is in the type of objects that come out of the analysis and design processes. The objects during OOA focus on the problem domain and generally represent some things or concepts in the problem. These objects are sometimes called *semantic objects* as they have a meaning in the problem domain [118]. The solution domain, on the other hand, consists of semantic objects as well as other objects. During design, as the focus is on finding and defining a solution, the semantic objects identified during OOA may be refined and extended from the point of view of implementation, and other objects are added that are specific to the solution domain. The solution domain objects include *interface, application*, and *utility* objects [118]. The interface objects deal with the user interface, which is not directly a part of the problem domain but represents some aspect of the solution desired by the user. The application objects specify the control mechanisms for the proposed solution. They are driver objects that are specific to the application needs. Utility objects are those needed to support the services of the semantic objects or to implement them efficiently (e.g., queues, trees, and tables). These objects are frequently general-purpose objects and are not application-dependent.

The basic goal of the analysis and design activities is to identify the classes in the system and their relationships, and frequently represented by class diagrams. However, the system has to support some functionality and behavior. Hence, in addition to concentrating on the static structure of the problem or solution domains, the dynamic behavior of the system has to be studied to make sure that the final design supports the desired dynamic behaviors. Due to this, some dynamic modeling of the system is desired before the design is complete. Whether this type of modeling is part of analysis or design, i.e., where in the overall OOAD process the boundary between analysis and design is, is not generally agreed on.

Another way to view the difference between modeling and design is that in design, a model is built for the (eventual) implementation. As a consequence, implementation issues drive the modeling process during design. While in analysis, comprehension and representation issues drive the process. This also results in OOA sometimes using primitives that are somewhat richer than the ones used in OOD, as the OOD primitives tend to be closely associated with the features of the programming language to be used for implementing the design. The models built during object-oriented analysis form the starting point of object-oriented design, and the model built by OOD forms the basis for object-oriented implementation.

7.2   OO Concepts

Here we discuss the main concepts behind object-orientation. Though these concepts were also used during object-oriented analysis, they are discussed in more concrete terms here, as a design deals with the solution domain and is therefore closer to the final implementation. As the discussion revolves around the OO concepts as supported in programming languages, readers who are very familiar with OO languages and their concepts can omit this section. In the following section we discuss some design concepts.

7.2.1 Classes and Objects

Classes and objects are the basic building blocks of an OOD, just like functions (and procedures) are for a function-oriented design. During design, we are not dealing just with abstractions of real-world objects (as is the case with analysis), but we are also dealing with abstract software objects. During analysis, we viewed an object as an entity in the problem domain that had clearly defined boundaries and behavior. During design, this has to be extended to accommodate software objects.

Encapsulation

In general, we consider objects entities that provide some services to be used by a client, which could be another object, program, or a user. The basic property of an object is *encapsulation*: it encapsulates the data and information it contains, and supports a well-defined abstraction. For this, an object provides some well-defined services its clients can use, with the additional constraint that a client can access the object only through these services. This encapsulation of information along with the implementation of the operations performed on the information such that from outside a set of services is available is a key concept in object orientation. The set of services that can be requested from outside the object forms the *interface* of the object. An object may have operations defined only for internal use that cannot be used from outside. Such operations do not form part of the interface. The interface defines all ways in which an object can be used from outside.

For example, consider an object `directory` of telephone numbers that has add-name(), change-number(), and find-number() operations as part of the interface. These are the operations that can be invoked from outside on the object `directory`. It may also have internal operations like hash() and insert() that are used to support the operations in the interface but do not form part of the interface. These operations can only be invoked from within the object `directory` (i.e., by the operations defined on the object). Note that objects of other classes may also have the same interface (see the discussion on inheritance later).

A major advantage of encapsulation is that access to the encapsulated data is limited to the operations defined on the data. Hence, it becomes much easier to ensure that the integrity of data is preserved, something very hard to do if any program from outside can directly manipulate the data structures of an object. This is an extremely desirable property when building large systems, without which things can be very chaotic. In function-oriented systems, this is usually supported through self-discipline by providing access functions to some data and requiring or suggesting that other programs access the information through the access functions. In OO languages, this is enforced by the language, and no program from outside can directly access the encapsulated data.

Encapsulation, leading to the separation of the interface and its implementation, has another major consequence. As long as the interface is preserved, implementation of an object can be changed without affecting any user of the object. For example, consider the `directory` object discussed earlier. Suppose the object uses an array of words to implement the operations defined on `directory`. Later, if the implementation is changed from the array to a B-tree or by using hashing, only the internals of the object need to be changed (i.e., the data definitions and the implementation of the operations). From the outside, the `directory` object can continue to be used in the same manner as before, because its interface is not changed.

State, Behavior, and Identity

An object has state, behavior, and identity [23, 124]. The encapsulated data for an object defines the *state* of the object. An important property of objects is that this state *persists*, in contrast to the data defined in a function or procedure, which is generally lost once the function stops being active (finishes its current execution). In an object, the state is preserved and it persists through the life of the object, i.e., unless the object is actively destroyed.

The various components of the information an object encapsulates can be viewed as "attributes" of the object. That is, an object can be viewed as having various attributes, whose values (together with the information about the relationship of the object to the other objects) form the state of the object. The relationship between attributes and encapsulated data is that the former is in terms of concepts that may have some meaning in the problem domain: they essentially represent the abstract information being modeled by the components of the data structures.

The state and services of an object together define its *behavior*. We can say that the behavior of an object is how an object reacts in terms of state changes when it is acted on, and how it acts upon other objects by requesting services and operations. Generally, for an object, the defined operations together specify the behavior of the object. However, it should be pointed out that although the operations specify the behavior, the actual behavior also depends on the state of the object as an operation acts on the state and the sequence of actions it performs can depend on the state. A side effect of performing an operation may be that the state of the object is modified. As operations are the only means by which some activity can be performed by the object, it should also be clear that the current state of an object represents the sequence of operations that have been performed on it.

Finally, an object has *identity*. Identity is the property of an object that distinguishes it from all other objects. In most programming languages, variable names are used to distinguish objects from each other. So, for example, one can declare objects s1, s2, ... of class type `Stack`. Each of these variables s1, s2, ... will refer to a unique stack having a state of its own (which depends on the operations performed on the stack represented by the variable).

Classes

Objects represent the basic run-time entities in an OO system; they occupy space in memory that keeps its state and is operated on by the defined operations on the object. A *class*, on the other hand, defines a possible set of objects. We have seen that objects have some attributes, whose values constitute much of the state of an object. What attributes an object has are defined by the class of the object. Similarly, the operations allowed on an object or the services it provides, are defined by the class of the object. But a class is merely a definition that does not create any objects and cannot hold any values. When objects of a class are created, memory for the objects is allocated.

A class can be considered a template that specifies the properties for objects of the class. Classes have [136]:

1. An interface that defines which parts of an object of a class can be accessed from outside and how

2. A class body that implements the operations in the interface

3. Instance variables that contain the state of an object of that class

Each object, when it is created, gets a private copy of the instance variables, and when an operation defined on the class is performed on the object, it is performed on the state of the particular object.

The relationship between a class and objects of that class is similar to the relationship between a type and elements of that type. A class represents a set of objects that share a common structure and a common behavior, whereas an object is an instance of a class. The interface of the objects of a class—the behavior and the state space (i.e., the states an object can take)—are all specified by the class. The class specifies the operations that can be performed on the objects of that class and the interface of each of the operations.

Note that classes can be viewed as *abstract data types*. Abstract data types (ADTs) were promulgated in the 1970s, and a considerable amount of work has been done on specification and implementation of ADTs. The major differences between ADTs and class are inheritance and polymorphism (discussed later). Classes without inheritance are essentially ADTs, but with inheritance, which is considered a central property of object orientation, their semantics are richer than that of an ADT.

Not all operations defined on a class can be invoked on objects of that class from outside the object—some operations are defined that are entirely for internal use. The case for data declarations within the class is similar. Although generally it is fully encapsulated, in some languages it is possible to have some data visible from outside. However, this distinction of what is visible from outside has to be enforced by the language. Using the C++ classification, the data and operations of a class (sometimes collectively referred to as *features*) can be declared as one of three types:

- *Public.* These are (data or operation) declarations that are accessible from outside the class to anyone who can access an object of this class.

- *Protected.* These are declarations that are accessible from within the class itself and from within subclasses (actually also to those classes that are declared as friends).

- *Private.* These are declarations that are accessible only from within the class itself (and to those classes that are declared as friends).

Different programming languages provide different access restrictions, but public and private separation are generally needed. At least one operation is needed to create (and initialize) an object and one is needed to destroy an object. The operation creating and initializing objects is called *constructor*, and the operation destroying objects is called *destructor*. The remaining

```
class List{
    private:
    // data definitions to implement bag
    int list[MAX];
    int size;

    public:
        List() {size = 0};
        add (number); // add a number
        int ispresent (number); //check if number is present
        int delete (number); // delete a number, if present
}
```

Figure 7.2: Class `List` of numbers.

operations can be broadly divided into two categories: modifiers and value-ops. Modifiers are operations that modify the state of the object, while value-ops are operations that access the object state but do not alter it. The operations defined on a class are also called *methods* of that class.

When a client requests some operations on an object, the request is actually bound to a method defined on the class of the object. Then that method is executed, using the state of the object on which the operation is to be executed. In other words, the object itself provides the state while the class provides the actual procedure for performing the operation on the object.

An Example

An example will illustrate these concepts. Suppose we need to have an object that represents a list of integers. The list consists of the numbers we put in it. We want it to be such that we can check if a number exists, and add or remove a number. In C++, the class definition List (to be used for obtaining the object list) could be something like Figure 7.2.

With this definition, a particular list, list, can be created by declaring List list. We can declare as many objects of the type List as we want. Whenever an object is declared of the type List, the constructor operator List() is executed, which sets the size of that list to 0. In C++, the operator with the same name as the name of the class is the constructor operator invoked to initialize the object whenever the object is created by declaration. We can add a number n to this bag by invoking list.add(n). The history of whatever numbers we add to list is preserved within the list (in its private data members). Much later, when we want to check if a number is present, it will return that the number is present if at any time in the past the number was added to list and it has not been deleted.

Note that the fact that the list is implemented as an array and a size pointer is not visible from outside. Other programs use lists by declaring objects of the type List and then performing operations on them. If at a later time, due to efficiency reasons we want to change the implementation of List to use a binary search tree, we will have to change the data structures and the code of the operations. However, no change needs to be made to the programs that declare and use various lists.

In C++, the interface of the object is whatever is defined as *public*. Generally, it will contain only the operations. The declarations in the private part can only be used from within the object; they cannot be accessed from outside. If some function is declared as private, then that function cannot be invoked from outside; it can only be used by the other operations defined on the class. The code for a function defined in a class can either be given with the definition of the function interface (as was done with the constructor List()) or defined elsewhere. If it is defined elsewhere, the definition has to be prefixed with the class name. For example, the function add(n) will be declared as List::add(int n).

7.2.2   Relationships Among Objects

An object, as a stand-alone entity, has very limited capabilities—it can only provide the services defined on it. Any complex system will be composed of many objects of different classes, and these objects will interact with each other so that the overall system objectives are met. In object-oriented systems, an object interacts with another by sending a *message* to the object to perform some service it provides. On receiving the message, the object invokes the requested service or the method and sends the result, if needed. Frequently, the object providing the service is called the *server* and the object requesting the service is called the *client*. This form of client-server interaction is a direct fall out of encapsulation and abstraction supported by objects.

If an object invokes some services in other objects, we can say that the two objects are *related* in some way to each other. All objects in a system are not related to all other objects. In fact, in most programming languages, an object cannot even access all objects, but can access only those objects that have been explicitly programmed or located for this purpose. During design, which objects are related has to be clearly defined so that the system can be properly implemented.

If an object uses some services of another object, there is an *association* between the two objects. This association is also called a *link*—a link exists from one object to another if the object uses some services of the other object. Links frequently show up as pointers when programming. A link captures the fact that a message is flowing from one object to another. However, when a link exists, though the message flows in the direction of the link, information can flow in both directions (e.g., the server may return some results).

With associations comes the issue of visibility, that is, which object is visible to which. This is an issue that is very pertinent for implementation and therefore comes up during design. However, this is not an important issue during analysis and is therefore rarely dealt with during OOA. The basic issue here is that if there is a link from object A to object B, for A to be able to send a message to B, B must be visible to A in the final program. There are different ways to provide this visibility. Some of the important possibilities are [23]:

- The supplier object is global to the client.

- The supplier object is a parameter to some operation of the client that sends the message.

- The supplier object is a part of the client object.

- The supplier object is locally declared in some operation.

Each of these has some consequences. For example, if the supplier object is a global object to the client, then the scoping of languages may make the client visible to many other objects. This is, in general, not very desirable, and should be done only when there is common information that many different classes need. If the supplier object is a parameter of a method, then the intention is to show that the object belongs elsewhere, and this object may access it only through this method. If the supplier object is a part of the client, it means that the supplier object is declared as a data member of this class. This implies that when the life of the client object finishes, the supplier object is also destroyed. This clearly can have implications on sharing of objects and services. Overall, how an object is made visible to an object that needs to access it is an important design issue to be kept in mind when designing associations.

If the supplier object is declared in the client object, there are different ways to implement associations. They can be implemented by a pointer in one of the objects (generally the client object) to the other object. The problem with this approach comes if the link is to be traversed in the reverse direction from the object to which it is pointed. For this, a search needs to be performed on all existing objects of the class with which this class has an association to find which object has the pointer to this object. Hence, this method of implementation should be used only if it is clear that the application is such that the reverse traversal of the link will never be needed.

Another way of implementing the association is by making the link bidirectional, which is what links generally mean in modeling. This can be done by keeping a pointer to the other object in each of the two objects. This is more expensive in terms of storage, but it solves the problem. However, care must be taken to see that the links are consistent; whenever one of the pointers is modified, the other pointer needs to be modified accordingly.

Yet another way of implementing association is to create a new object, whose only duty is to keep track of the links between objects. This approach separates the link maintenance job from the two objects. This is useful when there are many links. Each object will register its link with this special-purpose object.

Links between objects capture the client/server type of relationship. Another type of relationship between objects is *aggregation*, which reflects the whole/part-of relationship.   Though not necessary, aggregation generally implies containment. That is, if an object A is an aggregation of objects B and C, then objects B and C will generally be within object A (though there are situations where the conceptual relationship of aggregation may not get reflected as actual containment of objects). The main implication of this is that a contained object cannot survive without its containing object. With links, that is not the case. An example of aggregation in C++ notation is shown next:

```
class Disk {
    private:
        Track *tracks;
        disk information
            :
};
```

```
class Track {
        private:
                Sector sectors[MAX];
                            :
};

Class Sector {
        private:
                        :
}
```

In this example, a class of type `Disk` is declared, which specifies that any object of this type will have within it a pointer to another object of class `Track`, and this pointer is private information of the object that cannot be accessed from outside the object. The definition of the class `Track` states that each object of this type will have an array of elements of class `Sector` within it as private data members. The example captures the fact that a disk consists of many tracks, and each track contains many sectors. As shown by class definitions, aggregation can be implemented by declaring the parts as objects within the class, as is done while defining the class `Track`. Or it can be implemented as a pointer to the part, as is done while defining `Disk`. The latter method is also used for defining aggregation; hence representing aggregation is used only for efficiency reasons or if the object is to be accessed by many other objects outside the container object.

7.2.3   Inheritance and Polymorphism

Inheritance is a concept unique to object orientation. Some of the other concepts, such as information hiding, can be supported by non-object-oriented languages through self-discipline, but inheritance cannot generally be supported by such languages. It is also the concept central to many of the arguments claiming that software reuse can be better supported with object orientation.

Inheritance is a relation between classes that allows for definition and implementation of one class based on the definition of existing classes [107]. Let us try to understand this better. When a class B inherits from another class A, B is referred to as the *subclass* or the *derived class* and A is referred to as the *superclass* or the *base class*. In general, a subclass B will have two parts: a derived part and an incremental part [107]. The derived part

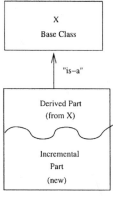

Figure 7.3: Inheritance.

is the part inherited from A and the incremental part is the new code and definitions that have been specifically added for B. This is shown in Figure 7.3 [107]. Objects of type B have the derived part as well as the incremental part. Hence, by defining only the incremental part and inheriting the derived part from an existing class, we can define objects that contain both.

Inheritance is often called an "is-a" relation, implying that an object of type B is also an instance of type A. That is, an instance of a subclass, though more than an instance of the superclass, is also an instance of the superclass.

In general, an inherited feature of A may be redefined in various forms in B. This redefinition may change the visibility of the operation (e.g., a public operation of A may be made private in B), changed (e.g., by defining a different sequence of instructions for this operation), renamed, voided, and so on.

The inheritance relation between classes forms a hierarchy. As inheritance represents an "is-a" relation, it is important that the hierarchy represent a structure present in the application domain and is not created simply to reuse some parts of an existing class. That is, the hierarchy should be such that an object of a class is also an object of all its super classes in the problem domain.

The power of inheritance lies in the fact that all common features of the subclasses can be accumulated in the superclass. In other words, a feature is placed in the higher level of abstractions. Once this is done, such features can be inherited from the parent class and used in the subclass directly.

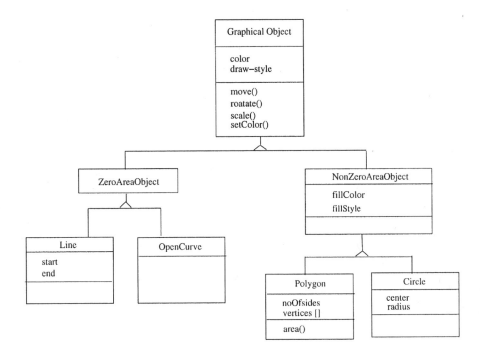

Figure 7.4: An inheritance example.

This implies that if there are many abstract class definitions available, when a new class is needed, it is possible that the new class is a specialization of one or more of the existing classes. In that case, the existing class can be tailored through inheritance to define the new class.

Inheritance promotes reuse by defining the common operations of the subclasses in a superclass. However, inheritance makes the subclasses dependent on the superclass, and a change in the superclass will directly affect the subclasses that inherit from it. As classes may change as design is refined, with each change in a class, its impact on the subclasses will also have to be analyzed. This also has an impact on the testing of classes. We will discuss the issue of testing later in the book.

Let us illustrate inheritance through the use of an example. Consider a graphics package that has the class GraphicalObject representing all graphical objects. A graphical object can have a zero area or a non-zero area, giving two subclasses ZeroAreaObject and NonZeroAreaObject. Line and Curve are two specific object classes of the first category, and Polygon and Circle are two specific object classes of the latter category. This hierarchy of classes is shown in Figure 7.4.

As we can see, the `GraphicalObject` has attributes of color and draw-style (which represents the style of drawing the figure)—both of which each graphical object has. It has many operations defined on it—move(), rotate(), scale(), etc.—the ones that are needed for every object by the graphics package. Note, however, that even though operations like rotate() and scale() are defined for an object, they are totally conceptual in that their exact specification depends on the nature of the object (e.g., rotate() on a circle has to do different things than rotate() on a line). Hence, these operations have to be defined for each object. In C++, such operations that are declared in a superclass and redefined in a subclass are declared as virtual in the superclass. If an operation specified in a class is always redefined in its subclass, then the operation can be defined as *pure virtual* (in C++, this is done by equating it to 0), implying that the operation has no body. The implication of existence of these operations is that no objects of this class can be created, as some of the operations declared in the class are not defined and hence cannot be performed. Such a class is sometimes called an *abstract base class*. The C++ class skeletons for this hierarchy are shown next:

```
class GraphicalObject {
    protected:
        unsigned int color;
        unsigned int draw_style;
    public:
        virtual void move( Point &newLocation );
        virtual void rotate(double angle );
        virtual void scale( double XScale , double YScale);
        void setColor( unsigned int col );
        void setDrawStyle( unsigned int style );
};

class ZeroAreaObject: public GraphicalObject {};

class NonZeroAreaObject: public  GraphicalObject {
    protected:
        unsigned int fillColor;
        unsigned int fillStyle;
    public:
        virtual fill();
};

class Line: public ZeroAreaObject {
```

```
    private:
        Point start, end;
    public:
        int length();
        Point &midPoint();
        // Inherited virtual features are given definition here
        void move(Point &newLocation );
        void rotate( double angle );
        void scale( double XScale, double YScale);
};

class OpenCurve: public ZeroAreaObject {
    private:
        Point *controlPoints;
    public:
        // Inherited virtual features are given definition here
};

class Polygon: public NonZeroAreaObject {
    private:
        Point *vertices;
        unsigned int noOfSides;
    public:
        double area();
        // Inherited virtual features are defined here
};

class Circle: public NonZeroAreaObject {
    private:
        Point centre;
        unsigned int radius;
    public:
        double area();
        // Inherited virtual features are defined here
};
```

Inheritance can be broadly classified as being of two types: strict inheritance and nonstrict inheritance [136]. In *strict inheritance* a subclass takes all the features from the parent class and adds additional features to specialize it. That is, all data members and operations available in the base class are also available in the derived class. This form supports the "is-a" relation and is the easiest form of inheritance. *Nonstrict inheritance* occurs when the sub-

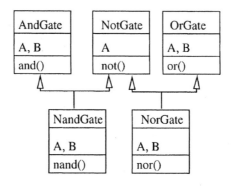

Figure 7.5: Multiple inheritance.

class does not have all the features of the parent class or some features have been redefined. This form of inheritance has consequences in the dynamic behavior and complicates testing.

A class hierarchy need not be a simple tree structure. It may be a graph, which implies that a class may inherit from multiple classes. This type of inheritance, when a subclass inherits from many superclasses, is called *multiple inheritance*. Consider part of the class hierarchy of logic gates for a system for simulating digital logic of circuits as shown in Figure 7.5. In this example, there are separate classes to represent And gates, Nor gates, and Or gates. The class for representing Nand gates inherits from both the class for And gates and the class for Not gates. That is, all the definitions (instances and operations) that have been declared as public (or protected) in the classes NotGate and AndGate are available for use to the class NandGate. Similarly, the class NorGate inherits from the OrGate and NotGate. Like in regular inheritance, a subclass can redefine any feature if it desires.

Multiple inheritance brings in some new issues. First, some features of two-parent classes may have the same name. So, for example, there may be an operation $O()$ in class A and class B. If a class C inherits from class A and class B, then when $O()$ is invoked from an object of class C, if $O()$ is not defined locally within C, it is not clear from where the definition of $O()$ should be taken—from class A or from class B. This ambiguity does not arise if there is no multiple inheritance; the operation of the closest ancestor in which $O()$ is defined is executed. Different language mechanisms or rules can be used to resolve this ambiguity. In C++, when such an ambiguity arises, the programmer has to resolve it by explicitly specifying the superclass from which the definition of the feature is to be taken.

Multiple inheritance also brings in the possibility of *repeated inheritance*,

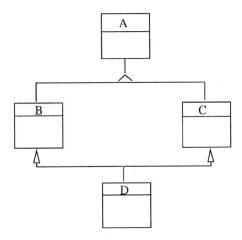

Figure 7.6: Repeated inheritance.

where a class inherits more than once from the same class [136]. For example, consider the situation shown in Figure 7.6 where classes B and C inherit from class A and class D inherits from both B and C. A situation like this means that effectively class D is inheriting twice from A—once through B and once through C. This form of inheritance is even more complex, as features of A may have been renamed in B and C, and can lead to run-time errors.

Due to the complexity that comes with multiple inheritance and its variations and the possibility of confusion that comes with them, it is generally advisable to avoid their usage.

Inheritance brings in *polymorphism*, a general concept widely used in type theory, that deals with the ability of an object to be of different types. In OOD, polymorphism comes in the form that a reference in an OO program can refer to objects of different types at different times. Here we are not talking about "type coercion," which is allowed in languages like C; these are features that can be avoided if desired. In object-oriented systems, with inheritance, polymorphism cannot be avoided—it must be supported. The reason is the "is-a" relation supported by inheritance—an object x declared to be of class B is also an object of any class A that is the superclass of B. Hence, anywhere an instance of A is expected, x can be used.

With polymorphism, an entity has a static type and a dynamic type [107]. The static type of an object is the type of which the object is declared in the program text, and it remains unchanged. The dynamic type of an entity, on the other hand, can change from time to time and is known only at reference time. Once an entity is declared, at compile time the set of types that this entity belongs to can be determined from the inheritance hierarchy that has been defined. The dynamic type of the object will be one of this set, but the actual dynamic type will be defined at the time of reference of the object. In the preceding example, the static type of x is B. Initially, its dynamic type is also B. Suppose an object y is declared of type A, and in some sequence of instructions there is an instruction $x := y$. Due to the "is-a" relation between A and B, this is a valid statement. After this statement is executed, the dynamic type of x will change to A (though its static type remains B). This type of polymorphism is called *object polymorphism* [136], in which wherever an object of a superclass can be used, objects of subclasses can be used.

This type of polymorphism requires *dynamic binding* of operations, which brings in *feature polymorphism*. Dynamic binding means that the code associated with a given procedure call is not known until the moment of the call [107]. Let us illustrate with an example. Suppose x is a polymorphic reference whose static type is B but whose dynamic type could be either A or B. Suppose that an operation O is defined in the class A, which is redefined in the class B. Now when the operation O is invoked on x, it is not known statically what code will be executed. That is, the code to be executed for the statement $x.O$ is decided at run time, depending on the dynamic type of x—if the dynamic type is A, the code for the operation O in class A will be executed; if the dynamic type is B, the code for operation O in class B will be executed. This dynamic binding can be used quite effectively during application development to reduce the size of the code. For example, take the case of the graphical object hierarchy discussed earlier. In an application, suppose the elements of a figure are stored in an array A (of `GraphicalObject` type). Suppose element 1 of this array is a line, element 2 is a circle, and so on. Now if we want to rotate each object in the figure, we simply loop over the array performing `A[i].rotate()`. For each A[i], the appropriate rotate function will be executed. That is, which function A[i].rotate() refers to is decided at run time, depending on the dynamic type of object A[i].

This feature polymorphism, which is essentially overloading of the feature (i.e., a feature can mean different things in different contexts and its exact meaning is determined only at run time) causes no problem in strict inheritance because all features of a superclass are available in the subclasses. But in nonstrict inheritance, it can cause problems, because a child may lose a feature. Because the binding of the feature is determined at run time, this can cause a run-time error as a situation may arise where the object is bound to the superclass in which the feature is not present.

7.3 Design Concepts

In an OO system, the basic module is a class, and during design the key activity is to identify and specify the modules that should be there in the system being built. The goal of the design activity is to create a design that, besides being correct, has other attributes that make it a good design.

There are many desirable attributes for an OO system. However, here we will focus on three main concepts. If we can create a design that is satisfactory from these three perspectives (and is correct,) then we can be fairly sure that we have a good design. These key concepts govern the quality of a design, and should therefore drive the design process and the design choices. The three concepts are cohesion, coupling, and open-closed principle. Our goal is to create a design in which the modules are low in coupling, high in cohesion (we will soon understand what low and high means), and which satisfy the open-closed principle. Besides these, we also discuss a few design guidelines that suggest more concrete ways of putting these principles in practice.

7.3.1 Coupling

As mentioned in the previous chapter, coupling is an inter-module concept which captures the strength of interconnection between modules. The more tightly coupled the modules are, the more dependent they are on each other, and the more difficult it is to understand and modify them. Low coupling is desirable for making the system more understandable and modifiable.

The degree of coupling between a module and another module depends on how much information is needed about the other module for understanding and modifying this module, and how complex and explicit this information is. Low coupling occurs when this information is as little as possible, as simple as possible, and is easily visible or identifiable. In the previous chapter we discussed this concept for systems with functional modules. Although the concept remains the same, its manifestation in OO systems is somewhat different as objects are semantically richer than functions. In OO systems, three different types of coupling exists between modules [53]

- Interaction coupling

- Component coupling

- Inheritance coupling

Interaction coupling occurs due to methods of a class invoking methods of other classes. Note that as we are looking at coupling between classes we focus on interaction between classes, and not within a class. In many ways, this situation is similar to a function calling another function and hence this coupling is similar to coupling between functional modules. Like with functions, the worst form of coupling here is if methods directly access internal parts of other methods. (This type of interaction is disallowed in many languages but is allowed where concepts like friend classes, which allow a friend to delve into the internals of a class, exist.)

Interaction coupling reduces, though is still very high, if methods of a class interact with methods in another class by directly manipulating instance variables or attributes of objects of the other class. This form of interaction is also bad as one has to understand the code of other classes to understand what changes they are making to the class. It also violates the encapsulation principle of OO. This form of interaction is worse if variables are used to communicate temporary data, that is, the variables are used not to hold the state of the object but to pass state of the computation from one object to another. If this temp-value holder variable happens to be in the super class, then the coupling worsens since the variable is visible to all sub classes.

Coupling is least (like in coupling with functional modules) if methods communicate directly through parameters. Within this category, coupling is lower if only data is passed, but is higher if control information is passed since the invoked method impacts the execution sequence in the calling method. Also, coupling is higher if the amount of data being passed is more. So, if whole data structures are passed when only some parts are needed, coupling is being unnecessarily increased. Similarly, if an object is passed to a method when only some of its component objects (or objects the passed object refers to) are used within the method, coupling increases unnecessarily. The least coupling situation therefore is when communication is with parameters only, with only necessary variables being passed, and these parameters only pass data.

Component coupling refers to the interaction between two classes where a class has variables of the other class. Three clear situations exist when this can happen. A class C can be component coupled with another class C, if C has an instance variable of type C, or C has a method whose parameter is of type C, or if C has a method which has a local variable of type C (which can then be passed as parameter to some method it invokes.) Note that when C is component coupled with C, it has the potential of being component coupled with all subclasses of C as at runtime an object of any subclass may actually be used. It should be clear that whenever there is component coupling, there is likely to be interaction coupling. Component coupling is considered to be weakest (i.e., most desired) if in a class C, the variables of class C are either in the signatures of the methods of C, or some attributes are of type C. If interaction is through local variables, then this interaction is not visible from outside, and therefore increases coupling.

Inheritance coupling is due to the inheritance relationship between classes. Two classes are considered inheritance coupled if one class is a direct or indirect subclass of the other. If inheritance adds coupling, one can ask the question why not do away with inheritance altogether. The reason is that inheritance may reduce the overall coupling in the system. Let us consider two situations. If a class A is coupled with another class B, and if B is a hierarchy with B and B as two subclasses, then if a method m is factored out of B and B and put in the super class B, the coupling reduces as A is now only coupled with B, whereas earlier it was coupled with both B and B. Similarly, if B is a class hierarchy which supports specialization-generalization relationship, then if new subclasses are added to B, no changes need to be made to a class A which calls methods in B. That is, for changing B's hierarchy, A need not be disturbed. Without this hierarchy, changes in B would most likely result in changes in A.

Within inheritance coupling there are some situations that are worse than others. The worst form is when a subclass B modifies the signature of a method in B (or deletes the method). This situation can easily lead to a run-time error, besides violating the true spirit of the is-a relationship. If the signature is preserved but the implementation of a method is changed, that also violates the is-a relationship, though may not lead to a run-time error, and should be avoided. The least coupling scenario is when a subclass only adds instance variables and methods but does not modify any inherited ones.

7.3.2 Cohesion

Whereas coupling is an inter-module concept, cohesion is an intra-module concept. It focuses on why elements of a module are together in the same module. The objective here is to have elements that are tightly related to belong to the same module. This will make the modules easier to understand,

and as they capture clear concepts and abstractions, easier to modify. Generally, higher cohesion will lead to lower coupling as many elements that need to interact a lot will reside together in strongly coupled modules, lessening the need for interaction with other modules. On the other hand, modules that have low cohesion will often need to interact with other modules to perform their task. Clearly, for making a system more understandable and modifiable, we would like it to consist of modules that are highly cohesive. In other words, the goal is to have a high degree of cohesion in the modules in the system. Cohesion in OO systems also has three aspects [53]:

- Method cohesion

- Class cohesion

- Inheritance cohesion

Method cohesion is same as cohesion in functional modules, which we discussed at length in the previous chapter. It focuses on why the different code elements of a method are together within the method. The highest form of cohesion is if each method implements a clearly defined function, and all statements in the method contribute to implementing this function. In general, with functionally cohesive methods, what the method does can be stated easily with a simple statement. That is, in a short and simple statement of the type "this method does...," we can express the functionality of the method.

Class cohesion focuses on why different attributes and methods are together in this class. The goal is to have a class that implements a single concept or abstraction with all elements contributing towards supporting this concept. In general, whenever there are multiple concepts encapsulated within a class, the cohesion of the class is not as high as it could be, and a designer should try to change the design to have each class encapsulate a single concept.

One symptom of the situation where a class has multiple abstractions is that the set of methods can be partitioned into two (or more) groups, each accessing a distinct subset of the attributes. That is, the set of methods and attributes can be partitioned into separate groups, each encapsulating a different concept. Clearly, in such a situation, by having separate classes encapsulating separate concepts, we can have modules with improved cohesion.

In many situations, even though two (or more) concepts may be encapsulated within a class, there are some methods that access attributes of both the encapsulated concepts. This happens, when the class represents different entities which have a relationship between them. For cohesion, it is best to represent them as two separate classes with relationship among them. That is, we should have multiple classes, with some methods in these classes accessing objects of the other class. In a way, this improvement in cohesion results in an increased coupling. However, for modifiability and understandability, it is better if each class encapsulates a single concept.

Inheritance cohesion focuses on why classes are together in an hierarchy. The two main reasons for inheritance are to model generalization-specialization relationship, and for code reuse. Cohesion is considered high if the hierarchy supports generalization-specialization of some concept (which is likely to naturally lead to reuse of some code). It is considered lower if the hierarchy is primarily for sharing code with weak conceptual relationship between superclass and subclasses. In other words, it is desired that in an OO system the class hierarchies should that they support clearly identified generalization-specializa

7.3.3 The Open

This is a design c ... he OO context. Like with cohesion and ... promote building of systems that are ... change happen frequently and a desig ... ange will result in systems that will die ... o the changing world.

The basic principle, a ... are entities should be open for extens ... A mod- ule being "open for extensi ... extended to accommodate new deman ... anges in requirements and system functi ... osed for mod- ification" means that the existin ... dule is not changed when making enhancements.

Then how does one make enha ... s to a module without changing the existing source code? This principle restricts the changes to modules to extension only, i.e., it allows addition of code, but disallows changing of existing code. If this can be done, clearly, the value is tremendous. Code changes involve heavy risk and to ensure that a change has not "broken"

Figure 7.7: Example without using subtyping.

things that were working often requires a lot of regression testing. This risk can be minimized if no changes are made to existing code. But if changes are not made, how will enhancements be made? This principle says that enhancements should be made by adding new code, rather than altering old code.

There is another side benefit of this. Programmers typically prefer writing new code rather than modifying old code. But the reality is that systems that are being built today are being built on top of existing software. If this principle is satisfied, then we can expand existing systems by mostly adding new code to old systems, and minimizing the need for changing code.

This principle can be satisfied in OO designs by properly using inheritance and polymorphism. Inheritance allows creating new classes that will extend the behavior of existing classes without changing the original class. And it is this property that can be used to support this principle. As an example consider an application in which a client object (of type Client) interacts with a printer object (of class Printer1) and invokes the necessary methods for completing its printing needs. The class diagram for this will be as shown in Figure 7.7.

In this design, the client directly calls the methods on the printer object for printing something. Now suppose the system has to be enhanced to allow another printer to be used by the client. Under this design, to implement this change, a new class Printer2 will have to be created and the code of the client class will have to be changed to allow using object of Printer2 type as well. This design does not support the open-closed principle as the Client class is not closed against change.

The design for this system, however, can be done in another manner that supports the open-closed principle. In this design, instead of directly implementing the Printer1 class, we create an abstract class Printer that defines the interface of a printer and specifies all the methods a printer object should support. Printer1 is implemented as a specialization of this class. In this design, when Printer2 is to be added, it is added as another subclass of type Printer. The client does not need to be aware of this subtype as it

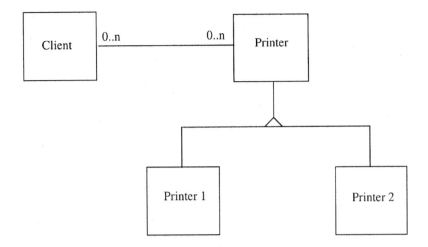

Figure 7.8: Example using subtyping.

interacts with objects of type Printer. That is, the client only deals with a generic Printer, and its interaction is same whether the object is actually of type Printer1 or Printer2. The class diagram for this is shown in Figure 7.8.

It is this inheritance property of OO that is leveraged to support the open-closed principle. The basic idea is to have a class encapsulate the abstraction of some concept. If this abstraction is to be extended, the extension is done by creating new subclasses of the abstraction, thereby keeping all the existing code unchanged.

If inheritance hierarchies are built in this manner, they are said to satisfy the Liskov Substitution Principle [112]. According to this principle, if a program is using object o1 of a (base) class C, that program should remain unchanged if o1 is replaced by an object o2 of a class C, where C is a subclass of C. If this principle is satisfied for class hierarchies, and hierarchies are used properly, then the open-closed principle can be supported. It should also be noted that recommendations for both inheritance coupling and inheritance cohesion support that this principle be followed in class hierarchies.

7.3.4 Some Design Guidelines

In an OO design, class definitions make up the bulk of the system definition. Therefore, the design of classes has a major impact on the overall quality of the design. Here we present a set of guidelines for class design that can be used to produce "good quality" classes [107], or reusable classes [103]. Most of these rules, and their intent, are self-explanatory and based on the preceding discussion of design concepts.

1. The public interface of a class should only contain the operations defined on the class. That is, the data definitions should not be a part of the public interface.

2. Only the operations that form the interface for a class, that is, the ones needed by the users of the class, should be the public members of the class.

3. An instance of a class should not send messages directly to components of another class. That is, if there is a class C defined inside a class B, then objects of a class A should not directly perform operations on objects of class C (though many languages will permit it).

4. Each operation defined on a class should be such that it either modifies or accesses some data defined in the class.

5. A class should be dependent on as few classes as possible.

6. The interaction between two classes should be explicit. That is, global objects should be avoided, and any objects needed by an object should be explicitly passed as a parameter or accessed through other explicitly defined means.

7. Each subclass should be developed as a specialization of the superclass with the public interface of the superclass becoming part of the public interface of the subclass.

8. The inheritance hierarchy should model some hierarchy that naturally exists, and the class definition at each level should represent some concept. The top of the hierarchy should be an abstract class.

9. Inside a class, case analysis on object type should be avoided. If this is needed, it should be done by sending messages.

10. The number of arguments and the size of methods should be kept small.

7.4 Unified Modeling Language (UML)

Most design approaches have two aspects to them—a language or a notation to express the design, particularly while it is being developed, and a methodology for developing the design. As design is a creative and iterative activity, a good notation should aid the designer during the design activity. This means that the notation should allow the designer to succinctly capture the key aspects of the design (and refine it later), and allow easy communication to encourage brainstorming. With good notation, often the methodology for design becomes a set of general rules, and the notation becomes the primary tool for creating the design.

Unified Modeling Language (UML) is a graphical notation for expressing object oriented designs [24, 124, 64]. It is called a modeling language and not a design notation as it allows representing various aspects of the system, not just the design that has to be implemented. For a design, a specification of the classes that exist in the system might suffice. However, while modeling, during the design process, the designer also tries to understand how the different classes are related and how they interact to provide the desired functionality. This aspect of modeling helps build designs that are more likely to satisfy all the requirements of the system. Due to the ability of UML to create different models, it has become an aid for understanding the system, designing the system, as well as a notation for representing design.

Though UML has now evolved into a fairly comprehensive and large modeling notation, we will focus on a few central concepts and notations relating to classes and their relationships and interactions. Though we have already seen some of the notation when discussing OO analysis, we discuss it here independently for sake of completeness. For a more detailed discussion on UML, the reader is referred to [24, 124, 64].

7.4.1 Class Diagram

The class diagram of UML is the central piece in a design or model. As the name suggests, these diagrams describe the classes that are there in the design. As the final code of an OO implementation is mostly classes, these diagrams have a very close relationship with the final code. There are many tools that translate the class diagrams to code skeletons, thereby avoiding errors that might get introduced if the class diagrams are manually translated to class definitions by programmers. A class diagram defines

1. *Classes that exist in the system*—besides the class name, the diagrams are capable of describing the key fields as well as the important methods of the classes.

2. *Associations between classes*—what types of associations exist between different classes.

3. *Subtype, supertype relationship*—classes may also form subtypes giving type hierarchies using polymorphism. The class diagrams can represent these hierarchies also.

A class itself is represented as a rectangular box which is divided into three areas. The top part gives the class name. By convention the class name is a word with the first letter in uppercase. (In general, if the class name is a combination of many words, then the first letter of each word is in uppercase.) The middle part lists the key attributes or fields of the class. These attributes are the state holders for the objects of the class. By convention, the name of the attributes starts with a lowercase, and if multiple words are joined, then each new word starts with an uppercase. The bottom part lists the methods or operations of the class. These represent the behavior that the class can provide. Naming conventions are same as for attributes but to show that it is a function, the names end with "( )". (The parameters of the methods can also be specified, if desired.)

Sometimes, designers may like to specify the responsibility of a class. The responsibility is what the entire class is meant to do using its attributes and methods. Some designers feel that cohesive classes have clearly defined responsibility. If responsibility needs to be specified, it is typically done by having a 4th part at the bottom of the class box and specifying the responsibility in it as plain text.

If a class is an interface (having specifications but no body,) this can be specified by marking the class with the stereotype "$<< interface >>$", which is generally written above the class name. Similarly, if a class/method/attribute has some properties that we want to specify, it can be done by tagging the entity by specifying the property next to the entity name within "{" and "}" or by putting some special symbol. Example of a class, an interface, and a class with some tagged values is shown in Figure 7.9.

The divided-box notation is to describe the key features of a class as a stand alone entity. However, classes have relationships between them, and objects of different classes interact. Therefore, to model a system or an application, we must represent relationship between classes. One common

Queue
{private} front: int {private} rear: int {readonly} MAX: int
{public} add(element: int) {public} remove(): int {protected} isEmpty(): boolean

<<interface>> Figure
area: double perimeter: double
calculateArea(): double calculatePerimeter(): double

Figure 7.9: Class, stereotypes, and tagged values.

relationship is the generalization-specialization relationship between classes, which finally gets reflected as the inheritance hierarchy. In this hierarchy, properties of general significance are assigned to a more general class—the superclass—while properties which can specialize an object further are put in the subclass. All properties of the superclass are inherited by the subclass, so a subclass contains its own properties as well as those of the superclass.

The generalization-specialization relationship is specified by having arrows coming from the subclass to the superclass, with the empty triangle shaped arrow-head touching to the superclass. Often, when there are multiple subclasses of a class, this may be specified by having one arrow head on the superclass, and then drawing lines from this to the different subclasses. In this hierarchy, often specialization is done on the basis of some *discriminator*—a distinguishing property that is used to specialize superclass into different subclasses. In other words, by using the discriminator, objects of the superclass type are partitioned into sets of objects of different subclass types. The discriminator used for the generalization-specialization relationship can be specified by labeling the arrow. An example of how this relationship is modeled in UML is shown in 7.10.

In this example, the IITKPerson class represents all people belonging to the IITK. These are broadly divided into two subclasses—Student and Employee, as both these types have many different properties (some common ones also) and different behavior. Similarly, students have two different subclasses, UnderGraduate and PostGraduate, both requiring some different attributes and having different constraints. The Employee class has subtypes representing the faculty, staff, and research staff. (This hierarchy is from an actual working system developed for the author's Institute.)

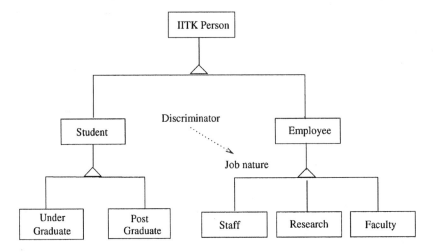

Figure 7.10: A class hierarchy.

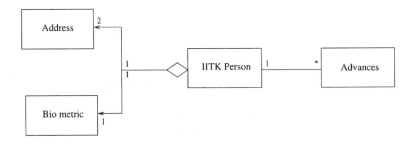

Figure 7.11: Aggregation and association among classes.

Besides the generalization-specialization relationship, another common relationship is association, which allows objects to communicate with each other. An association between two classes means that an object of one class needs some services from objects of the other class to perform its own service. The relationship is that of peers in that objects of both the classes can use services of the other. The association is shown by a line between the two classes. An association may have a name which can be specified by labeling the association line. (The association can also be assigned some attributes of its own.) And if the roles of the two ends of the association need to be named, that can also be done. In an association, an end may also have multiplicity allowing relationships like 1 to 1, or 1 to many be modeled. Where there is a fixed multiplicity, it is represented by putting a number at that end; a zero or many multiplicity is represented by a *.

Another type of relationship is the part-whole relationship which represents the situation when an object is composed of many parts, each part itself is an object. This situation represents containment or aggregation—i.e. object of a class are contained inside the object of another class. (Containment and aggregation can be treated separately and shown differently, but we will consider them as the same.) For representing this aggregation relationship, the class which represents the "whole" is shown at the top and a line emanating from a little diamond connecting it to classes which represent the parts. Often in an implementation this relationship is implemented in the same manner as an association, hence, this relationship is also sometimes modeled as an association.

The association and aggregation are shown in Figure 7.11, expanding the example given above. An object of `IITKPerson` type contains two objects of type `Address`, representing the permanent address and the current address. It also contains an object of type `BiometricInfo`, which keeps information like the person's picture and signature. As these objects are common to all people, they belong in the parent class rather than a subclass. An IITKPerson is allowed to take some advances from the Institute to meet expenses for travel, medical , etc. Hence, `Advances` is a different class (which, incidently, has a hierarchy of its own) to which `IITKPerson` class as a 1 to m association. (These relations are also from the system.)

Class diagrams focus on classes, and should not be confused with *object diagram*. Objects are specific instances of classes. Sometimes, it is desirable to model specific objects and relationship between them, and for that object diagrams are used. An object is represented like a class, except that its name also specifies the name of the class to which it belongs. Generally, the object name starts with lowercase, and the class name is specified after a colon. To further clarify, the entire name is underlined. An example is, myList: List. The attributes of an object may have specific values. These values can be specified by giving them along with the attribute name (E.g. name = "John").

7.4.2   Sequence and Collaboration Diagrams

Class diagrams represent the static structure of the system, or they capture what is the structure of the code that may implement it, and how the different classes in the code are related. Class diagrams, however, do not represent the dynamic behavior of the system. That is, how the system behaves when it performs some of its functions cannot be represented by class diagrams.

This is done through *sequence diagrams* or *collaboration diagrams*, together called *interaction diagrams*. An interaction diagram typically captures the behavior of a use case and models how the different objects in the system collaborate to implement the use case. Let us first discuss sequence diagrams, which is perhaps more common of the two interaction diagrams.

A sequence diagram shows the series of messages exchanged between some objects, and their temporal ordering, when objects collaborate to provide some desired system functionality (or implement a use case). The sequence diagram is generally drawn to model the interaction between objects for a particular use case. Note that in a sequence diagram (and also in collaboration diagrams), it is objects that participate and not classes. When capturing dynamic behavior, the role of classes are limited as during execution it is objects that exist.

In a sequence diagram, all the objects that participate in the interaction are shown at the top as boxes with object names. For each object, a vertical bar representing its lifeline is drawn downwards. A message from one object to another is represented as an arrow from the lifeline of one to the lifeline of the other. Each message is labeled with the message name, which typically should be the name of a method in the class of the target object. An object can also make a self call, which is shown as an message starting and ending in the same objects lifeline. To clarify the sequence of messages and relative timing of each, time is represented as increasing as one moves farther away downwards from the object name in the object life. That is, time is represented by the y-axis, increasing downwards.

Using the lifeline of objects and arrows, one can model objects lives and how messages flow from one object to another. However, frequently a message is sent from one object to another only under some condition. This condition can be represented in the sequence diagram by specifying it within brackets before the message name. If a message is sent to multiple receiver objects, then this multiplicity is shown by having a "*" before the message name.

Each message has a return, which is when the operation finishes and returns the value (if any) to the invoking object. Though often this message can be implied, sometimes it may be desirable to show the return message explicitly. This is done by showing a dashed arrow. A sequence diagram for an example is shown in Figure 7.12. This example is for printing the graduation report for students. The object for GradReport (which has the responsibility for printing the report) sends a message to the Student objects for the relevant information, which request the CourseTaken objects for the

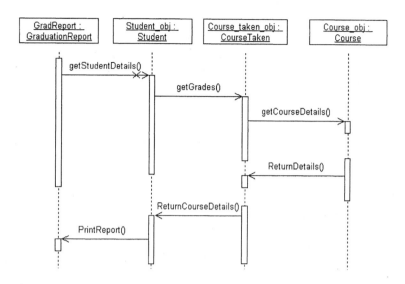

Figure 7.12: Sequence diagram for printing a graduation report.

courses the student has taken. These objects get information about the courses from the **Course** objects. (This example is discussed in greater length later in Chapter 9, where this implementation is improved through refactoring. The class diagram is also given in that Chapter in Figure 9.5.)

A collaboration diagram also shows how objects communicate. Instead of using a timeline-based representation that is used by sequence diagrams, a collaboration diagram looks more like a state diagram. Each object is represented in the diagram, and the messages sent from one object to another are shown as *numbered* arrows from one object to the other. In other words, the chronological ordering of messages is captured by message numbering, in contrast to a sequence diagram where ordering of messages is shown pictorially. As should be clear, the two types of interaction diagrams are semantically equivalent and have the same representation power. The collaboration diagram for the above example is shown in Figure 7.13. Over the years, however, sequence diagrams have become more popular, as people find the visual representation of sequencing quicker to grasp.

As we can see, an interaction diagram models the internal dynamic behavior of the system, when the system performs some function. The internal dynamics of the system is represented in terms of how the objects interact with each other. Through an interaction diagram, one can clearly see how a system internally implements an operation, and what messages are sent

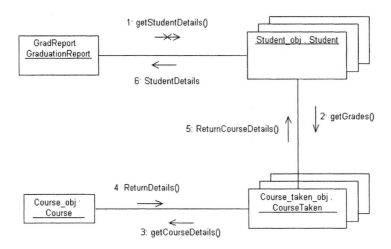

Figure 7.13: Collaboration diagram for printing a graduation report.

between different objects. If a convincing interaction diagram cannot be constructed for a system operation with the classes that have been identified in the class diagram, then it is safe to say that the system structure is not capable of supporting this operation and that it must be enhanced. So, it can be used to validate if the system structure being designed through class diagrams is capable of providing the desired services.

As a system has many functions, each involving different objects in different ways, there will be a dynamic model for each of these functions or use cases. In other words, whereas one class diagram can capture the structure of the system's code, for the dynamic behavior many diagrams are needed. Many systems may be performing many functions and it may not be feasible or practical to draw the interaction diagram for each of these. Typically, during design, interaction diagram of some key use cases or functions will be drawn to make sure that the classes that exist can indeed support the desired use cases, and to understand their dynamics. So, while creating the design, it should be kept in mind that while one class diagram is needed to represent the structure of the system, an interaction diagram represents interactions of objects for one of the many scenarios.

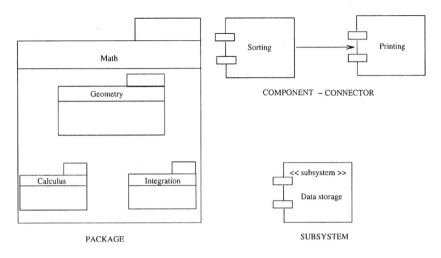

Figure 7.14: Subsystems, Components, and packages.

7.4.3 Other Diagrams and Capabilities

UML is an extensible and quite elaborate modeling notation. Above we have discussed notation related to two of the most common models developed while modeling a system—class diagrams and interaction diagrams. These two together help model the static structure of the system as well as the dynamic behavior. There are, however, many other aspects that might need to be modeled for which extra notation is required. UML provides notation for many different types of models.

In modeling and building systems, often instead of classes, components are used. Components often encapsulate "larger" elements, and are semantically simpler than classes. Components often encapsulate subsystems and provide clearly defined interfaces through which these components can be used by other components in the system. While designing an architecture, as we have seen, components are very useful. UML provides a notation for specifying a component. UML also provides a separate notation for a subsystem. In a large system, many classes may be combined together to form packages, where a package is a collection of many elements, possibly of different types. UML also provides a notation to specify packages. These are shown in Figure 7.14.

In the chapter on Architecture we discussed the deployment view of the system, which may be quite different from the component or module view. In deployment view, the focus is what software element uses which hardware, that is, how is the system deployed. UML has notation for representing a deployment view. The main element is a *node*, represented as a named cube, which represents a computing resource like the CPU which physically exists. The name of the cube identifies the resource as well as its type. Within the cube for the node the software elements it deploys (which can be components, packages, classes, etc.) are shown using their respective notation. If different nodes communicate with each other, this is shown by connecting the nodes by lines.

The notation for packages and deployment view provide structural views of the system from different perspectives. UML also provides notation to express different types of behavior. A *state diagram* is a model in which the entity being modeled is viewed as a set of states, with transitions between the states taking place when some event occurs. A state is represented as a rectangle with rounded edges or as ellipses or circles; transitions are represented by arrows connecting two states. Details can also be attached to transitions. State diagrams are often used to model the behavior of objects of a class—the state represents the different states of the object and transition captures the performing of the different operations on that object. So, whereas interaction diagrams capture how objects collaborate, a state diagram models how an object itself evolves as operations are performed on it. This can help clearly elucidate and specify the behavior of a class. We will discuss it further in the next chapter, as we view state diagrams as helping in doing the detailed design of a class.

Activity Diagrams provide another method for modeling dynamic behavior. These diagrams model a system by modeling the activities that take place in it when the system executes for performing some function. Each activity is represented like an oval, with the name of the activity within it. From the activity, the system proceeds to other activities. Often, which activity to perform next depends on some decision. This decision is shown as a diamond leading to multiple activities (which are the options for this decision). Repeated execution of some activities can also be shown, These diagrams are like flow charts, but also have notation to specify parallel execution of activities in a system by specifying an activity splitting into multiple activities or many activities joining (synchronizing) after their completion.

UML is an extensible notation allowing a modeler the flexibility to represent newer concepts as well. There are many situations in which a modeler needs some notation which is similar to an existing one but is not exactly the same. For example, in some cases, one may want to specify if a class is an abstract class or an interface. Instead of having special notation for these concepts, UML has the concept of a stereotype, through which existing notation can be used to model different concepts. An existing notation, for example of a class, can be used to represent some other similar concept by specifying it as a stereotype by giving the name of the new concept within $<<$ and $>>$. We have already seen an example earlier. A metaclass can be specified in a similar manner; and so can a utility class (one which has some utility functions which are directly used and whose objects are not created).

Tagged values can be used to specify additional properties of the elements to which they are attached. They can be attached to any name, and are specified within "{ }". Though tagged values can be anything a modeler wants, it is best to limit its use to a few clearly defined (and pre-agreed) properties like *private, abstract, query,* and *readonly.* Notes can also be attached to the different elements in a model. We have earlier seen the use of some tagged values in Figure 7.9.

We discussed use cases and use case diagrams in an earlier chapter. Use case diagrams are part of the UML. However, as discussed earlier, use case diagrams add little additional information that use cases do not provide. They are mostly used for providing a high-level summary of use cases.

7.5 A Design Methodology

Many design and analysis methodologies have been proposed. Some of the earlier ones are [23, 37, 95, 133]. As we stated earlier, a methodology basically uses the concepts (of OO in this case) to provide guidelines and notation for the design activity. Though methodologies are useful, they do not reduce the activity of design to a sequence of steps that can be followed mechanically. Due to this, the overall approach and the principles behind it are often more useful than the details of the methodologies. In fact, most experienced designers tailor the methodology to suit their way of thinking and working. We will discuss only one particular methodology here, as at an abstract level most methodologies start to seem very similar and vary mostly in details. Even though it is one of the earlier methodologies, its basic concepts are still applicable.

We assume that during architecture design the system has been broken into high-level subsystems or components. The problem we address is how to produce an object-oriented design for a subsystem, which can itself be viewed as a system.

As we discussed earlier, the OO design of consists of specification of all the classes and objects that will exist in the system implementation. A complete OO design should be such that in the implementation phase only further details about methods or attributes need to be added. A few low-level objects may be added later, but most of the classes and objects and their relationships are identified during design.

In OO design, the OO analysis forms the starting step. Using the model produced during analysis, a detailed model of the final system is built. As we discussed earlier, in an object-oriented approach, the separation between analysis and design is not very clear and depends on the perception. We will follow what we defined in Chapter 4 regarding what constitutes the output of an OOA—a class diagram of the problem. The OMT methodology that we discuss for design considers dynamic modeling and functional modeling parts of the analysis [133]. As these two models have little impact on the object model produced in OOA or on the SRS, we view these modeling as part of the design activity. Hence, performing the object modeling can be viewed as the first step of design. With this point of view, the design methodology for producing an OO design consists of the following sequence of steps:

- Produce the class diagram

- Produce the dynamic model and use it to define operations on classes

- Produce the functional model and use it to define operations on classes

- Identify internal classes and operations

- Optimize and package

We discussed object-oriented modeling in Chapter 4, along with a methodology for performing the modeling. Any methodology can be followed, as long as the output of the modeling activity is the class diagram representing the problem structure. Hence, the first step of the design is generally performed during the requirements phase when the problem is being modeled for producing the SRS. Briefly, during analysis, the basic goal is to produce a class diagram of the problem domain. This requires identification of object types in the problem domain, the structures between classes (both inheritance and aggregation), attributes of the different classes, associations between the different classes, and the services each class needs to provide to support the system. For further details, the reader should refer to Chapter 4.

7.5.1 Dynamic Modeling

The class diagram models the static structure of the system, However, just modeling the static structure is not sufficient for designing the system, as the desired effect of the events on the system state will also impact the final structure of the system. So, a better understanding of the dynamic behavior of the system will help in further refining the design.

The dynamic model of a system aims to specify how the state of various objects changes when events occur. An event is something that happens at some time instance. For an object, an event is essentially a request for an operation. An event typically is an occurrence of something and has no time duration associated with it. Each event has an initiator and a responder. Events can be internal to the system, in which case the event initiator and the event responder are both within the system. An event can be an external event, in which case the event initiator is outside the system (e.g., the user or a sensor).

A scenario is a sequence of events that occur in a particular execution of the system, as we have seen while discussing use cases in Chapter 3. From the scenarios, the different events being performed on different objects can be identified, which are then used to identify services on objects. The different scenarios together can completely characterize the behavior of the system. If the design is such that it can support all the scenarios, we can be sure that the desired dynamic behavior of the system can be supported by the design. This is the basic reason for performing dynamic modeling. With use cases, dynamic modeling involves preparing interaction diagrams for the important scenarios, identifying events on classes, ensuring that events can be supported, and perhaps build state models for the classes.

It is best to start by modeling scenarios being triggered by external events. The scenarios should not necessarily cover all possibilities, but the major ones should be considered. First the main success scenarios should be modeled, then scenarios for "exceptional" cases should be modeled. For example, in the system for a restaurant that we discussed in Chapter 4, the main success scenario for placing an order could be:

> Customer reads the menu.
> Customer places the order.
> Order is sent to the kitchen for preparation.
> Ordered items are served.
> Customer requests for a bill for the order.
> Bill is prepared for this order;
> Customer is given the bill;
> Customer pays the bill.

An "exception" scenario could be if the ordered item was not available or if the customer cancels his order. From each scenario, events have to be identified. Events are interactions with the outside world and object-to-object interactions. All the events that have the same effect on the flow of control in the system are grouped as a single event type. Each event type is then allocated to the object classes that initiate it and that service the event. With this done, a scenario can be represented as a sequence (or collaboration) diagram showing the events that will take place on the different objects if the execution corresponding to the scenario takes place. A possible sequence diagram of the preceding scenario is given in Figure 7.15.

Once the main scenarios are modeled, various events on objects that are needed to support executions corresponding to the various scenarios are known. This information is then used to expand our view of the classes in the design. The main reason for performing dynamic modeling is that scenarios and sequence diagrams extend the initial design. Generally speaking, for each event in the sequence diagrams, there will be an operation on the object on which the event is invoked. So, by using the scenarios and sequence diagrams we can further refine our view of the objects and add operations that are needed to support some scenarios but may not have been identified during initial modeling. For example, from the event trace diagram in Figure 7.15, we can see that "placeOrder" and "getBill" will be two operations required on the object of type Order if this interaction is to be supported.

The effect of these different events on a class itself can be modeled using the state diagrams. We believe that the state transition diagram is of limited use during system design but may be more useful during detailed design. Hence, we will discuss state modeling of classes in the next chapter.

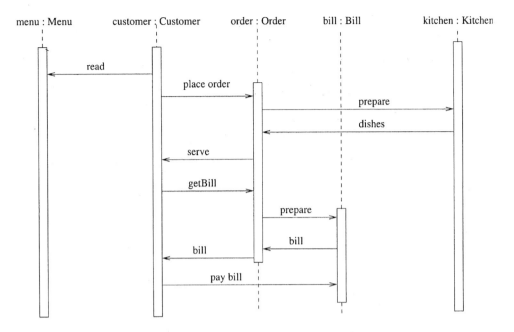

Figure 7.15: A sequence diagram for the restaurant.

7.5.2 Functional Modeling

The functional model describes the computations that take place within a system. It is the third dimension in modeling—object modeling looks at the static structure of the system, dynamic modeling looks at the events in the system, and functional modeling looks at the functionality of the system. In other words, the functional model of a system specifies what happens in the system, the dynamic model specifies when it happens, and the class model specifies what it happens to [133].

A functional model of a system specifies how the output values are computed in the system from the input values, without considering the control aspects of the computation. This represents the functional view of the system—the mapping from inputs to outputs and the various steps involved in the mapping. Generally, when the transformation from the inputs to outputs is complex, consisting of many steps, the functional modeling is likely to be useful. In systems where the transformation of inputs to outputs is not complex, the functional model is likely to be straightforward.

As we have seen, the functional model of a system (either the problem domain or the solution domain) can be represented by a data flow diagram

(DFD). We have used DFDs in problem modeling, and the structured design methodology, discussed in Chapter 6. Just as with dynamic modeling, the basic purpose of doing functional modeling, when the goal is to obtain an object oriented design for the system, is to use the model to make sure that the object model can perform the transformations required from the system. As processes represent operations and in an object-oriented system, most of the processing is done by operations on classes, all processes should show up as operations on classes. Some operations might appear as single operations on an object; others might appear as multiple operations on different classes, depending on the level of abstraction of the DFD. If the DFD is sufficiently detailed, most processes will occur as operations on classes. The DFD also specifies the abstract signature of the operations by identifying the inputs and outputs.

7.5.3   Defining Internal Classes and Operations

The classes identified so far are the ones that come from the problem domain. The methods identified on the objects are the ones needed to satisfy all the interactions with the environment and the user and to support the desired functionality. However, the final design is a blueprint for implementation. Hence, implementation issues have to be considered. While considering implementation issues, algorithm and optimization issues arise. These issues are handled in this step.

First, each class is critically evaluated to see if it is needed in its present form in the final implementation. Some of the classes might be discarded if the designer feels they are not needed during implementation.

Then the implementation of operations on the classes is considered. For this, rough algorithms for implementation might be considered. While doing this, a complex operation may get defined in terms of lower-level operations on simpler classes. In other words, effective implementation of operations may require heavy interaction with some data structures and the data structure to be considered an object in its own right. These classes that are identified while considering implementation concerns are largely support classes that may be needed to store intermediate results or to model some aspects of the object whose operation is to be implemented. The classes for these objects are called *container classes.*

Once the implementation of each class and each operation on the class has been considered and it has been satisfied that they can be implemented, the system design is complete. The detailed design might also uncover some very low-level objects, but most such objects should be identified during system design.

7.5.4 Optimize and Package

In the design methodology used, the basic structure of the design was created during analysis. As analysis is concerned with capturing and representing various aspects of the problem, some inefficiencies may have crept in. In this final step, the issue of efficiency is considered, keeping in mind that the final structures should not deviate too much from the logical structure produced by analysis, as the more the deviation, the harder it will be to understand a design. Some of the design optimization issues are discussed next [133].

Adding Redundant Associations. The association in the initial design may make it very inefficient to perform some operations. In some cases, these operations can be made more efficient by adding more associations. Consider the example where a Company has a relationship to a person (a company employs many persons) [133]. A person may have an attribute languages-spoken, which lists the languages the person can speak. If the company sometimes needs to determine all its employees who know a specific language, it has to access each employee object to perform this operation. This operation can be made more efficient by adding an index in the Company object for different languages, thereby adding a new relationship between the two types of objects. This association is largely for efficiency. For such situations, the designer must consider each operation and determine how many objects in an association are accessed and how many are actually selected. If the hit ratio is low, indexes can be considered.

Saving Derived Attributes. A derived attribute is one whose value can be determined from the values of other attributes. As such an attribute is not independent, it may not have been specified in the initial design. However, if it is needed very often or if its computation is complex, its value can be computed and stored once and then accessed later. This may require new objects to be created for the derived attributes. However, it should be kept in mind that by doing this the consistency between derived attributes and base attributes will have to be maintained and any changes to the base attributes may have to be reflected in the derived attributes.

Use of Generic Types. A language like C++ allows "generic" classes to be declared where the base type or the type of some attribute is kept "generic" and the actual type is specified only when the object is actually defined. (The approach of C++ does not support true generic types, and this type of definition is actually handled by the compiler.) By using generic types, the code size can be reduced. For example, if a list is to be used in different contexts, a generic list can be defined and then instantiated for an integer, real, and char types.

Adjustment of Inheritance. Sometimes the same or similar operations are defined in various classes in a class hierarchy. By making the operation slightly more general (by extending interface or its functionality), it can be made a common operation that can be "pushed" up the hierarchy. The designer should consider such possibilities. Note that even if the same operation has to be used in only some of the derived classes, but in other derived classes the logic is different for the operation, inheritance can still be used effectively. The operation can be pushed to the base class and then redefined in those classes where its logic is different.

Another way to increase the use of inheritance, which promotes reuse, is to see if abstract classes can be defined for a set of existing classes and then the existing classes considered as a derived class of that. This will require identifying common behavior and properties among various classes and abstracting out a meaningful common superclass. Note that this is useful only if the abstract superclass is meaningful and the class hierarchy is "natural." A superclass should not be created simply to pack the common features on some classes together in a class.

Besides these, the general design principles discussed earlier should be applied to improve the design—to make it more compact, efficient, and modular. Often these goals will conflict. In that case, the designer has to use his judgment about which way to go. In general, as we stated earlier in the chapter, understandability and modularity should be given preference over efficiency and compactness.

7.5.5 Examples

Before we apply the methodology on some examples, it should be remembered again that no design methodology reduces the activity of producing a design to a series of steps that can be mechanically executed; each step requires some amount of engineering judgment. Furthermore, the design produced by following a methodology should not be considered the final design. The design can and should be modified using the design principles and the ultimate objectives of the project in mind. Methodologies are essentially guidelines to help the designer in the design activity; they are not hard-and-fast rules. The examples we give here are relatively small, and all aspects of

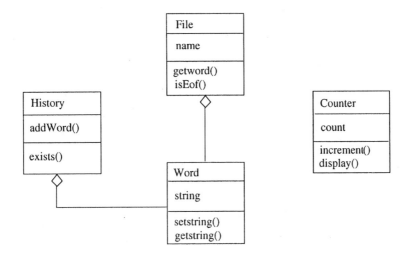

Figure 7.16: Class diagram for the word counting problem.

the methodology do not get reflected in them. However, the design of the case studies, given at the end of the chapter, will provide a more substantial example for design.

The Word-Counting Problem

Let us first consider the word counting problem discussed in Chapter 6 (for which the structured design was done). The initial analysis clearly shows that there is a `File` object, which is an aggregation of many `Word` objects. Further, one can consider that there is a `Counter` object, which keeps track of the number of different words. It is a matter of preference and opinion whether `Counter` should be an object, or counting should be implemented as an operation. If counting is treated as an operation, the question will be to which object it belongs. As it does not belong "naturally" to either the class `Word` nor the class `File`, it will have to be "forced" into one of the classes. For this reason, we have kept `Counter` as a separate object. The basic problem statement finds only these three objects. However, further analysis for services reveals that some history mechanism is needed to check if the word is unique. The class diagram obtained after doing the initial modeling is shown in Figure 7.16.

Now let us consider the dynamic modeling for this problem. This is essentially a batch processing problem, where a file is given as input and some output is given by the system. Hence, the use case and scenario for

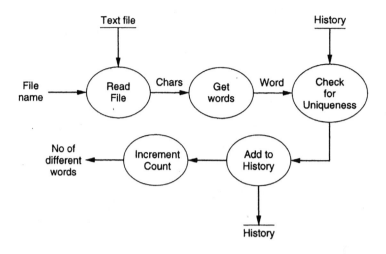

Figure 7.17: Functional Model for the word counting problem.

this problem are straightforward. For example, the scenario for the "normal" case can be:

System prompts for the file name; user enters the file name.
System checks for existence of the file.
System reads the words from the file.
System prints the count.

From this simple scenario, no new operations are uncovered, and our object diagram stays unchanged. Now we consider the functional model. One possible functional model is shown in Figure 7.17. The model reinforces the need for some object where the history of what words have been seen is recorded. This object is used to check the uniqueness of the words. It also shows that various operations like increment(), isunique(), and addToHistory() are needed. These operations should appear as operations in classes or should be supported by a combination of operations. In this example, most of these processes are reflected as operations on classes and are already incorporated in the design.

Now we are at the last two steps of design methodology, where implementation and optimization concerns are used to enhance the object model. The first decision we take is that the history mechanism will be implemented by a binary search tree. Hence, instead of the class History, we have a different class Btree. Then, for the class Word, various operations are needed to compare different words. Operations are also needed to set the string value for a word and retrieve it. The final class diagram is similar in structure to the one shown in Figure 7.16, except for these changes.

The final step of the design activity is to specify this design. This is not a part of the design methodology, but it is an essential step, as the design specification is what forms the major part of the design document. The design specification, as mentioned earlier, should specify all the classes that are in the design, all methods of the classes along with their interfaces. We use C++ class structures for our specification. The final specification of this problem is given next. This specification can be reviewed for design verification and can be used as a basis of implementing the design.

```
class Word  {
    private :
        char *string; // string representing the word
    public:
        bool operator == ( Word ); // Checks for equality
        bool operator < ( Word );
        bool operator > ( Word );
        Word operator = ( Word ); // The assignment operator
        void setWord ( char * ); // Sets the string for the word
        char *getWord ( ); // gets the string for the word
};

class File {
    private:
        FILE inFile;
        char *fileName;
    public:
        Word getWord ( ); // get a word; Invokes operations of Word
        bool isEof ( ); // Checks for end of file
        void fileOpen ( char * );
};

class Counter {
    private:
        int counter;
    public:
        void increment ( );
```

```
            void display ( );
};

class Btree: GENERIC in <ELEMENT_TYPE>  {
    private:
        ELEMENT_TYPE element;
        Btree < ELEMENT_TYPE > *left;
        Btree < ELEMENT_TYPE > *right;
    public:
        void insert( ELEMENT_TYPE ); // to insert an element
        bool lookup( ELEMENT_TYPE ); // to check if an element exists
};
```

As we can see, all the class definitions complete with data members and operations and all the major declarations are given in the design specification. Only the implementation of the methods are not provided. This design was later implemented in C++. The conversion to code required only minor additions and modifications to the design. The final code was about 240 lines of C++ code (counting noncomment and nonblank lines only).

Rate of Returns Problem

Let us consider a slightly larger problem: that of determining the rate of returns on investments. An investor has made investments in some companies. For each investment, in a file, the name of the company, all the money he has invested (in the initial purchase as well as in subsequent purchases), and all the money he has withdrawn (through sale of shares or dividends) are given, along with the dates of each transaction. The current value of the investment is given at the end, along with the date. The goal is to find the rate of return the investor is getting for each investment, as well as the rate of return for the entire portfolio. In addition, the amounts he has invested initially, amounts he has invested subsequently, amounts he has withdrawn, and the current value of the portfolio also is to be output.

This is a practical problem that is frequently needed by investors (and forms the basis of our second Case Study). The computation of rate of return is not straightforward and cannot be easily done through spreadsheets. Hence, such a software can be of practical use. Besides the basic functionality given earlier, the software needs to be robust and catch errors that can be caught in the input data.

We start with the analysis of the problem. Initial analysis clearly shows that there are a few object classes of interest—Portfolio, Investment,

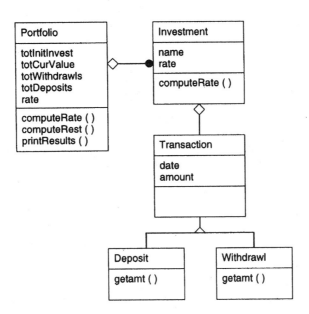

Figure 7.18: Class diagram for rate of return problem.

and `Transaction`. A portfolio consists of many investments, and an investment consists of many transactions. Hence, the class `Portfolio` is an aggregation of many `Investments`, and an `Investment` s an aggregation of many `Transactions`. A transaction can be of `Withdrawal` type or `Deposit` type, resulting in a class hierarchy, with `Investment` being the superclass and `Withdrawal` and `Deposit` subclasses.

For an object of class `Investment`, the major operation we need to perform is to find the rate of return. For the class `Portfolio` we need to have operations to compute rate of return, total initial investment, total withdrawal, and total current value of the portfolio. Hence, we need operations for these. The class diagram obtained from analysis of the problem is shown in Figure 7.18.

In this problem, as the interaction with the environment is not much, the dynamic model is not significant. Hence, we omit the dynamic modeling for this problem. A possible functional model is given in Figure 7.19. The classes are then enhanced to make sure that each of the processes of the functional model is reflected as operations on various objects. As we can see, most of the processes already exist as operations.

Now we have to perform the last two steps of the design methodology,

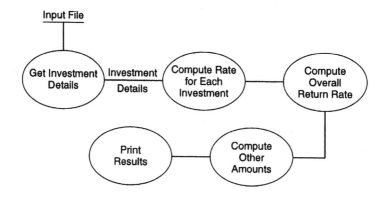

Figure 7.19: Functional model for the rate of return problem.

where implementation and optimization concerns are used to enhance the classes. While considering the implementation of computation of total initial investment, computation of overall return rate, overall withdrawals and so on, we notice that for all of these, appropriate data from each investment is needed. Hence, to the class `Investments`, appropriate operations need to be added. Further, we note that all the computations for total initial investment, total current value, and so on are all done together, and each of these is essentially adding values from various investments. Hence, we combine them in a single operation in `Portfolio` and a corresponding single operation in `Investment`. Studying the class hierarchy, we observe that the only difference in the two subclasses `Withdrawal` and `Deposit` is that in one case the amount is subtracted and in the other it is added. In such a situation, the two types can be easily considered a single type by keeping the amount as negative for a withdrawal and positive for a deposit. So we remove the subclasses, thereby simplifying the design and implementation. Instead of giving the class diagram for the final design, we provide the specification of the classes:

```
class Transaction {
    private:
        int amount; // money amount for the transaction
        int month; // month of the transaction
        int year; // year of the transaction
```

```
    public:
        getAmount();
        getMonth();
        getYear();
        Transaction(amount, month, year); // sets values
};


class Investment {
    private:
        char *investmentName; // Name of the company
        Transaction *transactArray; // List of transactions
        int noOfTransacts; // Total number of transactions
        float rateOfReturn; // rate of return
    public:
        getTransactDetails();  // Set details of transactions
        computeRate();
        float getRate(); // Return the rate of the returns
        compute(initVal, totWithdrawls, totCurVal, totDeposits);
                // Returns these values for this investment
};

class Portfolio {
    private:
        Investment *investArray; // List of investments
        int noOfInvestments; // Total number of investments
        int totalInitInvest;
        int totalDeposits;
        int totalCurVal;
        int totalWithdrawl;
        float RateOfReturns; // Overall rate of returns
    public:
        getInvestDetails( char * fname ); // Parse the input file
        computeRate(); // Compute rates of return
        compute(); // Compute other totals
        printResults(); // Print return rates, total values, etc.
};
```

The design is self-explanatory. This design was later implemented in C++
code, and we found that only minor implementation details were added
during the implementation, showing the correctness and completeness of
the design. The final size of the program was about 470 lines of C++ code
(counting noncomment and nonblank lines only).

7.6   Metrics

We have already seen that the basic paradigm behind OOD is fundamentally different from the paradigm of function-oriented design. This has brought in a different building block and concepts related to this building block. The definition of modularity has also changed for this new building block, and new methodologies have been proposed for creating designs using this paradigm. It is, therefore, natural to expect that a new set of metrics will be required to evaluate an OO design. A few attempts have been made to propose metrics for object-oriented software [1, 32, 111].

Here we present some metrics that have been proposed for evaluating the complexity of an OOD. As design of classes is the central issue in OOD and the major output of any OOD methodology is the class definition, these metrics focus on evaluating classes. Note that for measuring the size of a system, conventional approaches, which measure the size in LOC or function points, can be used, even if OO is used for design. It is the metrics for evaluating the quality or complexity of the design that need to be redefined for OOD. The metrics discussed were proposed in [32], and the discussion is based on this work. The results of an experiment described in [6] for validating these metrics and the metrics data presented in [32] are used to discuss the role of these metrics.

Weighted Methods per Class (WMC)

The effort in developing a class will in some sense be determined by the number of methods the class has and the complexity of the methods. Hence, a complexity metric that combines the number of methods and the complexity of methods can be useful in estimating the overall complexity of the class. The weighted methods per class (WMC) metric does precisely this.

Suppose a class C has methods $M_1, M_2, ..., M_n$ defined on it. Let the complexity of the method M_i be c_i. As a method is like a regular function or procedure, any complexity metric that is applicable for functions can be used to define c_i (e.g., estimated size, interface complexity, and data flow complexity). The WMC is defined as:

$$WMC = \sum_{i=1}^{i=n} c_i.$$

If the complexity of each method is considered 1, WMC gives the total number of methods in the class.

The data given in [6, 32], which is based on evaluation of some existing programs, shows that in most cases, the classes tend to have only a small number of methods, implying that most classes are simple and provide some specific abstraction and operations. Only a few classes have many methods defined on them. The analysis in [6] showed that the WMC metric has a reasonable correlation with fault-proneness of a class. As can be expected, the larger the WMC of a class the better the chances that the class is fault-prone.

Depth of Inheritance Tree (DIT)

Inheritance is, as we have mentioned, one of the unique features of the object-oriented paradigm. As we have said before, inheritance is one of the main mechanisms for reuse in OOD—the deeper a particular class is in a class hierarchy, the more methods it has available for reuse, thereby providing a larger reuse potential. At the same time, as we have mentioned, inheritance increases coupling, which makes changing a class harder. In other words, a class deep in the hierarchy has a lot of methods it can inherit, which makes it difficult to predict its behavior. For both these reasons, it is useful to have some metric to quantify inheritance. The depth of inheritance tree (DIT) is one such metric.

The DIT of a class C in an inheritance hierarchy is the depth from the root class in the inheritance tree. In other words, it is the length of the shortest path from the root of the tree to the node representing C or the number of ancestors C has. In case of multiple inheritance, the DIT metric is the maximum length from a root to C.

The data in [6, 32] suggests that most classes in applications tend to be close to the root, with the maximum DIT metric value (in the applications studied) being around 10. Most the classes have a DIT of 0 (that is, they are the root). This seems to suggest that the designers tend to keep the number of abstraction levels (reflected by the levels in the inheritance tree) small, presumably to aid understanding. In other words, designers (of the systems evaluated) might be giving up on reusability in favor of comprehensibility. The experiments in [6] show that DIT is very significant in predicting defect-proneness of a class: the higher the DIT the higher the probability that the class is defect-prone.

Number of Children (NOC)

The number of children (NOC) metric value of a class C is the number of immediate subclasses of C. This metric can be used to evaluate the degree of reuse, as a higher NOC number reflects reuse of the definitions in the superclass by a larger number of subclasses. It also gives an idea of the direct influence of a class on other elements of a design—the larger the influence of a class, the more important that the class is correctly designed. In the empirical observations, it was found that classes generally had a small NOC metric value, with a vast majority of classes having no children (i.e., NOC is 0). This suggests that in the systems analyzed, inheritance was not used very heavily. However, the data in [6] seems to suggest that the larger the NOC, the lower the probability of detecting defects in a class. That is, the higher NOC classes are less defect-prone. The reasons for this are not definitive.

Coupling Between Classes (CBC)

As discussed earlier, coupling between modules of a system, in general, reduces modularity and makes module modification harder. In OOD, as the basic module is a class, it is desirable to reduce the coupling between classes. The less coupling of a class with other classes, the more independent the class, and hence it will be more easily modifiable. Coupling between classes (CBC) is a metric that tries to quantify coupling that exists between classes.

The CBC value for a class C is the total number of other classes to which the class is coupled. Two classes are considered coupled if methods of one class use methods or instance variables defined in the other class. In general, whether two classes are coupled can easily be determined by looking at the code and the definitions of all the methods of the two classes. However, note that there are indirect forms of coupling (through pointers, etc.) that are hard to identify by evaluating the code.

The experimental data indicates that most of the classes are self-contained and have a CBC value of 0, that is, they are not coupled with any other class, including superclasses [32]. Some types of classes, for example the ones that deal with managing interfaces (called interface objects earlier), generally tend to have higher CBC values. The data in [6] found that CBC is significant in predicting the fault-proneness of classes, particularly those that deal with user interfaces.

Response for a Class (RFC)

Although the CBC for a class captures the number of other classes to which this class is coupled, it does not quantify the "strength" of interconnection. In other words, it does not explain the degree of connection of methods of a class with other classes. Response for a class (RFC) tries to quantify this by capturing the total number of methods that can be invoked from an object of this class.

The RFC value for a class C is the cardinality of the response set for a class. The response set of a class C is the set of all methods that can be invoked if a message is sent to an object of this class. This includes all the methods of C and of other classes to which any method of C sends a message. It is clear that even if the CBC value of a class is 1 (that is, it is coupled with only one class), the RFC value may be quite high, indicating that the "volume" of interaction between the two classes is very high. It should be clear that it is likely to be harder to test classes that have higher RFC values.

The experimental data found that most classes tend to invoke a small number of methods of other classes. Again, classes for interface objects tend to have higher RFC values. The data in [6] found that RFC is very significant in predicting the fault-proneness of a class—the higher the RFC value the larger the probability that the class is defect-prone.

Lack of Cohesion in Methods (LCOM)

This last metric in the suite of metrics proposed in [32] tries to quantify cohesion of classes. As we have seen, along with low coupling between modules, high cohesion is a highly desirable property for modularity. For classes, cohesion captures how closely bound are the different methods of the class. One way to quantify this is given by the LCOM metric.

Two methods of a class C can be considered "cohesive" if the set of instance variables of C that they access have some elements in common. That is, if I_1 and I_2 are the set of instance variables accessed by the methods M_1 and M_2, respectively, then M_1 and M_2 are similar if $I_1 \cap I_2 \neq \phi$. Let Q be the set of all cohesive pairs of methods, that is, all (M_i, M_j) such that I_i and I_j have a non-null intersection. Let P be the set of all noncohesive pairs of methods, that is, pairs such that the intersection of sets of instance variables they access is null. Then LCOM is defined as

$$LCOM = |P| - |Q|, \text{if } |P| > |Q| \; 0 \; \text{otherwise.}$$

If there are n methods in a class C, then there are $n(n-1)$ pairs, and LCOM is the number of pairs that are non cohesive minus the number of pairs that are cohesive. The larger the number of cohesive methods, the more cohesive the class will be, and the LCOM metric will be lower. A high LCOM value may indicate that the methods are trying to do different things and operate on different data entities, which may suggest that the class supports multiple abstractions, rather than one abstraction. If this is validated, the class can be partitioned into different classes. The data in [6] found little significance of this metric in predicting the fault-proneness of a class.

In [6], the first five metrics, which were found to be significant in predicting the fault-proneness of classes, were combined to predict the fault-proneness of classes. The experiments showed that the first five metrics, when combined (in this case the coefficients for combination were determined by multivariate analysis of the fault and metric data) are very effective in predicting fault-prone classes. In their experiment, out of a total of 58 faulty classes, 48 classes were correctly predicted as fault-prone. The prediction missed 10 classes and predicted 32 extra classes as fault-prone, although they were not so.

7.7 Summary

In the previous chapter we studied how a software system can be designed using functional abstraction as the basic unit. In this chapter, we looked at how a system can be designed using objects and classes as the basic unit. The fundamental difference in this approach from functional approaches is that an object encapsulates state and provides some predefined operations on that state. That is, state (or data) and operations (i.e., functions) are considered together, whereas in the function-oriented approach the two are kept separate.

When using an object-oriented approach, an object is the basic design unit. For objects, during design, the class for the objects is identified. A class represents the type for the object and defines the possible state space for the objects of that class and the operations that can be performed on the objects. An object is an instance of a class and has state, behavior, and identity. Objects in a system do not exist in isolation but are related to each other. One of the goals of design is to identify the relationship between the objects of different classes.

Universal Modeling Language (UML) has become the de-facto standard for building models of object-oriented systems. UML has various types of diagrams to model different types of properties, and allows both static structure as well as dynamic behavior to be modeled. It is an extensible notation that allows new types to be added.

For representing the static structure, the main diagram is the class diagram, which represents the classes in the system and relationships between the classes. The relationship between the classes may be *generalization-specialization*, which leads to class hierarchies. The relationship may be that of an *aggregation* which models the "whole-part of" relationship. Or it may be an *association*, which models the client-serve type of relationship between classes.

For modeling the dynamic behavior, sequence or collaboration diagrams (together called interaction diagrams) may be used. These diagrams represent how a scenario is implemented by involving different objects. The focus is on capturing the messages that are exchanged between objects to implement a scenario.

There are many other diagrams that UML has proposed that can be used to model other aspects. For example, the state diagram can be used to model behavior of a class. Activity diagrams can model the activities that take place in a system during some execution. For static structure, it provides notation for specifying subsystems, packages, and components.

To ensure that the design is modular, some general properties should be satisfied. The three properties we have discussed are cohesion, coupling, and open-closed principle. Coupling is an inter-class concept and captures how closely the different classes interact with each other and how much they depend on each other. Cohesion is an intra-class concept and captures how strongly the elements of a class are related. Open-closed principle states that the classes should be designed in a manner that they are closed for modification but are open for extension. A good design should have low coupling, high cohesion, and should satisfy the open-closed principle—these make the design more modular and easier to change.

A good modeling notation and principles to evaluate a design are the key necessities for creating good design. Design methodologies help by providing some guidelines of how to create a design. We discussed the object modeling technique for design, which first creates a class model for the system, and then refines it through dynamic modeling, and functional modeling. Identifying the internal classes and optimization are the final steps in this methodology for creating a design.

Finally, we discussed some metrics that can be used to study the complexity of an object-oriented design. We presented one suite of metrics that were proposed, along with some data regarding their validation. The metric weighted methods per class is defined as the sum of complexities of all the methods and gives some idea about how much effort might be needed to develop the class. The depth of inheritance tree of a class is defined as the maximum depth in the class hierarchy of this class, and can represent the potential of reuse that exists for a class, and the degree of coupling between the class and its parent classes. The number of children metric is the number of immediate subclasses of a class, and it can be used to capture the degree of reuse of a class. Coupling of a class is the number of classes whose methods it uses or who use its methods. The response for a class metric is the number of methods that can be invoked by sending a message to this class. It tries to capture the strength of interconnection between classes. Finally, the lack of cohesion metric represents the number of method pairs whose set of access variables have nothing in common minus the number of method pairs that have some common instance variable.

Unlike in previous chapters, we have not discussed verification methods here. The reason is that verification methods discussed in the previous chapters are general techniques that are not specific to function-oriented approaches. Hence, the same general techniques can be used for object-oriented design.

Exercises

1. What is the relationship between abstract data types and classes?

2. Why are private parts of a superclass generally not made accessible to subclasses?

3. In C++, *friends* of a class C can access the private parts of C. For declaring a class F a friend of C, where should it be declared—in C or in F? Why?

4. What are the different ways in which an object can access another object in a language like C++? (Do not consider the access allowed by being a friend.)

5. What are the potential problems that can arise in software maintenance due to different types of inheritance?

6. What is the relationship between OOA, SRS, and OOD?

7. In the word-counting example, a different functional model was used from the one proposed in Chapter 6. Use the model given in Chapter 6 and modify the OO design.

8. Suppose a simulator for a disk is to be written (for teaching an Operating Systems course). Use OMT to design the simulator.

9. If an association between classes has some attributes of its own, how will you implement it?

10. If we were to use the method described in Chapter 5 to identify error-prone and complex modules, which of the metrics will you use and why (you may also combine the metrics).

11. Design an experiment to validate your proposal for predicting error-prone modules. Specify data collection and analysis.

12. Compare the OO designs and the structured design of the case study to obtain some observations for comparing the two design strategies (this can be considered a research problem).

Case Studies

As with previous chapters, we end this chapter by performing the object-oriented design of the case studies. Here we discuss the application of the design process on the case study, i.e., how the design for the case studies is created. The final design specifications are given on the Web site. While discussing the creation of design, we provide only the main steps to give an idea of the design activity.

Case Study 1—Course Scheduling

We start the design activity by identifying classes of objects in the problem domain and relationship between the classes. From the problem specification, given in Chapter 3, we can clearly identify the following objects: TimeTable, Course, Room, LectureSlot, CToBeSched (course to be scheduled), InputFile_1, and InputFile_2. From the problem, it is clear that TimeTable, an important object in the problem domain, is an aggregation of many TimeTableEntry, each of which is a collection of a Course, a Room where the course is scheduled, and a LectureSlot in which the course is scheduled.

On looking at the description of file 1, we find that it contains a list of rooms, courses, and time slots that is later used to check the validity of entries in file 2. This results in the objects RoomDB, CourseDB, and SlotDB, each of which is an aggregation of many members of Room, Course, and Slot, respectively. Similarly, on looking at the description of file 2, we find that it contains a TableOfCToBeSched, which is an aggregation of many CToBeSched.

On studying the problem further and considering the scheduling constraints imposed by the problem, it is clear that for scheduling, the courses have to be divided into four different types—depending on whether the course is a UG course or a PG course, and whether or not preferences are given. In other words, we can specialize CToBeSched to produce four subclasses: PGwithPref, UGwithPref, PGwithoutPref, and UGwithoutPref. The classes that represent courses with preferences will contain a list of preferences, which is a list of LectureSlots. This is the only hierarchy that is evident from examining the problem.

Considering the attributes of the object classes, the problem clearly specifies that a Room has the attributes *roomNo* and *capacity*; a LectureSlot has one major attribute, the *slot* it represents; and a Course has *courseName* as an attribute. A `CToBeSched` contains a `Course` and has *enrollment* as an attribute.

Considering the services for the classes, we identify from the problem specification services like *scheduleAll()* on `TableOfCToBeSched`, which schedules all the courses, *printTable()* for the `TimeTable`, *setentry()* and *getentry()* for a `TimeTableEntry`, and *insert()* and *lookup()* operations for the various lists. The initial class diagram is shown in Figure 7.20.

The system here is not an interactive system; hence dynamic modeling is rather straightforward. The normal scenario is that the inputs are given and the outputs are produced. There are at least two different normal scenarios possible, depending on whether there are any conflicts (requiring conflicts and their reasons to be printed) or not (in which case only the timetable is printed). The latter normal scenario does not reveal any new operations. However, a natural way to model the first scenario is to have an object `ConflictTable` into which different conflicts for the different time slots of different courses are stored, and from where they are later printed. Hence, we add this object and model it as an aggregation of `ConflictTableEntry`, with an operation *insertEntry()* to add a conflict entry in the table and an operation *printTable()* to print the conflicts. Then there are a number of exception scenarios—one for each possible error in the input. In each case, the scenario shows that a proper error message is to be output. This requires that operations needed on objects like `Room`, `Course` and `Slot` check their formats for correctness. Hence, validation operations are added to these objects.

The functional model for the problem was given in Chapter 6. It shows that from file 1, `roomDB`, `courseDB`, and `slotDB` need to be formed and the entries for each of these have to be obtained from the file and validated. As validation functions are already added, this adds the function for producing the three lists, called *build_CRS_DBs()*. Similarly, the DFD clearly shows that on `InputFile_2` a function to build the table of courses to be scheduled is needed, leading to the adding of the operation *buildCtoBeSched()*. While building this table, this operation also divides them into the four groups of courses, as done in the DFD. The DFD shows that an operation to schedule the courses is needed. This operation (*scheduleAll()*) is already there. Although the high-level DFD does not show, but a further refinement of the bubble for "schedule" shows that bubbles are needed for scheduling PG courses with preferences, UG courses with preferences, PG courses without preferences, and UG courses without preferences (they are reflected in the structure chart as modules). These bubbles get reflected as *schedule()* op-

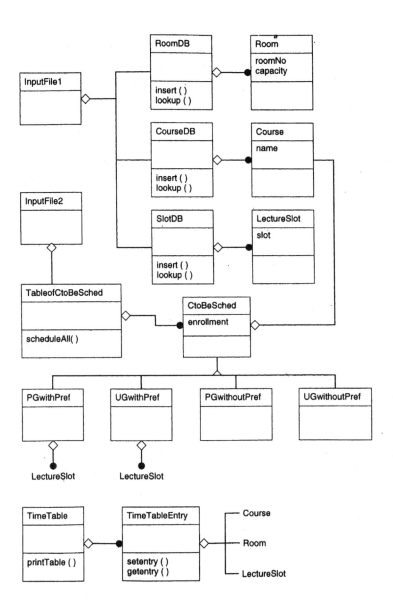

Figure 7.20: Initial class diagram for the case study.

erations on all four subclasses—`PGwithPref`, `UGwithPref`, `PGwihoutPrefs`, and `UGwithoutPrefs`. The DFD also has bubbles for printing the timetable and conflicts. These get translated into print operations on `TimeTable`, `TimeTableEntry`, `ConflictTable`, and `ConflictTableEntry`.

Now we come to the last steps of considering implementation concerns. Many new issues come up here. First, we decided to have a generic template class, which can be used to implement the various DBs, as all DBs are performing similar functions. Hence, we defined a template class `List`. When considering the main issue of scheduling, we notice that scheduling UG courses with preferences, as discussed in the Chapter 6, is not straightforward, as the system has to ensure that it does not make any PG course without preference "unschedulable." To handle this, we take a simple approach of having a data structure that will reserve slots for PG courses and will then be used to check for the safety of an assignment while scheduling PG courses with preferences. This adds an internal class `PGReserve`, with operations like *isAllotmentSafe()* (to check if making an allotment for UG course is "safe"), *Initialize()* (to initially "mark" all possible slots where `PGwithoutPref` courses can be scheduled). The structure is then used to schedule the PG courses without preferences after the UG courses with preferences are scheduled, leading to the operation *getSuitableSchedule()*.

To implement the scheduling operation, we decided to use the dynamic binding capability. For each subclass, the *schedule()* operation that has been defined is made to have the same signature, and a corresponding virtual function is added in the superclass `CtoBeScheduled`. With this, when the courses are to be scheduled, we can just go over all the courses that need to be scheduled and call the schedule operation. Dynamic binding will ensure that the appropriate schedule operation is called, depending on the type of course (i.e., to which of the four subclasses it belongs). All schedule operations will interact with the `TimeTable` for checking the conditions specified in the requirements. Various functions are added on `TimeTable` for this.

Having considered the scheduling operation, we considered the major operation on the files. It becomes clear that to implement these operations, various parsing functions are needed on the two files. These functions are then added. As these operations are only needed to implement the externally visible operations on the class, they are defined as private operations. Considering the public operations on these files reinforce the need for *insert()* and *lookup()* operations in the different DBs, these operations require operations to set the attributes of the independent object of which they are an aggregation. Hence, these operations are added. In a similar manner, while considering implementation issues various other operations on the different object classes were revealed. Various other operations are revealed when considering implementation of other operations. The final class diagram after the design is given in the design document available from the Web site.

As we can see, the class diagram, even for this relatively small system, is quite complex and not easily manageable. Furthermore, it is not practical to properly capture the parameters of the various operations in object diagrams. The types of the various attributes is also frequently not shown to keep the diagram compact. Similarly, all associations do not get reflected. Hence, for specifying the design precisely, this class diagram is translated to a precise specification of the classes. The final design specifications are also given in the design document available from the Web site.

Case Study 2—PIMS

The requirements for this case study have been given before. After reviewing the use cases, the following classes clearly emerge.

- Investment

- Portfolio

- Security

- Transaction

- GUI

- NetLoader

- Current Value System

- Alerts

- SecurityManager

- DataRepository

The relationship between them is relatively straightforward. The class diagram containing some of the classes is shown in Figure 7.21. Though this initial class structure was evolved during modeling, later the subtypes

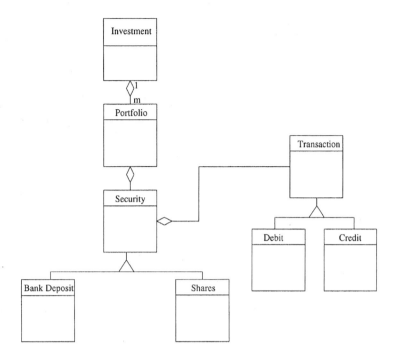

Figure 7.21: Class diagram for PIMS

of transaction were eliminated as they provided little useful value. Subtypes of security type were also eliminated.

There are many use cases specified in the SRS for this system. After the initial modeling of these classes and their methods, sequence diagrams for some of the scenarios of some of the use cases are drawn. From this exercise, the specifications of the classes is refined. Some of the sequence diagrams and the specifications of the classes are given in the design document which is available from the Web site.

8

Detailed Design

In previous chapters we discussed two different approaches for system design. In system design we concentrate on the modules in a system and how they interact with each other. Once a module is precisely specified, the internal logic that will implement the given specifications can be decided, and is the focus of this chapter. In this chapter we discuss methods for developing and specifying the detailed design of a module. We also discuss the metrics that can be extracted from a detailed design.

8.1 Detailed Design and PDL

Most design techniques, like structured design, identify the major modules and the major data flow among them. The methods used to specify the system design typically focus on the external interfaces of the modules and cannot be extended to specify the internals. Process design language (PDL) is one way in which the design can be communicated precisely and completely to whatever degree of detail desired by the designer. That is, it can be used to specify the system design and to extend it to include the logic design. PDL is particularly useful when using top-down refinement techniques to design a system or module.

8.1.1 PDL

One way to communicate a design is to specify it in a natural language, like English. This approach often leads to misunderstanding, and such imprecise communication is not particularly useful when converting the design into code. The other extreme is to communicate it precisely in a formal language,

```
minmax(infile)

ARRAY a

        DO UNTIL end of input
                READ an item into a
        ENDDO
        max, min := first item of a
        DO FOR each item in a
                IF max < item THEN set max to item
                IF min > item THEN set min to item
        ENDDO
END
```

Figure 8.1: PDL description of the minmax program.

like a programming language. Such representations often have great detail, which is necessary for implementation but not important for communicating the design. These details are often a hindrance to easy communication of the basic design. Ideally we would like to express the design in a language that is as precise and unambiguous as possible without having too much detail and that can be easily converted into an implementation. This is what PDL attempts to do.

PDL has an overall outer syntax of a structured programming language and has a vocabulary of a natural language (English in our case). It can be thought of as "structured English." Because the structure of a design expressed in PDL is formal, using the formal language constructs, some amount of automated processing can be done on such designs. As an example, consider the problem of finding the minimum and maximum of a set of numbers in a file and outputting these numbers in PDL as shown in Figure 8.1.

Notice that in the PDL program we have the entire logic of the procedure, but little about the details of implementation in a particular language. To implement this in a language, each of the PDL statements will have to be converted into programming language statements. Let us consider another example. Text is given in a file with one blank between two words. It is to be formatted into lines of 80 characters, except the last line. A word is not to be divided into two lines, and the numbers of blanks needed to fill the line are added at the end, with no more than two blanks between words. The PDL program is shown in Figure 8.2. Notice the use of procedure to express

```
Initialize buf to empty
DO FOREVER
      DO UNTIL (#chars in buf ≥ 80 & word boundary is reached)
                OR (end-of-text reached)
            read chars in buf
      ENDDO
      IF #chars > 80 THEN
            remove last word from buf
            PRINT-WITH-FILL (buf)
            set buf to last word ELSEIF #chars = 80 THEN
            print (Buf)
            set buf to empty
      ELSE EXIT the loop
ENDDO

PROCEDURE PRINT-WITH-FILL (buf)

Determine #words and #character in buf
#of blanks needed = 80 - #character
DO FOR each word in the buf
      print (word)
      if #printed words ≥ (#word - #of blanks needed) THEN
            print (two blanks)
      ELSE print (single blank)
ENDDO
```

Figure 8.2: PDL description of text-formatter.

the design.

With PDL, a design can be expressed in whatever level of detail that is suitable for the problem. One way to use PDL is to first generate a rough outline of the entire solution at a given level of detail. When the design is agreed on at this level, more detail can be added. This allows a successive refinement approach, and can save considerable cost by detecting the design errors early during the design phase. It also aids design verification by phases, which helps in developing error-free designs. The structured outer syntax of PDL also encourages the use of structured language constructs while implementing the design.

The basic constructs of PDL are similar to those of a structured language. The first is the IF construct. It is similar to the if-then-else construct of Pascal. However, the conditions and the statements to be executed need not be stated in a formal language. For a general selection, there is a CASE statement. Some examples of CASE statements are:

CASE OF transaction type
CASE OF operator type

The DO construct is used to indicate repetition. The construct is indicated by:

> DO iteration criteria
> > one or more statements
> ENDDO

The iteration criteria can be chosen to suit the problem, and unlike a formal programming language, they need not be formally stated. Examples of valid uses are:

> DO WHILE there are characters in input file
> DO UNTIL the end of file is reached
> DO FOR each item in the list EXCEPT when item is zero

A variety of data structures can be defined and used in PDL such as lists, tables, scalar, and integers. Variations of PDL, along with some automated support, are used extensively for communicating designs.

8.1.2   Logic/Algorithm Design

The basic goal in detailed design is to specify the logic for the different modules that have been specified during system design. Specifying the logic will require developing an algorithm that will implement the given specifications. Here we consider some principles for designing algorithms or logic that will implement the given specifications.

The term *algorithm* is quite general and is applicable to a wide variety of areas. Essentially, an algorithm is a sequence of steps that need to be performed to solve a given problem. The problem need not be a programming problem. We can, for example, design algorithms for such activities as cooking dishes (the recipes are nothing but algorithms) and building a table. In the software development life cycle we are only interested in algorithms related to software. For this, we define an algorithm to be an unambiguous procedure for solving a problem [74]. A *procedure* is a finite sequence of well-defined steps or operations, each of which requires a finite amount of memory and time to complete. In this definition we assume that termination is an essential property of procedures. From now on we will use procedures, algorithms, and logic interchangeably.

There are a number of steps that one has to perform while developing an algorithm [74]. The starting step in the design of algorithms is *statement of the problem*. The problem for which an algorithm is being devised has to be precisely and clearly stated and properly understood by the person responsible for designing the algorithm. For detailed design, the problem statement comes from the system design. That is, the problem statement is already available when the detailed design of a module commences. The next step is development of a mathematical *model* for the problem. In modeling, one has to select the mathematical structures that are best suited for the problem. It can help to look at other similar problems that have been solved. In most cases, models are constructed by taking models of similar problems and modifying the model to suit the current problem. The next step is the *design of the algorithm*. During this step the data structure and program structure are decided. Once the algorithm is designed, its correctness should be verified.

No clear procedure can be given for designing algorithms. Having such a procedure amounts to automating the problem of algorithm development, which is not possible with the current methods. However, some heuristics or methods can be provided to help the designer design algorithms for modules. The most common method for designing algorithms or the logic for a module is to use the *stepwise refinement technique* [148].

The stepwise refinement technique breaks the logic design problem into a series of steps, so that the development can be done gradually. The process starts by converting the specifications of the module into an abstract description of an algorithm containing a few abstract statements. In each step, one or several statements in the algorithm developed so far are decomposed into more detailed instructions. The successive refinement terminates when all instructions are sufficiently precise that they can easily be converted into programming language statements. During refinement, both data and instructions have to be refined. A guideline for refinement is that in each step the amount of decomposition should be such that it can be easily handled

```
int count (file)
FILE file;
word_list wl;
{
    read file into wl
    sort (wl);
    count = different_words (wl);
    printf (count);
}
```

Figure 8.3: Strategy for the first step in stepwise refinement.

and that represents one or two design decisions.

The stepwise refinement technique is a top-down method for developing detailed design. We have already seen top-down methods for developing system designs. To perform stepwise refinement, a language is needed to express the logic of a module at different levels of detail, starting from the specifications of the module. We need a language that has enough flexibility to accommodate different levels of precision. Programming languages typically are not suitable as they do not have this flexibility. For this purpose, PDL is very suitable. Its formal outer syntax ensures that the design being developed is a "computer algorithm" whose statements can later be converted into statements of a programming language. Its flexible natural language-based inner syntax allows statements to be expressed with varying degrees of precision and aids the refinement process.

An Example: Let us again consider the problem of counting different words in a text file. Suppose that in the high-level structure chart of a large text processing system, a COUNT module is specified whose job is to determine the count of different words. During detailed design we have to determine the logic of this module so that the specifications are met. We will use the stepwise refinement method for this. For specification we will use PDL, adapted to C-style syntax. A simple strategy for the first step is shown in Figure 8.3.

This strategy is simple and easy to understand. This is the strategy that we proposed in the data flow graph earlier. The "primitive" operations used in this strategy are very high-level and need to be further refined. Specifically, there are three operations that need refinement. These are (1) read file into the word list, whose purpose is to read all the words from the

```
read_from_file (file, wl)
FILE file;
word_list wl;
{
      initialize wl to empty;
      while not end-of-file {
      get_a_word from file
      add word to wl
}
```

Figure 8.4: Refinement of the reading operation.

file and create a word list, (2) sort(wl), which sorts the word list in ascending order, and (3) count different words from a sorted word list. So far, only one data structure is defined: the word list. As refinement proceeds, more data structures might be needed.

In the next refinement step, we should select one of the three operations to be refined and further elaborate it. In this step we will refine the reading procedure. One strategy for implementing the read module is to read words and add them to the word list. This is shown in Figure 8.4.

This is a straightforward strategy, simple enough to be easily handled in one refinement step. Another strategy could be to read large amounts of data from the file in a buffer and form the word list from this buffer. This might lead to a more efficient implementation. For the next refinement step we select the counting function. A strategy for implementing this function is shown in Figure 8.5.

Similarly, we can refine the sort function. Once these refinements are done, we have a design that is sufficiently detailed and needs no further refinement. For more complex problems many successive refinements might be needed for a single operation. Design for such problems can proceed in two ways—depth first or breadth first. In the depth first approach, when an operation is being refined, its refinement is completely finished (which might require many levels of refinement) before refinement of other operations begins. In the breadth first approach, all operations needing refinement are refined once. Then all the operations specified in this refinement are refined once. This is done until no refinement is needed. A combination of the two approaches could also be followed.

It is worth comparing the structure of the PDL programs produced by

```
int different_words (wl)
word_list wl;
{
     word last, cur;
     int cnt;

     last = first word in wl
     cnt = 1;
     while not end of list {
          cur = next word from wl
          if (cur <> last) {
               cnt = cnt + 1;
               last = cur;
          }
     }
     return (cnt)
}
```

Figure 8.5: Refinement of the function different_words.

this method as compared to the structure produced using the structured design methodology. The two structures are not the same. The basic difference is that in stepwise refinement, the function sort is subordinate to the main module, while in the design produced by using structured design methodology, it is a subordinate module to the input module. This is not just a minor point; it points to a difference in approaches. In stepwise refinement, in each refinement step we specify the operations that are needed (as we do while drawing the data flow diagram). In structured design, the focus is on partitioning the problem into input, output, and transform modules, which usually results in a different structure.

8.1.3   State Modeling of Classes

For object-oriented design, the approach just discussed for obtaining the detailed design may not be sufficient, as it focuses on specifying the logic or the algorithm for the modules identified in the (function-oriented) high-level design. But a class is not a functional abstraction and cannot be viewed as an algorithm. A method of a class can be viewed as a functional module, and the methods can be used to specify the logic for the methods.

The technique for getting a more detailed understanding of the class as a whole, without talking about the logic of different methods, has to be different from the refinement-based approach. An object of a class has some state and many operations on it. To better understand a class, the relationship between the state and various operations and the effect of interaction of various operations have to be understood. This can be viewed as one of the objectives of the detailed design activity for object-oriented development. Once the overall class is better understood, the algorithms for its various methods can be developed. Note that the axiomatic specification approach for a class, discussed earlier in this chapter, also takes this view. Instead of specifying the functionality of each operation, it specifies, through axioms, the interaction between different operations.

A method to understand the behavior of a class is to view it as a finite state automata (FSA). An FSA consists of states and transitions between states, which take place when some events occur. When modeling an object, the state is the value of its attributes, and an event is the performing of an operation on the object. A *state diagram* relates events and states by showing how the state changes when an event is performed. A state diagram for an object will generally have an initial state, from which all states in the FSA are reachable (i.e., there is a path from the initial state to all other states).

A state diagram for an object does not represent all the actual states of the object, as there are many possible states. A state diagram attempts to represent only the logical states of the object. A *logical state* of an object is a combination of all those states from which the behavior of the object is similar for all possible events. Two logical states will have different behavior for at least one event. For example, for an object that represents a stack, all states that represent a stack of size more than 0 and less than some defined maximum are similar as the behavior of all operations defined on the stack will be similar in all such states (e.g., push will add an element, pop will remove one, etc.). However, the state representing an empty stack is different as the behavior of top and pop operations are different now (an error message may be returned). Similarly, the state representing a full stack is different. The state model for this bounded size stack is shown in Figure 8.6.

The finite state modeling of objects is an aid to understand the effect of various operations defined on the class on the state of the object. A good understanding of this can aid in developing the logic for each of the operations. To develop the logic of operations, regular approaches for algorithm development can be used. The model can also be used to validate if the logic for an

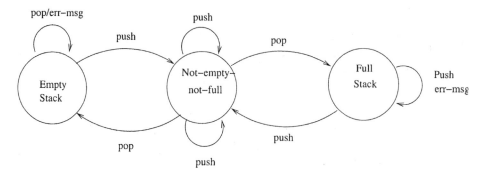

Figure 8.6: FSA model of a stack.

operation is correct. As we have seen, for a class, typically the input-output specification of the operations is not provided. Hence, the FSA model can be used as a reference for validating the logic of the different methods. As we will see in Chapter 10, a state model can be used for generating test cases for validation.

State modeling of classes has also been proposed as a technique for analysis [133]. However, we believe that it has limited use during analysis, and its role is more appropriate during detailed design when the detailed working of a class needs to be understood. Even here, the scope of this modeling is limited. It is likely to be more of use if the interaction between the methods through the state is heavy and there are many states in which the methods need to behave differently.

8.2   Verification

There are a few techniques available to verify that the detailed design is consistent with the system design. The focus of verification in the detailed design phase is on showing that the detailed design meets the specifications laid down in the system design. Validating that the system as designed is consistent with the requirements of the system is not stressed during detailed design. The three verification methods we consider are design walkthroughs, critical design review, and consistency checkers.

8.2.1   Design Walkthroughs

A *design walkthrough* is a manual method of verification. The definition and use of walkthroughs change from organization to organization. Here we describe one walkthrough model. A design walkthrough is done in an informal meeting called by the designer or the leader of the designer's group. The walkthrough group is usually small and contains, along with the designer, the group leader and/or another designer of the group. The designer might just get together with a colleague for the walkthrough or the group leader might require the designer to have the walkthrough with him.

In a walkthrough the designer explains the logic step by step, and the members of the group ask questions, point out possible errors or seek clarification. A beneficial side effect of walkthroughs is that in the process of articulating and explaining the design in detail, the designer himself can uncover some of the errors.

Walkthroughs are essentially a form of peer review. Due to its informal nature, they are usually not as effective as the design review.

8.2.2 Critical Design Review

The purpose of *critical design review* is to ensure that the detailed design satisfies the specifications laid down during system design. The critical design review process is same as the inspections process in which a group of people get together to discuss the design with the aim of revealing design errors or undesirable properties. The review group includes, besides the author of the detailed design, a member of the system design team, the programmer responsible for ultimately coding the module(s) under review, and an independent software quality engineer. While doing design review it should be kept in mind that the aim is to uncover design errors, not try to fix them. Fixing is done later.

The use of checklists, as with other reviews, is considered important for the success of the review. The checklist is a means of focusing the discussion or the "search" of errors. Checklists can be used by each member during private study of the design and during the review meeting. For best results, the checklist should be tailored to the project at hand, to uncover project-specific errors. Here we list a few general items that can be used to construct a checklist for a design review [52].

A Sample Checklist

- Does each of the modules in the system design exist in detailed design?

- Are there analyses to demonstrate that the performance requirements can be met?

- Are all the assumptions explicitly stated, and are they acceptable?

- Are all relevant aspects of system design reflected in detailed design?

- Have the exceptional conditions been handled?

- Are all the data formats consistent with the system design?

- Is the design structured, and does it conform to local standards?

- Are the sizes of data structures estimated? Are provisions made to guard against overflow?

- Is each statement specified in natural language easily codable?

- Are the loop termination conditions properly specified?

- Are the conditions in the loops OK?

- Are the conditions in the if statements correct?

- Is the nesting proper?

- Is the module logic too complex?

- Are the modules highly cohesive?

8.2.3   Consistency Checkers

Design reviews and walkthroughs are manual processes; the people involved in the review and walkthrough determine the errors in the design. If the design is specified in PDL or some other formally defined design language, it is possible to detect some design defects by using consistency checkers.

Consistency checkers are essentially compilers that take as input the design specified in a design language (PDL in our case). Clearly, they cannot produce executable code because the inner syntax of PDL allows natural language and many activities are specified in the natural language. However, the module interface specifications (which belong to outer syntax) are specified formally. A consistency checker can ensure that any modules invoked or used by a given module actually exist in the design and that the interface used by the caller is consistent with the interface definition of the called module. It can also check if the used global data items are indeed defined globally in the design.

Depending on the precision and syntax of the design language, consistency checkers can produce other information as well. In addition, these tools can be used to compute the complexity of modules and other metrics, because these metrics are based on alternate and loop constructs, which have a formal syntax in PDL. The trade-off here is that the more formal the design language, the more checking can be done during design, but the cost is that the design language becomes less flexible and tends towards a programming language.

8.3 Metrics

After the detailed design the logic of the system and the data structures are largely specified. Only the implementation-oriented details, which are often specific to the programming language used, need to be further defined. Hence, many of the metrics that are traditionally associated with code can be used effectively after detailed design. During detailed design all the metrics covered during the system design are applicable and useful. With the logic of modules available after detailed design, it is meaningful to talk about the complexity of a module. Traditionally, complexity metrics are applied to code, but they can easily be applied to detailed design as well. Here we describe some metrics applicable to detailed design.

8.3.1 Cyclomatic Complexity

Based on the capability of the human mind and the experience of people, it is generally recognized that conditions and control statements add complexity to a program. Given two programs with the same size, the program with the larger number of decision statements is likely to be more complex. The simplest measure of complexity, then, is the number of constructs that represent branches in the control flow of the program, like if then else, while do, repeat until, and goto statements.

A more refined measure is the *cyclomatic complexity measure* proposed by McCabe, which is a graph-theoretic–based concept. For a graph G with n nodes, e edges, and p connected components, the cyclomatic number $V(G)$ is defined as

$$V(G) = e - n + p.$$

To use this to define the cyclomatic complexity of a module, the control flow graph G of the module is first drawn. To construct a control flow graph of a

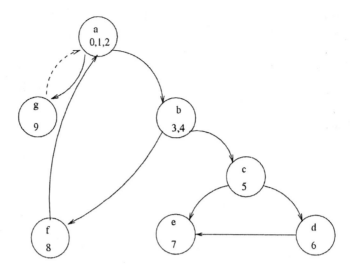

Figure 8.7: Flow graph of the example.

program module, break the module into blocks delimited by statements that affect the control flow, like if, while, repeat, and goto. These blocks form the nodes of the graph. If the control from a block i can branch to a block j, then draw an arc from node i to node j in the graph. The control flow of a program can be constructed mechanically. As an example, consider the C-like function for bubble sorting, given next. The control flow graph for this is given in Figure 8.7.

```
0.  {
1.        i = 1;
2.        while (i <= n) {
3.                j = i;
4.                while (j <= i) {
5.                        if (A[i] < A[j])
6.                                swap(A[i], A[j]);
7.                        j = j + 1; }
8.        i = i + 1; }
9.  }
```

The graph of a module has an entry node and an exit node, corresponding to the first and last blocks of statements (or we can create artificial nodes for simplicity, as in the example). In such graphs there will be a path from the entry node to any node and a path from any node to the exit node (assuming the program has no anomalies like unreachable code). For such a graph, the cyclomatic number can be 0 if the code is a linear sequence of statements without any control statement. If we draw an arc from the exit node to the entry node, the graph will be strongly connected because there is a path between any two nodes. The cyclomatic number of a graph for any program will then be nonzero, and it is desirable to have a nonzero complexity for a simple program without any conditions (after all, there is some complexity in such a program). Hence, for computing the cyclomatic complexity of a program, an arc is added from the exit node to the start node, which makes it a strongly connected graph. For a module, the *cyclomatic complexity* is defined to be the cyclomatic number of such a graph for the module.

As it turns out the cyclomatic complexity of a module (or cyclomatic number of its graph) is equal to the maximum number of linearly independent circuits in the graph. A set of circuits is linearly independent if no circuit is totally contained in another circuit or is a combination of other circuits. So, for calculating the cyclomatic number of a module, we can draw the graph, make it connected by drawing an arc from the exit node to the entry node, and then either count the number of circuits or compute it by counting the number of edges and nodes. In the graph shown in Figure 8.7, the cyclomatic complexity is

$$V(G) = 10 - 7 + 1 = 4.$$

The independent circuits are:

> ckt 1: b c e b
> ckt 2: b c d e b
> ckt 3: a b f a
> ckt 4: a g a

It can also be shown that the cyclomatic complexity of a module is the number of decisions in the module plus one, where a decision is effectively any conditional statement in the module [41]. Hence, we can also compute the cyclomatic complexity simply by counting the number of decisions in the module. For this example, as we can see, we get the same cyclomatic complexity for the module if we add 1 to the number of decisions in the module. (The module has three decisions: two in the two `while` statements and one in the `if` statement.)

The cyclomatic number is one quantitative measure of module complexity. It can be extended to compute the complexity of the whole program, though it is more suitable at the module level. McCabe proposed that the cyclomatic complexity of modules should, in general, be kept below 10. The cyclomatic number can also be used as a number of paths that should be tested during testing. Cyclomatic complexity is one of the most widely used complexity measures. Experiments indicate that the cyclomatic complexity is highly correlated to the size of the module in LOC (after all, the more lines of code the greater the number of decisions). It has also been found to be correlated to the number of faults found in modules.

8.3.2   Data Bindings

We have seen that coupling and cohesion are important concepts for evaluating a design. However, to be truly effective, metrics are needed to "measure" the coupling between modules or the cohesion of a module. During system design, we tried to quantify coupling based on information flow between modules. Now that the logic of modules is also available, we can come up with metrics that also consider the logic. One metric that attempts to capture the module-level concept of coupling is data binding. Data bindings are measures that capture the data interaction across portions of a software system [90]. In other words, data bindings try to specify how strongly coupled different modules in a software system are. Different types of data bindings are possible [90].

A *potential data binding* is defined as a triplet (p, x, q), where p and q are modules and x is a variable within the static scope of both p and q. This reflects the possibility that the modules p and q may communicate with each other through the shared variable x. This binding does not consider the internals of p and q to determine if the variable x is actually accessed in any of the modules. This binding is based on data declaration.

A *used data binding* is a potential binding where both p and q use the variable x for reference or assignment. This is harder to compute than potential data binding and requires more information about the internal logic of a module.

An *actual data binding* is a used data binding with the additional restriction that the module p assigns a value to x and q references x. It is the hardest to compute, and it signifies the situation where information may flow from the module p to module q through the shared variable x. Computation of actual data binding requires detailed logic descriptions of modules p and q.

All of these data bindings attempt to represent the strength of interconnections among modules. The greater the number of bindings between two modules, the higher the interconnection between these modules. For a particular type of binding, a matrix can be computed that contains the number of bindings between different modules. This matrix can be used for further statistical analysis to determine the interconnection strength of the system or a subsystem.

8.3.3 Cohesion Metric

Here we discuss one attempt at quantifying the cohesion of a module [54]. To compute the value of the cohesion metric for a module M, a flow graph G is constructed for M. Each vertex in G is an executable statement in M. For each node, we also record the variable referenced in the statement. An arc exists from a node s_i to another node s_j if the statement s_j can immediately follow the statement s_i in some execution of the module. In addition to these, we add an initial node I from where the execution of the module starts, and a final node T, at which the execution of the module terminates. For termination statements (e.g., return, exit) we draw an arc from the statement to T.

From G a *reduced* flow graph is constructed by deleting those nodes that do not refer to any variable (such as unconstrained gotos). All the arcs coming in the deleted node are redirected to the node that is the successor of the deleted node (such nodes will have only one successor).

Assume that the variables are sequentially numbered as 1, 2, ..., n. For a variable i, R_i is the reference set, which is the set of all the executable statements that refer to the variable i. The union of all the R_is is the set of all the nodes in the graph (minus the node for T, which is a nonexecuting node). Let $| G |$ refer to the (number of nodes - 1) for the reduced graph.

The cohesion of a set of statements S is defined as

$$C(S) = \frac{| S |\ dim(S)}{| G |\ dim(G)}$$

where $dim()$ is the dimension of a set of statements, which is the maximum number of linearly independent paths from I to T that pass through any element of S. Thus, the dimension of a set of statements S is the count of all the independent paths from the start statement to the end statement of a module that includes at least one statement from the set. If S is the set of all the statements in the module (if S is the same as G), then dim S is the same as the cyclomatic complexity of the module.

The cohesion of a module is defined as the average cohesion of the reference sets of the different statements or nodes in (reduced) G. Hence the cohesion of the module C(M) is

$$C(M) = \frac{\sum_{i=1}^{i=n} C(R_i)}{n}.$$

Essentially, this metric is trying to measure cohesion of a module by seeing how many independent paths of the module go through the different statements. The idea is that if a module has high cohesion, most of the variables will be used by statements in most paths. Hence for a high-cohesion module, the cohesion of the reference set of each variable will be high. The highest cohesion number achievable by this is when the dimension of all the reference sets is all the independent paths, thus the same as the cyclomatic complexity. In other words, the highest cohesion is when all the independent paths use all the variables of the module.

8.4   Summary

Detailed design starts after the module specifications are available, as part of the output of the system design. The goal of this activity is to develop the internal logic of the modules.

To express the internal logic of a module, we need a design language. The design language should be such that it is flexible enough to be easily usable, yet precise enough to be easily convertible into code. We have described a language, process design language (PDL), that satisfies the requirements. PDL can be used to express the detailed design of systems. It has a formal outer syntax and a flexible inner syntax and vocabulary, giving it a balance between formalism and ease of expression. Stepwise refinement and other algorithm development techniques can be used along with PDL to design as well as specify the logic.

For objects, state modeling can be used to understand the behavior of an object, as functional means are not sufficient. With state modeling, the state of an object is captured with methods causing transitions between states.

Like any phase, we need some metrics to evaluate the effectiveness of the phase and to evaluate the output of that phase. We considered a metric called cyclomatic complexity for evaluating the complexity of modules from their detailed design. This metric can be also used to assess the overall complexity of the system, or it can be used to identify the most complex modules, which are more likely to be "error-prone." In a module the cyclomatic complexity equals the number of decisions in the module plus one. We also discussed the data binding metric and a cohesion metric.

A few techniques exist for verifying the detailed design. The most common are design walkthroughs and critical design review. Automated tools can be used for some consistency checking if a well-defined design language, like PDL, is used. Even with automated consistency checkers, reviews and walkthroughs remain the most important methods for verifying the detailed design. We have described the review process and given a sample checklist that can be used in the review.

The detailed design activity is is frequently not performed formally because a detailed design description of the modules does not always adds much value, and experienced programmers feel that they can go directly to coding. Furthermore, the detailed design document has little archival value as it is almost impossible to keep the detailed design document consistent with the code. Hence the primary use of the detailed design phase is to help the programmer who can specify the logic and get it verified before writing the code. Due to this, developing the detailed design is of value mostly for the more complex and important modules. Even for these, the detailed design is often done informally by the programmer as part of the personal process of developing code. Due to these reasons, we will not give the detailed design of the case study.

Exercises

1. The detailed design of a system can involve many persons, each developing the detailed design of a set of modules. Draw a process diagram for this method of detailed design development.

2. Extend the PDL with constructs to support classes. Then write the detailed design for classes String, Btree, SymbolTable.

3. Do a state modeling of these classes: String, Btree, and SymbolTable.

4. What features would you like to add to PDL if the target source language supports data abstraction?

5. If cyclomatic complexity of a module is much higher than the suggested limit of 10, what will you do? Give reasons and guidelines for whatever you propose.

6. Design an experiment to study the relationship between the cyclomatic complexity and size in LOC of modules. Collect a set of programs and then perform the experiment and determine the nature of the relationship between them for these programs.

7. Design an experiment to study the relation between cyclomatic complexity and "error-proneness" of modules. If you can collect error data, execute the experiment on the data you can collect.

9

Coding

The goal of the coding or programming activity is to implement the design in the best possible manner. The coding activity affects both testing and maintenance profoundly. As we saw earlier, the time spent in coding is a small percentage of the total software cost, while testing and maintenance consume the major percentage. Thus, it should be clear that the goal during coding should *not* be to reduce the implementation cost, but the goal should be to reduce the cost of later phases, even if it means that the cost of this phase has to increase. In other words, the goal during this phase is *not* to simplify the job of the programmer. Rather, the goal should be to simplify the job of the tester and the maintainer.

This distinction is important, as programmers are often concerned about how to finish their job quickly, without keeping the later phases in mind. During coding, it should be kept in mind that the programs should not be constructed so that they are easy to write, but so that they are easy to read and understand. A program is read a lot more often and by a lot more people during the later phases.

There are many different criteria for judging a program, including readability, size of the program, execution time, and required memory. Having readability and understandability as a clear objective of the coding activity can itself help in producing software that is more maintainable. A famous experiment by Weinberg showed that if programmers are specified a clear objective for the program, they usually satisfy it [143]. In the experiment, five different teams were given the same problem for which they had to develop programs. However, each of the teams was specified a different objective, which it had to satisfy. The different objectives given were: minimize the

	Resulting Rank (1 = Best)				
	O1	O2	O3	O4	O5
Minimize effort to complete (O1)	1	4	4	5	3
Minimize number of statements (O2)	2–3	1	2	3	5
Minimize memory required (O3)	5	2	1	4	4
Maximize program clarity (O4)	4	3	3	2	2
Maximize output clarity (O5)	2–3	5	5	1	1

Figure 9.1: The Weinberg experiment.

effort required to complete the program, minimize the number of statements, minimize the memory required, maximize the program clarity, and maximize the output clarity. It was found that in most cases each team did the best for the objective that was specified to it. The rank of the different teams for the different objectives is shown in Figure 9.1.

The experiment clearly shows that if objectives are clear, programmers tend to achieve that objective. Hence, if readability is an objective of the coding activity, then it is likely that programmers will develop easily understandable programs. For our purposes, ease of understanding and modification are the basic goals of the programming activity.

In this chapter we will first discuss some programming practices and guidelines, in which we will also discuss some common coding errors to make students aware of them. Then we discuss some processes that are followed while coding. Refactoring is discussed next, which is done during coding but is a distinct activity. We then discuss some verification methods, followed by discussion of some metrics. We end the chapter with a discussion of the implementation of the case studies.

9.1   Programming Principles and Guidelines

The main task before a programmer is to write quality code with few bugs in it. The additional constraint is to write code quickly. Writing solid code is a skill that can only be acquired by practice. However, based on experience, some general rules and guidelines can be given for the programmer. Good programming (producing correct and simple programs) is a practice independent of the target programming language, although well-structured programming languages make the programmer's job simpler. In this section, we will discuss some concepts and practices that can help a programmer write higher quality code. As a key task of a programmer is to avoid errors in the programs, we first discuss some common coding errors.

9.1.1 Common Coding Errors

Software errors (we will use the terms errors, defects and bugs interchangeably in our discussion here; precise definitions are given in the next chapter) are a reality that all programmers have to deal with. Much of effort in developing software goes in identifying and removing bugs. There are various practices that can reduce the occurrence of bugs, but regardless of the tools or methods we use, bugs are going to occur in programs. Though errors can occur in a wide variety of ways, some types of errors are found more commonly. Here we give a list of some of the commonly occurring bugs. The main purpose of discussing them is to educate programmers about these mistakes so that they can avoid them. The compilation is based on various published articles on the topic (e.g., [28, 87, 57, 55, 150]), and a more detailed compilation is available in the TR [141].

Memory Leaks

A memory leak is a situation where the memory is allocated to the program which is not freed subsequently. This error is a common source of software failures which occurs frequently in the languages which do not have automatic garbage collection (like C, C++). They have little impact in short programs but can have catastrophic effect on long running systems. A software system with memory leaks keeps consuming memory, till at some point of time the program may come to an exceptional halt because of the lack of free memory. An example of this error is:

```c
char* foo(int s)
{
        char *output;
        if (s>0)
          output=(char*) malloc (size);
        if (s==1)
          return NULL; /* if s==1 then mem leaked */
        return(output);
}
```

Freeing an Already Freed Resource

In general, in programs, resources are first allocated and then freed. For example, memory is first allocated and then deallocated. This error occurs when the programmer tries to free the already freed resource. The impact of this common error can be catastrophic. An example of this error is:

```
main()
{
   char *str;
   str=(char *)malloc(10);
   if (global==0)
         free(str);
   free(str); /* str is already freed
}
```

The impact of this error can be more severe if we have some malloc statement between the two free statements—there is a chance that the first freed location is now allocated to the new variable and the subsequent free will deallocate it!

NULL Dereferencing

This error occurs when we try to access the contents of a location that points to NULL. This is a commonly occurring error which can bring a software system down. It is also difficult to detect as it the NULL dereferencing may occur only in some paths and only under certain situations. Often improper initialization in the different paths leads to the NULL reference statement. It can also be caused because of aliases—for example, two variables refer to the same object, and one is freed and an attempt is made to dereference the second. This code segment shows two instances of NULL dereference.

```
char *ch=NULL;
if (x>0)
{
   ch='c';
}
printf("\%c", *ch); /* ch may be NULL
*ch=malloc(size);
ch = 'c'; /* ch will be NULL if malloc returns NULL
```

Similar to NULL dereference is the error of accessing uninitialized memory. This often occurs if data is initialized in most cases, but some cases do not get covered. they were not expected. An example of this error is:

```
switch( i )
{
        case 0: s=OBJECT_1; break;
        case 1: s=OBJECT_2;break;
}
return (s); /* s not initialized for values
                other than 0 or 1 */
```

Lack of Unique Addresses

Aliasing creates many problems, and among them is violation of unique addresses when we expect different addresses. For example in the string concatenation function, we expect source and destination addresses to be different. If this is not the case, as is the situation in the code segment below, it can lead to runtime errors.

```
strcat(src,destn);
/* In above function, if src is aliased to destn,
 * then we may get a runtime error */
```

Synchronization Errors

In a parallel program, where there are multiple threads possibly accessing some common resources, then synchronization errors are possible [43, 55]. These errors are very difficult to find as they don't manifest easily. But when they do manifest, they can cause serious damage to the system. There are different categories of synchronization errors, some of which are:

1. Deadlocks

2. Race conditions

3. Inconsistent synchronization

Deadlock is a situation in which one or more threads mutually lock each other. The most frequent reason for the cause of deadlocks is inconsistent locking sequence—the threads in deadlock wait for resources which are in turn locked by some other thread. Race conditions occur when two threads try to access the same resource and the result of the execution depends on the order of the execution of the threads. Inconsistent synchronization is also a common error representing the situation where there is a mix of locked and unlocked accesses to some shared variables, particularly if the access involves updates. Some examples of these errors are given in the [141].

Array Index Out of Bounds

Array index often goes out of bounds, leading to exceptions. Care needs to be taken to see that the array index values are not negative and do not exceed their bounds.

Arithmetic exceptions

These include errors like divide by zero and floating point exceptions. The result of these may vary from getting unexpected results to termination of the program.

Off by One

This is one of the most common errors which can be caused in many ways. For example, starting at 1 when we should start at 0 or vice versa, writing $<= N$ instead of $< N$ or vice versa, and so on.

Enumerated data types

Overflow and underflow errors can easily occur when working with enumerated types, and care should be taken when assuming the values of enumerated data types. An example of such an error is:

```
typedef enum {A, B,C, D} grade;
void foo(grade x)
{
        int l,m;
        l=GLOBAL_ARRAY[x-1]; /* Underflow possible */
        m=GLOBAL_ARRAY[x+1]; /* Overflow possible */
}
```

Illegal use of & instead of &&

This bug arises if non short circuit logic (like & or |) is used instead of short circuit logic (&& or ||). Non short circuit logic will evaluate both sides of the expression. But short circuit operator evaluates one side and based on the result, it decides if it has to evaluate the other side or not. An example is:

```
if(object != null & object.getTitle() != null)
/* Here second operation can cause a null dereference */
```

String handling errors

There are a number of ways in which string handling functions like strcpy, sprintf, gets etc can fail. Examples are one of the operands is NULL, the string is not NULL terminated, or the source operand may have greater size than the destination. String handling errors are quite common.

Buffer overflow

Though buffer overflow is also a frequent cause of software failures, in todays world its main impact is that it is a security flaw that can be exploited by a malicious user for executing arbitrary code.

When a program takes an input which is being copied in a buffer, by giving a large (and malicious) input, a malicious user can overflow the buffer on the stack. By doing this, the return address can get rewritten to whatever the malicious user has planned. So, when the function call ends, the control goes to where the malicious user has planned, which is typically some malicious code to take control of the computer or do some harmful actions. Basically, by exploiting the buffer overflow situation, a malicious user can execute arbitrary code. The following code fragment illustrates buffer overflow:

```
void mygets(char *str){
      int ch;
      while(ch=getchar() !='\n' && ch!='\0')
            *(str++)=ch;
      *str='\0';
}
main(){
      char s2[4];
      mygets(s2);
```

```
}
```

Here there is a possible buffer overflow attack. If the input given is large, it can overflow the buffer s2, and by carefully crafting the bytes that go on the stack the return address of mygets() can be replaced by an address of a malicious program. For further discussion on buffer overflow and on writing code that is secure, the reader is referred to [88].

9.1.2 Structured Programming

As stated earlier the basic objective of the coding activity is to produce programs that are easy to understand. It has been argued by many that structured programming practice helps develop programs that are easier to understand. The structured programming movement started in the 1970s, and much has been said and written about it. Now the concept pervades so much that it is generally accepted—even implied—that programming should be structured. Though a lot of emphasis has been placed on structured programming, the concept and motivation behind structured programming are often not well understood. Structured programming is often regarded as "goto-less" programming. Although extensive use of gotos is certainly not desirable, structured programs *can* be written with the use of gotos. Here we provide a brief discussion on what structured programming is.

A program has a static structure as well as a dynamic structure. The static structure is the structure of the text of the program, which is usually just a linear organization of statements of the program. The dynamic structure of the program is the sequence of statements executed during the execution of the program. In other words, both the static structure and the dynamic behavior are sequences of statements; where the sequence representing the static structure of a program is fixed, the sequence of statements it executes can change from execution to execution.

The general notion of correctness of the program means that when the program executes, it produces the desired behavior. To show that a program is correct, we need to show that when the program executes, its behavior is what is expected. Consequently, when we argue about a program, either formally to prove that it is correct or informally to debug it or convince ourselves that it works, we study the static structure of the program (i.e., its code) but try to argue about its dynamic behavior. In other words, much of the activity of program understanding is to understand the dynamic behavior of the program from the text of the program.

It will clearly be easier to understand the dynamic behavior if the structure in the dynamic behavior resembles the static structure. The closer the correspondence between execution and text structure, the easier the program is to understand, and the more different the structure during execution, the harder it will be to argue about the behavior from the program text. The goal of structured programming is to ensure that the static structure and the dynamic structures are the same. That is, the objective of structured programming is to write programs so that the sequence of statements executed during the execution of a program is the same as the sequence of statements in the text of that program. As the statements in a program text are linearly organized, the objective of structured programming becomes developing programs whose control flow during execution is linearized and follows the linear organization of the program text.

Clearly, no meaningful program can be written as a sequence of simple statements without any branching or repetition (which also involves branching). So, how is the objective of linearizing the control flow to be achieved? By making use of structured constructs. In structured programming, a statement is not a simple assignment statement, it is a structured statement. The key property of a structured statement is that it has a *single-entry* and a *single-exit*. That is, during execution, the execution of the (structured) statement starts from one defined point and the execution terminates at one defined point. With single-entry and single-exit statements, we can view a program as a sequence of (structured) statements. And if all statements are structured statements, then during execution, the sequence of execution of these statements will be the same as the sequence in the program text. Hence, by using single-entry and single-exit statements, the correspondence between the static and dynamic structures can be obtained. The most commonly used single-entry and single-exit statements are:

>*Selection:* if B then S1 else S2
>   if B then S1
>*Iteration:* While B do S
>   repeat S until B
>*Sequencing:* S1; S2; S3;...

It can be shown that these three basic constructs are sufficient to program any conceivable algorithm. Modern languages have other such constructs that help linearize the control flow of a program, which, generally speaking, makes it easier to understand a program. Hence, programs should be written so that, as far as possible, single-entry, single-exit control constructs are used. The basic goal, as we have tried to emphasize, is to make the logic of the program simple to understand. No hard-and-fast rule can be formulated that will be applicable under all circumstances. Structured programming practice forms a good basis and guideline for writing programs clearly.

It should be pointed out that the main reason structured programming was promulgated is formal verification of programs. As we will see later in this chapter, during verification, a program is considered a sequence of executable statements, and verification proceeds step by step, considering one statement in the statement list (the program) at a time. Implied in these verification methods is the assumption that during execution, the statements will be executed in the sequence in which they are organized in the program text. If this assumption is satisfied, the task of verification becomes easier. Hence, even from the point of view of verification, it is important that the sequence of execution of statements is the same as the sequence of statements in the text.

A final note about the structured constructs. Any piece of code with a single-entry and single-exit cannot be considered a structured construct. If that is the case, one could always define appropriate units in any program to make it appear as a sequence of these units (in the worst case, the whole program could be defined to be a unit). The basic objective of using structured constructs is to linearize the control flow so that the execution behavior is easier to understand and argue about. In linearized control flow, if we understand the behavior of each of the basic constructs properly, the behavior of the program can be considered a composition of the behaviors of the different statements. For this basic approach to work, it is implied that we can clearly understand the behavior of each construct. This requires that we be able to succinctly capture or describe the behavior of each construct. Unless we can do this, it will not be possible to compose them. Clearly, for an arbitrary structure, we cannot do this merely because it has a single-entry and single-exit. It is from this viewpoint that the structures mentioned earlier are chosen as structured statements. There are well-defined rules that specify how these statements behave during execution, which allows us to argue about larger programs.

Overall, it can be said that structured programming, in general, leads to programs that are easier to understand than unstructured programs, and that such programs are easier (relatively speaking) to formally prove. However, it should be kept in mind that structured programming is not an end in itself. Our basic objective is that the program be easy to understand. And structured programming is a safe approach for achieving this objective. Still, there are some common programming practices that are now well understood that make use of unstructured constructs (e.g., break statement, continue statement). Although efforts should be made to avoid using statements that effectively violate the single-entry single-exit property, if the use of such statements is the simplest way to organize the program, then from the point of view of readability, the constructs should be used. The main point is that any unstructured construct should be used only if the structured alternative is harder to understand. This view can be taken only because we are focusing on readability. If the objective was formal verifiability, structured programming will probably be necessary.

9.1.3 Information Hiding

A software solution to a problem always contains data structures that are meant to represent information in the problem domain. That is, when software is developed to solve a problem, the software uses some data structures to capture the information in the problem domain.

In general, only certain operations are performed on some information. That is, a piece of information in the problem domain is used only in a limited number of ways in the problem domain. For example, a ledger in an accountant's office has some very defined uses: debit, credit, check the current balance, etc. An operation where all debits are multiplied together and then divided by the sum of all credits is typically not performed. So, any information in the problem domain typically has a small number of defined operations performed on it.

When the information is represented as data structures, the same principle should be applied, and only some defined operations should be performed on the data structures. This, essentially, is the principle of information hiding. The information captured in the data structures should be hidden from the rest of the system, and only the access functions on the data structures that represent the operations performed on the information should be visible. In other words, when the information is captured in data structures and then on the data structures that represent some information, for each operation on the information an access function should be provided. And as the rest of the system in the problem domain only performs these defined operations on the information, the rest of the modules in the software should only use these access functions to access and manipulate the data structures.

Information hiding can reduce the coupling between modules and make the system more maintainable. Information hiding is also an effective tool for managing the complexity of developing software—by using information hiding we have separated the concern of managing the data from the concern of using the data to produce some desired results.

Many of the older languages, like Pascal, C, and FORTRAN, do not provide mechanisms to support data abstraction. With such languages, information hiding can be supported only by a disciplined use of the language. That is, the access restrictions will have to be imposed by the programmers; the language does not provide them. Most modern OO languages provide linguistic mechanisms to implement information hiding.

9.1.4   Some Programming Practices

The concepts discussed above can help in writing simple and clear code with few bugs. There are many programming practices that can also help towards that objective. We discuss here a few rules that have been found to make code easier to read as well as avoid some of the errors. Some of these practices are from [141].

Control Constructs: As discussed earlier, it is desirable that as much as possible single-entry, single-exit constructs be used. It is also desirable to use a few standard control constructs rather than using a wide variety of constructs, just because they are available in the language.

Gotos: Gotos should be used sparingly and in a disciplined manner. Only when the alternative to using gotos is more complex should the gotos be used. In any case, alternatives must be thought of before finally using a goto. If a goto must be used, forward transfers (or a jump to a later statement) is more acceptable than a backward jump.

Information Hiding: As discussed earlier, information hiding should be supported where possible. Only the access functions for the data structures should be made visible while hiding the data structure behind these functions.

User-Defined Types: Modern languages allow users to define types like the enumerated type. When such facilities are available, they should be exploited where applicable. For example, when working with dates, a type can be defined for the day of the week. Using such a type makes the program much clearer than defining codes for each day and then working with codes.

Nesting: If nesting of if-then-else constructs becomes too deep, then the logic become harder to understand. In case of deeply nested if-then-elses, it is often difficult to determine the if statement to which a particular else clause is associated. Where possible, deep nesting should be avoided, even if it means a little inefficiency. For example, consider the following construct of nested if-then-elses:

```
if C1 then S1
    else if C2 then S2
        else if C3 then S3
            else if C4 then S4;
```

If the different conditions are disjoint (as they often are), this structure can be converted into the following structure:

```
if C1 then S1;
if C2 then S2;
if C3 then S3;
if C4 then S4;
```

This sequence of statements will produce the same result as the earlier sequence (if the conditions are disjoint), but it is much easier to understand. The price is a little inefficiency.

Module Size: We discussed this issue during system design. A programmer should carefully examine any function with too many statements (say more than 100). Large modules often will not be functionally cohesive. There can be no hard-and-fast rule about module sizes the guiding principle should be cohesion and coupling.

Module Interface: A module with a complex interface should be carefully examined. As a rule of thumb, any module whose interface has more than five parameters should be carefully examined and broken into multiple modules with a simpler interface if possible.

Side Effects: When a module is invoked, it sometimes has side effects of modifying the program state beyond the modification of parameters listed in the module interface definition, for example, modifying global variables. Such side effects should be avoided where possible, and if a module has side effects, they should be properly documented.

Robustness: A program is robust if it does something planned even for exceptional conditions. A program might encounter exceptional conditions in such forms as incorrect input, the incorrect value of some variable, and overflow. If such situations do arise, the program should not just "crash" or "core dump"; it should produce some meaningful message and exit gracefully.

Switch case with default: If there is no default case in a "switch" statement, the behavior can be unpredictable if that case arises at some point of time which was not predictable at development stage. Such a practice can result in a bug like NULL dereference, memory leak, as well as other types of serious bugs. It is a good practice to always include a default case.

```
switch (i){
      case 0 : {s=malloc(size)
      }
  s[0] = y; /* NULL dereference if default occurs*/
```

Empty Catch Block: An exception is caught, but if there is no action, it may represent a scenario where some of the operations to be done are not performed. Whenever exceptions are caught, it is a good practice to take some default action, even if it is just printing an error message.

```
try {
      FileInputStream fis = new
      FileInputStream("InputFile");
}
catch (IOException ioe) { }
      // not a good practice
```

Empty if, while Statement: A condition is checked but nothing is done based on the check. This often occurs due to some mistake and should be caught. Other similar errors include empty finally, try, synchronized, empty static method, etc. Such useless checks should be avoided.

```
if (x == 0) {}  /* nothing is done after checking x */
else {
   :
}
```

Read Return to be Checked: Often the return value from reads is not checked, assuming that the read returns the desired values. Sometimes the result from a read can be different from what is expected, and this can cause failures later. There may be some cases where neglecting this condition may result in some serious error. For example, if read from scanf() is more than expected, then it may cause a buffer overflow. Hence the value of read should be checked before accessing the data read. (This is the reason why most languages provide a return value for the read operation.)

Return From Finally Block: One should not return from finally block, as cases it can create false beliefs. For example, consider the code

```
public String foo() {
    try {
            throw new Exception( "An Exception" );
    }
    catch (Exception e) {
            throw e;
    }
    finally {
            return "Some value";
            }
    }
```

In this example, a value is returned both in exception and nonexception scenarios. Hence at the caller site, the user will not be able to distinguish between the two. Another interesting case arises when we have a return from try block. In this case, if there is a return in finally also, then the value from finally is returned instead of the value from try.

Correlated Parameters: Often there is an implicit correlation between the parameters. For example, in the code segment given below, "length" represents the size of BUFFER. If the correlation does not hold, we can run into a serious problem like buffer overflow (illustrated in the code fragment below). Hence, it is a good practice to validate this correlation rather than assuming that it holds. In general, it is desirable to do some counter checks on implicit assumptions about parameters.

```
void (char *src, int length, char destn[]) {
        strcpy (destn, src); /* Can cause buffer overflow
                        if length > MAX_SIZE */
    }
```

Trusted Data sources: Counter checks should be made before accessing the input data, particularly if the input data is being provided by the user or is being obtained over the network. For example, while doing the string copy operation, we should check that the source string is null terminated, or that its size is as we expect. Similar is the case with some network data which may be sniffed and prone to some modifications or corruptions. To avoid problems due to these changes, we should put some checks, like parity checks, hashes, etc. to ensure the validity of the incoming data.

Give Importance to Exceptions: Most programmers tend to give less attention to the possible exceptional cases and tend to work with the main flow of events, control, and data. Though the main work is done in the main path, it is the exceptional paths that often cause software systems to fail. To make a software system more reliable, a programmer should consider all possibilities and write suitable exception handlers to prevent failures or loss when such situations occur.

9.1.5 Coding Standards

Programmers spend far more time reading code than writing code. Over the life of the code, the author spends a considerable time reading it during debugging and enhancement. People other than the author also spend considerable effort in reading code because the code is often maintained by someone other than the author. In short, it is of prime importance to write code in a manner that it is easy to read and understand. Coding standards provide rules and guidelines for some aspects of programming in order to make code easier to read. Most organizations who develop software regularly develop their own standards.

In general, coding standards provide guidelines for programmers regarding naming, file organization, statements and declarations, and layout and comments. To give an idea of coding standards (often called conventions or style guidelines), we discuss some guidelines for Java, based on publicly available standards (from www.geosoft.no or java.sun.com/docs).

Naming Conventions

Some of the standard naming conventions that are followed often are:

- Package names should be in lower case (e.g., mypackage, edu.iitk.maths)

- Type names should be nouns and should start with uppercase (e.g., Day, DateOfBirth, EventHandler)

- Variable names should be nouns starting with lower case (e.g., name, amount)

- Constant names should be all uppercase (e.g., PI, MAX_ITERATIONS)

- Method names should be verbs starting with lowercase (e.g., getValue())

- Private class variables should have the _ suffix (e.g., "private int value_"). (Some standards will require this to be a prefix.)

- Variables with a large scope should have long names; variables with a small scope can have short names; loop iterators should be named i, j, k, etc.

- The prefix *is* should be used for boolean variables and methods to avoid confusion (e.g., isStatus should be used instead of status); negative boolean variable names (e.g., isNotCorrect) should be avoided.

- The term *compute* can be used for methods where something is being computed; the term *find* can be used where something is being looked up (e.g., computeMean(), findMin().)

- Exception classes should be suffixed with *Exception* (e.g., OutOfBound-Exception.)

Files

There are conventions on how files should be named, and what files should contain, such that a reader can get some idea about what the file contains. Some examples of these conventions are:

- Java source files should have the extension .java—this is enforced by most compilers and tools.

- Each file should contain one outer class and the class name should be same as the file name.

- Line length should be limited to less than 80 columns and special characters should be avoided. If the line is longer, it should be continued and the continuation should be made very clear.

Statements

These guidelines are for the declaration and executable statements in the source code. Some examples are given below. Note, however, that not everyone will agree to these. That is why organizations generally develop their own guidelines that can be followed without restricting the flexibility of programmers for the type of work the organization does.

- Variables should be initialized where declared, and they should be declared in the smallest possible scope.

- Declare related variables together in a common statement. Unrelated variables should not be declared in the same statement.

- Class variables should never be declared public.

- Use only loop control statements in a for loop.

- Loop variables should be initialized immediately before the loop.

- Avoid the use of *break* and *continue* in a loop.

- Avoid the use of *do ... while* construct.

- Avoid complex conditional expressions—introduce temporary boolean variables instead.

- Avoid executable statements in conditionals.

Commenting and Layout

Comments are textual statements that are meant for the program reader to aid the understanding of code. The purpose of comments is not to explain in English the logic of the program—if the logic is so complex that it requires comments to explain it, it is better to rewrite and simplify the code instead. In general, comments should explain what the code is doing or why the code is there, so that the code can become almost standalone for understanding the system. Comments should generally be provided for blocks of code, and in many cases, only comments for the modules need to be provided.

Providing comments for modules is most useful, as modules form the unit of testing, compiling, verification and modification. Comments for a module are often called *prologue* for the module, which describes the functionality and the purpose of the module, its public interface and how the module is to be used, parameters of the interface, assumptions it makes about the parameters, and any side effects it has. Other features may also be included. It should be noted that prologues are useful only if they are kept consistent with the logic of the module. If the module is modified, then the prologue should also be modified, if necessary.

Java provides *documentation comments* that are delimited by "/** ... */", and which could be extracted to HTML files. These comments are mostly used as prologues for classes and its methods and fields, and are meant to provide documentation to users of the classes who may not have access to the source code. In addition to prologue for modules, coding standards may specify how and where comments should be located. Some such guidelines are:

- Single line comments for a block of code should be aligned with the code they are meant for.

- There should be comments for all major variables explaining what they represent.

- A block of comments should be preceded by a blank comment line with just "/*" and ended with a line containing just "*/".

- Trailing comments after statements should be short, on the same line, and shifted far enough to separate them from statements.

Layout guidelines focus on how a program should be indented, how it should use blank lines, white spaces, etc. to make it more easily readable. Indentation guidelines are sometimes provided for each type of programming construct. However, most programmers learn these by seeing the code of others and the code fragments in books and documents, and many of these have become fairly standard over the years. We will not discuss them further except saying that a programmer should use some conventions, and use them consistently.

9.2 Coding Process

The coding activity starts when some form of design has been done and the specifications of the modules to be developed are available. With the design, modules are usually assigned to individual developers for coding. In a top-down implementation, we start by assigning modules at the top of the hierarchy and proceed to the lower levels. In a bottom-up implementation, the development starts with first implementing the modules at the bottom of the hierarchy and proceeds up. The impact of how we proceed is on integration and testing.

When modules are assigned to developers, they use some process for developing the code. We now look at some processes that developers use during coding, or that have been suggested.

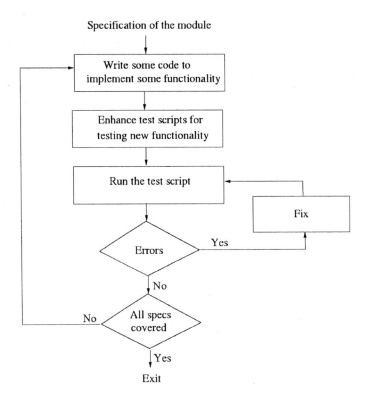

Figure 9.2: An incremental coding process.

9.2.1   An Incremental Coding Process

The process followed by many developers is to write the code for the currently assigned module, and when done, perform unit testing on it and fix the bugs found. Then the code is checked in the project repository to make it available to others in the project. (We will explain the process of checking in later.)

A better process for coding, that is often followed by experienced developers, is to develop the code incrementally. That is, write code for implementing only part of the functionality of the module. This code is compiled and tested with some quick tests to check the code that has been written so far. When the code passes these tests, the developer proceeds to add further functionality to the code, which is then tested again. In other words, the code is built incrementally by the developers, testing it as it is built. This coding process is shown in Figure 9.2.

The basic advantage of developing code incrementally with testing being done after every round of coding is to facilitate debugging—an error found in some testing can be safely attributed to code that was added since last successful testing. For following this process, it is essential that there be automated test scripts that can run the test cases with the click of a button. With these test scripts, testing can be done as frequently as desired, and new test cases can be added easily. These test scripts are a tremendous aid when code is enhanced in future due to requirement changes—through the test scripts it can be quickly checked that the earlier functionality is still working. These test scripts can also be used with some enhancements for the final unit testing that is often done before checking in the module.

9.2.2 Test Driven Development

Test Driven Development (TDD) [11] is a coding process that turns around the common approach to coding. In TDD, a programmer first writes the test scripts, and then writes the code to pass the tests. The whole process is done incrementally, with tests being written based on the specifications and code being written to pass the tests. The TDD process is shown in Figure 9.3.

This is a relatively new approach, which has been adopted in the extreme programming (XP) methodology [10]. The concept of TDD is, however, general and not tied to any particular methodology. The discussion of TDD here is based on [11].

A few points are worth noting about TDD. First, the approach says that you write just enough code to pass the tests. By following this, the code is always in sync with the tests. This is not always the case with the code-first approach, in which it is all too common to write a long piece of code, but then only write a few tests which cover only some parts of the code. By encouraging that code is written only to pass the tests, the responsibility of ensuring that required functionality is built is being passed to the activity of writing the test cases. That is, it is the task of test cases to check that the code that will be developed has all the functionality needed.

This writing of test cases before the code is written makes the development usage-driven. That is, first the focus is to determine how the code to be developed will be used. This is extracted from the specifications and the usage interface is specified precisely when the test cases are written. This helps ensure that the interfaces are from the perspective of the user of the code and that some key usage scenarios have been enunciated before the code is written. The focus is on the users of the code and the code is written to satisfy the users. This can reduce interface errors.

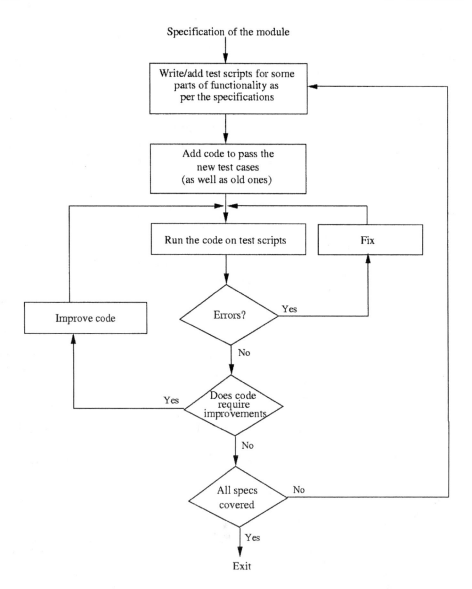

Figure 9.3: Test driven development process.

In TDD, some type of prioritization for code development naturally happens. It is most likely that the first few tests are likely to focus on using the main functionality. Generally, the test cases for lower priority features or functionality will be developed later. Consequently, code for high priority features will be developed first and lower priority items will be developed later. This has the benefit that higher priority items get done first, but has the drawback that some of the lower priority features or some special cases for which test cases are not written may not get handled in the code.

As the code is written to satisfy the test cases, the completeness of the code depends on the thoroughness of the test cases. Often it is hard and tedious to write test cases for all the scenarios or special conditions, and it is highly unlikely that a developer will write test cases for all the special cases. In TDD, as the goal is to write enough code to pass the test cases, such special cases may not get handled. Also, as at each step code is being written primarily to pass the tests, it may later be found that earlier algorithms were not well suited. In that case, the code should be improved before new functionality is added, as shown in Figure 9.3.

9.2.3 Pair Programming

Pair programming is also a coding process that has been proposed as a key technique in extreme programming (XP) methodology [10]. In pair programming, code is not written by individual programmers but by a pair of programmers. That is, the coding work is assigned not to an individual but to a pair of individuals. This pair together writes the code.

The process envisaged is that one person will type the program while the other will actively participate and constantly review what is being typed. When errors are noticed, they are pointed out and corrected. When needed, the pair discuss the algorithms, data structures, or strategies to be used in the code to be written. The roles are rotated frequently making both equal partners and having similar roles.

The basic motivation for pair programming is that as code reading and code reviews have been found to be very effective in detecting defects, by having a pair do the programming we have the situation where the code is getting reviewed as it is being typed. That is, instead of writing code and then getting it reviewed by another programmer, we have a programmer who is constantly reviewing the code being written. Like incremental development and testing, we now have incremental reviewing taking place.

Besides ongoing code review, having two programmers apply themselves to the programming task at hand is likely to result in better decisions being taken about the data structures, algorithms, interfaces, logic, etc. Special conditions, which frequently result in errors, are also more likely to be dealt with in a better manner.

The potential drawback of pair programming is that it may result in loss of productivity by assigning two people for a programming task. It is clear that a pair will produce better code as compared to code being developed by a single programmer. The open question is whether this increase in productivity due to improved code quality offsets the loss incurred by putting two people on a task. There are also issues of accountability and code ownership, particularly when the pairs are not fixed and rotate (as has been proposed in XP). Impact of pair programming is an active area of research, particularly for experimental software engineering.

9.2.4   Source Code Control and Build

In a project many different people develop source code. Each programmer creates different source files, which are eventually combined together to create executables. Programmers keep changing their source files as the code evolves, as we have seen in the processes discussed above, and often make changes in other source files as well. In order to keep control over the sources and their evolution, source code control is almost always used in projects using tools like the CVS on UNIX (www.cvshome.org) or visual source safe (VSS) on Windows (msdn.microsoft.com/vstudio/previous/ssafe) Here we give a brief description of how these tools are used in the coding process. Earlier in Chapter 2 we have discussed the concepts of a general CM process. Our discussion is based on CVS.

A modern source code control system contains a repository, which is essentially a controlled directory structure, which keeps the full revision history of all the files. For efficiency, a file history is generally kept as deltas or increments from the base file. This allows any older version of the file to be recreated, thereby giving the flexibility to easily discard a change, should the need arise. The repository is also the "official" source for all the files.

For a project, a repository has to be set up with permissions for different people in the project. The files the repository will contain are also specified—these are the files whose evolution the repository maintains. Programmers use the repository to make their source files changes available, as well as obtain other source files. Some of the types of commands that are generally performed by a programmer are:

Get a local copy. A programmer in a project works on a local copy of the file. Commands are provided to make a local copy from the repository. Making a local copy is generally called a *checkout*. An example command is *cvs checkout < module >*, which copies a set of files that belongs to the *< module >* on the local machine. A user will get the latest copy of the file. However, if a user wants, any older version of a file can be obtained from the repository, as the complete history is maintained. Many users can check out a file.

Make changes to file(s). The changes made to the local file by a programmer remain local until the changes are *committed* back on the repository. By committing (e.g., by *cvs commit < file >*) the changes made to the local file are made to the repository, and are hence available to others. This operation is also referred to as *check in*.

Update a local copy. Changes committed by project members to the repository are not reflected in the local copies that were made before the changes were committed. For getting the changes, the local copies of the files have to be updated (e.g., by *cvs update* command). By an update, all the changes made to the files are reflected in the local copy.

Get Reports. Source control tools provide a host of commands to provide different reports on the evolution of the files. These include reports like the difference between the local file and the latest version of the file, all changes made to a file along with the dates and reasons for change (which are typically provided while committing a change).

Note that once the changes are committed, they become available to all members of the team, who are generally supposed to use the source files from the repository for checking their own programs. Hence, it is essential that a programmer commits a source file only when it is in a state that it is usable by others. In steady state, the normal behavior of a project member will be as follows: check out the latest version of the files to be changed; make the planned changes to them; validate that the changes have the desired effect (for which all the files may be copied and the system tried out locally); commit the changes back to the repository.

It should be clear that if two people check out some file and then make changes, there is a possibility of a conflict—different changes are made to the same parts of the file. All tools will detect the conflict when the second person tries to commit the changes, and will inform the user. The user has to manually resolve the conflit, i.e., make the file such that the changes do not conflict with existing changes, and then commit the file. Conflicts are usually rare as they occur only if different changes are made to the same lines in a file.

With a source code control system, a programmer does not need to maintain all the versions—at any time if some changes need to be undone, older

versions can be easily recovered. The repositories are always backed up, so
they also provide protection against accidental loss. Furthermore, a record
of changes is maintained—who made the change and when, why was the
change made, what were the actual changes, etc. Most importantly, the
repository provides a central place for the latest and authoritative files of
the project. This is invaluable for products that have a long life and that
evolve over many years.

Besides using the repository for maintaining the different versions, it is
also used for constructing the software system from the sources—an activity
often called *build*. The build gets the latest version (or the desired version
number) of the sources from the repository, and creates the executables from
the sources.

Building the final executables from the source files is often done through
tools like the Makefile [62], which specify the dependence between files and
how the final executables are constructed from the source files. These tools
are capable of recognizing that files have changed and will recompile whenever files are changed for creating the executables. With source code control,
these tools will generally get the latest copy from the repository, then use it
for creating executables.

This is one of the simplest approaches to source code control and build.
Often, when large systems are being built, more elaborate methods for source
code control and build are needed. Such methods often have a hierarchy of
controlled areas, each having different levels of control and different sources,
with the top of the hierarchy containing all the files needed to build the "official" system. Lower levels of the hierarchy can be used by different groups
to create "local" builds for testing and other purposes. In such a system,
forward integration and reverse integration is needed to pass changes back
and forth between the controlled areas at different levels of the hierarchy.
An advanced tool like ClearCase provides such capabilities.

9.3   Refactoring

We have seen that coding often involves making changes to some existing
code. Code also changes when requirements change or when new functionality is added. Due to the changes being done to modules, even if we started
with a good design, with time we often end up with code whose design is
not as good as it could be. And once the design embodied in the code becomes complex, then enhancing the code to accommodate required changes

becomes more complex, time consuming, and error prone. In other words, the productivity and quality starts decreasing.

Refactoring is the technique to improve existing code and prevent this design decay with time. Refactoring is part of coding in that it is performed during the coding activity, but is not regular coding. Refactoring has been practiced in the past by programmers, but recently it has taken a more concrete shape, and has been proposed as a key step in the Extreme Programming practice [10]. Refactoring also plays an important role in test driven development—code improvement step in the TDD process is really doing refactoring. Here we discuss some key concepts and some methods for doing refactoring. The discussion here is based on the book on this topic by Fowler [65].

9.3.1 Basic Concepts

Refactoring is defined as a change made to the internal structure of software to make it easier to understand and cheaper to modify without changing its observable behavior [65]. A key point here is that the change is being made to the design embodied in the source code (i.e., the internal structure) exclusively for improvement purposes.

The basic objective of refactoring is to improve the design. However, note that this is not about improving a design during the design stages for creating a design which is to be later implemented (which is the focus of design methodologies), but about improving the design of code that already exists. In other words, refactoring, though done on source code, has the objective of improving the design that the code implements. Therefore, the basic principles of design guide the refactoring process. Consequently, a refactoring generally results in one or more of the following:

1. Reduced coupling

2. Increased cohesion

3. Better adherence to open-closed principle (for OO systems)

Refactoring involves changing the code to improve one of the design properties, while keeping the external behavior the same. Refactoring is often triggered by some coding changes that have to be done. If some enhancements are to be made to the existing code, and it is felt that if the code structure was different (better) then the change could have been done easier, that is the time to do refactoring to improve the code structure.

Even though refactoring is triggered by the need to change the software (and its external behavior), it should not be confused or mixed with the changes for enhancements. It is best to keep these two types of changes separate. So, while developing code, if refactoring is needed, the programmer should cease to write new functionality, and first do the refactoring, and then add new code.

The main risk of refactoring is that existing working code may "break" due to the changes being made. This is the main reason why most often refactoring is not done. (The other reason is that it may be viewed as an additional and unnecessary cost.) To mitigate this risk, the two golden rules are:

1. Refactor in small steps

2. Have test scripts available to test existing functionality

If a good test suite is available, then whether refactoring preserves existing functionality can be checked easily. Refactoring cannot be done effectively without an automated test suite as without such a suite determining if the external behavior has changed or not will become a costly affair. By doing refactoring in a series of small steps, and testing after each step, mistakes in refactoring can be easily identified and rectified. With this, each refactoring makes only a small change, but a series of refactorings can significantly transform the program structure.

With refactoring, code becomes continuously improving. That is, the design, rather than decaying with time, evolves and improves with time. With refactoring, the quality of the design improves, making it easier to make changes to the code as well as find bugs. The extra cost of refactoring is paid for by the savings achieved later in reduced testing and debugging costs, higher quality, and reduced effort in making changes.

If refactoring is to be practiced, its usage can also ease the design task in the design stages. Often the designers spend considerable effort in trying to make the design as good as possible, try to think of future changes and try to make the design flexible enough to accommodate all types of future changes they can envisage. This makes the design activity very complex, and often results in complex designs. With refactoring, the designer does not have to be terribly worried about making the best or most flexible design—the goal is to try to come up with a good and simple design. And later if new changes are required that were not thought of before, or if shortcomings are found in the design, the design is changed through refactoring. More often than not,

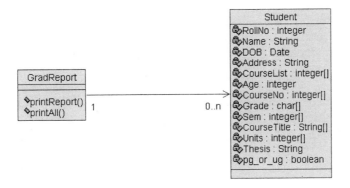

Figure 9.4: Initial class diagram.

the extra flexibility envisaged and designed is never needed, resulting in a system that is unduly complex.

Note that refactoring is not a technique for bug fixing or for improving code that is in very bad shape. It is done to code that is mostly working— the basic purpose is to make the code live longer by making its structure healthier. It starts with healthy code and instead of letting it become weak, it continues to keep it healthy.

9.3.2 An example

Let us illustrate the refactoring process by an example. Let us consider a simplified system to produce a graduation report for a student. A student in a university takes a set of courses, and perhaps, writes a thesis. This system checks the whether a student has completed the graduation requirements, and prints the result along with the list of courses the students has taken, the thesis the student may have done, the student's cumulative grade points (referred to as CPI or cumulative point index), and other information about the student. A student may be a graduate student (referred to as PG or postgraduate) or an undergraduate (UG). To keep the example simple, the graduation requirements for the two are only in terms of number of courses they have to take, and that graduate students have to do a thesis.

Consider a simple implementation for this, whose design is shown in the class diagram in Figure 9.4. (The full code for this implementation as well as code after refactorings is available on the book's Web site.)

There is an array of student objects, which is accessed by printReport(). The object for a students contains all the information about the student,

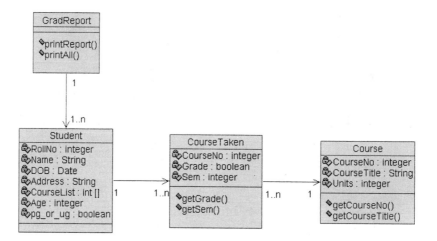

Figure 9.5: Class diagram after first refactoring.

which also provides a host of methods (not shown in the diagram) to provide the required information to a client object. All the logic for producing the report is in PrintReport()—it gets info about the student, perform suitable checks depending on whether the student is a UG or a PG, and prints the data about the student, the report, the list of courses, and computes and prints the grade point (called CPI).

This implementation has poor cohesion (one class encapsulates every-thing), very strong coupling between the two classes, and adding another category of student (e.g., having a separate category for PhD students) will require making changes in existing code. Clearly, this poor design can be improved through refactoring.

As refactoring involves frequent testing, before refactoring, it is best to have an automated test script which can be used to test the changes as they are made. For this implementation, we have created a test script using JUnit (we will discuss this more later in the chapter). The test script essentially first creates a few students and sets suitable values (through a constructor), then invokes printReport() to print the report on a file, and then uses different assertions provided in JUnit to check if the output is as expected. (The test script is also available from the Web site.) This script will be executed every time a refactoring is done to check if anything is "broken." As refactoring should not change external behavior, it should be possible to use the earlier test scripts.

To improve this design, we will perform a series of refactoring steps. In

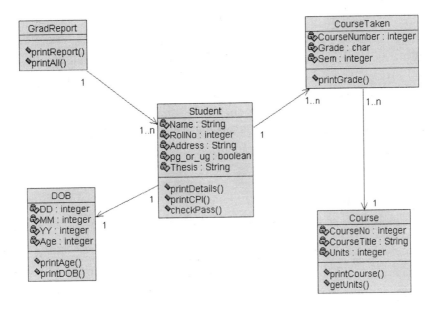

Figure 9.6: Class diagram after second refactoring.

the first step, we improve the cohesion by creating a new class for Course, which contains all information about the course, and a class CourseTaken which contains information related to a student taking a course (for example, the semester in which the course is taken and the grade the student gets). The responsibilities are also suitably shifted to these classes (and the constructor of Student also distributes the necessary construction activities among constructors of the different classes). The design after this refactoring is shown in 9.5.

With this refactoring, arrays in the earlier code have been converted into objects. Furthermore, redundancy in course information, which existed in earlier design (information about a course was replicated in each Student object that had that course) has also been eliminated.

The code after this refactoring can be tested using the test script for the original code. In other words, the earlier test script can be executed directly with this refactored code.

This design, though much improved, can still be improved. We can see that though date of birth of a student is information about a student, we can easily create an object to represent dates. This will be a more flexible and cohesive design. Also, the responsibility of printing different parts still rests within the main printReport() function, even though some of the information that is to be printed resides now with different objects. This increases coupling as the GradReport object will have to invoke methods on different objects to get the information it needs, and then print it. In this refactoring, functionality is distributed among objects such that the functionality resides where it belongs, that is, the functionality is performed in the object that has most of the information needed to perform the required function. This has been done with some printing functions as well as calculation of the grade point average. The design after this refactoring is shown in Figure 9.6. Again, as the external interface is preserved, the earlier test script can be used to execute this program and check that it passes.

In the final refactoring, we make use of inheritance. We note that in this design, coupling has been reduced and cohesion has been improved, the open-closed principle is still violated. If we were to add another class of student, then the code will have to be changed—we cannot handle it by extending the classes. This is because we are considering all students together and are separating the UG and PG students using a flag field. Using the power of inheritance, we can create a hierarchy in which we have different types of students as specializations of the base student class. This is what is done in this refactoring, and the final design is shown in 9.7. Now that we have PG as a separate class, as thesis is done only by PG students, thesis also has been made a separate class. Responsibilities have been suitably distributed. Due to the use of polymorphism, the flag variable (ug-or-pg) now disappears, and the conditionals using this flag have been replaced with suitable use of polymorphism.

Once again, the main interface remains the same and the code after this refactoring can be tested using the initial test script, thereby ensuring that whatever worked in the start (at least to the extent determined by the test script) continues to work after refactoring. For this example, the original code, code after each refactoring, and the Junit test script are all available from the Web site.

9.3.3 Bad Smells

We now discuss the signs in the code that can tell us that refactoring may be called for. These are sometimes called "bad smells" [65]. Basically, these are some easy to spot signs in the code that often indicate that some of the desirable design properties may be getting violated or that there is potential of improving the design. In other words, if you "smell" one of these "bad

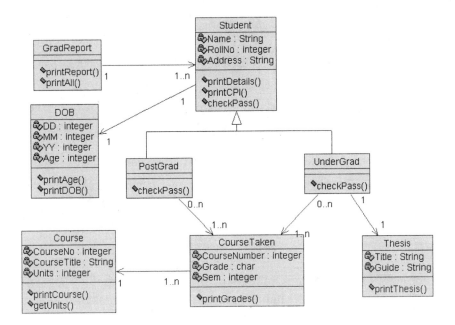

Figure 9.7: Class diagram after final refactoring.

smells" it may be a sign that refactoring is needed. Of course, whether refactoring is indeed needed will have to be decided on a case-by-case basis by looking at the code and the opportunities that may exist for improving the code. Some of these bad smells from [65] are given here.

1. *Duplicate Code.* This is quite common. One reason for this is that some small functionality is being executed at multiple places (e.g., the age from date of birth may be computed in each place that needs the date). Another common reason is that when there are multiple subclasses of a class, then each subclass may end up doing a similar thing. Duplicate code means that if this logic or function has to be changed, it will have to be changed in all the places it exists, making changes much harder and costlier.

2. *Long Method.* If a method is large, it often represents the situation where it is trying to do too many things and therefore is not cohesive.

3. *Long Class.* Similarly, a large class may indicate that it is encapsulating multiple concepts, making the class not cohesive.

4. *Long Parameter List.* Complex interfaces are clearly not desirable—they make the code harder to understand. Often, the complexity is not intrinsic but a sign of improper design.

5. *Switch Statements.* In object-oriented programs, if the polymorphism is not being used properly, it is likely to result in a switch statement everywhere the behavior is to be different depending on the property. Presence of similar switch statements in different places is a sign that instead of using class hierarchy, switch statement is being used. Presence of switch statement makes it much harder to extend code—if a new category is to be added, all the switch statements will have to be modified.

6. *Speculative Generality.* Some class hierarchies may exist because the objects in subclasses seem to be different. However, if the behavior of objects of the different subclasses is the same, and there is no immediate reason to think that behaviors might change, then it is a case of unnecessary complexity.

7. *Too Much Communication Between Objects.* If methods in one class are making many calls to methods of another object to find out about its state, this is a sign of strong coupling. It is possible that this may be unnecessary and hence such situations should be examined for refactoring.

8. *Message Chaining.* One method calls another method, which simply passes this call to another object, and so on. This chain potentially results in unnecessary coupling.

These bad smells in general are indicative of a poor design. We can note that many of these smells existed in our example above.

9.3.4   Common Refactorings

Clearly there are unlimited possibilities of how code can be refactored to improve its design. A catalog of common refactorings, and steps for performing each of them is presented in [65]. New refactorings are continually being listed in www.refactoring.com. As discussed above, a refactoring should help make the code easier to understand and modify. To achieve this objective, many refactorings focus on improving the methods, classes, or class hierarchies. Here we discuss briefly some of the refactorings suggested in [65] in each of these three groups. There are other refactorings that deal with reducing the message chains, which we do not discuss.

The general process of refactoring is the same for all of these—one refactoring step is performed, and then the new code is tested (with automated test scripts) to make sure that refactoring has not altered any behavior and old tests still pass. If multiple refactorings are to be applied, they should be applied one at a time, and a new one should be done only after the current one has been successfully tested.

Improving Methods

We have seen earlier that a method may not be cohesive and a method may perform many different functions. A main goal of refactoring to improve methods is to simplify them and make them more cohesive. The level of coupling by a method depends considerably on its interface and by simplifying the interface, the coupling can be reduced.

1. *Extract Method.* This refactoring is often done if a method is too long, indicating that it may not be cohesive and may be performing multiple functions. The objective is to have short methods whose signatures give a fairly accurate idea to the users about what the methods do. During this refactoring, a piece of code from a method is extracted out as a new method. The variables referred to in this code that are in the scope of original method become the parameters to the new method. Any variables declared in this code but used elsewhere will have to be defined in the original method. In the original method, the extracted code is replaced by an invocation to the new method. Sometimes, the new method may be a function returning a value. An illustration of this refactoring was given in the example above.

   Similarly, if there is a method that returns a value but also changes the state of some objects, then this method should be converted into two methods—one that returns the desired value, and the other to make the desired state change. Having a method that only returns a value and has no side effect generally has a strong functional cohesion. (This refactoring is called *separate query from modifier*.)

2. *Add/Remove Parameter.* If a method needs more information from its caller, perhaps because the scope of what the method has to do has expanded, then new parameters need to be added. However, this

should be done only if the existing parameters cannot provide the information that is needed. The dual of this is parameter removal. Sometimes, for the sake of future extension or flexibility, information is asked for but is not used. For the sake of simplicity, parameters that are not being used should be removed. But if a class is part of a hierarchy, this has to be done carefully to make sure that hierarchy relationships are not disturbed. Or the change will have to be done at higher/lower levels of the hierarchy as well.

Improving Classes

Most refactorings under this category focus on improving cohesion of classes or reducing coupling between classes. Enhancing the cohesion of classes often results in moving fields and methods from one class to another such that logically connected data items and methods that access them are all encapsulated together in one object. Coupling reduction often requires changes in classes to reduce the degree of interaction between them.

1. *Move Method.* In this a method is moved from one class to another. This is a very important refactoring, and is generally done when a method in class A seems to be interacting too heavily with another object of class B, indicating that perhaps the natural home for the method is class B and not class A. Often it is not initially clear where a method may belong, and the designer may assign it to class A. However, later, if it is seen that the natural home is class B, then it should be moved.

   Initially, it is better to leave the source method as a delegating method which just invokes the new method. This way, the change is limited only to the two methods. However, whenever possible, the references or calls to the methods should be redirected to the new method and the old method should be eliminated. If the original method was not a private method, then this will imply that all the classes that used the method will have to be changed.

2. *Move Field.* If a field in class A is being used more often by methods in class B, then the field should be moved to class B. This will reduce the coupling between A and B, and enhance the encapsulation of both the classes. This refactoring is similar to the one above—in Move Method the behavior is being reassigned and in this one state is being

reassigned. Assuming that the field was private, after moving the field from class A to B, all reference to the field in methods in A will have to be changed to suitable method calls to class B for getting the state.

3. *Extract Class.* Often a designer starts with a class and as the need for new features arise, the classes are extended to do more, sometimes resulting in large classes that do not have clear abstraction and are holding too many responsibilities. If there is a large class that seems to be holding multiple responsibilities or encapsulating more than one concept, then this refactoring is applied. A new class is created and the relevant fields and methods are moved to the new class. The refactoring is justified if the new classes have crisper abstraction than the large class, and the responsibilities of both can be clearly and succinctly stated. The class extraction should not result in too much coupling between the two classes, which will indicate an artificial partitioning. If the large class was holding multiple responsibilities, the chances are that different subsets of its methods are primarily accessing different subsets of its state.

   One way to perform this refactoring is to first create the new class and create a link from the old class to the new one. Then the move field and move method refactorings can be repeatedly applied to move the fields and methods that belong to the new class.

4. *Replace Data Value with Object.* This is similar to the Extract Class refactoring. Often some data items are treated as fields of the class initially. As development proceeds, these data items become semantically richer with more operations being performed on them. Examples of such data items are date, telephone numbers, social security number, address etc. If multiple operations are being performed within the class on these data items, then it may make sense to convert the data into an object.

Improve Hierarchies

Class hierarchy is a key object oriented concept that is the foundation for the open-closed principle. In order to support this principle, it is imperative that polymorphism be used effectively. The goal of refactorings here is to leverage polymorphism to make classes more amenable to easy extension later, and to use polymorphism to create designs that more naturally represent the problem.

1. *Replace Conditional with Polymorphism.* If we have a class in which the behavior of some methods depends on value of some type-code, we essentially have a situation where a traditional, function-oriented approach is still being used. Polymorphism can, and should, be used to capture the situation more naturally. Presence of case statement (or equivalent) within a method, or some type codes declared in the class, are good indicators that this refactoring may be needed. An example of this was given earlier, when in the method printReport() of GradReport class, which has to deal with behavior of PG and UG students. In refactoring, a class hierarchy was created where PG and UG are modeled into two different classes. These objects have some common functionality inherited from their base class Student, apart from having their specialized methods. So the object of base class can now point dynamically to one of the derived classes which got rid of the case statement. The difference in behavior was captured by the different sub classes and hence there is no need of an explicit switch statement.

2. *Pull up Field/Method.* An important factor in having a good hierarchy is to have common elements belonging to parent class while the variable elements belonging to the sub classes. Consequently, when there is a situation that multiple subclasses have the same field, the field should be pulled up to the superclass. Similarly, if there are methods in subclasses that are producing identical results (perhaps even with different code/algorithm) we have a situation where functionality is being duplicated. And duplicate code is one of the key factors that makes making changes much harder. Hence, such a situation exists, the structure is improved if the method is moved up to the superclass. If the subclasses have constructors which are similar, then they can also be pulled up into the superclass and be called from the subclass constructor.

   The inverse of pull up is push down, giving us push down field/method refactorings. If a superclass contains a field that is used only by some subclass, it is best to push that field down to the class that uses it. Similarly, if there is some method in the superclass that is relevant only to some subclass, then it should be moved down to the subclass.

9.4 Verification

Once a programmer has written the code for a module, it has to be verified before it is used by others. So far we have assumed that testing is the means by which this verification is done. Though testing is the most common method of verification, there are other effective techniques also. Here we discuss a few common ones. It should be pointed out that by verification we do not mean proving correctness of programs, which for our purposes is only *one* method for program verification.

Here we will focus on techniques that are now widely used in practice—inspections (including code reading), unit testing, and program checking. We will also discuss a formal verification approach, though formal verification is less widely used and is applied mostly in special situations.

Though we are focusing on verifying individual programs written by programmers, some of the techniques like program checking are applicable at the complete system level also.

9.4.1 Code Inspections

Inspection, which is a general verification approach that can be applied to any document, has been widely used for detecting defects. It was started for detecting defects in the code, and was later applied for design, requirements, plans, etc. The general inspection process was discussed earlier, and for code inspection also it remains the same.

Code inspections are usually held after code has been successfully compiled and other forms of static tools have been applied. The main motivation for this is to save human time and effort, which would otherwise be spent detecting errors that a compiler or static analyzer can detect.

The documentation to be distributed to the inspection team members includes the code to be reviewed and the design document. The team for code inspection should include the programmer, the designer, and the tester.

The aim of code inspections is to detect defects in code. In addition to defects, there are quality issues which code inspections usually look for, like efficiency, compliance to coding standards, etc. Often the type of defects the code inspection should focus on is contained in a checklist that is provided to the inspectors. Some of the items that can be included in a checklist for code reviews are [52]:

A Sample Checklist:

- Do data definitions exploit the typing capabilities of the language?

- Do all the pointers point to some object? (Are there any "dangling pointers"?)

- Are the pointers set to NULL where needed?

- Are pointers being checked for NULL when being used?

- Are all the array indexes within bound?

- Are indexes properly initialized?

- Are all the branch conditions correct (not too weak, not too strong)?

- Will a loop always terminate (no infinite loops)?

- Is the loop termination condition correct?

- Is the number of loop executions "off by one"?

- Where applicable, are the divisors tested for zero?

- Are imported data tested for validity?

- Do actual and formal interface parameters match?

- Are all variables used? Are all output variables assigned?

- Can statements placed in the loop be placed outside the loop?

- Are the labels unreferenced?

- Will the requirements of execution time be met?

- Are the local coding standards met?

Inspection are very effective for detecting defects and are widely used in many commercial organizations. However, inspections also tends to be very expensive as it uses time of many people. Consequently, for some code segments the cost may not be justified. In these situations, instead of a group inspection, review by one person can be performed. One approach for doing this is to have the person inspecting the code apply some structured code reading technique, which we briefly discuss now.

Code reading involves careful reading of the code by the reviewer to detect any discrepancies between the design specifications and the actual implementation. It involves determining the abstraction of a module and then comparing it with its specifications. The process is the reverse of design. In design, we start from an abstraction and move toward more details. In code reading we start from the details of a program and move toward an abstract description.

The process of code reading is best done by reading the code inside-out, starting with the innermost structure of the module. First determine its abstract behavior and specify the abstraction. Then the higher-level structure is considered, with the inner structure replaced by its abstraction. This process is continued until we reach the module or program being read. At that time the abstract behavior of the program/module will be known, which can then be compared to the specifications to determine any discrepancies.

Code reading is very useful and can detect errors often not revealed by testing. Reading in the manner of stepwise abstraction also forces the programmer to code in a manner conducive to this process, which leads to well-structured programs. Code reading is sometimes called *desk review*.

9.4.2 Static Analysis

There are many techniques for verification now available that are not testing-based, but directly check the programs through the aid of analysis tools. This general area is called program checking. Three forms of checking are becoming popular—model checking, dynamic analysis, and static analysis. (Program verification can also be treated as a form of program checking, but is generally not performed through tools. We discuss it separately later in the section.)

In model checking, an abstract model of the program being verified is first constructed. The model captures those aspects that affect the properties that are to be checked. The desired properties are also specified and a model checker checks whether the model satisfies the stated properties. A discussion of model checking is available in [56, 42]. In dynamic analysis, the program is instrumented and then executed with some data. The value of variables, branches taken, etc. are recorded during the execution. Using the data recorded, it is evaluated if the program behavior is consistent with some of the dynamic properties. A discussion of dynamic analysis is available in [117, 3]. Perhaps the most widely used program checking technique is static analysis, which is becoming increasingly popular with more tools becoming available. In this section we focus primarily on static analysis.

Analysis of programs by methodically analyzing the program text is called *static analysis*. Static analysis is usually performed mechanically by the aid of software tools. During static analysis the program itself is not executed, but the program text is the input to the tools. The aim of static analysis is to detect errors or potential errors in the code and to generate information that can be useful in debugging. (Static analyzers can also generate information for documentation, but we will not discuss this aspect.)

Many compilers perform some limited static analysis. However, the analysis performed by compilers focuses around code generation and not defect detection. Static analysis tools, on the other hand, explicitly focus on detecting errors. Two approaches are possible. The first is to detect patterns in code that are "unusual" or "undesirable" and which are likely to represent defects. The other is to directly look for defects in the code, that is, look for those conditions that can cause programs to fail when executing.

In either case, a static analyzer, as it is trying to identify defects (i.e. which can cause failures on execution) without running the code but only by analyzing the code, sometimes identifies situations as errors which are not actually errors (i.e. false positives), and sometimes fails to identify some errors. These limitations of a static analyzer is characterized by its *soundness* and *completeness*.   Soundness captures the occurrence of false positives in the errors the static analyzer identifies, and completeness characterizes how many of the existing errors are missed by the static analyzer. As full soundness and completeness is not possible, the goal is to have static analyzers be as sound and as complete as possible. Usually there is a trade off involved—a higher level of completeness often implies less soundness (i.e., more false positives). Due to imperfect soundness, the errors identified by static analyzers are actually "warnings"—the program possibly has a defect, but there is a possibility that the warning may not be a defect.

The first form of static analysis is looking for unusual patterns in code. This is often done through data flow analysis and control flow analysis. One of the early approaches focusing of data flow anamolies is described in [63]. Here, our discussion is based on checkers described in [150], which identify redundancies in the programs. These redundancies usually go undetected by the compiler, and often represent errors caused due to carelessness in typing, lack of clear understanding of the logic, or some other reason. At the very least, presence of such redundancies implies poor coding. Hence, if a program has these redundancies it is a cause of concern, and their presence should be carefully examined. Some of the redundancies that the checkers identify are:

- Idempotent operations

- Assignments that were never read

- Dead code

- Conditional branches that were never taken

Idempotent operations occur in situations like when a variable is assigned to itself, divided by itself, or performs a boolean operation with itself. Redundant assignments occur when a variable is assigned some value but the variable is not used after the assignment, that is, either the function exits or a new assignment is done without using the variable. Dead code occurs when there is a piece of code that cannot be reached in any path and consequently will never be executed. Redundant conditionals occur if a branching construct contains a condition that is always true or false, and hence is redundant. All these situations represent redundancies in programs that should normally not occur in well thought out programs. Hence, they are candidates for presence of errors.

Some examples of errors identified by these checks will illustrate the use of techniques. Small program fragments from large public domain software systems which contained these redundancies are shown in Figure 9.8 [150]. In these examples the presence of these redundancies actually represents some type of error in the program.

These checkers are efficient and can be applied on large code bases. Experiments on many widely used software systems have shown that the warnings generated by the static analyzer has reasonable levels of "false positives" (about 20% to 50% of the warnings are false positives). Experiments also showed that the presence of these redundancies correlate highly with actual errors in programs.

The second approach for static analysis is to directly look for errors in the programs—bugs that can cause failures when the programs execute. These approaches focus on some types of defects that are otherwise hard to identify or test. Many tools of this type are commercially available or have been developed in-house by large software organizations. Here we base our discussion on the tool called PREfix [28], which has been used on some very large software systems and in some large commercial software companies. As they directly look for errors, the level of false positives generated by this tool tends to be low. Some of the errors PREfix identifies are:

```
/* idempotent operation */
for (i=0; i< size; i++) {
    if (pv[i]!= -1 && pv[i] >= val)
    pv[i] = pv[i]++; /* error */
}

/* Redundant assignment */
do {
    ...
    if (signal\_pending(current))
    { err = - ERRSTARTSYS; break; }
    ...
} while (condition);
return 0; /*value of err lost*/

/* Dead code */
for (c1; c2; c3) {
...
if (C) {
    ...
    break; }
else {
    ...
    break; }
stmt;  /*this is unreachable*/

/* Unnecessary check */
if (!(error && ... && ...))
{   ...
    return -1; }
if (error) /*redundant check*/
    { ... }
}
```

Figure 9.8: Examples of redundant operations.

- Using uninitialized memory

- Dereferencing uninitialized pointer

- Dereferencing NULL pointer

- Dereferencing invalid pointer

- Dereferencing or returning pointer to freed memory

- Leaking memory or some other resource like a file

```
1.    #include <stdlib.h>
2.    #include <stdio.h>

3.    char *f(int size)
4.    {
5.         char *result;

6.         if (size>0)
7.             result = (char *)malloc(size);
8.         if (size==1)
9.             return NULL;
10.        result[0] = 0;
11.        return result;
12.   }
```

Figure 9.9: An example program.

- Returning pointer to local stack variable

- Divide by zero

As we can see, these are all situations that can cause failure of the software during execution. Also, as we have discussed earlier, some of these errors are made commonly by programmers and are often hard to detect through testing. In other words, many of these errors occur commonly and are hard to detect, but can be detected easily and cheaply by the use of this tool.

To identify these errors, PREfix simulates the execution of functions by tracing some distinct paths in the function. As the number of paths can be infinite, a maximum limit is set on the number of paths that will be simulated. As it turns out, most of the errors get detected within a limit of about 100 paths. During simulation of the execution, it keeps track of the memory state, which it also examines at the end of the path and reports the memory problems it identifies. (As we can see from the list above, the focus is quite heavily on memory related errors.)

For complete programs, it first simulates the lowest level functions in the call graph, and then moves up the graph. For a called function, a model is built by simulation, which is then used in simulation of the called function. The model of a function consists of the list of external variables that affect the function (parameters, global variables, etc.) or that the function affects (return values, global variables, etc.), and a set of possible outcomes. Each outcome consists of a guard which specifies the pre-condition for this outcome, constraints, and the result (which is essentially the post-conidition). By simulating called functions and using their outcomes in the simulation of a called function allows the tool to identify inter-function problems—their experiments showed that more than 90% of the errors fall in this category where more than one function is involved. Details of how the analysis is done are given in the paper [28]. An example of the types of errors identified will illustrate what the tool does. Consider the program given in Figure 9.9 [28]. The tool will generate three warnings for this program:

```
8: leaking memory (path: 5 6 7 8)
9: dereferencing uninitialized pointer 'result'
   (path: 5 7 9)
9: dereferencing NULL pointer 'result'
   (path: 5 6 7 9)
```

The first warning catches the error that if size is 1, then the allocated memory is not freed, and hence we have a memory leak. The second warning catches the error that if size is less than or equal to 0, then line 6 will not be executed, and hence result is not defined and we access an uninitialized pointer. If this path is followed in an execution of the program, a runtime error will be generated at line 9. Similarly, if malloc() cannot allocate memory and returns a NULL pointer in line 6, then there will be a runtime error of trying to dereference a NULL pointer at line 9.

All these are runtime errors that are detected not by executing the program but by analyzing the program text. Besides the nature of the error found, the tool gives the path in whose execution the tool found the error—this helps the programmer in understanding under which situation the error occurs. The tool provides a lot more information to help the programmer clearly identify the error.

As static analysis is performed with the help of software tools, it is a very cost-effective way of discovering errors. An added advantage of static analysis is that it detects the errors directly and not just the presence of errors, as is the case with testing. Consequently, little debugging is needed after the presence of error is detected. The main issue with using these tools is the presence of "false positives" in the warnings the tool generates. The presence of false positives means that a programmer has to also examine the false positives and then discard them, leading to wastage of effort. More importantly, they cause a doubt in the minds of the programmer on the warnings which can lead to even correct errors being discarded as false positives. Still, the use of static analysis is increasing in commercial setups as they provide a cost effective and scalable technique of detecting errors in the code which are often hard to detect through testing.

The general area of program checking is an active area of research. There are many commercial and public domain tools available for performing different types of analysis.

9.4.3 Proving Correctness

Many techniques for verification aim to reveal errors in the programs, because the ultimate goal is to make programs correct by removing the errors. In proof of correctness, the aim is to prove a program correct. So, correctness is directly established, unlike the other techniques in which correctness is never really established but is implied (and hoped) by the absence of detection of any errors. Proofs are perhaps more valuable during program construction, rather than after the program has been constructed. Proving while developing a program may result in more reliable programs that can be proved more easily. Proving a program not constructed with formal verification in mind can be quite difficult.

Any proof technique must begin with a formal specification of the program. No formal proof can be provided if what we have to prove is not stated or is stated informally in an imprecise manner. So, first we have to state formally what the program is supposed to do. A program will usually not operate on an arbitrary set of input data and may produce valid results only for some range of inputs. Hence, it is often not sufficient merely to state the goal of the program, but we should also state the input conditions in which the program is to be invoked and for which the program is expected to produce valid results. The assertion about the expected final state of a program is called the *post-condition* of that program, and the assertion about the input condition is called the *pre-condition* of the program. Often, determining the pre-condition for which the post-condition will be satisfied is the goal of proof. Here we will briefly describe a technique for proving correctness called the *axiomatic method*, which was proposed by Hoare [86]. It is often also called the *Floyd-Hoare proof method*, as it is based on Floyd's inductive assertion technique.

The Axiomatic Approach

In principle, all the properties of a program can be determined statically from the text of the program, without actually executing the program. The first requirement in reasoning about programs is to state formally the properties of the elementary operations and statements that the program uses. In the axiomatic model of Hoare [86], the goal is to take the program and construct a sequence of assertions, each of which can be inferred from previously proved assertions and the rules and axioms about the statements and operations in the program. For this, we need a mathematical model of a program and all the constructs in the programming language. Using Hoare's notation, the basic assertion about a program segment is of the form:

$$P\{S\}Q.$$

The interpretation of this is that if assertion P is true before executing S, then assertion Q will be true after executing S, if the execution of S terminates. Assertion P is the pre-condition of the program and Q is the post-condition. These assertions are about the values taken by the variables in the program before and after its execution. The assertions generally do not specify a particular value for the variables, but they specify the general properties of the values and the relationships among them.

To prove a theorem of the form $P\{S\}Q$, we need some rules and axioms about the programming language in which the program segment S is written. Here we consider a simple programming language, which deals only with integers and has the following types of statements: (1) assignment, (2) conditional statement, and (3) an iterative statement. A program is considered a sequence of statements. We will now discuss the rules and axioms for these statements so that we can combine them to prove the correctness of programs.

Axiom of Assignment: Assignments are central to procedural languages. In our language no state change can be accomplished without the assignment statement. The axiom of assignment is also central to the axiomatic approach. In fact, only for the assignment statement do we have an independent axiom; for the rest of the statements we have rules. Consider the assignment statement of the form

$$x := f$$

where x is an identifier and f is an expression in the programming language without any side effects. Any assertion that is true about x after the assignment must be true of the expression f before the assignment. In other words, because after the assignment the variable x contains the value computed by the expression f, if a condition is true after the assignment is made, then the condition obtained by replacing x by f must be true before the assignment. This is the essence of the axiom of assignment. The axiom is stated next:

$$P_f^x \{x := f\} P$$

P is the post-condition of the program segment containing only the assignment statement. The pre-condition is P_f^x, which is an assertion obtained by substituting f for all occurrences of x in the assertion P. In other words, if P_f^x is true before the assignment statement, P will be true after the assignment.

This is the only axiom we have in Hoare's axiomatic model besides the standard axioms about the mathematical operators used in the language (such as commutativity and associativity of the $+$ operator). The reason that we have only one axiom for the assignment statement is that this is the only statement in our language that has any effect on the state of the system, and we need an axiom to define what the effect of such a statement is. The other language constructs, like alternation and iteration, are for flow control, to determine which assignment statements will be executed. For such statements rules of inference are provided.

Rule of Composition: Let us first consider the rule for sequential composition, where two statements S1 and S2 are executed in sequence. This rule is called *rule of composition*, and is shown next:

$$\frac{P\{~S1\}Q, Q\{S2\}R}{P\{S1; S2\}R}$$

The explanation of this notation is that if what is stated in the numerator can be proved, the denominator can be inferred. Using this rule, if we can prove P{S1}Q and Q{S2}R, we can claim that if before execution the pre-condition P holds, then after execution of the program segment S1;S2 the post-condition R will hold. In other words, to prove P{S1;S2}R, we have to find some Q and prove that P{S1}Q and Q{S2}R. This rule is dividing the problem of determining the semantics of a sequence of statements into determining the semantics of individual statements. In other words, from the proofs of simple statements, proofs of programs (i.e., sequence of statements) will be constructed. Note that the rule handles a strict sequence of statements only (recall the earlier discussion on structured programming).

Rule for Alternate Statement: Let us now consider the rules for an `if` statement. For formal verification, the entire `if` statement is treated as one construct, the semantics of which have to be determined. This is the way in which other structured statements are also handled. There are two types of if statement, one with an else clause and one without. The rules for both are given next:

$$\frac{P \wedge B\{S\}Q, P \wedge \sim B \Rightarrow Q}{P \ \{\text{if B then S}\}Q}$$

$$\frac{P \wedge B\{S1\}Q, P \wedge B\{S2\}Q}{P\{\text{if B then S1 else S2}\}Q}$$

Let us consider the if-then-else statement. We want to prove a post-condition for this statement. However, depending on the evaluation of B, two different statements can be executed. In both cases the post-condition must be satisfied. Hence if we can show that starting in the state where $P \wedge B$ is true and executing S1 or starting in a state where $P \wedge \sim B$ is true and executing the statement S2, both lead to the post-condition Q, then the following can be inferred: if the if-then-else statement is executed with pre-condition P, the post-condition Q will hold after execution of the statement. Similarly, for the if-then statement, if B is true then S is executed; otherwise the control goes straight to the end of the statement. Hence, if we can show that starting from a state where $P \wedge B$ is true and executing S leads to a state where Q is true and before the if statement if $P \wedge \sim B$ implies Q, then we can say that starting from P before the if statement we will always reach a state in which Q is true.

Rules of Consequence: To be able to prove new theorems from the ones we have already proved using the axioms, we require some rules of inference. The simplest inference rule is that if the execution of a program ensures that an assertion Q is true after execution, then it also ensures that every assertion logically implied by Q is also true after execution. Similarly, if a pre-condition ensures that a post-condition is true after execution of a program, then every condition that logically implies the pre-condition will also ensure that the post-condition holds after execution of the program. These are called *rules of consequence*, and they are formally stated here:

$$\frac{P\{S\}R, R \Rightarrow Q}{P\{S\}Q}$$

$$\frac{P \Rightarrow R, R\{S\}Q}{P\{S\}Q}$$

Rule of Iteration: Now let us consider iteration. Loops are the trickiest construct when dealing with program proofs. We will consider only the `while` loop of the form `while B do S`. We have to determine the semantics of the whole construct.

In executing this loop, first the condition B is checked. If B is false, S is not executed and the loop terminates. If B is true, S is executed and B is tested again. This is repeated until B evaluates to false. We would like to be able to make an assertion that will be true when the loop terminates. Let this assertion be P. As we do not know how many times the loop will be executed, it is easier to have an assertion that will hold true irrespective of how many times the loop body is executed. In that case P will hold true after every execution of statement S, and will be true before every execution of S, because the condition that holds true after an execution of S will be the condition for the next execution of S (if S is executed again). Furthermore, we know that the condition B is false when the loop terminates and is true whenever S is executed. These properties have been used in the rule for iteration:

$$\frac{P \wedge B\{S\}P}{P\{\text{while B do S}\}P \wedge \sim B}$$

As the condition P is unchanging with the execution of the statements in the loop body, it is called the *loop invariant*. Finding loop invariants is the thorniest problem in constructing proofs of correctness. One method for getting the loop invariant that often works is to extract $\sim B$ from the post-condition of the loop and try the remaining assertion as the loop invariant. Another method is to try replacing the variable that binds the loop execution with the loop counter. Thus if the loop has a counter i, which goes from 0 to n, and if the post-condition of the loop contains n, then replace n by i and try the assertion as a loop invariant.

An Example

Although in a theorem of the form $P\{S\}Q$, we say that if P is true at the start and the execution of S terminates, Q will be true after executing S, to prove a theorem of this sort we work backwards. That is, we do not start with the pre-condition; we work our way to the end of the program to determine the post-condition. Instead we start with the post-condition and work our way back to the start of the program, and determine the pre-condition. We use the axiom of assignment and other rules to determine the pre-condition of a statement for a given post-condition. If the pre-condition we obtain by doing this is implied by P, then by rules of consequence we can say that P\{S\}Q is a theorem. Let us consider a simple example of

(* Remainder of x/y *)
1. **begin**
2.   q := 0;
3.   r := x;
4.   **while** r ≥ y **do**
5.   **begin**
6.   r := r - y ;
7.   q := q + 1 ;
8.   **end**;
9.**end**.

Figure 9.10: Program to determine the remainder.

determining the remainder in integer division, by repeated subtraction. The program is shown in Figure 9.10.

The pre-condition and post-condition of this program are given as

$$P = \{x \geq 0 \wedge y > 0\}$$

$$Q = \{x = qy + r \wedge 0 \leq r < y\}$$

We have to prove that P {Program} Q is a theorem. We start with Q. The first statement before the end of the program is the loop. We invent the loop invariant by removing ~B from the Q, which is also the output assertion of the loop. For this we factor Q into a form like $I \wedge \sim B$, then choose I as the invariant. For this program we have $\sim B = \{r < y\}$, and $Q = \{x = qy + r \wedge 0 \leq r \wedge r < y\}$, hence our trial invariant I is $\{x = qy + r \wedge 0 \leq r\}$.

Let us now see if this invariant is appropriate for this loop, that is, starting with this, we get a pre-condition of the form $I \wedge B$. Starting with I, we use the assignment axiom and the pre-condition for statement 7 is

$$x = (q + 1)y + r \wedge 0 \leq r\{q := q + 1\}I$$

Using the assignment axiom for statement 6, we get the pre-condition for 6 as

$$x = (q + 1)y + (r - y) \wedge 0 \leq (r - y),$$

which is the same as $x = qy + r \wedge y \leq r$. Using the rule of composition (for statements 6 and 7), we can say

$$x = qy + r \wedge y \leq r\{r := r - y; q := q + 1\}I.$$

Because $x = qy + r \wedge y \leq r \Rightarrow I \wedge B$, by rule of consequence and the rule for the `while` loop, we have

$$I\{\text{while loop in program}\}I \wedge \sim (r \geq y)$$

where I is $x = qy + r \wedge 0 \leq r$.

Now let us consider the statements before the loop (i.e., statements 2 and 3). The post-condition for these statements is I. Using the axiom of assignment, we first replace r with x, and then we replace q with 0 to get

$$(x = x \wedge 0 \leq x) \Rightarrow (0 \leq x).$$

By composing these statements with the `while` statement, we get

$$0 \leq x\{\text{the entire program}\}I \wedge \sim B.$$

Because, $(I \wedge \sim B)$ is the post-condition Q of the program and $0 \leq x$ is the pre-condition, we have proved the program to be correct.

Discussion

In the axiomatic method, to prove P{S}Q, we assume that S will terminate. So, by proving that the program will produce the desired post-condition using the axiomatic method, we are essentially saying that *if* the program terminates, it will provide the desired post-condition. The axiomatic proof technique cannot prove whether or not a program terminates. For this reason, the proof using the axiomatic technique is called the proof of *partial correctness*.

This is in contrast to the proof of *total correctness*, where termination of a program is also proved. Termination of programs is of considerable interest for obvious reason of avoiding infinite loops. With the axiomatic method, additional techniques have to be used to prove termination. One common method is to define a well-ordered set that has a smallest member and then add an expression to the assertions that produces a value in the set. If after an execution of the loop body, it can be shown that the value of the expression is less than it was on the entry, then the loop must terminate. There are other methods of proving correctness that aim to prove total correctness.

Proofs of correctness have obvious theoretical appeal and a considerable body of literature exists in the area. Despite this, the practical use of these formal methods of verification has been limited. In the software development industry proving correctness is not generally used as a means of verification. Their use, at best, is limited to proving correctness of some critical modules.

There are many reasons for the lack of general use of formal verification. Constructing proofs is quite hard, and even for relatively modest problems, proofs can be quite large and difficult to comprehend. As much of the work must be done manually (even if theorem provers are available), the techniques are open to clerical errors. In addition, the proof methods are usually limited to proving correctness of single modules. When procedures and functions are used, constructing proofs of correctness becomes extremely hard. In essence, the technique of proving correctness does not scale up very well to large programs. Despite these shortcomings, proof techniques offer an attractive formal means for verification and hold promise for the future.

9.4.4   Unit Testing

Unit testing is another approach for verifying the code that a programmer is written. Unit testing is like regular testing where programs are executed with some test cases except that the focus is on testing smaller programs or modules called units. In the programming processes we discussed earlier, the testing was essentially unit testing. A unit may be a function, a small collection or functions, a class, or a small collection of classes. Most often, it is the unit a programmer is writing code for, and hence unit testing is most often done by a programmer to test the code that he or she has written. Testing, however, is a general technique that can also be used for validating complete systems. We will discuss testing in more detail in the next chapter.

Testing of modules or software systems is a difficult and challenging task. Selection of test cases is a key issue in any form of testing. We will discuss the problem of test case selection in detail in the next chapter when we discuss testing. For now, it suffices that during unit testing the tester, who is generally the programmer, will execute the unit for a variety of test cases and study the actual behavior of the units being tested for these test cases. Based on the behavior, the tester decides whether the unit is working correctly or not. If the behavior is not as expected for some test case, then the programmer finds the defect in the program (an activity called *debugging*), and fixes it. After removing the defect, the programmer will generally execute the test case that caused the unit to fail again to ensure that the fixing has indeed made the unit behave correctly.

For a functional unit, unit testing will involve testing the function with different test data as input. In this, the tester will select different types of test data to exercise the function. Typically, the test data will include some data representing the normal case, that is, the one that is most likely to occur. In addition, test data will be selected for special cases which must be dealt with by the program and which might result in special or exceptional result.

An issue with unit testing is that as the unit being tested is not a complete system but just a part, it is not executable by itself. Furthermore, in its execution it may use other modules that have not been developed yet. Due to this, unit testing often requires drivers or stubs to be written. Drivers play the role of the "calling" module and are often responsible for getting the test data, executing the unit with the test data, and then reporting the result. Stubs are essentially "dummy" modules that are used in place of the actual module to facilitate unit testing. So, if a module M uses services from another module M' that has not yet been developed, then for unit testing M, some stub for M' will have to be written so M can invoke the services in some manner on M' so that unit testing can proceed. The need for stubs can be avoided, if coding and testing proceeds in a bottom-up manner—the modules at lower levels are coded and tested first such that when modules at higher levels of hierarchy are tested, the code for lower level modules is already available.

If incremental coding is practiced, as discussed above, then unit testing needs to be performed every time the programmer adds some code. Clearly, for this, automated scripts for unit testing are essential. With automated scripts, whether the programs pass the unit tests or not can be determined simply by executing a script. For incremental testing it is desirable that the programmer develops this unit testing script and keeps enhancing it with additional test cases as the code evolves. That is, instead of executing the unit by executing it and manually inputting the test data, it is better if execution of the unit with the chosen test data is all programmed. Then this program can be executed every time testing needs to be done. Some tools are available to facilitate this.

In object-oriented programs, the unit to be tested is usually an object of a class. Testing of objects can be defined as the process of exercising the routines provided by an object with the goal of uncovering errors in the implementation of the routines or state of the object or both [137]. For an object, we can test a method using approaches for testing functions, but we cannot test the object using these approaches, as the issue of state comes in. To test an object, we also have to test the interaction between the methods provided on the object.

State-based testing is a technique that can be used for unit testing an object. In the simplest form, a method is tested in all possible states that the object can assume, and after each invocation the resulting state is checked to see whether or not the method takes the object under test to the expected state. For state-based testing to be practical, the set of states in which a method is tested has to be limited. State modeling of classes can help here [24, 64], or the tester can determine the important states of the object. Once the different object states are decided, then a method is tested in all those states that form valid input for it. We will discuss selection of test cases based on a state model in the next chapter.

To test a class, the programmer needs to create an object of that class, take the object to a particular state, invoke a method on it, and then check whether the state of the object is as expected. This sequence has to be executed many times for a method, and has to be performed for all the methods. All this is facilitated if we use frameworks like the Junit (www.junit.org). Though Junit itself is for Java, similar frameworks have been developed for other languages like C++ and C#. Here we briefly describe how Junit can be used for testing a class and give an example.

For testing of a class CUT (class under test) with Junit, the tester has to create another class which inherits from Junit (e.g., `class CUTtest extends Junit`). The Junit framework has to be imported by this class. This class is the driver for testing CUT. It must have a constructor in which the objects that are needed for the test cases are created; a setUp() method which is typically used for creating any objects and setting up values before executing a test case; a suite(), and a main () that executes the suite() using a TestRunner provided by Junit. Besides these methods, all other methods are actually test cases.

Most of these methods are often named `testxxxx()`. Such a method typically focuses on testing a method under some state (typically the name of the method and/or the state is contained in xxx). This method first sets up the state if not already setup (by setup()), and then executes the method to be tested. To check the results, Junit provides two special methods AssertTrue(boolean_expression) and AssertFalse(boolean_expression). By using functions and having a logical expression on the state of the object, the tester can test if the state is correct or not. If all the assertions in all the methods succeed, then Junit declares that the test has passed. If any assert statements fail, Junit declares that testing has failed and specifies the assertion that has failed.

To get an idea of how it works, consider the testing of a class Matrix.java,

```
class Matrix {
    private double [][] matrix;  //Matrix elements
    private int row, col;       //Order of Matrix

    public Matrix(); // Constructor
    public Matrix(int i,int j); // Sets #rows and #cols
    public Matrix(int i,int j,double[][] a); // Sets from 2D array
    public Matrix(Matrix a); //Constructs matrix from another
    public void read(); //read elts from console and set up matrix
    public void setElement(int i,int j,double value); // set elt i,j
    public int noOfRows(); // returns no of rows
    public int noOfCols(); // returns no of cols
    public Matrix add(Matrix a); // add a to matrix
    public Matrix sub(Matrix a); // subtracts a from matrix
    public Matrix mul(Matrix b); // multiplies b to matrix
    public Matrix transpose(); // transposes the matrix
    public Matrix minor(int a, int b); // returns a x b sub-matrix
    public double determinant(); // determinant of the matrix
    public Matrix inverse() throws Exception; // inverse of the matrix
    public void print(); // prints matrix on console
    public boolean equals(Matrix m); // checks for equality with m
}
```

Figure 9.11: Class Matrix.java

which provides standard operations on matrices. The main attributes of the class and the main methods are given in Figure 9.11.

For unit testing the Matrix class, clearly we need to test standard operations like creation of a matrix, setting of values, etc. We also need to test whether the operations like add, subtract, multiply, determinant are performing as expected. Each test case we want to execute is programmed by setting the values and then performing the operation. The result of the operation is checked through the assert statements. For example, for testing add(), we create a method testAdd() in which a matrix is added to another. The correct result is stored apriori in another matrix. After addition, it is checked if the result obtained by performing add() is equal to the correct result. The method for this is shown in Figure 9.12. The programmer may want to perform more tests for add(), for which more test methods will be needed. Similarly, methods are written for testing other methods. Some of these tests are also shown in Figure 9.12. The complete script has over 30 assertions spread over more than 20 test methods. The complete code for classes Matrix.java and MatrixTest.java can be found on the book's Web

```
import junit.framework.*;
public class MatrixTest extends TestCase {

    Matrix A, B, C, D, E, res;            /* test matrices */

    public MatrixTest(String testcase)
    {
        super(testcase);

        double a[][]=new double[][]{{9,6},{7,5}};
        A = new Matrix(2,2,a);
        double b[][]=new double[][]{{16,21},{3,12}};
        B = new Matrix(2,2,b);
        double d[][]=new double[][]{{2,2,3},{4,8,6},{7,8,9}};
        res=new Matrix();
    }

    public void testAdd()
    {
        double c[][]=new double[][]{{25,27},{10,17}};
        C = new Matrix(2,2,c);
        res=A.add(B);
        assertTrue(res!=null);
        assertTrue(C.equals(res));
    }

    public void testSetGet()
    {
        C=new Matrix(2,2);
        for (int i=0;i<2;i++)
           for (int j=0;j<2;j++)
              C.setElement(i,j,A.getElement(i,j));
        assertTrue(C.equals(A));
    }

    public void testMul()
    {
        double c[][]=new double[][]{{162,261},{127,207}};
        C = new Matrix(2,2,c);
        res=A.mul(B);
        assertTrue(res!=null);
        assertTrue(C.equals(res));
    }
}
```

Figure 9.12: Testing the matrix class with Junit.

```
public void testTranspose()
{
   res=A.transpose();
   res=res.transpose();
   assertTrue(res.equals(A));
}

public void testInverseCorrectness()
{
   try{
      res=null;
      res=A.inverse();
      res=res.mul(A);
      double dd[][]=new double[][]{{1,0},{0,1}};
      Matrix DD=new Matrix(2,2,dd);
      assertTrue(res.equals(DD));
   }
   catch (Exception e)
   {assertTrue(false);
   }
}
}
```

Figure 9.12: Testing the matrix class with Junit (contd.)

site.

As we can see, Junit encourages automated testing. Not only is the execution of test cases automated, the checking of the results is also automated. This makes running tests fully automatic. By building testing scripts, and continuously updating them as the class evolves, we always have a test script which can be run quickly. So, whenever we make any changes to the code, we can quickly check if the past test cases are running on the click of a button. This becomes almost essential if incremental coding or test driven development (discussed earlier in the chapter) is to be practiced.

9.4.5 Combining Different Techniques

After discussing various techniques for verification it is natural to ask how these techniques compare with each other, and how they should be combined for applying it on a project. We will first address the comparison issue. For this purposes we consider two approaches to testing—white box or structural testing separately. We will discuss these in detail in next chapter. For now,

Defect	Technique				
	Code Review	Static Analysis	Proof	White box Test	Black box Test
Computational	Med	Med	High	High	Med
Logic	Med	Med	High	High	Med
I/O	High	Med	Low	Med	High
Data handling	High	High	Med	Low	High
Interface	High	High	low	High	Med
Data Definition	Med	Med	Med	Low	Med
Database	High	Low	Low	Med	Med

Figure 9.13: Comparison of the different techniques.

it is sufficient to say that black box testing is done without the knowledge of the internals of the programs while white box testing is driven by the internal structure of the programs.

By effectiveness, we mean the fault detecting capability. The effectiveness of a technique for testing a particular software will, in general, depend on the type of errors that exist in the software, as, in general, no one strategy does better than another strategy for all types of errors. Based on the nature of the techniques one can make some general observations about the effectiveness for different types of errors. One such comparison is given in Figure 9.13 [52].

As we can see, according to this comparison, different techniques have different strengths and weaknesses. For example, white box testing, as one would expect, is good for detecting logic errors, but not very good for detecting data handling errors. For data handling type errors, static analysis is quite good. Similarly, black box testing is good for input/output errors as it focuses on the external behavior, but it is not as good for detecting logic errors. As the figure shows, no one technique is good at detecting all types of errors, and hence no one technique can suffice for proper verification and validation. If high reliability is desired for the software, a combination of these techniques will have to be used. From the table, one can see that if code reviews, white box testing, and black box testing are all used, then together they have a high capability of detecting errors in all the categories described earlier.

Another way of measuring effectiveness is to consider the "cost effectiveness" of different strategies, that is, the cost of detecting an error by using a particular strategy. And the cost includes all the effort required to plan, execute the verification approach, and evaluate the results. In cost effectiveness, static analysis fares the best, as without any human effort it can detect anomalies that have a high probability of containing errors. However, as many of these tools also have "false positives" which have to be evaluated before they can be identified as false positives, the effort required is not as small as it may look.

Code reviews can also be cost effective as they find faults directly, unlike in testing where only the failure is detected and the fault has to be found through debugging. Furthermore, no test case planning, test case generation, or test case execution is needed. However, reviews require considerable effort by a group of reviewers reviewing the code. Testing tends to be very cost effective for detecting the earlier defects, but as the remaining defects reduce, uncovering defects by testing becomes much harder. Formal verification is generally the most expensive as it is mostly human effort, and quite intense.

Let us now discuss how these techniques can be combined. It is clear from the comparison in Figure 9.13 and from the nature of white box and black box testing approaches, that the two basic approaches to testing are actually complementary. One looks at one program from the outside, the other from the inside. Hence, for effective testing of programs, both techniques should be applied. An approach to combine them is to start with selecting a set of test cases for performing the black box testing. These test cases will provide some coverage but may not provide the desired level of coverage. The set of test cases is then augmented with additional test cases so that the desired coverage level is achieved.

Overall, first the available tools should be applied first, as they are probably the least expensive in terms of detecting defects. If unit testing and inspections both are to be done, then which one should be done first will probably depend on the situation. Generally, it is believed that inspections should be done first and then unit testing should be done. However, as inspections tend to be expensive and may be done only on critical code, it may be appropriate if inspections are done after some amount of unit testing has been done. Proofs of correctness are very labor intensive and are applied only for very critical programs.

9.5 Metrics

Traditionally, work on metrics has focused on the final product, namely the code. In a sense, all metrics for intermediate products of requirements and design are basically used to ensure that the final product has a high quality and the productivity of the project stays high. That is, the basic goal of metrics for intermediate products is to predict or get some idea about the metrics of the final product. For the code, the most commonly used metrics are size, complexity, and reliability. We will discuss reliability in the next chapter, as most reliability models use test data to assess reliability. Here we discuss a few size and complexity measures.

9.5.1 Size Measures

Size of a product is a simple measure, which can be easy to calculate. The main reason for interest in size measures is that size is the major factor that affects the cost of a project. Size in itself is of little use; it is the relationship of size with the cost and quality that makes size an important metric. It is also used to measure productivity during the project (e.g., KLOC per person-month). Final quality delivered by a process is also frequently normalized with respect to size (number of defects per KLOC). For these reasons, size is one of the most important and frequently used metrics.

The most common measure of size is delivered lines of source code, or the number of lines of code (LOC) finally delivered. The trouble with LOC is that the number of lines of code for a project depends heavily on the language used. For example, a program written in assembly language will be large compared to the same program written in a higher-level language, if LOC is used as a size measure. Even for the same language, the size can vary considerably depending on how lines are counted. Despite these deficiencies, LOC remains a handy and reasonable size measure that is used extensively. Currently, perhaps the most widely used counting method for determining the size is to count non-comment, non-blank lines only.

Halstead [79] has proposed metrics for length and volume of a program based on the number of operators and operands. In a program we define the following measurable quantities:

- n_1 is the number of distinct operators

- n_2 is the number of distinct operands

- $f_{1,j}$ is the number of occurrences of the jth most frequent operator

- $f_{2,j}$ is the number of occurrences of the jth most frequent operand

Then the vocabulary n of a program is defined as

$$n = n_1 + n_2.$$

With the measurable parameters listed earlier, two new parameters are defined:

$$N_1 = \sum f_{1,j}, N_2 = \sum f_{2,j}.$$

N_1 is the total occurrences of different operators in the program and N_2 is the total occurrences of different operands. The length of the program is defined as

$$N = N_1 + N_2.$$

From the length and the vocabulary, the volume V of the program is defined as

$$V = Nlog_2(n).$$

This definition of the volume of a program represents the minimum number of bits necessary to represent the program. $Log_2(n)$ is the number of bits needed to represent every element in the program uniquely, and N is the total occurrences of the different elements. Volume is used as a size metric for a program. Experiments have shown that the volume of a program is highly correlated with the size in LOC.

9.5.2 Complexity Metrics

The productivity, if measured only in terms of lines of code per unit time, can vary a lot depending on the complexity of the system to be developed. Clearly, a programmer will produce a lesser amount of code for highly complex system programs, as compared to a simple application program. Similarly, complexity has great impact on the cost of maintaining a program. To quantify complexity beyond the fuzzy notion of the ease with which a program can be constructed or comprehended, some metrics to measure the complexity of a program are needed.

Some metrics for complexity were discussed in Chapter 8. The same metrics that are applicable to detailed design can be applied to code. One such complexity measure discussed in the previous chapter is *cyclomatic complexity*, in which the complexity of a module is the number of independent cycles in the flow graph of the module. A number of metrics have been proposed for quantifying the complexity of a program [80], and studies have been done to correlate the complexity with maintenance effort. Here we discuss a few more complexity measures. Most of these have been proposed in the context of programs, but they can be applied or adapted for detailed design as well.

Size Measures

A complexity measure tries to capture the level of difficulty in understanding a module. In other words, it tries to quantify a cognitive aspect of a program. It is well known that, in general, the larger a module, the more difficult it is to comprehend. Hence, the size of a module can be taken as a simple measure of the complexity of the module. It can be seen that, on an average, as the size of the module increases, the number of decisions in it are likely to increase. This means that, on an average, as the size increases the cyclomatic complexity also increases. Though it is clearly possible that two programs of the same size have substantially different complexities, in general, size is quite strongly related to some of the complexity measures.

Halstead's Measure

Halstead also proposed a number of other measures based on his software science [79]. Some of these can be considered complexity measures. As given earlier, a number of variables are defined in software science. These are n_1 (number of unique operators), n_2 (number of unique operands), N_1 (total frequency of operators), and N_2 (total frequency of operands). As any program must have at least two operators—one for function call and one for end of statement—the ratio $n_1/2$ can be considered the relative level of difficulty due to the larger number of operators in the program. The ratio N_2/n_2 represents the average number of times an operand is used. In a program in which variables are changed more frequently, this ratio will be larger. As such programs are harder to understand, *ease of reading or writing* is defined as

$$D = \frac{n_1 * N_2}{2 * n_2}.$$

Halstead's complexity measure focused on the internal complexity of a module, as does McCabe's complexity measure. Thus the complexity of the module's connection with its environment is not given much importance. In Halstead's measure, a module's connection with its environment is reflected in terms of operands and operators. A call to another module is considered an operator, and all the parameters are considered operands of this operator.

Live Variables

In a computer program, a typical assignment statement uses and modifies only a few variables. However, in general the statements have a much larger context. That is, to construct or understand a statement, a programmer must keep track of a number of variables, other than those directly used in the statement. For a statement, such data items are called *live variables*. Intuitively, the more live variables for statements, the harder it will be to understand a program. Hence, the concept of live variables can be used as a metric for program complexity.

First let us define *live variables* more precisely. A variable is considered live from its first to its last reference within a module, including all statements between the first and last statement where the variable is referenced. Using this definition, the set of live variables for each statement can be computed easily by analysis of the module's code. The procedure of determining the live variables can easily be automated.

For a statement, the number of live variables represents the degree of difficulty of the statement. This notion can be extended to the entire module by defining the average number of live variables. The average number of live variables is the sum of the count of live variables (for all executable statements) divided by the number of executable statements. This is a complexity measure for the module.

Live variables are defined from the point of view of data usage. The logic of a module is not explicitly included. The logic is used only to determine the first and last statement of reference for a variable. Hence, this concept of complexity is quite different from cyclomatic complexity, which is based entirely on the logic and considers data as secondary.

Another data usage-oriented concept is *span*, the number of statements between two successive uses of a variable. If a variable is referenced at n different places in a module, then for that variable there are $(n-1)$ spans. The average span size is the average number of executable statements between two successive references of a variable. A large span implies that the reader of the program has to remember a definition of a variable for a larger period of time (or for more statements). In other words, span can be considered a complexity measure; the larger the span, the more complex the module.

Knot Count

A method for quantifying complexity based on the locations of the control transfers of the program has been proposed in [149]. It was designed largely for FORTRAN programs, where explicit transfer of control is shown by the use of goto statements. A programmer, to understand a given program, typically draws arrows from the point of control transfer to its destination, helping to create a mental picture of the program and the control transfers in it. According to this metric, the more intertwined these arrows become, the more complex the program. This notion is captured in the concept of a "knot."

A *knot* is essentially the intersection of two such control transfer arrows. If each statement in the program is written on a separate line, this notion can be formalized as follows. A jump from line a to line b is represented by the pair (a, b). Two jumps (a, b) and (p, q) give rise to a knot if either min (a, b) < min (p, q) < max (a, b) and max (p, q) > max (a, b); or min (a, b) < max (p, qa) < max (a, b) and min (p, q) < min (a, b).

Problems can arise while determining the knot count of programs using structured constructs. One method is to convert such a program into one that explicitly shows control transfers and then compute the knot count. The basic scheme can be generalized to flow graphs, though with flow graphs only bounds can be obtained.

Topological Complexity

A complexity measure that is sensitive to the nesting of structures has been proposed in [31]. Like cyclomatic complexity, it is based on the flow graph of a module or program. The complexity of a program is considered its maximal intersect number *min*.

To compute the maximal intersect, a flow graph is converted into a strongly connected graph (by drawing an arrow from the terminal node to the initial node). A strongly connected graph divides the graph into a finite number of regions. The number of regions is (edges - nodes + 2). If we draw a line that enters each region exactly once, then the number of times this line intersects the arcs in the graph is the maximal intersect *min*, which is taken to be the complexity of the program.

9.6 Summary

The goal of the coding activity is to develop correct programs that are also clear and simple. As reading programs is a much more common activity than writing programs, the goal of the coding activity is to produce simple programs that are easy to understand and modify and that are free from errors. Ease of understanding and freedome from defects are the key properties of high quality code. The focus of this chapter is to discuss approaches that can be used for developing high quality code.

We discussed some principles whose application can help improve code quality. These include structured programming and information hiding. In structured programs, the program is a sequence of single-entry, single-exit statements, and the control flow during execution is linearized. This makes the dynamic structure of a program similar to the static structure, and hence easy to understand and verify. In information hiding, the data structures are hidden behind access functions, thereby raising the level of abstraction and hiding complexity. We also described some common coding errors to make the programmer aware about them, and some programming practices that can help reduce errors. We briefly discussed coding standards that help improve readability as well as reduce errors.

There are different ways a programmer can proceed with developing code. We discussed a few processes that can be followed by a programmer. One is the incremental process in which the programmer writes code in small increments and tests and debugs each increment before writing more code. Test driven development is a programming approach in which test cases are written first and then code is written to pass these test cases. When the code succeeds, the programmer writes another small set of test cases and then the code to implement it. Test driven development is also an incremental programming approach. Pair programming is another approach, in which coding is done by a pair of programmers. Both programmers together discuss the strategy, data structures, and algorithms to be used. When one programmer does the actual coding, the other reviews it as it is being typed. Regardless of the approach the programmer follows, source code control is an important part of the coding process. We briefly discussed how source code control is used by programmers.

Code evolves and changes over time as systems evolve. Often due to these changes the design of the software becomes too complex making changing harder. Refactoring is an approach in which during the coding activity, effort is spent in refactoring the existing code to improve its design so that changes become easier to make. During refactoring no new functionality is added—only improvement is done so that the design of the code improves by reduction of coupling, increase in cohesion, and better use of hierarchies. We have discussed the refactoring process and various techniques for doing refactoring, and have given a detailed example.

The code written by a programmer should be verified before it is incorporated in the overall system. The most commonly used techniques for verification are static analysis, code inspections, and unit testing. In static analysis, the source code is examined for anomalies and situations that can represent bugs through suitable tools. It is a very efficient way of detecting errors and static analyzers can detect a variety of defects. However, warnings given by a static analyzers also have "false positives," requiring further analysis by the programmers to identify actual defects. Code inspections, using a standard inspection process, is a very effective approach for finding errors. It can, however, be expensive, and hence is sometimes replaced with code reading or one-person review. Unit testing the code is a very popular and most often used practice by programmers. In this drivers and stubs are written to test the program the programmer had developed. Unit testing can benefit from tools, and we have briefly discussed how unit testing can be done with the Junit tool. Formal verification is another approach that is sometimes used for very critical portions of the system. We have discussed one approach for formal verification also.

A number of metrics exist for quantifying different qualities of the code. The most commonly used are size metrics, because they are used to assess the productivity of people and are often used in cost estimation. The most common size measure is lines of code (LOC), which is also used in most cost models. There are also other measures for size. The goal of complexity metrics is to quantify the complexity of software. Complexity is an important factor affecting the productivity of projects and is a factor in cost estimation. A number of different metrics exist. Perhaps the most common is the cyclomatic complexity, which is based on the internal logic of the program and defines complexity as the number of independent cycles in the flow graph of the program.

Exercises

1. What is structured programming and how does it help improve code quality?

2. If you have all the tools available, how will you do the verification of the programs you write?

3. For memory and resource related errors (memory leaks, null dereferencing, etc.) compare the effectiveness and efficiency of the different verification techniques.

4. Buffer overflow is a common error which is also a main security flaw. What are some of the coding practices that will help minimize this error? What other types of errors these practices will impact?

5. Draw a flow diagram describing your own personal process. Critically evaluate it and suggest modifications that will help improve the quality of the code you write.

6. Work on some programs alone. Then, along with a friend, develop some other programs using pair programming. Compare the productivity and code quality achieved in the two approaches.

7. In your next project, develop a few classes using your standard approach. Then use Junit and develop a few classes using an incremental approach. Record effort and defect data and then compare the average development time, productivity, and defects found.

8. Do a similar experiment with TDD. How does it compare with your regular development process?

9. What are the major concepts that help make a program more readable?

10. Consider the following program to determine the product of two integers x and y:

```
if (x = 0) or (y = 0) then
       p := 0
else begin
       p := x;
       i := 1;
       while (i != y) do begin
              p := p * x;
              i := i + 1;
       end;
end;
```

Write formal specifications for a program to compute the product of two numbers. Then, using the axiomatic method, prove that this program is correct.

11. Consider the following two algorithms for searching an element E in a sorted array A, which contains n integers. The first procedure implements a simple linear search algorithm. The second performs a binary search. Binary search is generally much more efficient in terms of execution time compared to the linear search.

```
function lin_search (A, E): boolean
var
```

```
            i : integer;
            found: boolean;
begin
            found := false;
            i := 1;
            while (not found) and (i ≤ n) do begin
            if (A[i] = E) then found := true;
            i := i + 1;
            end;
            lin_search := found;
end;


function bin_search (A, E): boolean
var
            low, high, mid, i, j : integer;
            found : boolean;
begin
            low := 1;
            high := n;
            found := false;
            while (low ≤ high) and (not found) do begin
                  mid := (low + high)/2;
                  if E < A[mid] then high := mid - 1
                        else if E > A[mid] then low := mid + 1
                        else found := true;
            end;
            bin_search := found;
end;
```

Determine the cyclomatic complexity and live variable complexity for these two functions. Is the ratio of the two complexity measures similar for the two functions?

12. What is Halstead's size measure for these two modules? Compare this size with the size measured in LOC.

13. Consider the size measure as the number of bytes needed to store the object code of a program. How useful is this size measure? Is it closer to LOC or Halstead's metric? Explain.

14. Not all control statements are equally complex. Assign complexity weights (0–10) to different control statements in Java, and then determine a formula to calculate the complexity of a program. How will you determine if this measure is better or worse than other complexity measures?

15. A combination of conditions in a decision makes a decision more complex. Such decisions should be treated as a combination of different decisions. Compared to the simple measure where each decision is treated as one, how much will the difference in the cyclomatic complexity of a program with 20% of its conditional statements having two conditions and 20% having three conditions be, when evaluated by this new approach?

16. Design an experiment to study the correlation between some of the complexity measures and between some of the size measures.

17. Design an experiment to study if the "error-proneness" of a module is related to a complexity measure for the module.

Case Studies

Implementation of Structured Design of Case Study 1

The programs were written in C on a Sun workstation, as required. The first version almost directly implemented the modules specified in the function-oriented design. The total size of the program was about 1320 lines. We determined various code based complexity and size metrics for this code using the tool complexity that we developed. This is shown below.

```
---------------------------------------------------------------
   MODULE                      SIZE   CYCLOMATIC COMPLEXITY
---------------------------------------------------------------
   validate_file2              111          18
   validate_dept_courses        88          17
   sched_ug_pref               104          16
   validate_class_rooms         92          15
   validate_lec_times           84          15
   print_conflicts              50          11
   print_TimeTable              42          10
   chk_fmt_time_slot            36          10
   sched_pg_pref                82           9
   separate_courses             46           9
---------------------------------------------------------------
Total Size:   1322    Total Cyclomatic Complexity:  243
Avg.  size:     33    Avg.  Cyclomatic Complexity:    6
---------------------------------------------------------------
```

From these metrics, it was clear that some of the modules were too large and had a high complexity value. Based on this information, we carefully reviewed some of these modules to see if their size or complexity could be reduced. During the reviews we found that in these modules some parts of the code were actually implementing some support functions that can be separated by forming clean, functionally cohesive modules.

As a result of this, a few new modules were formed. The complexity of many of the modules was reduced, and there was a general decline in the average complexity. It is worth noting that the total size and complexity is reduced by this exercise, besides the reduction in the complexity and size of the individual modules. That is, by this exercise we did not just redistribute the complexity, we actually reduced the overall complexity. The overall figures after the changes are:

```
-----------------------------------------------------------
Total Size:  1264    Total Cyclomatic Complexity:  235
Avg.  Size:    30    Avg.  Cyclomatic Complexity:    5
-----------------------------------------------------------
```

OO Design Implementation of Case Study 1

The object-oriented design of the case study given earlier was implemented in C++. The implementation did extend the design a little, as is to be expected, but the extension was mostly in the addition of data members and some methods. No major design changes were required due to implementation issues. The code could have been analyzed by using some of the metrics and then modified, as was done in the code implementing the structured design. However, this was not done for this implementation for three reasons. First, we did not have tools to analyze the C++ programs. Secondly, some of the tools that were available for use through other sources worked on a different version of C++ (our implementation is in GNU C++). And finally, the OO metrics are still relatively new, and not much data about their use is available.

The C++ code for the case study is also available from the home page of the book.

Implementation of Case Study 2

This case study was implemented in Java on a PC. Some unit testing was done on some of the modules using Junit. The unit testing report is available from the Web site.

The entire code for this case study is also available from the Web site.

10

Testing

In a software development project, errors can be introduced at any stage during development. Though errors are detected after each phase by techniques like inspections, some errors remain undetected. Ultimately, these remaining errors will be reflected in the code. Hence, the final code is likely to have some requirements errors and design errors, in addition to errors introduced during the coding activity. Testing is the activity where the errors remaining from all the previous phases must be detected. Hence, testing performs a very critical role for ensuring quality. The focus of this chapter is primarily on system testing in which the entire software system is tested, though testing is also performed on individual programs written by programmers and the concepts discussed are also applicable for individual program testing.

During testing, the software to be tested is executed with a set of test cases, and the behavior of the system for the test cases is evaluated to determine if the system is performing as expected. Clearly, the success of testing in revealing errors depends critically on the test cases. Much of this chapter is devoted to test case selection, criteria for selecting test cases, and their effect on testing.

We begin this chapter by discussing some definitions and concepts pertinent to testing. Then we discuss the two basic approaches to testing—black box or functional testing and white-box or structural testing. Aspects of testing process is discussed next, followed by a discussion on how testing data can be used for defect prevention. Then we discuss reliability estimation, as reliability is the main metric of interest during testing. This chapter ends with case studies.

10.1   Testing Fundamentals

In this section we will first define some of the terms that are commonly used when discussing testing. Then we will discuss some basic issues relating to how testing can proceed, the need for oracles for testing, the importance of psychology of the tester, and some desirable properties for the criteria used for testing. Once these are discussed, we will proceed with the issue of selection of test cases.

10.1.1   Error, Fault, and Failure

So far, we have used the intuitive meaning of the term *error* to refer to problems in requirements, design, or code. Sometimes error, fault, and failure are used interchangeably, and sometimes they refer to different concepts. Let us start by defining these concepts clearly. We follow the IEEE definitions [91] for these terms.

The term *error* is used in two different ways. It refers to the discrepancy between a computed, observed, or measured value and the true, specified, or theoretically correct value. That is, error refers to the difference between the actual output of a software and the correct output. In this interpretation, error is essentially a measure of the difference between the actual and the ideal. Error is also used to refer to human action that results in software containing a defect or fault. This definition is quite general and encompasses all the phases.

Fault is a condition that causes a system to fail in performing its required function. A fault is the basic reason for software malfunction and is synonymous with the commonly used term *bug*. The term error is also often used to refer to defects (taking a variation of the second definition of error). In this book we will continue to use the terms in the manner commonly used, and no explicit distinction will be made between errors and faults, unless necessary. It should be noted that the only faults that a software has are "design faults"; there is no wear and tear in software.

Failure is the inability of a system or component to perform a required function according to its specifications. A software failure occurs if the behavior of the software is different from the specified behavior. Failures may be caused due to functional or performance reasons. A failure is produced only when there is a fault in the system. However, presence of a fault does not guarantee a failure. In other words, faults have the potential to cause failures and their presence is a necessary but not a sufficient condition for failure to occur. Note that the definition does not imply that a failure must be *observed*. It is possible that a failure may occur but not be detected.

Note also that what is called a "failure" is dependent on the project, and its exact definition is often left to the tester or project manager. For example, is a misplaced line in the output a failure or not? Clearly, it depends on the project; some will consider it a failure and others will not. Take another example. If the output is not produced within a given time period, is it a failure or not? For a real-time system this may be viewed as a failure, but for an operating system it may not be viewed as a failure. This means that there can be no general definition of failure, and it is up to the project manager or end user to decide what will be considered a failure for reliability purposes. Note that in the example of a misplaced line, a defect might be recorded, and even corrected later, but its occurrence might not be considered a failure.

There are some implications of these definitions. Presence of an error (in the state) implies that a failure must have occurred, and the observance of a failure implies that a fault must be present in the system. However, the presence of a fault does not imply that a failure must occur. The presence of a fault in a system only implies that the fault has a *potential* to cause a failure to occur. Whether a fault actually manifests itself in a certain time duration depends on many factors. This means that if we observe the behavior of a system for some time duration and we do not observe any errors, we cannot say anything about the presence or absence of faults in the system. If, on the other hand, we observe some failure in this duration, we can say that there are some faults in the system.

There are direct consequences of this on testing. In testing, system behavior is observed, and by observing the behavior of a system or a component during testing, we determine whether or not there is a failure. Because of this fundamental reliance on behavior observation, testing can only reveal the presence of faults, not their absence. By observing failures of the system we can deduce the presence of faults; but by not observing a failure during our observation (or testing) interval we cannot claim that there are no faults in the system. An immediate consequence of this is that it becomes hard to decide for how long we should test a system without observing any failures before deciding to stop testing. This makes "when to stop testing" one of the hard issues in testing.

During the testing process, only failures are observed, by which the presence of faults is deduced. That is, testing only reveals the presence of faults. The actual faults are identified by separate activities, commonly referred

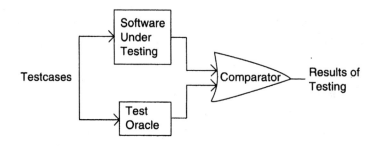

Figure 10.1: Testing and test oracles.

to as "debugging." In other words, for identifying faults, after testing has revealed the presence of faults, the expensive task of debugging has to be performed. This is one of the reasons why testing is an expensive method for identification of faults, compared to methods that directly observe faults.

10.1.2   Test Oracles

To test any program, we need to have a description of its expected behavior and a method of determining whether the observed behavior conforms to the expected behavior. For this we need a *test oracle.*

A test oracle is a mechanism, different from the program itself, that can be used to check the correctness of the output of the program for the test cases. Conceptually, we can consider testing a process in which the test cases are given to the test oracle and the program under testing. The output of the two is then compared to determine if the program behaved correctly for the test cases, as shown in Figure 10.1.

Test oracles are necessary for testing. Ideally, we would like an automated oracle, which always gives a correct answer. However, often the oracles are human beings, who can make mistakes. As a result, when there is a discrepancy between the results of the program and the oracle, we have to verify the result produced by the oracle, before declaring that there is a fault in the program.

The human oracles generally use the specifications of the program to decide what the "correct" behavior of the program should be. However, the specifications themselves may contain errors, be imprecise, or contain ambiguities. Such shortcomings in the specifications are the major cause of situations where one party claims that a particular condition is not a failure while the other claims it is. There is no easy solution to this problem, as testing does require some specifications against which the given system is tested.

There are some systems where oracles are automatically generated from specifications of programs or modules. With such oracles, we are assured that the output of the oracle is consistent with the specifications. These oracles also eliminate the effort of determining the expected behavior for a test case. However, even this approach does not solve all our problems, because of the possibility of errors in the specifications. Consequently, an oracle generated from the specifications will only produce correct results if the specifications are correct, and it will not be dependable in the case of specification errors. Furthermore, such systems that generate oracles from specifications are likely to require formal specifications, which are frequently not generated during design.

10.1.3 Test Cases and Test Criteria

Having test cases that are good at revealing the presence of faults is central to successful testing. The reason for this is that if there is a fault in a program, the program can still provide the expected behavior for many inputs. Only for the set of inputs that exercise the fault in the program will the output of the program deviate from the expected behavior. Hence, it is fair to say that testing is as good as its test cases.

Ideally, we would like to determine a set of test cases such that successful execution of all of them implies that there are no errors in the program. This ideal goal cannot usually be achieved due to practical and theoretical constraints. Each test case costs money, as effort is needed to generate the test case, machine time is needed to execute the program for that test case, and more effort is needed to evaluate the results. Therefore, we would also like to minimize the number of test cases needed to detect errors. These are the two fundamental goals of a practical testing activity—maximize the number of errors detected and minimize the number of test cases (i.e., minimize the cost). As these two are frequently contradictory, the problem of selecting the set of test cases with which a program should be tested becomes more complex.

While selecting test cases the primary objective is to ensure that if there is an error or fault in the program, it is exercised by one of the test cases. An ideal test case set is one that succeeds (meaning that its execution reveals no errors) only if there are no errors in the program. One possible ideal set of test cases is one that includes all the possible inputs to the program. This is often called *exhaustive* testing. However, exhaustive testing is impractical and infeasible, as even for small programs the number of elements in the input domain can be extremely large.

So, how should we select our test cases? On what basis should we include some element of the program domain in the set of test cases and not include others? For this *test selection criterion* (or simply *test criterion*) can be used.   For a given program P and its specifications S, a test selection criterion specifies the conditions that must be satisfied by a set of test cases T. The criterion becomes a basis for test case selection. For example, if the criterion is that all statements in the program be executed at least once during testing, then a set of test cases T satisfies this criterion for a program P if the execution of P with T ensures that each statement in P is executed at least once.

There are two fundamental properties for a testing criterion: reliability and validity [73]. A criterion is reliable if all the sets (of test cases) that satisfy the criterion detect the same errors. That is, it is insignificant which of the sets satisfying the criterion is chosen; every set will detect exactly the same errors. A criterion is valid if for any error in the program there is some set satisfying the criterion that will reveal the error. A fundamental theorem of testing is that if a testing criterion is valid and reliable, if a set satisfying the criterion succeeds (revealing no faults), then the program contains no errors [73]. However, it has been shown that no algorithm exists that will determine a valid criterion for an arbitrary program.

Getting a criterion that is reliable and valid and that can be satisfied by a manageable number of test cases is usually not possible. So, often criteria are chosen that are not valid or reliable like "90% of the statements should be executed at least once." Often a criterion is not even clearly specified, as in "all special values in the domain must be included" (what is a "special value"?).

Even when the criterion is specified, generating test cases to satisfy a criterion is not simple. In general, generating test cases for most of the criteria cannot be automated. For example, even for a simple criterion like "each statement of the program should be executed," it is extremely hard to construct a set of test cases that will satisfy this criterion for a large program, even if we assume that all the statements can be executed (i.e., there is no part that is not reachable).

A criterion C_1 includes (or subsumes) the criterion C_2 if for every program P and its specification S, any set of test cases that satisfy C_1 also satisfy C_2 [145, 67]. This relation is represented as $C_1 \Rightarrow C_2$, and is a transitive relation. One may think that if $C_1 \Rightarrow C_2$, testing based on C_1 will always be better than testing based on C_2. Unfortunately, this is not the case. The reason is that the fault-detection capability of a set of test cases T that satisfy a criterion C depends on the actual test cases in T and not just C (i.e., the criterion is not valid). In other words, if T_1 and T_2 both satisfy C for a program P, it does not mean that T_1 and T_2 will execute the same paths of P and detect the same faults in P. Because the actual test cases also play a role in whether or not an error in a program is detected, in general, it is possible to have a situation where $C_1 \Rightarrow C_2$, T_1 satisfies C_1, T_2 satisfies C_2, but T_2 detects an error that T_1 does not. However, if similar methods are used for test case generation then, generally speaking, C_1 will be better for testing than C_2 if $C_1 \Rightarrow C_2$.

The intent of the preceding discussion is to illustrate that no single criterion will serve the purpose of detecting a reasonable number of errors in a program. Though frequently the focus is on the criterion, to use a criterion for testing, the strategy for generating test cases to satisfy a criterion is also important. As it is generally known that all the faults in a program cannot be practically revealed by testing, and due to the limitations of the test criterion, it is best that during testing more than one criterion be used.

10.1.4 Psychology of Testing

As we have seen, devising a set of test cases that will guarantee that all errors will be detected is not feasible. Moreover, there are no formal or precise methods for selecting test cases. Even though there are a number of heuristics and rules of thumb for deciding the test cases, selecting test cases is still a creative activity that relies on the ingenuity of the tester. Because of this, the psychology of the person performing the testing becomes important.

The basic purpose of testing is to detect the errors that may be present in the program. Hence, one should not start testing with the intent of showing that a program works; but the intent should be to show that a program does not work. With this in mind we can define testing as the process of executing a program with the intent of finding errors [121].

This emphasis on proper intent of testing is not a trivial matter because test cases are designed by human beings, and human beings have a tendency to perform actions to achieve the goal they have in mind. So, if the goal is to demonstrate that a program works, we may consciously or subconsciously

select test cases that will try to demonstrate that goal and that will beat
the basic purpose of testing. On the other hand, if the intent is to show
that the program does not work, we will challenge our intellect to find test
cases toward that end, and we are likely to detect more errors. Testing is
essentially a destructive process, where the tester has to treat the program
as an adversary that must be beaten by the tester by showing the presence
of errors. With this in mind, a test case is "good" if it detects an as-yet-
undetected error in the program, and our goal during designing test cases
should be to design such "good" test cases.

One of the reasons many organizations require a product to be tested
by people not involved with developing the program before finally delivering
it to the customer is this psychological factor. It is hard to be destructive
to something we have created ourselves, and we all like to believe that the
program we have written "works." So, it is not easy for someone to test his
own program with the proper frame of mind for testing. Another reason for
independent testing is that sometimes errors occur because the programmer
did not understand the specifications clearly. Testing of a program by its
programmer will not detect such errors, whereas independent testing may
succeed in finding them.

This approach towards testing is suitable for earlier stages of testing,
where indeed the objective is to reveal errors. However, often the last stages
of testing are meant more for evaluating the product. In these types of
testing, test cases are selected primarily to mimic the user behavior or user
scenarios.

10.2   Black-Box Testing

There are two basic approaches to testing: black-box and white-box. In
black-box testing the structure of the program is not considered. Test cases
are decided solely on the basis of the requirements or specifications of the
program or module, and the internals of the module or the program are not
considered for selection of test cases. In this section, we will present some
techniques for generating test cases for black-box testing. White-box testing
is discussed in the next section.

In black-box testing, the tester only knows the inputs that can be given
to the system and what output the system should give. In other words,
the basis for deciding test cases in functional testing is the requirements or
specifications of the system or module. This form of testing is also called

functional or behavioral testing.

The most obvious functional testing procedure is exhaustive testing, which as we have stated, is impractical. One criterion for generating test cases is to generate them randomly. This strategy has little chance of resulting in a set of test cases that is close to optimal (i.e., that detects the maximum errors with minimum test cases). Hence, we need some other criterion or rule for selecting test cases. There are no formal rules for designing test cases for functional testing. In fact, there are no precise criteria for selecting test cases. However, there are a number of techniques or heuristics that can be used to select test cases that have been found to be very successful in detecting errors. Here we mention some of these techniques.

10.2.1 Equivalence Class Partitioning

Because we cannot do exhaustive testing, the next natural approach is to divide the input domain into a set of equivalence classes, so that if the program works correctly for a value then it will work correctly for all the other values in that class. If we can indeed identify such classes, then testing the program with one value from each equivalence class is equivalent to doing an exhaustive test of the program.

However, without looking at the internal structure of the program, it is impossible to determine such ideal equivalence classes (even with the internal structure, it usually cannot be done). The equivalence class partitioning method [121] tries to approximate this ideal. An equivalence class is formed of the inputs for which the behavior of the system is specified or expected to be similar. Each group of inputs for which the behavior is expected to be different from others is considered a separate equivalence class. The rationale of forming equivalence classes like this is the assumption that if the specifications require the same behavior for each element in a class of values, then the program is likely to be constructed so that it either succeeds or fails for each of the values in that class. For example, the specifications of a module that determines the absolute value for integers specify one behavior for positive integers and another for negative integers. In this case, we will form two equivalence classes—one consisting of positive integers and the other consisting of negative integers.

For robust software, we must also consider invalid inputs. That is, we should define equivalence classes for invalid inputs also.

Equivalence classes are usually formed by considering each condition specified on an input as specifying a valid equivalence class and one or more invalid equivalence classes. For example, if an input condition specifies a range of values (say, $0 <$ count $<$ Max), then form a valid equivalence class with that range and two invalid equivalence classes, one with values less than the lower bound of the range (i.e., count < 0) and the other with values higher than the higher bound (count $>$ Max). If the input specifies a set of values and the requirements specify different behavior for different elements in the set, then a valid equivalence class is formed for each of the elements in the set and an invalid class for an entity not belonging to the set.

One common approach for determining equivalence classes is as follows. If there is reason to believe that the entire range of an input will not be treated in the same manner, then the range should be split into two or more equivalence classes, each consisting of values for which the behavior is expected to be similar. For example, for a character input, if we have reasons to believe that the program will perform different actions if the character is an alphabet, a number, or a special character, then we should split the input into three valid equivalence classes.

Another approach for forming equivalence classes is to consider any special value for which the behavior could be different as an equivalence class. For example, the value 0 could be a special value for an integer input.

Also, for each valid equivalence class, one or more invalid equivalence classes should be identified.

It is often useful to consider equivalence classes in the output. For an output equivalence class, the goal is to have inputs such that the output for that test case lies in the output equivalence class. As an example consider a program for determining rate of return for some investment. There are three clear output equivalence classes—positive rates—positive rate of return, negative rate of return, and zero rate of return. During testing, it is important to test for each of these, that is, give inputs such that each of these three outputs are generated. Determining test cases for output classes may be more difficult, but output classes have been found to reveal errors that are not revealed by just considering the input classes.

Once equivalence classes are selected for each of the inputs, then the issue is to select test cases suitably. There are different ways to select the test cases. One strategy is to select each test case covering as many valid equivalence classes as it can, and one separate test case for each invalid equivalence class. A somewhat better strategy which requires more test cases is to have a test case cover at most one valid equivalence class for each input, and have one separate test case for each invalid equivalence class. In

Input	Valid Equivalence Classes	Invalid Equivalence Classes
s	EQ1: Contains numbers EQ2: Contains lower case letters EQ3: Contains upper case letters EQ4: Contains special characters EQ5: String length between 0-N	IEQ1: non-ASCII characters IEQ2: String length > N
n	EQ6: Integer in valid range	IEQ3: Integer out of range

Table 10.1: Valid and invalid equivalence classes.

the latter case, the number of test cases for valid equivalence classes is equal to the largest number of equivalence classes for any input, plus the total number of invalid equivalence classes.

As an example consider a program that takes two inputs—a string s of length up to N and an integer n. The program is to determine the top n highest occurring characters in s. The tester believes that the programmer may deal with different types of characters separately. One set of valid and invalid equivalence classes for this is shown in Table 10.1.

With these as the equivalence classes, we have to select the test cases. A test case for this is a pair of values for s and n. With the first strategy for deciding test cases, one test case could be: s as a string of length less than N containing lower case, upper case, numbers, and special characters; and n as the number 5. This one test case covers all the valid equivalence classes (EQ1 through EQ6). Then we will have one test case each for covering IEQ1, IEQ2, and IEQ3. That is, a total of 4 test cases is needed.

With the second approach, in one test case we can cover one equivalence class for one input only. So, one test case could be: a string of numbers, and 5. This covers EQ1 and EQ6. Then we will need test cases for EQ2 through EQ5, and separate test cases for IEQ1 through IEQ3.

10.2.2 Boundary Value Analysis

It has been observed that programs that work correctly for a set of values in an equivalence class fail on some special values. These values often lie on the boundary of the equivalence class. Test cases that have values on the boundaries of equivalence classes are therefore likely to be "high-yield" test cases, and selecting such test cases is the aim of the boundary value analysis. In boundary value analysis [121], we choose an input for a test case from an equivalence class, such that the input lies at the edge of the equivalence classes. Boundary values for each equivalence class, including the equivalence classes of the output, should be covered. Boundary value test cases are also called "extreme cases." Hence, we can say that a boundary value test case is a set of input data that lies on the edge or boundary of a class of input data or that generates output that lies at the boundary of a class of output data.

In case of ranges, for boundary value analysis it is useful to select the boundary elements of the range and an invalid value just beyond the two ends (for the two invalid equivalence classes). So, if the range is $0.0 \leq$ x ≤ 1.0, then the test cases are 0.0, 1.0 (valid inputs), and -0.1, and 1.1 (for invalid inputs). Similarly, if the input is a list, attention should be focused on the first and last elements of the list.

We should also consider the outputs for boundary value analysis. If an equivalence class can be identified in the output, we should try to generate test cases that will produce the output that lies at the boundaries of the equivalence classes. Furthermore, we should try to form test cases that will produce an output that does not lie in the equivalence class. (If we can produce an input case that produces the output outside the equivalence class, we have detected an error.)

Like in equivalence class partitioning, in boundary value analysis we first determine values for each of the variables that should be exercised during testing. If there are multiple inputs, then how should the set of test cases be formed covering the boundary values? Suppose each input variable has a defined range. Then there are 6 boundary values—the extreme ends of the range, just beyond the ends, and just before the ends. If an integer range is min to max, then the six values are $min - 1, min, min + 1, max - 1, max, max + 1$. Suppose there are n such input variables. There are two strategies for combining the boundary values for the different variables in test cases.

In the first strategy, we select the different boundary values for one variable, and keep the other variables at some nominal value. And we select one test case consisting of nominal values of all the variables. In this case, we will have $6n + 1$ test cases. For two variables X and Y, the 13 test cases will be as shown in Figure 10.2.

A second strategy is to try all possible combinations for the values for the different variables. As there are 7 values for each variable (6 boundary values and one nominal value), if there are n variables, there will be a total

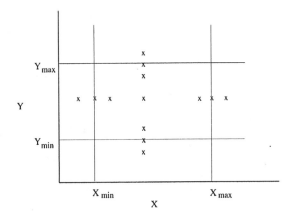

Figure 10.2: Test cases for BVA.

of 7^n test cases.

10.2.3   Cause-Effect Graphing

One weakness with the equivalence class partitioning and boundary value methods is that they consider each input separately. That is, both concentrate on the conditions and classes of one input. They do not consider combinations of input circumstances that may form interesting situations that should be tested. One way to exercise combinations of different input conditions is to consider all valid combinations of the equivalence classes of input conditions. This simple approach will result in an unusually large number of test cases, many of which will not be useful for revealing any new errors. For example, if there are n different input conditions, such that any combination of the input conditions is valid, we will have 2^n test cases.

Cause-effect graphing [121] is a technique that aids in selecting combinations of input conditions in a systematic way, such that the number of test cases does not become unmanageably large. The technique starts with identifying causes and effects of the system under testing. A *cause* is a distinct input condition, and an *effect* is a distinct output condition. Each condition forms a node in the cause-effect graph. The conditions should be stated such that they can be set to either true or false. For example, an input condition can be "file is empty," which can be set to true by having an empty input file, and false by a nonempty file. After identifying the causes and effects, for each effect we identify the causes that can produce that effect and how the conditions have to be combined to make the effect true. Conditions are combined using the Boolean operators "and," "or," and "not," which are represented in the graph by &, |, and ~. Then for each effect, all combinations of the causes that the effect depends on which will make the effect true are generated (the causes that the effect does not depend on are essentially "don't care"). By doing this, we identify the combinations of conditions that make different effects true. A test case is then generated for each combination of conditions, which make some effect true.

Let us illustrate this technique with a small example. Suppose that for a bank database there are two commands allowed:

credit	acct_number	transaction_amount
debit	acct_number	transaction_amount

The requirements are that if the command is credit and the acct_number is valid, then the account is credited. If the command is debit, the acct_number is valid, and the transaction_amount is valid (less than the balance), then the account is debited. If the command is not valid, the account number is not valid, or the debit amount is not valid, a suitable message is generated. We can identify the following causes and effects from these requirements:

Causes:
   c1. Command is credit
   c2. Command is debit
   c3. Account number is valid
   c4. Transaction_amt is valid

Effects:
   e1. Print "invalid command"
   e2. Print "invalid account_number"
   e3. Print "Debit amount not valid"
   e4. Debit account
   e5. Credit account

The cause-effect of this is shown in Figure 10.3. In the graph, the cause-effect relationship of this example is captured. For all effects, one can easily determine the causes each effect depends on and the exact nature of the dependency. For example, according to this graph the effect e5 depends on the causes c2, c3, and c4 in a manner such that the effect e5 is enabled when all c2, c3, and c4 are true. Similarly, the effect e2 is enabled if c3 is false.

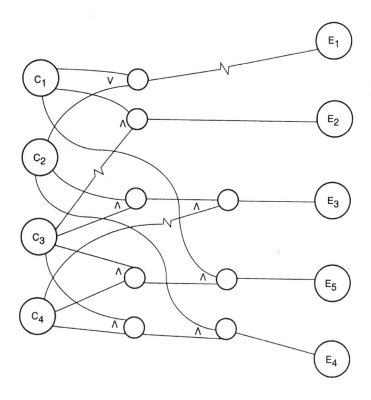

Figure 10.3: The cause-effect graph.

From this graph, a list of test cases can be generated. The basic strategy is to set an effect to 1 and then set the causes that enable this condition. The condition of causes forms the test case. A cause may be set to false, true, or don't care (in the case when the effect does not depend at all on the cause). To do this for all the effects, it is convenient to use a decision table. The decision table for this example is shown in Figure 10.4.

This table lists the combinations of conditions to set different effects. Each combination of conditions in the table for an effect is a test case. Together, these condition combinations check for various effects the software should display. For example, to test for the effect e3, both c2 and c4 have to be set. That is, to test the effect "Print debit amount not valid," the test case should be: Command is debit (setting c2 to True), the account number is valid (setting c3 to False), and the transaction money is not proper (setting c4 to False).

SNo.	1	2	3	4	5
c1	0	1	x	x	1
C2	0	x	1	1	x
c3	x	0	1	1	1
c4	x	x	0	1	1
e1	1				
e2		1			
e3			1		
e4				1	
e5					1

Figure 10.4: Decision table for the cause-effect graph.

Cause-effect graphing, beyond generating high-yield test cases, also aids the understanding of the functionality of the system, because the tester must identify the distinct causes and effects. There are methods of reducing the number of test cases generated by proper traversing of the graph. Once the causes and effects are listed and their dependencies specified, much of the remaining work can also be automated.

10.2.4   Pair-wise Testing

There are generally many parameters that determine the behavior of a software system. These parameters could be direct input to the software or implicit settings like those for devices. These parameters can take different values, and for some of them the software may not work correctly. Many of the defects in software generally involve one condition, that is, some special value of one of the parameters. Such a defect is called single-mode fault [125]. Simple examples of single mode fault are a software not able to print for a particular type of printer, a software that cannot compute fare properly when the traveller is a minor, a telephone billing software that does not compute the bill properly for a particular country.

Single-mode faults can be detected by testing for different values of different parameters. So, if there are n parameters for a system, and each one of them can take m different values (or m different classes of values, each class being considered as same for purposes of testing as in equivalence class partitioning), then with each test case we can test one different value of each parameter. In other words, we can test for all the different values in m test cases.

However, all faults are not single-mode and there are combinations of inputs that reveal the presence of faults. For example, a telephone billing software that does not compute correctly for night time calling (one parameter) to a particular country (another parameter). Or an airline ticketing system that has incorrect behavior when a minor (one parameter) is travelling business class (another parameter) and not staying over the weekend (third parameter). These multi-mode faults can be revealed during testing by trying different combinations of the parameter values—an approach called combinatorial testing.

Unfortunately, full combinatorial testing is often not feasible. For a system with n parameters, each having m values, the number of different combinations is n^m. For a simple system with 5 parameters, each having 5 different values the total number of combinations is 3,125. And if testing each combination takes 5 minutes, it will take over one month to test all combinations. Clearly, for complex systems that have many parameters and each parameter may have many values, a full combinatorial testing is not feasible and practical techniques are needed to reduce the number of tests.

Some research has suggested that most software faults are revealed on some special single values or by an interaction of pair of values [40]. That it, most faults tend to be either single-mode or double-mode. For testing for double-mode faults, we need not test the system with all the combinations of parameter values, but need to test such that all combinations of values for each pair of parameters is exercised. This is called *pair-wise testing*.

In pair-wise testing, all pairs of values have to be exercised during testing. If there are n parameters, each with m values, then between each two parameter we have $m*m$ pairs. The first parameter will have these many pairs with each of the remaining $n-1$ parameters, the second one will have new pairs with $n-2$ parameters (as its pairs with the first are already included in the first parameter pairs), the third will have pairs with $n-3$ parameters and so on. That is, the total number of pairs are $m*m*n*(n-1)/2$.

The objective of pair-wise testing is to have a set of test cases that cover all the pairs. As there are n parameters, a test case is a combination of values of these parameters and will cover $(n-1)+(n-2)+...=n(n-1)/2$ pairs. In the best case when each pair is covered exactly once by one test case, m^2 different test cases will be needed to cover all the pairs.

As an example consider a software product being developed for multiple platforms that uses the browser as its interface. Suppose the software is being designed to work for three different operating systems and three different browsers. In addition, as the product is memory intensive there is a desire

A	B	C	Pairs
a1	b1	c1	(a1,b1) (a1,c1) (b1,c1)
a1	b2	c2	(a1,b2) (a1,c2) (b2,c2)
a1	b3	c3	(a1,b3) (a1,c3) (b3,c3)
a2	b1	c2	(a2,b1) (a2,c2) (b1,c2)
a2	b2	c3	(a2,b2) (a2,c3) (b2,c3)
a2	b3	c1	(a2,b3) (a2,c1) (b3,c1)
a3	b1	c3	(a3,b1) (a3,c3) (b1,c3)
a3	b2	c1	(a3,b2) (a3,c1) (b2,c1)
a3	b3	c2	(a3,b3) (a3,c2) (b3,c2)

Table 10.2: Test cases for pair-wise testing.

to test its performance under different levels of memory. So, we have the following three parameters with their different values:

```
Operating System: Windows, Solaris, Linux
Memory Size: 128M, 256M, 512M
Browser: IE, Netscape, Mozilla
```

For discussion, we can say that the system has three parameters: A (operating system), B (memory size), and C (browser). Each of them can have three values which we will refer to as $a_1, a_2, a_3, b_1, b_2, b_3$, and c_1, c_2, c_3. The total number of pair-wise combinations is 9*3 = 27. The number of test cases, however, to cover all the pairs is much less. A test case consisting of values of the three parameters covers three combinations (of A-B, B-C, and A-C). Hence, in the best case, we can cover all 27 combinations by 27/3=9 test cases. These test cases are shown in Table 10.2, along with the pairs they cover.

As should be clear, generating test cases to cover all the pairs is not a simple task. The minimum set of test cases are those in which each pair is covered by exactly one test case. Often, it will not be possible to generate the minimum set of test cases, particularly when the number of values for different parameters is different. Various algorithms have been proposed, and some programs are available online to generate the test cases to cover all the pairs.

For many situations where manual generation is feasible, the following approach can be followed. Start with one combination of parameter values. Keep adding new combinations, choosing values such that no two values exist together in any earlier test case, until all pairs are covered. When selecting such values is not possible, select the values that has the fewest values that have existed together in an earlier test case. Essentially we are generating a test case that can cover as many as new pairs as possible. By avoiding covering pairs multiple times, we can produce a small set of test cases that cover all pairs. Efficient algorithms of generating the smallest number of test cases for pair-wise testing exist. In [40] an example is given in which for 13 parameters, each having three distinct values, all pairs are covered in merely 15 test cases, while the total number of combinations is over 1 million!

Pair-wise testing is a practical way of testing large software systems that have many different parameters with distinct functioning expected for different values. An example would be a billing system (for telephone, hotel, airline, etc.) which has different rates for different parameter values. It is also a practical approach for testing general purpose software products that are expected to run on different platforms and configurations, or a system that is expected to work with different types of systems.

10.2.5 Special Cases

It has been seen that programs often produce incorrect behavior when inputs form some special cases. The reason is that in programs, some combinations of inputs need special treatment, and providing proper handling for these special cases is easily overlooked. For example, in an arithmetic routine, if there is a division and the divisor is zero, some special action has to be taken, which could easily be forgotten by the programmer. These special cases form particularly good test cases, which can reveal errors that will usually not be detected by other test cases.

Special cases will often depend on the data structures and the function of the module. There are no rules to determine special cases, and the tester has to use his intuition and experience to identify such test cases. Consequently, determining special cases is also called *error guessing*.

The psychology is particularly important for error guessing. The tester should play the "devil's advocate" and try to guess the incorrect assumptions the programmer could have made and the situations the programmer could have overlooked or handled incorrectly. Essentially, the tester is trying to identify error prone situations. Then test cases are written for these situations. For example, in the problem of finding the number of different words in a file (discussed in earlier chapters) some of the special cases can be: file is empty, only one word in the file, only one word in a line, some empty lines in the input file, presence of more than one blank between words, all words are the same, the words are already sorted, and blanks at the start and end of the file.

Incorrect assumptions are usually made because the specifications are not complete or the writer of specifications may not have stated some properties, assuming them to be obvious. Whenever there is reliance on tacit understanding rather than explicit statement of specifications, there is scope for making wrong assumptions. Frequently, wrong assumptions are made about the environments. However, it should be pointed out that special cases depend heavily on the problem, and the tester should really try to "get into the shoes" of the designer and coder to determine these cases.

10.2.6   State-Based Testing

There are some systems that are essentially state-less in that for the same inputs they always give the same outputs or exhibit the same behavior. Many batch processing systems, computational systems, and servers fall in this category. In hardware, combinatorial circuits fall in this category. At a smaller level, most functions are supposed to behave in this manner. There are, however, many systems whose behavior is state-based in that for identical inputs they behave differently at different times and may produce different outputs. The reason for different behavior is the state of the system, that is, the behavior and outputs of the system depend not only on the inputs provided, but also on the state of the system. The state of the system depends on the past inputs the system has received. In other words, the state represents the cumulative impact of all the past inputs on the system. In hardware the sequential systems fall in this category. In software, many large systems fall in this category as past state is captured in databases or files and used to control the behavior of the system. For such systems, another approach for selecting test cases is the state-based testing approach [34].

Theoretically, any software that saves state can be modeled as a state machine. However, the state space of any reasonable program is almost infinite, as it is a cross product of the domains of all the variables that form the state. For many systems the state space can be partitioned into a few states, each representing a logical combination of values of different state variables which share some property of interest [16]. If the set of states of a system is manageable, a state model of the system can be built. A state model for a system has four components:

- *States.* Represent the impact of the past inputs to the system.

- *Transitions.* Represent how the state of the system changes from one state to another in response to some events.

- *Events.* Inputs to the system.

- *Actions.* The outputs for the events.

The state model shows what state transitions occur and what actions are performed in a system in response to events. When a state model is built from the requirements of a system, we can only include the states, transitions, and actions that are stated in the requirements or can be inferred from them. If more information is available from the design specifications, then a richer state model can be built.

For example, consider the student survey example discussed in Chapter 4. According to the requirements, a system is to be created for taking a student survey. The student takes a survey and is returned the current result of the survey. The survey result can be up to five surveys old. We consider the last architecture given in Figure 4.11, which had a cache between the server and the database, and in which the survey and results are cached and updated only after 5 surveys, on arrival of a request. The proposed architecture has a database at the back, which may go down.

To create a state machine model of this system, we notice that of a series of six requests, the first 5 may be treated differently. Hence, we divide into two states: one representing the the receiving of 1-4 requests (state 1), and the other representing the receiving of request 5 (state 2). Next we see that the database can be up or down, and it can go down in any of these two states. However, the behavior of requests, if the database is down may be different. Hence, we create another pair of states (states 3 and 4). Once the database has failed, then the first 5 requests are serviced using old data. When a request is received after receiving 5 requests, the system enters a failed state (state 5), in which it does not give any response. When the system recovers from the failed state, it must update its cache immediately, hence is goes to state 2. The state model for this system is shown in Figure 10.5 (*i* represents an input from the user for taking the survey).

Note that we are assuming that the state model of the system can be created from its specifications or design. This is how most state modeling is done, and that is how the model was built in the example. Once the state model is built, we can use it to select test cases. When the design is implemented, these test cases can be used for testing the code. It is because of this we treat state-based testing as a black box testing strategy.

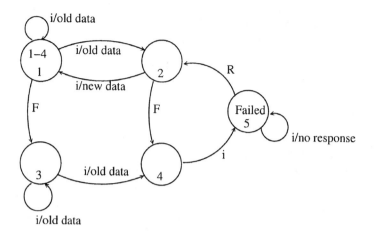

Figure 10.5: State model for the student survey system.

However, the state model often requires information about the design of the system. In the example above, some knowledge of the architecture is utilized. Sometimes making the state model may require detailed information about the design of the system. For example, for a class, we have seen that the state modeling is done during design, and when a lot is already known about the class, its attributes, and its methods. Due to this, the state-based testing may be considered as somewhat between black-box and white-box testing. Such strategies are sometimes called *gray box testing.*

Given a state model of a system how should test cases be generated? Many coverage criteria have been proposed [123]. We discuss only a few here. Suppose the set of test cases is T. Some of the criteria are:

- **All transition coverage (AT).** T must ensure that every transition in the state graph is exercised.

- **All transitions pair coverage (ATP).** T must execute all pairs of adjacent transitions. (An adjacent transition pair comprises of two transitions: an incoming transition to a state and an outgoing transition from that state.)

- **Transition tree coverage (TT).** T must execute all simple paths, where a simple path is one which starts from the start state and reaches a state that it has already visited in this path or a final state.

The first criterion states that during testing all transitions get fired. This will also ensure that all states are visited. The transition pair coverage is a

S.No.	Transition	Test case
1	$1 \rightarrow 2$	req()
2	$1 \rightarrow 2$	req();req();req();req();req();req()
3	$2 \rightarrow 1$	seq for 2; req()
4	$1 \rightarrow 3$	req();fail()
5	$3 \rightarrow 3$	req();fail();req()
6	$3 \rightarrow 4$	req();fail();req();req();req();req();req()
7	$4 \rightarrow 5$	seq for 6; req()
8	$5 \rightarrow 2$	seq for 6; req();recover()

Table 10.3: Test cases for a state based testing criteria.

stronger criterion requiring that all combinations of incoming and outgoing transitions for each state must be exercised by T. If a state has two incoming transitions t1 and t2, and two outgoing transitions t3 and t4, then a set of test cases T that executes t1;t3 and t2;t4 will satisfy AT. However, to satisfy ATP, T must also ensure execution of t1;t4 and t2;t3. The transition tree coverage is named in this manner as a transition tree can be constructed from the graph and then used to identify the paths. In ATP, we are going beyond transitions, and stating that different paths in the state diagram should be exercised during testing. ATP will generally include AT.

For the example above, the set of test cases for AT are given below in Table 10.3. Here req() means that a request for taking the survey should be given, fail() means that the database should be failed, and recover() means that the failed database should be recovered.

As we can see, state-based testing draws attention to the states and transitions. Even in the above simple case, we can see different scenarios get tested (e.g., system behavior when the database fails, and system behavior when it fails and recovers thereafter). Many of these scenarios are easy to overlook if test cases are designed only by looking at the input domains. The set of test cases is richer if the other criteria are used. For this example, we leave it as an exercise to determine the test cases for other criteria.

10.3   White-Box Testing

In the previous section we discussed black-box testing, which is concerned with the function that the tested program is supposed to perform and does not deal with the internal structure of the program responsible for actually implementing that function. Thus black-box testing is concerned with functionality rather than implementation of the program. White-box testing, on the other hand is concerned with testing the implementation of the program. The intent of this testing is not to exercise all the different input or output conditions (although that may be a by-product) but to exercise the different programming structures and data structures used in the program. White-box testing is also called *structural testing*, and we will use the two terms interchangeably.

To test the structure of a program, structural testing aims to achieve test cases that will force the desired coverage of different structures. Various criteria have been proposed for this. Unlike the criteria for functional testing, which are frequently imprecise, the criteria for structural testing are generally quite precise as they are based on program structures, which are formal and precise. Here we will discuss three different approaches to structural testing: control flow-based testing, data flow-based testing, and mutation testing.

10.3.1   Control Flow-Based Criteria

Most common structure-based criteria are based on the control flow of the program. In these criteria, the control flow graph of a program is considered and coverage of various aspects of the graph are specified as criteria. Hence, before we consider the criteria, let us precisely define a control flow graph for a program.

Let the *control flow graph* (or simply *flow graph*) of a program P be G. A node in this graph represents a block of statements that is always executed together, i.e., whenever the first statement is executed, all other statements are also executed. An edge (i, j) (from node i to node j) represents a possible transfer of control after executing the last statement of the block represented by node i to the first statement of the block represented by node j. A node corresponding to a block whose first statement is the start statement of P is called the *start* node of G, and a node corresponding to a block whose last statement is an exit statement is called an *exit* node [129]. A *path* is a finite sequence of nodes $(n_1, n_2, ..., n_k), k > 1$, such that there is an edge (n_i, n_{i+1}) for all nodes n_i in the sequence (except the last node n_k). A *complete path* is a path whose first node is the start node and the last node is an exit node.

Now let us consider control flow-based criteria. Perhaps the simplest coverage criteria is *statement coverage*, which requires that each statement of the program be executed at least once during testing. In other words, it requires that the paths executed during testing include all the nodes in the graph. This is also called the *all-nodes* criterion [129].

This coverage criterion is not very strong, and can leave errors undetected. For example, if there is an `if` statement in the program without having an `else` clause, the statement coverage criterion for this statement will be satisfied by a test case that evaluates the condition to true. No test case is needed that ensures that the condition in the `if` statement evaluates to false. This is a serious shortcoming because decisions in programs are potential sources of errors. As an example, consider the following function to compute the absolute value of a number:

```
int abs (x)
int x;
{
        if (x >= 0) x = 0 - x;
        return (x)
}
```

This program is clearly wrong. Suppose we execute the function with the set of test cases { x=0 } (i.e., the set has only one test case). The statement coverage criterion will be satisfied by testing with this set, but the error will not be revealed.

A little more general coverage criterion is *branch coverage*, which requires that each edge in the control flow graph be traversed at least once during testing. In other words, branch coverage requires that each decision in the program be evaluated to true and false values at least once during testing. Testing based on branch coverage is often called *branch testing*. The 100% branch coverage criterion is also called the *all-edges* criterion [129]. Branch coverage implies statement coverage, as each statement is a part of some branch. In other words, $C_{branch} \Rightarrow C_{stmt}$. In the preceding example, a set of test cases satisfying this criterion will detect the error.

The trouble with branch coverage comes if a decision has many conditions in it (consisting of a Boolean expression with Boolean operators *and* and *or*). In such situations, a decision can evaluate to true and false without actually exercising all the conditions. For example, consider the following function that checks the validity of a data item. The data item is valid if it lies between 0 and 100.

```
int check(x)
int x;
{
   . if ((x >= ) && (x <= 200))
         check = True;
      else check = False;
}
```

The module is incorrect, as it is checking for $x \leq 200$ instead of 100 (perhaps a typing error made by the programmer). Suppose the module is tested with the following set of test cases: { x = 5, x = -5 }. The branch coverage criterion will be satisfied for this module by this set. However, the error will not be revealed, and the behavior of the module is consistent with its specifications for all test cases in this set. Thus, the coverage criterion is satisfied, but the error is not detected. This occurs because the decision is evaluating to true and false because of the condition ($x \geq 0$). The condition ($x \leq 200$) never evaluates to false during this test, hence the error in this condition is not revealed.

This problem can be resolved by requiring that all conditions evaluate to true and false. However, situations can occur where a decision may not get both true and false values even if each individual condition evaluates to true and false. An obvious solution to this problem is to require decision/condition coverage, where all the decisions and all the conditions in the decisions take both true and false values during the course of testing.

Studies have indicated that there are many errors whose presence is not detected by branch testing because some errors are related to some combinations of branches and their presence is revealed by an execution that follows the path that includes those branches. Hence a more general coverage criterion is one that requires all possible paths in the control flow graph be executed during testing. This is called the *path coverage* criterion or the *all-paths* criterion, and the testing based on this criterion is often called *path testing*. The difficulty with this criterion is that programs that contain loops can have an infinite number of possible paths. Furthermore, not all paths in a graph may be "feasible" in the sense that there may not be any inputs for which the path can be executed. It should be clear that $C_{path} \Rightarrow C_{branch}$.

As the path coverage criterion leads to a potentially infinite number of paths, some efforts have been made to suggest criteria between the branch coverage and path coverage. The basic aim of these approaches is to select a set of paths that ensure branch coverage criterion and try some other paths that may help reveal errors. One method to limit the number of paths is to consider two paths the same if they differ only in their subpaths that are caused due to the loops. Even with this restriction, the number of paths can be extremely large.

Another such approach based on the cyclomatic complexity has been proposed in [116]. The test criterion is that if the cyclomatic complexity of a module is V, then at least V distinct paths must be executed during testing. We have seen that cyclomatic complexity V of a module is the number of independent paths in the flow graph of a module. As these are independent paths, all other paths can be represented as a combination of these basic paths. These basic paths are finite, whereas the total number of paths in a module having loops may be infinite.

It should be pointed out that none of these criteria is sufficient to detect all kind of errors in programs. For example, if a program is missing some control flow paths that are needed to check for a special value (like pointer equals nil and divisor equals zero), then even executing all the paths will not necessarily detect the error. Similarly, if the set of paths is such that they satisfy the all-path criterion but exercise only one part of a compound condition, then the set will not reveal any error in the part of the condition that is not exercised. Hence, even the path coverage criterion, which is the strongest of the criteria we have discussed, is not strong enough to guarantee detection of all the errors.

10.3.2 Data Flow-Based Testing

Now we discuss some criteria that select the paths to be executed during testing based on data flow analysis, rather than control flow analysis. In the previous chapter, we discussed use of data flow analysis for static testing of programs. In the data flow-based testing approaches, besides the control flow, information about where the variables are defined and where the definitions are used is also used to specify the test cases. The basic idea behind data flow-based testing is to make sure that during testing, the definitions of variables and their subsequent use is tested. Just like the all-nodes and all-edges criteria try to generate confidence in testing by making sure that at least all statements and all branches have been tested, the data flow testing tries to ensure some coverage of the definitions and uses of variables. Approaches for use of data flow information have been proposed in [109, 129]. Our discussion here is based on the family of data flow-based testing criteria that were proposed in [129]. We discuss some of these criteria here.

For data flow-based criteria, a *definition-use graph* (*def/use* graph, for short) for the program is first constructed from the control flow graph of the program. A statement in a node in the flow graph representing a block of code has variable occurrences in it. A variable occurrence can be one of the following three types [129]:

- *def* represents the definition of a variable. The variable on the left-hand side of an assignment statement is the one getting defined.

- *c-use* represents computational use of a variable. Any statement (e.g., read, write, an assignment) that uses the value of variables for computational purposes is said to be making c-use of the variables. In an assignment statement, all variables on the right-hand side have a c-use occurrence. In a read and a write statement, all variable occurrences are of this type.

- *p-use* represents predicate use. These are all the occurrences of the variables in a predicate (i.e., variables whose values are used for computing the value of the predicate), which is used for transfer of control.

Based on this classification, the following can be defined [129]. Note that c-use variables may also affect the flow of control, though they do it indirectly by affecting the value of the p-use variables. Because we are interested in the flow of data between nodes, a c-use of a variable x is considered *global c-use* if there is no def of x within the block preceding the c-use. With each node i, we associate all the global c-use variables in that node. The p-use is associated with edges. If $x_1, x_2, ..., x_n$ had p-use occurrences in the statement of a block from where two edges go to two different blocks j and k (e.g., with an if then else), then $x_1, ..., x_n$ are associated with the two edges (i, j) and (i, k).

A path from node i to node j is called a *def-clear* path with respect to (w.r.t.) a variable x if there is no def of x in the nodes in the path from i to j (nodes i and j may have a def). Similarly, a def-clear path w.r.t. x from a node i to an edge (j, k) is one in which no node on the path contains a definition of x. A def of a variable x in a node i is a *global def*, if it is the last def of x in the block being represented by i, and there is a def-clear path from i to some node with a global c-use of x. Essentially, a def is a global def if it can be used outside the block in which it is defined.

The def/use graph for a program P is constructed by associating sets of variables with edges and nodes in the flow graph. For a node i, the set $def(i)$ is the set of variables for which there is a global def in the node i, and the set $c\text{-}use(i)$ is the set of variables for which there is a global c-use in the node i. For an edge (i, j), the set $p\text{-}use(i, j)$ is the set of variables for which there is a p-use for the edge (i, j).

Suppose a variable x is in $def(i)$ of a node i. Then, $dcu(x, i)$ is the set of nodes, such that each node has x in its c-use, $x \in def(i)$, and there is a def-clear path from i to j. That is, dcu(x, i) represents all those nodes in which the (global) c-use of x uses the value assigned by the def of x in i. Similarly, $dpu(x, i)$ is the set of edges, such that each edge has x in its p-use, $x \in def(i)$, and there is a def-clear path from i to (j, k). That is, dpu(x, i) represents all those edges in which the p-use of x uses the value assigned by the def of x in i.

Based on these definitions proposed in [129], a family of test case selection criteria was proposed in [129], a few of which we discuss here. Let G be the def/use graph for a program, and let P be a set of complete paths of G (i.e., path representing a complete execution of the program). A test case selection criterion defines the contents of P.

P satisfies the *all-defs* criterion if for every node i in G and every x in $def(i)$, P includes a def-clear path w.r.t. x to some member of $dcu(x, i)$ or some member of $dpu(x, i)$. This criterion says that for the def of every variable, one of its uses (either p-use or c-use) must be included in a path. That is, we want to make sure that during testing the use of the definitions of all variables is tested.

The *all-p-uses* criterion requires that for every $x \in def(i)$, P include a def-clear path w.r.t. x from i to some member of $dpu(x, i)$. That is, according to this criterion all the p-uses of all the definitions should be tested. However, by this criterion a c-use of a variable may not be tested. The *all-p-uses, some-c-uses* criterion requires that all p-uses of a variable definition must be exercised, and some c-uses must also be exercised. Similarly, the *all-c-uses, some-p-uses* criterion requires that all c-uses of a variable definition be exercised, and some p-uses must also be exercised.

The *all-uses* criterion requires that all p-uses and all c-uses of a definition must be exercised. That is, the set P must include, for every node i and every $x \in def(i)$, a def-clear path w.r.t. x from i to all elements of $dcu(x, i)$ and to all elements of $dpu(x, i)$. A few other criteria have been proposed in [129].

In terms of the number of test cases that might be needed to satisfy the

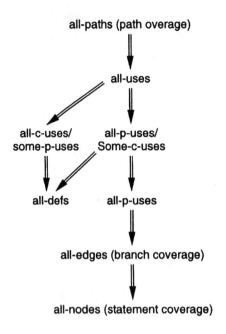

Figure 10.6: Relationship between different criteria.

data flow-based criteria, it has been shown that though the theoretical limit on the size of the test case set is up to quadratic in the number of two-way decision statements in the program, the actual number of test cases that satisfy a criterion is quite small in practice [146]. Empirical observation in [146] seems to suggest that in most cases the number of test cases grows linearly with the number of two-way decisions in the program.

As mentioned earlier, a criterion C_1 includes another criterion C_2 (represented by $C_1 \Rightarrow C_2$) if any set of test cases that satisfy criterion C_1 also satisfy the criterion C_2. The inclusion relationship between the various data flow criteria and the control flow criteria is given in Figure 10.6 [129].

It should be quite clear that all-paths will include all-uses and all other structure-based criteria. All-uses, in turn, includes all-p-uses, all-defs, and all-edges. However, all-defs does not include all-edges (and the reverse is not true). The reason is that all-defs is focusing on all definitions getting used, while all-edges is focusing on all decisions evaluating to both true and false. For example, a decision may evaluate to true and false in two different test cases, but the use of a definition of a variable x may not have been exercised. Hence, the all-defs and all-edges criteria are, in some sense, incomparable.

As mentioned earlier, inclusion does not imply that one criterion is always better than another. At best, it means that if the test case generation strategy for two criteria C_1 and C_2 is similar, and if $C_1 \Rightarrow C_2$, then statistically speaking, the set of test cases satisfying C_1 will be better than a set of test cases satisfying C_2. The experiments reported in [67] show that no one criterion (out of a set of control flow-based and data flow-based criteria) does significantly better than another consistently. However, it does show that testing done by using all-branch or all-uses criterion generally does perform better than randomly selected test cases.

10.3.3   An Example

Let us illustrate the use of some of the control flow-based and data flow-based criteria through the use of an example. Consider the following example of a simple program for computing x^y for any integer x and y [129]:

```
1. scanf(x, y); if (y < 0)
2.      pow = 0 - y;
3. else pow = y;
4. z = 1.0;
5. while (pow != 0)
6.      { z = z * x; pow = pow - 1; }
7. if (y < 0)
8.      z = 1.0/z;
9. printf(z);
```

The def/use graph for this program is given in the Figure 10.7 [129]. In the graph, the line numbers given in the code segment are used to number the nodes (each line contains all the statements of that block). For each node, the def set (i.e., the set of variables defined in the block) and the c-use set (i.e., the set of variables that have a c-use in the block) are given along with the node. For each edge, if the p-use set is not empty, it is given in the graph.

The various sets are easily determined from the block of code representing a node. To determine the dcu and dpu the graph has to be traversed. The dcu for various node and variable combination is given next:

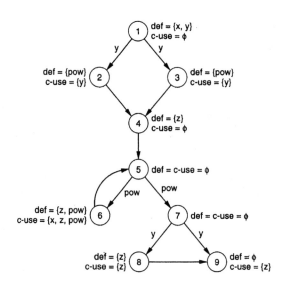

Figure 10.7: def/use graph for the example.

(node, var)	dcu	dpu
(1, x)	{6}	ϕ
(1, y)	{2, 3}	{(1,2), (1,3), (7, 8), (7, 9)}
(2, pow)	{6}	{(5, 6), (5, 7)}
(3, pow)	{6}	{(5, 6), (5, 7)}
(4, z)	{6, 8, 9}	ϕ
(6, z)	{6, 8, 9}	ϕ
(6, pow)	{6}	{(5, 6), (5, 7)}
(8, z)	{9}	ϕ

Now let us discuss the issue of generating test cases for this program using
various criteria. We can divide the problem of test case selection into two
parts. First we identify some paths that together satisfy the chosen criterion.
Then we identify the test cases that will execute those paths. As the first
issue is more relevant when discussing coverage criteria, frequently in testing
literature only the paths that satisfy the criterion are discussed. While
selecting paths that satisfy a given coverage brings us to the question of
whether the path is *feasible*, that is, if it is possible to have some test data
that will execute that path. It is known that a program may contain paths

that are not feasible. A simple example is in a program with a `for` loop. In such a program, no path that executes the loop fewer than the number of times specified by the `for` loop is feasible. In general, the issue of feasibility of paths cannot be solved algorithmically, as the problem is undecidable. However, the programmer can use his judgment and knowledge about the program to decide whether or not a particular path is infeasible. With the presence of infeasible paths, it is not possible to fully satisfy the criterion like all-uses, and the programmer will have to use his judgment to avoid considering the infeasible paths.

Let us first consider the all-edges criterion, which is the same as 100% branch coverage. In this we want to make sure that each edge in the graph is traversed during testing. For this, if the paths executed by the test cases include the following paths, we can see that all edges are indeed covered:

$$(1; 2; 4; 5; 6; 7; 8; 9), (1; 3; 4; 5; 7; 9)$$

Here we could have chosen a set of paths with (1; 2; 4; 5; 6; 7; 9) as one of them. But a closer examination of the program will tell us that this path is not feasible, as going from 1 to 2 implies that y is negative, which in turn implies that from 7 we must go to 8 and cannot go directly to 9. As can be seen even from this simple example, it is very easy to have paths that are infeasible. To execute the selected paths (or paths that include these paths), the following two test cases will suffice: $(x = 3, y = 1)$ and $(x = 3, y = -1)$. That is, a set consisting of these two test cases will satisfy the all-edges criterion.

Now let us consider the all-defs criterion, which requires that for all definitions of all variables, at least one use (c-use or p-use) must be exercised during testing. First let us observe that the set of paths given earlier for the all-edges criterion does not satisfy the all-uses criterion. The reason is that to satisfy all-uses, we must have some path in which the defs in node 6 (i.e., for z and pow) also get used. As the only way to get the def of pow in node 6 to be used is to visit 6 again, these paths fail to satisfy the criterion. The following set of paths will satisfy the all-defs criterion:

$$(1; 2; 4; 5; 6; 5; 6; 7; 8; 9), (1; 3; 4; 5; 6; 7; 9)$$

Let's consider the first path in this. The prefix 1; 2; 4; 5; 6; ensures that all the defs of nodes 1, 2, and 4 have been used. Having another 5; 6 after this ensures that the defs in node 6 are used. This is not needed by the branch coverage, but it comes because of the def-use constraints. It can also be easily seen that the set of test cases selected for the branch coverage will not suffice here. The following two test cases will satisfy the criteria: $(x = 3, y = 4)$ and $(x = 3, y = -2)$.

Let us finally consider the all-uses criterion, which requires that all p-uses and all c-uses of all variable definitions be tried during testing. In other words, we have to construct a set of paths that include a path from any node having a def to all nodes in its dcu and its dpu. The dcu and dpu sets for all nodes were given earlier. In this example, as it turns out, the paths given earlier for all-defs also satisfy the all-uses criterion. Hence, the corresponding test cases will also suffice. We leave the details of this as an exercise for the reader.

10.3.4   Mutation Testing

Mutation testing is another structural testing technique that differs fundamentally from the approaches discussed earlier. In control flow-based and data flow-based testing, the focus was on which paths to execute during testing. Mutation testing does not take a path-based approach. Instead, it takes the program and creates many mutants of it by making simple changes to the program. The goal of testing is to make sure that during the course of testing, each mutant produces an output different from the output of the original program. In other words, the mutation testing criterion does not say that the set of test cases must be such that certain paths are executed; instead it requires the set of test cases to be such that they can distinguish between the original program and its mutants. The description of mutation testing given here is based on [50, 115].

In hardware, testing is based on some fault models that have been developed and that model the actual faults closely. The fault models provide a set of simple faults, combination of which can model any fault in the hardware. In software, however, no such fault model exists. That is why most of the testing techniques try to guess where the faults might lie and then select the test cases that will reveal those faults. In mutation testing, faults of some pre-decided types are introduced in the program being tested. Testing then tries to identify those faults in the mutants. The idea is that if all these "faults" can be identified, then the original program should not have these faults; otherwise they would have been identified in that program by the set of test cases.

Clearly this technique will be successful only if the changes introduced in the main program capture the most likely faults in some form. This is assumed to hold due to the *competent programmer hypothesis* and the *coupling effect.* The competent programmer hypothesis says that programmers are generally very competent and do not create programs at random, and for a given problem, a programmer will produce a program that is very "close" to a correct program. In other words, a correct program can be constructed from an incorrect program with some minor changes in the program. The coupling effect says that the test cases that distinguish programs with minor differences with each other are so sensitive that they will also distinguish programs with more complex differences. In [115], some experiments are cited in which it has been shown that the test data that can distinguish mutants created by simple changes can also distinguish up to 99% of the mutants that have been created by applying a series of simple changes.

Now let us discuss the mutation testing approach in a bit more detail. For a program under test P, mutation testing prepares a set of *mutants* by applying *mutation operators* on the text of P. The set of mutation operators depends on the language in which P is written. In general, a mutation operator makes a small unit change in the program to produce a mutant. Examples of mutation operators are: replace an arithmetic operator with some other arithmetic operator, change an array reference (say, from A to B), replace a constant with another constant of the same type (e.g., change a constant to 1), change the label for a goto statement, and replace a variable by some special value (e.g., an integer or a real variable with 0). Each application of a mutation operator results in one mutant. As an example, consider a mutation operator that replaces an arithmetic operator with another one from the set $\{+, -, *, **, /\}$. If a program P contains an expression

$$a = b * (c - d),$$

then this particular mutation operator will produce a total of eight mutants (four by replacing '*' and four by replacing '-'). The mutation operators that make exactly one syntactic change in the program to produce a mutant are said to be of *first order*. If the coupling effect holds, then the first-order mutation operators should be sufficient, and there is no need for higher-order mutation operators.

Mutation testing of a program P proceeds as follows. First a set of test cases T is prepared by the tester, and P is tested by the set of test cases in T. If P fails, then T reveals some errors, and they are corrected. If P does not fail during testing by T, then it could mean that either the program P is correct or that P is not correct but T is not sensitive enough to detect the faults in P. To rule out the latter possibility (and therefore to claim that the confidence in P is high), the sensitivity of T is evaluated through mutation testing and more test cases are added to T until the set is considered sensitive enough for "most" faults. So, if P does not fail on T, the following steps are performed [115]:

1. Generate mutants for P. Suppose there are N mutants.

2. By executing each mutant and P on each test case in T, find how many mutants can be distinguished by T. Let D be the number of mutants that are distinguished; such mutants are called *dead*.

3. For each mutant that cannot be distinguished by T (called a *live* mutant), find out which of them are equivalent to P. That is, determine the mutants that will always produce the same output as P. Let E be the number of equivalent mutants.

4. The *mutation score* is computed as $D/(N - E)$.

5. Add more test cases to T and continue testing until the mutation score is 1.

In this approach, for the mutants that have not been distinguished by T, their equivalence with P has to be determined. As determining the equivalence of two programs is undecidable, this cannot be done algorithmically and will have to be done manually (tools can be used to aid the process). There are many situations where this can be determined easily. For example, if a condition $x <= 0$ (in a program to compute the absolute value, say) is changed to $x < 0$, we can see immediately that the mutant produced through this change will be equivalent to the original program P, as it does not matter which path the program takes when the value of x is 0. In other situations, it may be very hard to determine equivalence. One thing is clear: the tester will have to compare P with all the live mutants to determine which are equivalent to P. This analysis can then be used to add further test cases to T in an attempt to kill those live mutants that are not equivalent.

Determining test cases to distinguish mutants from the original program is also not easy. In an attempt to form a test case to kill a mutant, a tester will have to examine the mutant (and the original program) and then reason which test case is likely to distinguish the mutant. This can be a complex exercise, depending on the complexity of the program being tested and the exact nature of the difference between the mutant and the original program. Suppose that a statement at line l of the program P has been mutated to produce the mutant M. The first property that a test case t needs to have to distinguish M and P is that the test case should force the execution to reach the statement at l. The test case t should also be such that after execution of the statement at l, different states are reached by P and M. Before reaching l, the state while executing the programs P and M will be the same as the programs are same until l. If the test case is such that after executing the statement at l, the execution of the programs P and M either takes a different path or the values in the state are different, then there is a possibility that this difference will be manifested in output being different. If the state after executing the statement at l continues to be the same in P and M, we will not be able to distinguish P and M. Finally, t should be such that when P and M terminate, their states are different (assuming that P and M output their complete state at the end only). As one can imagine, constructing a test case that will satisfy these three properties is not going to be, in general, an easy task.

Finally, let us discuss the issue of detecting errors in the original program P, which is one of the basic goals of testing. In mutation testing, errors in the original program are frequently revealed when test cases are being designed to distinguish mutants from the original program. If no errors are detected and the mutation score reaches 1, then the testing is considered *adequate* by the mutation testing criterion. It should be noted that even if no errors have been found in the program under test during mutation testing, the confidence in the testing increases considerably if the mutation score of 1 is achieved, as we know that the set of test case with which P has been tested has been able to kill all (nonequivalent) mutants of P. This suggests that if P had an error, one of its mutants would have been closer to the correct program, and then the test case that distinguished the mutant from P would have also revealed that P is incorrect (it is assumed that the output of all test cases are evaluated to see if P is behaving correctly).

One of the main problems of mutation testing relates to its performance. The number of mutants that can be generated by applying first-order mutation operators is quite large and depends on the language and the size of the mutation operator set. For a FORTRAN program containing L lines of code to which the mutation operator can be applied, the total number of mutants is of the order of L^2 [115]. These many programs have to be compiled and executed on the selected test case set. This requires an enormous amount of computer time. For example, for a 950-line program, it was estimated that a total of about 900,000 mutants will be produced, the testing of which would take more than 70,000 hours of time on a Sun SPARC station [115].

Further, the tester might have to spend considerable time, as he will have to examine many mutants, besides the original program, to determine whether or not they are equivalent. These performance issues make mutation testing impractical for large programs.

10.3.5   Test Case Generation and Tool Support

Once a coverage criterion is decided, two problems have to be solved to use the chosen criterion for testing. The first is to decide if a set of test cases satisfy the criterion, and the second is to generate a set of test cases for a given criterion. Deciding whether a set of test cases satisfy a criterion without the aid of any tools is a cumbersome task, though it is theoretically possible to do manually. For almost all the structural testing techniques, tools are used to determine whether the criterion has been satisfied. Generally, these tools will provide feedback regarding what needs to be tested to fully satisfy the criterion.

To generate the test cases, tools are not that easily available, and due to the nature of the problem (i.e., undecidability of "feasibility" of a path), a fully automated tool for selecting test cases to satisfy a criterion is generally not possible. Hence, tools can, at best, aid the tester. One method for generating test cases is to randomly select test data until the desired criterion is satisfied (which is determined by a tool). This can result in a lot of redundant test cases, as many test cases will exercise the same paths.

As test case generation cannot be fully automated, frequently the test case selection is done manually by the tester by performing structural testing in an iterative manner, starting with an initial test case set and selecting more test cases based on the feedback provided by the tool for test case evaluation. The test case evaluation tool can tell which paths need to be executed or which mutants need to be killed. This information can be used to select further test cases.

Even with the aid of tools, selecting test cases is not a simple process. Selecting test cases to execute some parts of as yet unexecuted code is often very difficult. Because of this, and for other reasons, the criteria are often weakened. For example, instead of requiring 100% coverage of statements and branches, the goal might be to achieve some acceptably high percentage (but less than 100%).

There are many tools available for statement and branch coverage, the criteria that are used most often. Both commercial and freeware tools are available for different source languages. These tools often also give higher level coverage data like function coverage, method coverage, and class coverage. To get the coverage data, the execution of the program during testing has be closely monitored. This requires that the program be instrumented so that required data can be collected. A common method of instrumenting is to insert some statements called *probes* in the program. The sole purpose of the probes is to generate data about program execution during testing that can be used to compute the coverage. With this, we can identify three phases in generating coverage data:

1. Instrument the program with probes

2. Execute the program with test cases

3. Analyze the results of the probe data

Probe insertion can be done automatically by a *preprocessor*. The execution of the program is done by the tester. After testing, the coverage data is displayed by the tool—sometimes graphical representations are also shown.

Tools for data flow-based testing and mutation testing are even more complex. Some tools have been built for aiding data flow-based testing [66, 81]. A data flow testing tool has to keep track of definitions of variables and their uses, besides keeping track of the control flow graph. For example, the ASSET tool for data flow testing [66] first analyzes a Pascal program unit to determine all the definition-use associations. It then instruments the program so that the paths executed during testing are recorded. After the program has been executed with the test cases, the recorded paths are evaluated for satisfaction of the chosen criterion using the definition-use associations generated earlier. The list of definition-use associations that have not yet been executed is also output, which can then be used by the tester to select further test cases.

It should be pointed out that when testing a complete program that consists of many modules invoked by each other, the presence of procedures considerably complicates data flow testing. The main reason is that the presence of global variable creates def-use pairs in which the statements may exist in different procedures, e.g., a (global) variable may be defined in one procedure and then used in another. To use data flow-based testing on complete programs (rather than just modules), inter-procedural data flow analysis will be needed. Though some methods have been developed for performing data flow-based testing on programs with procedures [83], the presence of multiple procedures complicates data flow-based testing. It should be noted that this problem does not arise with statement coverage and branch coverage, where there are no special linkages between modules. The statement or branch coverage of a program can be computed simply from the statement or branch coverage of its modules. This is one of the reasons for the popularity of these coverage measures and tools.

In mutation testing, the tool is generally given a program P and a set of test cases T. The tool has to first use the mutation operations for the language in which P is written to produce the mutants. Then P and all the mutants and P are executed with T. Based on the output of different programs, the mutation score, and the number and identity of dead and live mutants are determined and reported to the tester. The score tells the tester the quality of T according to the mutation criterion, and the set of live mutants give the feedback to the tester for selecting further test cases to increase the mutation score. Some mutation testing tools have also been built [27, 49].

10.4   Testing Process

The basic goal of the software development process is to produce software that has no errors or very few errors. In an effort to detect errors soon after they are introduced, each phase ends with a verification activity such as a review. However, most of these verification activities in the early phases of software development are based on human evaluation and cannot detect all the errors. This unreliability of the quality assurance activities in the early part of the development cycle places a very high responsibility on testing. In other words, as testing is the last activity before the final software is delivered, it has the enormous responsibility of detecting any type of error that may be in the software.

Furthermore, we know that software typically undergoes changes even after it has been delivered. And to validate that a change has not affected some old functionality of the system, regression testing is done. In regression testing, old test cases are executed with the expectation that the same old results will be produced. Need for regression testing places additional requirements on the testing phase; it must provide the "old" test cases and their outputs.

In addition, as we have seen in the discussions in this chapter, testing has its own limitations. These limitations require that additional care be taken while performing testing. As testing is the costliest activity in software

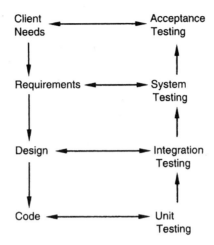

Figure 10.8: Levels of testing.

development, it is important that it be done efficiently.

All these factors mean that testing should not be done on-the-fly, as is sometimes done. It has to be carefully planned and the plan has to be properly executed. The testing process focuses on how testing should proceed for a particular project. Having discussed various methods of selecting test cases, we turn our attention to the testing process.

10.4.1 Levels of Testing

Testing is usually relied upon to detect the faults remaining from earlier stages, in addition to the faults introduced during coding itself. Due to this, different levels of testing are used in the testing process; each level of testing aims to test different aspects of the system.

The basic levels are unit testing, integration testing, and system and acceptance testing. These different levels of testing attempt to detect different types of faults. The relation of the faults introduced in different phases, and the different levels of testing are shown in Figure 10.8.

The first level of testing is called *unit testing*. In this, different modules are tested against the specifications produced during design for the modules. Unit testing is essentially for verification of the code produced during the coding phase, and hence the goal is to test the internal logic of the modules.

It is typically done by the programmer of the module. A module is considered for integration and use by others only after it has been unit tested satisfactorily. We have discussed it in more detail the previous chapter.

The next level of testing is often called *integration testing*. In this, many unit tested modules are combined into subsystems, which are then tested. The goal here is to see if the modules can be integrated properly. Hence, the emphasis is on testing interfaces between modules. This testing activity can be considered testing the design.

The next levels are *system testing* and *acceptance testing*. Here the entire software system is tested. The reference document for this process is the requirements document, and the goal is to see if the software meets its requirements. This is essentially a validation exercise, and in many situations it is the only validation activity. Acceptance testing is sometimes performed with realistic data of the client to demonstrate that the software is working satisfactorily. Testing here focuses on the external behavior of the system; the internal logic of the program is not emphasized. Consequently, mostly functional testing is performed at these levels.

These levels of testing are performed when a system is being built from the components that have been coded. There is another level of testing, called *regression testing*, that is performed when some changes are made to an existing system. We know that changes are fundamental to software; any software must undergo changes. Frequently, a change is made to "upgrade" the software by adding new features and functionality. Clearly, the modified software needs to be tested to make sure that the new features to be added do indeed work. However, as modifications have been made to an existing system, testing also has to be done to make sure that the modification has not had any undesired side effect of making some of the earlier services faulty. That is, besides ensuring the desired behavior of the new services, testing has to ensure that the desired behavior of the old services is maintained. This is the task of regression testing.

For regression testing, some test cases that have been executed on the old system are maintained, along with the output produced by the old system. These test cases are executed again on the modified system and its output compared with the earlier output to make sure that the system is working as before on these test cases. This frequently is a major task when modifications are to be made to existing systems.

A consequence of this is that the test cases for systems should be properly documented for future use in regression testing. In fact, for many systems that are frequently changed, regression testing scripts are used, which automate performing regression testing after some changes. A regression testing script executes a suite of test cases. For each test case, it sets the system state for testing, executes the test case, determines the output or some aspect of system state after executing the test case, and checks the system state or output against expected values. These scripts are typically produced during system testing, as regression testing is generally done only for complete systems. When the system is modified, the scripts are executed again, giving the inputs specified in the scripts and comparing the outputs with the outputs given in the scripts. Given the scripts, through the use of tools, regression testing can be largely automated.

Even with testing scripts, regression testing of large systems can take a considerable amount of time, particularly because execution and checking of all the test cases cannot be automated. If a small change is made to the system, often executing the entire suite of test cases is not justified, and the system is tested only with a subset of test cases. This requires *prioritization of test cases*. For prioritization, generally more data about each test case is recorded, which is then used during a regression testing to prioritize. For example, one approach is to record the set of blocks that each test case executes. If some part of the code has changed, then the test cases that execute the changed portion get the highest priority for regression testing. Test case prioritization is an active research area and many different approaches have been proposed in literature for this. We will not discuss it any further.

10.4.2 Test Plan

In general, testing commences with a *test plan* and terminates with acceptance testing. A test plan is a general document for the entire project that defines the scope, approach to be taken, and the schedule of testing as well as identifies the test items for the entire testing process and the personnel responsible for the different activities of testing. The test planning can be done well before the actual testing commences and can be done in parallel with the coding and design activities. The inputs for forming the test plan are: (1) project plan, (2) requirements document, and (3) system design document. The project plan is needed to make sure that the test plan is consistent with the overall quality plan for the project and the testing schedule matches that of the project plan. The requirements document and the design document are the basic documents used for selecting the test units and deciding the approaches to be used during testing. A test plan should contain the following:

- Test unit specification

- Features to be tested

- Approach for testing

- Test deliverables

- Schedule and task allocation

One of the most important activities of the test plan is to identify the test units. A *test unit* is a set of one or more modules, together with associated data, that are from a single computer program and that are the object of testing. A test unit can occur at any level and can contain from a single module to the entire system. Thus, a test unit may be a module, a few modules, or a complete system.

As seen earlier, different levels of testing have to be used during the testing activity. The levels are specified in the test plan by identifying the test units for the project. Different units are usually specified for unit, integration, and system testing. The identification of test units establishes the different levels of testing that will be performed in the project. Generally, a number of test units are formed during the testing, starting from the lower-level modules, which have to be unit-tested. That is, first the modules that have to be tested individually are specified as test units. Then the higher-level units are specified, which may be a combination of already tested units or may combine some already tested units with some untested modules. The basic idea behind forming test units is to make sure that testing is being performed *incrementally*, with each increment including only a few aspects that need to be tested.

An important factor while forming a unit is the "testability" of a unit. A unit should be such that it can be easily tested. In other words, it should be possible to form meaningful test cases and execute the unit without much effort with these test cases. For example, a module that manipulates the complex data structure formed from a file input by an input module might not be a suitable unit from the point of view of testability, as forming meaningful test cases for the unit will be hard, and driver routines will have to be written to convert inputs from files or terminals that are given by the tester into data structures suitable for the module. In this case, it might be better to form the unit by including the input module as well. Then the file input expected by the input module can contain the test cases.

Features to be tested include all software features and combinations of features that should be tested. A software feature is a software characteristic specified or implied by the requirements or design documents. These may include functionality, performance, design constraints, and attributes.

The *approach* for testing specifies the overall approach to be followed in the current project. The techniques that will be used to judge the testing effort should also be specified. This is sometimes called the *testing criterion* or the criterion for evaluating the set of test cases used in testing. In the previous sections we discussed many criteria for evaluating and selecting test cases.

Testing deliverables should be specified in the test plan before the actual testing begins. Deliverables could be a list of test cases that were used, detailed results of testing including the list of defects found, test summary report, and data about the code coverage. In general, a *test case specification* report, *test summary report*, and a *list of defects* should always be specified as deliverables. Test case specification is discussed later. The test summary report summarizes the results of the testing activities and evaluates the results. It defines the items tested, the environment in which testing was done, and a summary of defects found during testing.

The test plan, if it is a document separate from the project management plan, typically also specifies the schedule and effort to be spent on different activities of testing. This schedule should be consistent with the overall project schedule. For detailed planning and execution, the different tasks in the test plan should be enumerated and allocated to *test resources* who are responsible for performing them. Many large products have separate testing teams and therefore a separate test plan. A smaller project may include the test plan as part of its quality plan in the project management plan.

10.4.3 Test Case Specifications

The test plan focuses on how the testing for the project will proceed, which units will be tested, and what approaches (and tools) are to be used during the various stages of testing. However, it does not deal with the details of testing a unit, nor does it specify which test cases are to be used.

Test case specification has to be done separately for *each unit*. Based on the approach specified in the test plan, first the features to be tested for this unit must be determined. The overall approach stated in the plan is refined

Requirement Number	Condition to be tested	Test data and settings	Expected output

Figure 10.9: Test case specifications.

into specific test techniques that should be followed and into the criteria to be used for evaluation. Based on these, the test cases are specified for testing the unit. Test case specification gives, for each unit to be tested, all test cases, inputs to be used in the test cases, conditions being tested by the test case, and outputs expected for those test cases. Test case specifications look like a table of the form shown in Figure 10.9.

Sometimes, a few columns are also provided for recording the outcome of different rounds of testing. That is, sometimes test case specifications document is also used to record the result of testing. In a round of testing, the outcome of all the test cases is recorded (i.e., pass or fail). Hopefully, in a few rounds all the entries will pass.

Test case specification is a major activity in the testing process. Careful selection of test cases that satisfy the criterion and approach specified is essential for proper testing. We have considered many methods of generating test cases and criteria for evaluating test cases. A combination of these can be used to select the test cases. It should be pointed out that test case specifications contain not only the test cases, but also the rationale of selecting each test case (such as what condition it is testing) and the expected output for the test case.

There are two basic reasons test cases are specified before they are used for testing. It is known that testing has severe limitations and the effectiveness of testing depends very heavily on the exact nature of the test cases. Even for a given criterion, the exact nature of the test cases affects the effectiveness of testing. Constructing "good" test cases that will reveal errors in programs is still a very creative activity that depends a great deal on the ingenuity of the tester. Clearly, it is important to ensure that the set of test cases used is of "high quality."

As with many other verification methods, evaluation of quality of test cases is done through "test case review." For any review, a formal document or work product is needed. This is the primary reason for having the test case specification in the form of a document. The test case specification document is reviewed, using a formal review process, to make sure that the test cases are consistent with the policy specified in the plan, satisfy the chosen criterion, and in general cover the various aspects of the unit to be tested. For this purpose, the reason for selecting the test case and the expected output are also given in the test case specification document. By looking at the conditions being tested by the test cases, the reviewers can check if all the important conditions are being tested. As conditions can also be based on the output, by considering the expected outputs of the test cases, it can also be determined if the production of all the different types of outputs the unit is supposed to produce are being tested. Another reason for specifying the expected outputs is to use it as the "oracle" when the test case is executed.

Besides reviewing, another reason for specifying the test cases in a document is that the process of sitting down and specifying all the test cases that will be used for testing helps the tester in selecting a good set of test cases. By doing this, the tester can see the testing of the unit in totality and the effect of the total set of test cases. This type of evaluation is hard to do in on-the-fly testing where test cases are determined as testing proceeds.

Another reason for formal test case specifications is that the specifications can be used as "scripts" during regression testing, particularly if regression testing is to be performed manually. Generally, the test case specification document itself is used to record the results of testing. That is, a column is created when test cases are specified that is left blank. When the test cases are executed, the results of the test cases are recorded in this column. Hence, the specification document eventually also becomes a record of the testing results.

10.4.4 Test Case Execution and Analysis

With the specification of test cases, the next step in the testing process is to execute them. This step is also not straightforward. The test case specifications only specify the set of test cases for the unit to be tested. However, executing the test cases may require construction of driver modules or stubs. It may also require modules to set up the environment as stated in the test plan and test case specifications. Only after all these are ready can the test cases be executed. Sometimes, the steps to be performed to execute the test cases are specified in a separate document called the *test procedure specification*. This document specifies any special requirements that exist for setting the test environment and describes the methods and formats for reporting the results of testing. Measurements, if needed, are also specified, along with methods to obtain them.

Various outputs are produced as a result of test case execution for the unit under test. These outputs are needed to evaluate if the testing has been satisfactory. The most common outputs are the *test summary report*, and the *error report*. The test summary report is meant for project management, where the summary of the entire test case execution is provided. The summary gives the total number of test cases executed, the number and nature of errors found, and a summary of the metrics data collected. The error report is the details of the errors found during testing.

Testing requires careful monitoring, as it consumes the maximum effort, and has a great impact on final quality. A few metrics are very useful for monitoring testing. *Testing effort* is the total effort actually spent by the team in testing activities, and is an indicator of whether or not sufficient testing is being performed. If inadequate testing is done, it will be reflected in a reduced testing effort or reduced testing schedule. From the plan and past experience we should know the expected effort and duration of testing. The estimated effort is used for monitoring. Such monitoring can catch the "miracle finish" cases, where the project "finishes" suddenly, soon after the coding is done. Such "finishes" occur for reasons such as unreasonable schedules, personnel shortages, and slippage of schedule. Such a finish usually implies that to finish the project the testing phase has been compressed too much, which is likely to mean that the software has not been evaluated properly.

Computer time consumed during testing is another measure that can give valuable information to project management. In general, in a software development project, the computer time consumption is low at the start, increases as time progresses, and reaches a peak. Thereafter it is reduced as the project reaches its completion. Maximum computer time is consumed during the latter part of coding and testing. By monitoring the computer time consumed, one can get an idea about how thorough the testing has been. Again, by comparing the previous buildups in computer time consumption, computer time consumption of the current project can provide valuable information about whether or not the testing is adequate.

The error report gives the list of all the defects found. The defects are generally also categorized into different categories. To facilitate reporting and tracking of defects found during testing (and other quality control activities), defects found must be properly recorded. This recording is generally

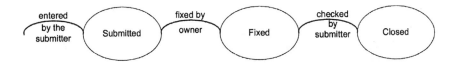

Figure 10.10: Life cycle of a defect.

done using tools. Let us now look at the defect logging and tracking activity, and how some simple analysis can be done on the defect data to aid project monitoring. With defect logging using tools, the error report is really a view of the logged defect data.

10.4.5 Defect Logging and Tracking

A large software project may include thousands of defects that are found by different people at different stages of the project. Often the person who fixes a defect is different than the person who finds or reports the defect. In such a scenario, defect reporting and closing cannot be done informally. The use of informal mechanisms may lead to defects being found but later forgotten, resulting in defects not getting removed or in extra effort in finding the defect again. Hence, defects found must be properly logged in a system and their closure tracked. Defect logging and tracking is considered one of the best practices for managing a project [26], and is followed by most software organizations.

Let us understand the life cycle of a defect. A defect can be found by anyone at anytime. When a defect is found, it is logged in a defect control system, along with sufficient information about the defect. The defect is then in the state "submitted," essentially implying that it has been logged along with information about it. The job of fixing the defect is then assigned to some person, who is generally the author of the document or code in which the defect is found. The assigned person does the debugging and fixes the reported defect, and the defect then enters the "fixed" state. However, a defect that is fixed is still not considered as fully done. The successful fixing of the defect is verified. This verification may be done by another person (often the submitter), or by a test team, and typically involves running some tests. Once the defect fixing is verified, then the defect can be marked as "closed." In other words, the general life cycle of a defect has three states—submitted, fixed, and closed, as shown in Figure 10.10. A defect that is not closed is also called open.

This is a typical life cycle of a defect which is used in many organizations (e.g. [97]). However, the life cycle can be expanded or contracted to suit the purposes of the project or the organization. For example, some organizations developing critical systems may have more stages in the life cycle to track the defect more closely. Similarly, in a small non-critical project, the life cycle may have only two states—open and closed.

When logging a defect, sufficient information has to be recorded so that the effects can be recreated and debugging and fixing can be done. However, just tracking each defect is not sufficient for most projects, as analysis of defect data can also be very useful for improving the quality. To permit such analysis, suitable information has to be recorded. What data is recorded depends on the organization, and an example from an organization can be found in [97].

To understand the nature of defects being found, frequently defects are categorized into a few types, and the type of each defect is recorded. Such a classification is essential if causes of defects are to be identified later and then removed in an attempt to prevent defects from occurring. The defects can be classified in many different ways, and many schemes have been proposed. The orthogonal defect classification scheme [33], for example, classifies defects in categories that include functional, interface, assignment, timing, documentation, and algorithm. Some of the defect types used in a commercial organization are: Logic, Standards, User Interface, Component Interface, Performance, and Documentation [97].

The severity of the defect with respect to its impact on the working of the system is also often divided into few categories. This information is important for project management. For example, if a defect impacts a lot of users or has a catastrophic effect, then a project leader will want to fix it urgently. Similarly, if a defect is of a minor nature, it may be scheduled at ease. Hence classification of defects with respect to severity is very important for managing a project. Recording severity of defects found is also a standard practice in most software organizations. Most often a four-level classification is used. One such classification is:

- *Critical.* Show stopper; affects a lot of users; can delay project.

- *Major.* Has a large impact but workaround exists; considerable amount of work needed to fix it, though schedule impact is less.

- *Minor.* An isolated defect that manifests rarely and with little impact.

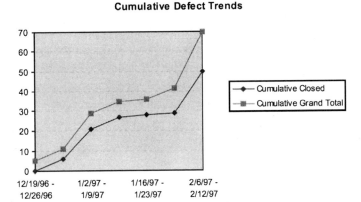

Figure 10.11: Defect arrival and closure trend.

- *Cosmetic.* Small mistakes that don't impact the correct working.

At the end of the project, ideally no open defects should remain. However, this ideal situation is often not practical for most large systems. Using severity classification, a project may have release criteria like "software can be released only if there are no critical and major bugs, and minor bugs are less than x per feature."

The defect data can be analyzed in other ways to improve project monitoring and control. A standard analysis done on almost all long lasting projects is to plot and observe the defect arrival and closure trend. Plotting both the arrival and removal can at a glance provide a view of the state of the quality control tasks in the project. An example of such a curve is shown in Figure 10.11 [97]. According to this curve, the gap between the total defects and the total closed defects is gradually increasing, although the increase is not too alarming. (In the project, this visibility prompted a change in the project schedule—development activity was slowed and resources were assigned to defect fixing such that the number of open defects was brought down.)

In addition to plotting the arrival and fixing, the volume of open defects can also be plotted. This gives a direct plot of how many defects are still not closed. This plot, generally increases with time first, and then starts decreasing. Towards project completion this plot should reach towards zero. For some intervals, the number of open defects might touch zero. That is, at some point during the project, all defects have been closed. Of course, this does not mean that there are no defects in the software—after reaching the zero open defect, further testing (and adding of code) may reveal defects. In other words, this plot is not monotonically decreasing, though it is expected that for most controlled projects its general trend will be downwards.

The defect data can also be analyzed for improving the process. One specific technique for doing this is defect prevention. We will discuss this further in the following section.

10.5   Defect Analysis and Prevention

We have seen that defects are introduced during development and are removed by the various quality control tasks in the process. Whereas the focus of the quality control tasks it to identify and remove the defects, the aim of defect prevention is to learn from defects found so far on the project and prevent defects from getting injected in the rest of the project. Some forms of defect prevention are naturally practiced and in a sense the goal of all standards, methodologies, and rules. is basically to prevent defects. However, when actual defect data is available, more effective defect prevention is possible through defect data analysis [76, 75]. Here we discuss an approach for doing focused defect prevention, based on practices of a commercial organization [97].

Defects analysis and prevention can be done at the organization level as well as at the project level. At the organization level, analysis of defects can lead to enhancements of organization-wide checklists, processes, or training. Defects analysis at the project level, aims to learn from defects found so far on the project and prevent defects in the rest of the project. Here we discuss only project-level analysis.

The main reason behind any defect prevention activity is to improve quality and improve productivity. Quality improves as with fewer defects injected, with the same effectiveness of quality control processes, the final system will have fewer defects. Productivity improves as lesser effort is spent on removing defects.

For a project, defect analysis for prevention can be done after some amount of coding has been done and a representative set of defects is known. If an iterative process is used, then the natural place for doing defect analysis will be after an iteration. The main tasks to be performed for doing defect prevention are: Do Pareto analysis to identify the main defect types, perform causal analysis to identify the causes of defects, and identify solutions to attack the causes.

10.5.1   Pareto Analysis

Pareto analysis is a common statistical technique used for analyzing causes, and is one of the primary tools for quality management [119, 139]. It is also sometimes called the 80-20 rule: 80% of the problems come from 20% of the possible sources. In software it can mean that 80% of the defects are caused by 20% of the root causes or that 80% of the defects are found in 20% of the code.

The first step for defect prevention is to draw a Pareto chart from the defect data. The number of defects found of different types is determined from the defect data and is plotted as a bar chart in the decreasing order. Along with the bar chart, a chart is also plotted on the same graph showing the cumulative number of defects as we move from types of defects given on the left of the x-axis to the right of the x-axis. The Pareto chart makes it immediately clear in visual as well as quantitative terms which are the main types of defects, and also which types of defects together form 80-85% of the total defects. If defects are being logged with information about their type, it is relatively easy to draw the Pareto chart.

As an example, consider the Pareto chart of the defect data for a project shown in Figure 10.12 [97]. This is a project in which features are being added to an existing system. The defects data for all enhancements done so far was used for this analysis. As can be seen, the logic defects are the most, followed by user interface defects, followed by standards defects. Defects in these three categories together account for more than 88% of the total defects, while the defects in the top two categories account for over 75% of the defects. Clearly, the target for defect prevention should be the top two or the top three categories such that defects in these categories can be reduced.

10.5.2   Perform Causal Analysis

The Pareto chart helps identify the main types of defects that have been found in the project so far, and are likely to be found in the rest of the project unless some action is taken. These can be treated as "effects" which we would like to minimize in future. For reducing these defects, we have to find the main causes for these defects and then try to eliminate these causes. Cause-effect (CE) diagram is a technique that can be used to determine the

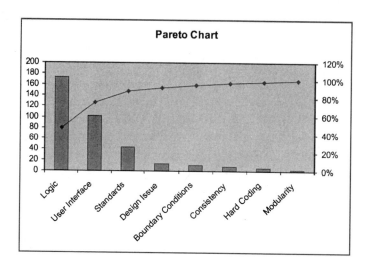

Figure 10.12: Pareto chart for defects found in ACE project.

causes of the observed effects [119, 139]. The understanding of the causes helps identify solutions to eliminate them.

The building of a CE diagram starts with identifying an effect whose causes we wish to understand. In the example above, the effect could be "too many GUI errors." To identify the causes, first some major categories of causes are established. For manufacturing, these major causes often are manpower, machines, methods, materials, measurement, and environment. One possible standard set of major causes in software can be process, people, technology, and training (this is used in an organization [97]). With the effect and major causes, the main structure of the diagram is made—effect as a box on the right connected by a straight horizontal line, and an angular line for each major cause connecting to the main line.

For analyzing the causes, the key is to continuously ask the question "Why does this cause produce this effect?" This is done for each of the major causes. The answers to these questions become the sub-causes and are represented as short horizontal lines joining the line for the major cause. Then the same question is asked for the causes identified. This "Why-Why-Why" process is repeated till all the root causes have been identified, i.e. the causes for which asking a "Why" does not make sense. When all the causes are marked in the diagram, the final picture looks like a fish-bone structure and hence the cause-effect diagram is also called the fish-bone diagram, or Ishikawa diagram after the name of its inventor.

The main steps in drawing a cause-effect diagram are as follows[139]:

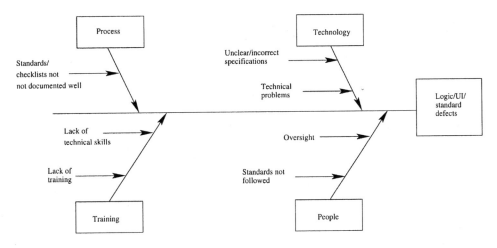

Figure 10.13: Cause-effect diagram for the example.

1. Clearly define the problem (i.e., the effect) that is to be studied. For defect prevention, it typically will be "too many defects of type X".

2. Draw an arrow from left to right with a box containing the effect drawn at the head. This is the backbone of this diagram.

3. Decide the major categories of causes. These could be the standard categories or some variation of it to suit the problem.

4. Write these major categories in boxes and connect them with diagonal arrows to the backbone. These form the major bones of the diagram.

5. Brainstorm for the sub-causes to these major causes by asking repeatedly, for each major cause, the question, "Why does this major cause produce the effect?"

6. Add the sub-causes to the diagram clustered around the bone of the major cause. Further sub-divide these causes, if necessary. Stop when no worthwhile answer to the question can be found.

Once the fishbone diagram is finished, we have identified all the causes for the effect under study. However, most likely the initial fishbone diagram will have too many causes. Clearly, some of the causes have a larger impact than others. Hence, before completing the root cause analysis, the top few causes are identified. This is done largely through discussion. For defect prevention, this whole exercise can be done for the top one or two categories of defects found in the Pareto analysis.

The fish bone diagram for this example is shown in Figure 10.13 .   In this analysis, causes of all the three major types of defects were discussed together. Hence, our effect is "too many logic/GUI/standards defects." When we asked the question "why do people and training cause too many logic or GUI or standards defects," some of the (almost obvious) reasons came out— lack of training, oversight, lack of technical skills. Similarly, when we asked the question "why do processes cause too many logic/GUI/standards defects," the answer came out as "standards not comprehensively documented" and "people not aware of standards." Similarly, for technology the causes were "unclear specifications" and "technical problems of tools." The brainstorming sessions for the causal analysis, of course, threw up many more causes. But after listing all the suggestions made during the meeting, they were prioritized. Prioritization can be done easily by considering each of the defects and identifying the causes for that defect. The causes that show up most frequently are the ones that are high priority, and are shown in Figure 10.13.

10.5.3   Develop and Implement Solutions

So far we have discussed how to identify the types of defects that are occurring frequently, and what are the root causes for the major defect categories. But no action has yet been taken to reduce the occurrence of defects. This is done in this phase.

Once the root causes are known, then the next natural step is to think of what can be done to attack the root causes, such that their manifestation in the form of defects is lessened. Some common prevention actions are are building/improving checklists, training programs, reviews, use of some specific tool. The solutions are developed through a brainstorming session. The cause-effect analysis also is done through brainstorming. Hence, frequently, these two steps might be done in the same session. There is one brainstorming session in which the cause-effect analysis is done and the preventive solutions are identified. The root causes and the preventive actions for the example are also shown in Table 10.4. The preventive actions proposed are self-explanatory.

The preventive solutions are action items which someone has to perform. Hence, the implementation of the solutions is the key. Unless the solutions are implemented, they are of no use at all. One way to ensure this is to treat

Root Cause	Preventive Actions
Standards not followed	Do a group reading of the standards. Ensure that standards are followed in mock projects.
Oversight	Effective self review Rigorous code reviews
Unclear/Incorrect Specifications	Conduct specification reviews
Lack of training	Every new entrant will do a mock project. A detailed specification and test plan will be made for the same.
Lack of techinical Skills	Develop tutorials for the key technologies. Have members do mock projects.

Table 10.4: Root causes and proposed solutions.

these as project activities, assign them to project members, and include them in the detailed project schedule.

An important part of implementing the solutions is to see if it is having the desired effect, that is, reducing the injection of defects and thereby reducing the rework effort expended in removing the defects. Analysis of defects some time after the solutions have been implemented can given some insight into this question. Generally, the next analysis for defect prevention can be used for this purpose. Besides tracking the impact, such follow-up analysis has tremendous reinforcing value—seeing the benefits convinces people like nothing else. Hence, besides implementation, the impact of implementation should also be analyzed.

10.6 Metrics—Reliability Estimation

After the testing is done and the software is delivered, the development is considered over. It will clearly be very desirable to know, in quantifiable terms, the reliability of the software being delivered. As testing directly impacts the reliability and most reliability models use data obtained during testing to predict reliability, reliability estimation is the main product metrics of interest at the end of the testing phase. We will focus our attention on this metric in this section.

Before we discuss the reliability modeling and estimation, let us briefly discuss a few main metrics that can be used for process evaluation at the end of the project.

Once the project is finished, one can look at the overall productivity achieved by the programmers during the project. As discussed earlier, productivity can be measured as lines of code (or function points) per person-month.

Another process metric of interest is *defect removal efficiency.* The *defect removal efficiency* of a defect removing process is defined as the percentage reduction of the defects that are present before the start of the process [104]. The *cumulative defect removal efficiency* of a series of defect removal processes is the percentage of defects that have been removed by this series. The defect removal efficiency cannot be determined exactly as the defects remaining in the system are not known. However, at the end of testing, as most defects have been uncovered, removal efficiencies can be estimated.

Let us now return to our main topic—software reliability modeling and assessment. Reliability of software often depends considerably on the quality of testing. Hence, by assessing reliability we can also judge the quality of testing. Alternatively, reliability estimation can be used to decide whether enough testing has been done. Hence, besides characterizing an important quality property of the product being delivered, reliability estimation has a direct role in project management—the reliability models being used by the project manager to decide when to stop testing.

Many models have been proposed for software reliability assessment, and a survey of many of the models is given in [71, 120, 61]. A discussion of the assumptions and consequent limitations on the models is given in [71]. Here we will discuss Musa's basic model, as it is one of the simplest models. The discussion of the model is based largely on the book [120]. It should, however, be pointed out that reliability models are not in widespread use and are used mostly in special situations.

10.6.1   Basic Concepts and Definitions

Reliability of a product specifies the probability of failure-free operation of that product for a given time duration. As we discussed earlier in this chapter, unreliability of any product comes due to failures or presence of faults in the system. As software does not "wear out" or "age" as a mechanical or an electronic system does, the unreliability of software is primarily due to bugs or design faults in the software. It is widely believed that with the current level of technology it is impossible to detect and remove all the faults in a large software system (particularly before delivery). Consequently, a software system is expected to have some faults in it.

Reliability is a probabilistic measure that assumes that the occurrence of failure of software is a random phenomenon. That is, if we define the life of a software system as a variable, this is a random variable that may assume different values in different invocations of the software. This randomness of the failure occurrences is necessary for reliability modeling. Here, by *randomness* all that is meant is that the failure cannot be predicted accurately. This assumption will generally hold for larger systems, but may not hold for small programs that have bugs (in which case one might be able to predict the failures). Hence, reliability modeling is more meaningful for larger systems (In [120] it is suggested that it should be applied to systems larger than 5000 LOC, as such systems will provide enough data points to do statistical analysis.)

Let X be the random variable that represents the life of a system. Reliability of a system is the probability that the system has not failed by time t. In other words,

$$R(t) = P(X > t).$$

The reliability of a system can also be specified as the *mean time to failure (MTTF)*. MTTF represents the expected lifetime of the system. From the reliability function, it can be obtained as [140]:

$$MTTF = \int_0^\infty R(x)dx.$$

Note that one can obtain the MTTF from the reliability function but the reverse is not always true. The reliability function can, however, be obtained from the MTTF if the failure process is assumed to be *Poisson*, that is, the life time has an *exponential distribution* [140]. With exponential distribution, if the failure rate of the system is known as λ, the MTTF is equal to $1/\lambda$.

Reliability can also be defined in terms of the number of failures experienced by the system by time t. Clearly, this number will also be random as failures are random. With this random variable, we define the *failure intensity* $\lambda(t)$ of the system as the number of expected failures per unit time at time t. With failure intensity, the number of failures that will occur between t and $t + \Delta t$ can be approximated as $\lambda(t)\Delta t$.

Let us define what is meant by time in these reliability models. There are three common definitions of time for software reliability models [120]: execution time, calendar time, and clock time. *Execution time* is the actual CPU time the software takes during its execution. *Calendar time* is the regular time we use, and *clock time* is the actual clock time that elapses while the software is executing (i.e., it includes the time the software waits in the system). Different models have used different time definitions, though the most commonly used are execution time and calendar time. It is now believed that execution time models are better and more accurate than calendar time models, as they more accurately capture the "stress" on the software due to execution.

Though faults are the cause of failures, the failure of software also depends critically on the environment in which it is executing [120]. It is well known that software frequently fails only if some types of inputs are given. In other words, if software has faults, only some types of input will exercise that fault to affect failures. Hence, how often these inputs cause failures during execution will decide how often the software fails. The *operational profile* of software captures the relative probability of different types of inputs being given to the software during its execution. As the definition of reliability is based on failures, which in turn depends on the nature of inputs, reliability is clearly dependent on the operational profile of the software. Hence, when we say that the reliability of software is $R(t)$, it assumes that this is for some operational profile. If the operational profile changes dramatically, then we will need to either recompute $R(t)$ or recalibrate it.

10.6.2   A Reliability Model

Let us now discuss one particular reliability model—Musa's basic execution time model. The description given here of the model is based on [120]. This is an execution time model, that is, the time taken during modeling is the actual CPU execution time of the software being modeled. The model is simple to understand and apply.

The model focuses on failure intensity while modeling reliability. It assumes that the failure intensity decreases with time, that is, as (execution) time increases, the failure intensity decreases. This assumption is generally true as the following is assumed about the software testing activity, during which data is being collected: during testing, if a failure is observed, the fault

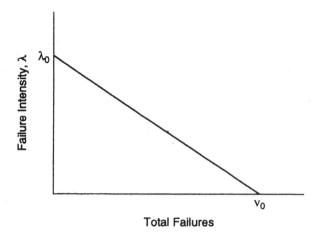

Figure 10.14: Failure intensity function.

that caused that failure is detected and the fault is removed. Consequently, the failure intensity decreases. Most other models make similar assumption which is consistent with actual observations.

In this model, it is assumed that each failure causes the same amount of decrement in the failure intensity. That is, the failure intensity decreases with a constant rate with the number of failures. That is, the failure intensity (number of failures per unit time) as a function of the number of failures is given as

$$\lambda(\mu) = \lambda_0(1 - \frac{\mu}{\nu_0}),$$

where λ_0 is the initial failure intensity at the start of execution (i.e., at time $t = 0$), μ is the expected number of failures by the given time t, and ν_0 is the total number of failures that would occur in infinite time. The total number of failures in infinite time is finite as it is assumed that on each failure, the fault in the software is removed. As the total number of faults in a given software whose reliability is being modeled is finite, this implies that the number of failures is finite. The failure intensity, as a function of the total number of failures experienced, is shown in Figure 10.14 [120].

The linear decrease in failure intensity as the number of failures observed increases is an assumption that is likely to hold for software for which the operational profile is uniform. That is, for software where the operational profile is such that any valid input is more or less equally likely, the assumption that the failure intensity decreases linearly generally holds. The intuitive rationale is that if the operational profile is uniform, any failure can occur at any time and all failures will have the same impact in failure intensity reduction. If the operational profile is not uniform, the failure intensity curves are ones whose slope decreases with the number of failures (i.e., each additional failure contributes less to the reduction in failure intensity). In such a situation the logarithmic model is better suited.

Note that the failure intensity decreases due to the nature of the software development process, in particular system testing, the activity in which reliability modeling is applied. Specifically, when a failure is detected during testing, the fault that caused the failure is identified and removed. It is removal of the fault that reduces the failure intensity. However, if the faults are not removed, as would be the situation if the software was already deployed in the field (when the failures are logged or reported but the faults are not removed), then the failure intensity would stay constant. In this situation, the value of λ would stay the same as at the last failure that resulted in fault removal, and the reliability will be given by $R(t) = e^{-\lambda\tau}$, where τ is the execution time.

The expected number of failures as a function of execution time τ (i.e., expected number of failures by time τ), $\mu(\tau)$, in the model is assumed to have an exponential distribution. That is,

$$\mu(\tau) = \nu_0(1 - e^{-\lambda_0/\nu_0 * \tau}).$$

By substituting this value in the equation for λ given earlier, we get the failure intensity as a function of time:

$$\lambda(\tau) = \lambda_0 * e^{-\lambda_0/\nu_0 * \tau}.$$

A typical shape of the failure intensity as it varies with time is shown in Figure 10.15 [120].

This reliability model has two parameters whose values are needed to predict the reliability of given software. These are the initial failure intensity λ_0 and the total number of failures ν_0. Unless the value of these are known, the model cannot be applied to predict the reliability of software. Most software reliability models are like this; they frequently will have a few parameters whose values are needed to apply the model.

It would be very convenient if these parameters had constant values for all software systems or if they varied in a manner that their values for a particular software can be determined easily based on some clearly identified

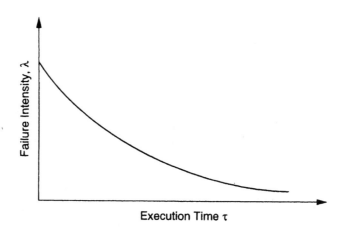

Figure 10.15: Failure intensity with time.

and easily obtained characteristic of the software (e.g., size or complexity). Some speculations have been made regarding how these parameters may depend on software characteristics. However, no such simple method is currently available that is dependable. The method that is currently used for all software reliability models is to *estimate* the value of these parameters for the particular software being modeled through the failure data for that software itself. In other words, the failure data of the software being modeled is used to obtain the value of these parameters. Some statistical methods are used for this, which we will discuss shortly.

The consequence of this fact is that, in general, for reliability modeling, the behavior of the software system is carefully observed during system testing and data of failures observed during testing is collected up to some time τ. Then statistical methods are applied to this collected data to obtain the value of these parameters. Once the values of the parameters are known, the reliability (in terms of failure intensity) of the software can be predicted. As statistical methods require that "enough" data points be available before accurate estimation of the parameters can be done, this implies that reliability can be estimated only after sufficient data has been collected. The requirement that there be a reasonably large failure data set before the parameters can be estimated is another reason reliability models cannot effectively be applied to software that is small in size (as it will not provide enough failure data points). Another consequence of this approach is that we can never determine the values of the parameters precisely. They will only be estimates, and there will always be some uncertainty with the values we compute. This uncertainty results in corresponding uncertainty in the reliability estimates computed using the models.

Let us assume that the failure data collection begins with system testing (as is usually the case). That is, time $\tau = 0$ is taken to be the commencement of system testing. The selection of the start of time is somewhat arbitrary. However, selecting the start of time where the assumptions about randomness and operational profile may not hold will cause the model to give incorrect estimates. This is why data of unit testing or integration testing, where the whole system is not being tested, is not considered. System testing, in which the entire system is being tested, is really the earliest point from where the data can be collected.

This model can be applied to compute some other values of interest that can help decide if enough testing has been done or how much more testing needs to be done to achieve a target reliability. Suppose the target reliability is specified in terms of desired failure intensity, λ_F. Let the present failure intensity be λ_P. Then the number of failures that we can expect to observe before the software achieves the desired reliability can be computed by computing $\lambda_F - \lambda_P$, which gives,

$$\Delta\mu = \frac{\nu_0}{\lambda_0}(\lambda_P - \lambda_F).$$

In other words, at any time we can now clearly say how many more failures we need to observe (and correct) before the software will achieve the target reliability. Similarly, we can compute the additional time that needs to be spent before the target reliability is achieved. This is given by

$$\Delta t = \frac{\nu_0}{\lambda_0} ln \frac{\lambda_P}{\lambda_F}.$$

That is, we can expect that the software needs to be executed for Δt more time before we will observe enough failures (and remove the faults corresponding to them) to reach the target reliability. This time can be converted to calendar time, which is what is used in projects, by incorporating some parameters about the software development environment. This issue will be discussed later.

10.6.3 Failure Data and Parameter Estimation

To apply the reliability model for a particular software, we need to obtain the value of the two parameters: λ_0 and ν_0. These parameters are not the same for all software and have to be estimated for the software being modeled using statistical techniques.

For statistical approaches to parameter estimation, data has to be collected about the failures of the software being modeled. Generally, the earliest point to start collecting data for reliability estimation is the start of system testing (a later point can also be taken, though it will reduce the number of failures that can be observed). The data can be collected in two different forms. The first form is to record the failure times (in execution time) of the failures observed during execution. This data will essentially be a sequence of (execution) times representing the first, second, and so on failures that are observed. The second form of data is to record the number of failures observed during execution in different time intervals (called *grouped failure data*). This form might sometimes be easier to collect if the unit is a clearly identified unit, like a day. In this form, the data will be in the form of a table, where the duration of the interval (in execution time) and the number of failures observed during that interval are given. We will only discuss the parameter estimation with the first form. For further details on parameter estimation, the reader is referred to [120].

There are many ways in which the model can be "fitted" to the data points to obtain the parameters or coefficients. One common method is the least squares approach in which the goal is to select the parameters for the model so that the square of the difference between the observed value and the one predicted by the model is minimized. This approach works well when the size of the data set is not very large.

For applying the least squares approach, we will consider the equation for the failure intensity as a function of the mean number of failures (i.e., $\lambda(\mu) = \lambda_0(1 - \mu/\nu_0)$). To determine parameters for this equation, we need a set of observed data points, each containing the value of the dependent variable and the value of the independent variable. In this case, this means that we need data points, each of which gives the failure intensity and the number of failures.

The data collected, as specified earlier, may be in the form of failure times or grouped failure data. The first thing that needs to be done is to convert the data to the desired form by determining the failure intensity for each failure. If the data about failure times is available, this conversion is done as follows [120]. Let the observation interval be $(0, t_e]$ (t_e is the time when the observations are stopped; it will generally be greater than the time of the last failure). We partition this observation interval at every kth failure occurrence. That is, this time interval is partitioned into sub-intervals, each (except the last one) containing k distinct failures. If the total number of failures observed until t_e is m_e, then the number of subintervals is p, where $p = \lceil m_e/k \rceil$. The observed failure intensity for an interval can now be computed by dividing the number of failures in that interval by the duration of the interval. That is, for an interval l, the observed failure intensity r_l is given by

$$r_l = \frac{k}{t_{kl} - t_{k(l-1)}}, l = 1, ..., p - 1.$$

For the last interval, the failure intensity is

$$r_p = \frac{m_e - k(p - 1)}{t_e - t_{k(l-1)}}.$$

These failure intensities are *independent* of each other as the different time intervals are disjoint. The estimate for the mean value for the lth interval, m_l, can be obtained by

$$m_l = k(l - 1).$$

(This takes the start value for the interval but has been found to be better than taking the average or midpoint value [120].) In this method, if k is chosen to be too small, large variations will occur in failure intensity. If the value of k is very large, too much smoothing may occur. A value of about five (i.e., $k = 5$) gives reasonable results [120].

Obtaining data in this form from grouped data is even easier. For each time interval for which failures were counted, dividing the number of failures by the duration of the interval will give the failure intensity of that interval. The total number of failures for an interval is the sum of all the failures of all the intervals before this interval.

In this manner, we can get from the collected data a set of p data points, each giving a failure intensity and the total number of failures observed. As the relationship between them is linear, a regression line can be fit in these data points. From the coefficients of the line, model parameters can be determined easily.

However, the approach of simple linear regression minimizes the sum of absolute errors (between the predicted value by the model and the actual value observed). This approach gives a higher weight to the data points with larger failure intensity. In other words, the coefficients will be influenced more by data points with larger failure intensity. A better approach is to consider *relative error*, which is absolute error divided by the value given by the model. The least squares approach here will be to minimize the sum of all the relative errors. With relative errors, each data point is given the same weight. However, with this, linear regression cannot be used, and closed-form equations for determining the coefficients are not available. For this approach, numerical methods must be used to determine the coefficients. The approach will be to obtain the derivatives of the equation for least squares (with relative error) with the two coefficients to be determined, set these to 0, and then solve these two simultaneous equations through some standard numerical technique like the Newton-Raphson method. For further discussion on this, the reader is referred to [120] or any numerical analysis text.

Once the parameters are known, we can also predict the number of faults in the delivered software using the reliability model (which can be used to predict faults per KLOC). As we don't otherwise know how many faults remain in software, generally, this data is available for a project only after the software has been in operation for a few years and most of its faults have been identified. By using the reliability model, we can predict this with some confidence.

The total failures experienced in infinity time by a software is related to the total faults in the system, as we are assuming that faults are generally removed after a failure is detected. However, the fault removal process may not be perfect and may introduce errors. In addition, each failure may not actually result in removing of a fault, as the information obtained on failure may not be sufficient for fault detection. If the total number of faults in the software is ω_0, we can get ν_0 from this by using the *fault reduction factor, B*:

$$\nu_0 = \frac{\omega_0}{B}$$

The fault reduction factor, B, is the ratio of the *net* fault reduction to the total number of failures experienced. If each failure resulted in exactly one fault being removed, then B would be 1. However, sometimes a failure is not sufficient to locate a fault or a fault removal adds some faults. Due to these, the fault reduction factor is not always 1. Currently available data suggests that B is close to 1, with an average value of about 0.95 [120]. This value can be used to predict the number of faults that remain in the software. Alternatively, the value of B can be computed from the data collected (additional data about fault correction will have to be compiled).

10.6.4   Translating to Calendar Time

The model discussed here is an execution-time model: all the times are the CPU execution time of the software. However, software development and project planning works in calendar time—hours, days, months, etc. Hence, we would like to convert the estimates to calendar time, particularly when we are trying to predict the amount of time still needed to achieve the desired reliability. In this case, it is clearly desirable to specify the time in calendar time, so that the project plan can be modified appropriately, if needed.

As reliability modeling is performed from system testing onward, the execution time can be related to the effort for testing, debugging, etc. The simplest way to do this is to determine an average ratio of the amount of effort to execution time and then to use this effort to estimate the calendar time. Alternatively, instead of giving one ratio, two ratios can be specified— one for the CPU time expended and one for the failures detected. These ratios can then be used to determine the total amount of effort.

Let us explain this approach with a simple example. Generally, the main resource during testing is the test team effort. For now, we consider this as the only resource of interest for modeling calendar time. Suppose the test team runs the software for 10 CPU hours, during which it detects 25 failures. Suppose that for each hour of CPU execution time, an average of 8 person-hours of the test team are consumed (ratio of effort to CPU time), and that on an average 4 person-hours is needed on each failure to analyze it (ratio of effort to failures). Hence, the total effort required for this is

$$10 * 8 + 25 * 4 = 180 \text{ person-hours.}$$

If the quantity of test team resources (i.e., the number of members in the test team) is three persons, this means that the calendar time for this is 60 hours. As the number of failures experienced is a function of time according to the Basic model, one overall ratio could also have been given with CPU time (or with number of failures). In this example, the overall ratio will be 18 person-hours per CPU hour.

10.6.5   An Example

Let us illustrate the use of the reliability model discussed earlier through the use of an example. In [120], times for more than 130 failures for a real

Time of Failure (in CPU sec)				
311	3089	5922	10,559	14,358
366	3565	6738	10,559	15,168
608	3623	8089	10,791	
676	4080	8237	11,121	
1098	4380	8258	11,486	
1278	4477	8491	12,708	
1288	4740	8625	13,251	
2434	5192	8982	13,261	
3034	5447	9175	13,277	
3049	5644	9411	13,806	
3085	5837	9442	14,185	
3089	5843	9811	14,229	

Table 10.5: Failure data for a real system.

system called T1 are given. For illustration purposes, we select about 50 data points from it, starting from after about 2000 CPU sec have elapsed (from the 21st failure). We define $\tau = 0$ after the first 2000 sec of [120] to illustrate that the choice of $\tau = 0$ is up to the reliability estimator and to eliminate the first few data points, which are likely to show a wider variation, as they probably represent the start of testing. The times of failures with this $\tau = 0$ are given in Table 10.5 [120].

As we can see, this is the failure times data. From this, using $k = 5$, we obtain the failure intensities and the cumulative failures as discussed earlier. The data points we get are:

$$(0.0045, 0), (0.0026, 5), (0.0182, 10), (0.0047, 15), (0.0040, 20),$$
$$(0.0020, 25), (0.0056, 30), (0.0032, 35), (0.0023, 40), (0.0035, 45)$$

For the purposes of this example, we will try to fit a regression line to this data using the regular least squares approach, for which parameter determination can be done in a simple manner. As discussed earlier, this method is likely to give poorer results compared to minimizing the square of relative errors. Using the regular regression line fitting approach, we get $\lambda_0 = 0.0074$ failure/CPU sec and $\nu_0 \approx 70$ failures. (If the complete data from [120] is used, then ν_0 comes out to about 136 failures. Because we are not counting the first 20, this means that by fitting a line on the complete data using the relative error approach, ν_0 would come out to be around 110. This error in our estimate is coming due to the smaller sample and the use of absolute error for determining the coefficients.) By the reliability model, the current reliability of the software (after 50 failures have been observed) is about 0.002 failure per CPU second.

We can see that the total number of estimated faults in the system at the start of the time is 70. Out of this, 50 faults have been removed (after observing the 50 failures). Hence, there are still 20 faults left in the software. Suppose the size of the final software was 20,000 LOC. If the failure data given earlier is until the end of system testing (i.e., the software is to be delivered after this) and this software development project is a typical project for the process that was followed, we can say that the capability of this process is to deliver software with a fault density of 1.0 per KLOC.

Now let's suppose the current failure intensity after 50 failures is not acceptable to the client. The desired failure intensity is 0.001 failure per CPU second. Using the model, we can say that to achieve this reliability, further testing needs to be done and the amount of CPU time that will be consumed in this extra testing can be estimated to be

$$70/0.0074 * ln(0.002/0.001) = 6,527 \text{ CPU} - \text{sec.}$$

That is, approximately 1.81 CPU hours of testing needs to be performed to achieve the target reliability. Suppose the limiting resource is only the testing personnel, there is one person assigned to test this software, and on an average 20 person-hours of testing personnel effort is spent for each hour of CPU time. In this case, we can say that more than 36 person-hours of testing need to be done. In other words, the calendar time needed to achieve the target reliability is about a week.

10.7 Summary

Testing plays a critical role in quality assurance for software. Due to the limitations of the verification methods for the previous phases, design and requirement faults also appear in the code. Testing is used to detect these errors, in addition to the errors introduced during the coding phase.

Testing is a dynamic method for verification and validation, where the system to be tested is executed and the behavior of the system is observed. Due to this, testing observes the failures of the system, from which the presence of faults can be deduced. However, separate activities have to be performed to identify the faults (and then remove them).

There are two approaches to testing: black-box and white-box. In black-box testing, the internal logic of the system under testing is not considered and the test cases are decided from the specifications or the requirements. It is often called functional testing. Equivalence class partitioning, boundary value analysis, and cause-effect graphing are examples of methods for selecting test cases for black-box testing. State-based testing is another approach in which the system is modeled as a state machine and then this model is used to select test cases using some transition or path based coverage criteria. State-based testing can also be viewed as grey-box testing in that it often requires more information than just the requirements.

In white-box testing, the test cases are decided entirely on the internal logic of the program or module being tested. The external specifications are not considered. Often a criterion is specified, but the procedure for selecting test cases is left to the tester. The most common control flow-based criteria are statement coverage and branch coverage, and the common data flow-based criteria are all-defs and all-uses. Mutation testing is another approach for white-box testing that creates mutants of the original program by changing the original program. The testing criterion is to kill all the mutants by having the mutant generate a different output from the original program.

As the goal of testing is to detect any errors in the programs, different levels of testing are often used. Unit testing is used to test a module or a small collection of modules and the focus is on detecting coding errors in modules. During integration testing, modules are combined into subsystems, which are then tested. The goal here is to test the system design. In system testing and acceptance testing, the entire system is tested. The goal here is to test the system against the requirements, and to test the requirements themselves. White-box testing can be used for unit testing, while at higher levels mostly black-box testing is used.

The testing process usually commences with a test plan, which is the basic document guiding the entire testing of the software. It specifies the levels of testing and the units that need to be tested. For each of the different units, first the test cases are specified and then they are reviewed. During the test case execution phase, the test cases are executed, and various reports are produced for evaluating testing. The main outputs of the execution phase are the test summary report and the error report.

The main metric of interest during testing is the reliability of the software under testing. Reliability of software depends on the faults in the software. To assess the reliability of software, reliability models are needed. To use

a model for a given software system, data is needed about the software
that can be used in the model to estimate the reliability of the software.
Most reliability models are based on the data obtained during the system
and acceptance testing. Data about time between failures observed during
testing are used by these models to estimate the reliability of the software.
We discussed one such reliability model in the chapter in some detail and
have discussed how the reliability model can be used in a project and what
the limitations of reliability models are.

Exercises

1. What are the different levels of testing and the goals of the different levels?
   For each level, specify which of the testing approaches is most suitable.

2. Testing, including debugging and fixing of bugs, is the most expensive task
   in a project. List the major activities in the entire testing process, and give
   your view on what % of the testing effort each consumes.

3. Suppose a software has three inputs, each having a defined valid range. How
   many test cases will you need to test all the boundary values?

4. For boundary value analysis, if the strategy for generating test cases is to
   consider all possible combinations for the different values, what will be the
   set of test cases for a software that has three inputs X, Y, and Z?

5. Take three variables A, B, and C, each having two values. Generate a set of
   test cases that will exercise all pairs.

6. Suppose a software has five different configuration variables that are set independently. If three of them are binary (have two possible values), and the
   rest have three values, how many test cases will be needed if pair-wise testing
   method is used?

7. Consider a vending machine that takes quarters and when it has received two
   quarters, gives a can of soda. Develop a state model of this system, and then
   generate sets of test cases for the various criteria.

8. Suppose you have to test a class for implementing a queue of integers. Using
   state-based approach (and one criteria for it), generate a set of test cases that
   you will use to test it. Assume standard operations like add, delete on the
   queue.

9. Consider a simple text formatter problem. Given a text consisting of words
   separated by blanks (BL) or newline (NL) characters, the text formatter has
   to covert it into lines, so that no line has more than MAXPOS characters,
   breaks between lines occurs at BL or NL, and the maximum possible number

- Testing will be suspended if during testing the test team encounters any critical defects, or a set of major defects which would prevent effective testing.

- The testing shall resume only when 100% of critical defects are fixed and at least 80% major defects are fixed.

- Testing shall end when all the test cases in the test plan have been executed.

- Defects identified will be notified to the development team regularly and all defect fixes received from the development team will be included for retesting.

For this case study, the system test plan was prepared with inputs from some software quality professionals from commercial organizations. So, in a sense, the test cases represent the type of testing that may be done by professionals. The test case specifications are available from the Web site.

Bibliography

[1] F. B. Abreu and R. Carapuca. Candidate metrics for object-oriented software wihin a taxonomy framework. *Journal of Systems and Software*, 26(1):87–96, Jan. 1994.

[2] A. J. Albrecht and J. E. Gaffney. Software function, source lines of code, and development effort prediction: A software science validation. *IEEE Transactions on Software Engineering*, 9(6):639–648, Nov. 1983.

[3] T. Ball. The concept of dynamic analysis. In *ESEC/FSE-7: Proceedings of the 7th European software engineering conference held jointly with the 7th ACM SIGSOFT international symposium on Foundations of software engineering*, pages 216–234, Toulouse, France, 1999. Springer-Verlag.

[4] S. Balsamo, A DiMarco, P. Inverardi, and M. Simeoni. Model-based performance prediction in software development: a survey. *IEEE Transactions on Software Engineering*, 30(5):295–310, May 2004.

[5] V. R. Basili. *Tutorial on models and metrics for software management and engineering*. IEEE Press, 1980.

[6] V. R. Basili, L. Briand, and W. L. Melo. A validation of object-oriented design metrics as quality indicators. *IEEE Transactions on Software Engineering*, 22(10):751–761, Oct 1996.

[7] V. R. Basili and A. Turner. Iterative enhancement, a practical technique for software development. *IEEE Transactions on Software Engineering*, SE-1(4), Dec. 1975.

[8] V. R. Basili and D. M. Weiss. Evaluation of a software requirements document by analysis of change data. In *5th Int. Conf. on Software Engineering*, pages 314–323. IEEE, 1981.

[9] L. Bass, P. Clements, and Rick Kazman. *Software Architecture in Practice, Second Edition*. Addison Wesley Professional, 2003.

[10] K. Beck. *Extreme Programming Explained*. Addison-Wesley, 2000.

[11] K. Beck. *Test Driven Development: by Example.* Addison-Wesley Professional, 2002.

[12] E. H. Bersoff. Elements of software configuration management. *IEEE Transactions of Software Engineering*, pages 79–87, Jan. 1984.

[13] E. H. Bersoff, V. D. Henderson, and S. G. Siegel. Software configuration management: A tutorial. *IEEE Computer*, pages 6–14, Jan. 1979.

[14] E. H. Bersoff, V. D. Henderson, and S. G. Siegel. *Software configuration management—an investment in product integrity.* Prentice-Hall, Inc., Englewood Cliffs, NJ, 1980.

[15] B. Beyer. *Object Oriented Software Construction.* Prentice Hall, 1988.

[16] R.V. Binder. *Testing Object-Oriented Systems—Model, Patterns, and Tools.* Addison Wesley, 1999.

[17] B. Boehm. Software engineering. *IEEE Transactions on Computers*, 25(12), Dec. 1976.

[18] B. Boehm. A spiral model of software development and enhancement. *IEEE Computer*, pages 61–72, May 1988.

[19] B. Boehm. *Tutorial: software risk management.* IEEE Computer Socity, Washington D.C., 1989.

[20] B. W. Boehm. *Software engineering economics.* Prentice Hall, Englewood Cliffs, NJ, 1981.

[21] B. W. Boehm. Software engineering economics. *IEEE Transactions on Software Engineering*, 10(1):135–152, Jan. 1984.

[22] B. W. Boehm. Improving software productivity. *IEEE Computer*, pages 43–57, Sept. 1987.

[23] G. Booch. *Object-oriented analysis and design.* The Benjamin/Cummings Publishing Company, Santa Clara, CA, 1994.

[24] G. Booch, J. Rumbaugh, and I. Jacobson. *The Unified Modeling Language User Guide.* Addison-Wesley, 1998.

[25] F. Brooks. *The Mytical Man Month.* Addison-Wesley, Reading, MA, 1975.

[26] N. Brown. Industrial-strength management strategies. *IEEE Software*, July 1996.

[27] T. A. Budd et al. The design of a prototype mutation system for program testing. In *National Computer Conference*, 1978.

[28] W. R. Bush, J. D. Pincus, and D. J. Sielaff. A static analyzer for finding dynamic programming errors. *Software Practice and Experience*, 30(7):775–802, June 2000.

[29] R.N. Charette. *Software Engineering Risk Analysis and Management*. Mc-Graw Hill, 1989.

[30] R.N. Charette. Large-scale project management is risk management. *IEEE Software*, July 1996.

[31] E. Chen. Program complexity and programmer productivity. *IEEE Transactions on Software Engineering*, SE-4:187–194, May 1978.

[32] S. R. Chidamber and C. F. Kemerer. A metrics suite for object-oriented design. *IEEE Transactions on Software Engineering*, 20(6):476–493, June 1994.

[33] R. Chillarege et al. Orthogonal defect classification—a concept for in-process measurements. *IEEE Transactions on Software Engineering*, 18(11):943–956, Nov 1992.

[34] T.S. Chow. Testing software design modeled by finite state machines. *IEEE Transactions on Software Engineering*, 4(3):178–187, 1978.

[35] P. Clements, F. Bachmann, L. Bass, D. Garlan, J. Ivers, R. Little, R. Nord, and J. Stafford. *Documenting Software Architectures: Views and Beyond*. Addison Wesley, 2003.

[36] P. Coad and E. Yourdon. *Object-oriented analysis*. Prentice Hall, 1990.

[37] P. Coad and E. Yourdon. *Object-oriented design*. Prentice Hall, 1991.

[38] A. Cockburn. *Agile Software Development*. Addison-Wesley, 2001.

[39] A. Cockburn. *Writing Effective Use Cases*. Addison-Wesley, 2001.

[40] D.M. Cohen, S.R. Dalal, M.L. Fredman, and G.C. Patton. The AETG system: An approach to testing based on combinatorial design. *IEEE Transactions on Software Engineering*, 23(7):437–443, 1997.

[41] S. D. Conte, H. E. Dunsmore, and V. Y. Shen. *Software engineering metrics and models*. The Benjamin/Cummings Publishing Company, 1986.

[42] J.C. Corbett et al. Bandera: extracting finite-state models from java source code. In *International Conference on Software Engineering*, pages 439–448, 2000.

[43] Cyrelli Artho. Jlint homepage: http://artho.com/jlint.

[44] A. M. Davis. Operational prototyping: A new development approach. *IEEE Software*, pages 70–78, Sept. 1992.

[45] A. M. Davis. *Software Requirements: Objects, Functions, and States*. Prentice Hall, Englewood Cliffs, NJ, 1993.

[46] A. M. Davis. Software prototyping. In *Advances in Computers, Vol. 40*, pages 39–63. Academic Press, 1995.

[47] J. S. Davis. Identification of errors in software requirements through use of automated requirements tools. *Information and Software Technology*, 31(9):472–476, Nov. 1989.

[48] T. DeMarco. *Structured analysis and system specification.* Yourdon Press, 1979.

[49] R. A. DeMillo et al. An extended overview of the MOTHRA testing environment. In *Workshop on Software Testing, Verification, and Analysis*, July 1988.

[50] R. A. DeMillo, R. A. Lipton, and F. G. Sayward. Hints on test data selection: Help for the practicing programmer. *IEEE Computer*, pages 34–41, Apr. 1978.

[51] L. Dobrica and E. Niemela. A survey on software architecture analysis methods. *IEEE Transactions on Software Engineering*, 28(7):638–653, 2002.

[52] R. H. Dunn. *Software defect removal.* McGraw-Hill Inc., 1984.

[53] J. Eder, G. Kappel, and M. Schrefl. Coupling and cohesion in object-oriented systems. Technical report, University of Klagenfurt, 1994.

[54] T. J. Emerson. A discriminating metric for module cohesion. In *Proc. of the 7th Int. Conf. on Software Engineering*, pages 294–303, 1984.

[55] D. Engler. Racerx: Effective, static detection of race conditions and deadlocks. Technical report, citeseer.ist.psu.edu/674744.html.

[56] D. Engler and M. Musuvathi. Static analysis versus software model checking for bug finding. In *5th Intl. Conference Verification, Model Checking and Abstract Interpretation (VMCAI '04)*, 2004.

[57] D. Evans. Static detection of dynamic memory errors. In *SIGPLAN Conference on Programming Language Design and Implementation (PLDI '96)*, 1996.

[58] M. E. Fagan. Design and code inspections to reduce errors in program development. *IBM System Journal*, (3):182–211, 1976.

[59] M. E. Fagan. Advances in software inspections. *IEEE Transactions on Software Engineering*, 12(7):744–751, July 1986.

[60] R. E. Fairly. *Software engineering concepts.* McGraw-Hill Inc., 1985.

[61] W. Farr. Software reliability modeling survey. In M. R. Lyu, editor, *Software Reliability Engineering*, pages 71–117. McGraw Hill and IEEE Computer Society, 1996.

[62] S. I. Feldman. Make—a program for maintaining computer programs. *Software Practice and Experience*, 9(3):255–265, March 1979.

[63] L. D. Fosdick and L. J. Osterweil. Dataflow analysis in software reliability. *ACM Computing Surveys*, 8(3), Sept. 1978.

[64] M. Fowler. *UML Distilled—A Brief Guide to the Standard Object Modeling Language*. Addison-Wesley Professional, 2003.

[65] M. Fowler, K. Beck, J. Brant, W. Opdyke, and D. Roberts. *Refactoring: Improving the Design of Existing Code*. Addison-Wesley, 1999.

[66] P. G. Frankl, S. Weiss, and E. J. Weyuker. ASSET: A system to select and evaluate tests. In *Proc. IEEE Conference on Software Tools*, pages 72–79, Apr. 1985.

[67] P. G. Frankl and E. J. Weyuker. Provable improvements on branch testing. *IEEE Transactions on Software Engineering*, 19(10):962–975, Oct. 1993.

[68] D. P. Freedman and G. M. Weinberg. *Handbook of Walkthroughs, Inspections, and Technical Reviews—Evaluating Programs, Projects, and Products*. Dorset House, 1990.

[69] E. Gamma, R. Helm, R. Johnson, and J. Vlissides. *Design Patterns—Elements of Reusable Object-Oriented Software*. Addison-Wesley Professional, 1995.

[70] T. Gilb and D. Graham. *Software Inspection*. Addison-Wesley, 1993.

[71] A. L. Goel. Software reliability models: Assumptions, limitations and applicability. *IEEE Transactions on Software Engineering*, SE-11:1411–1423, Dec. 1985.

[72] H. Gomma and D. B. H. Scott. Prototyping as a tool in the specification of user requirements. In *Fifth Int. Conf. on Software Engineering*, pages 333–341, 1981.

[73] J. Goodenough and S. L. Gerhart. Towards a theory of test data selection. *IEEE Transactions on Software Engineering*, SE-1:156–173, 1975.

[74] S. E. Goodman and S. T. Hedetniemi. *Introduction to the design and analysis of algorithms*. McGraw-Hill Inc., 1977.

[75] R. Grady. *Practical Software Metrics for Project Management and Process Improvement*. Prentice Hall, 1992.

[76] R. Grady and D. Caswell. *Software Metrics: Establishing a Company-wide Program*. Prentice Hall, 1987.

[77] R. B. Grady and T. V. Slack. Key lessons learned in achieving widespread inspection use. *IEEE Software*, pages 48–57, July 1994.

[78] E.M. Hall. *Managing Risk: Methods for Software Development and Enhancement*. Addison-Wesley, 1998.

[79] M. Halstead. *Elements of Software Science*. Eslevier North-Holland, New York, 1977.

[80] W. Harrison, K. Magel, R. Kluczny, and A. DeKock. Applying software complexity metrics to program maintenance. *IEEE Computer*, pages 65–79, Sept. 1982.

[81] M. J. Harrold and P. Kolte. Combat: A compiler based data flow testing system. In *Proc. of the Pacific Northwest Quality Conference*, pages 311–323, 1992.

[82] M. J. Harrold and G. Rothermel. Performing data flow testing on classes. In *ACM Foundations on Software Engineering*, pages 154–163, 1994.

[83] M. J. Harrold and M. L. Soffa. Interprocedural data flow testing. In *Proc. of the 3rd Testing, Analysis, and Verification Symposium*, pages 158–167, 1989.

[84] S. Henry and D. Kafura. Software structure metrics based on information flow. *IEEE Transactions on Software Engineering*, 7(5):510–518, 1981.

[85] S. Henry and D. Kafura. The evaluation of software systems' structures using quantitative software metrics. *Software Practice and Experience*, 14(6):561–573, June 1984.

[86] C. A. R. Hoare. An axiomatic basis for computer programming. *Communications of the ACM*, 12(3):335–355, 1969.

[87] D. Hovemeyer and W. Pugh. Finding bugs is easy. In *Proceedings, OOPSLA 2004; also findbugs.sourceforge.net*, 2004.

[88] M. Howard and D. LeBlanc. *Writing Secure Code (2nd ed.)*. Microsoft Press, 2002.

[89] W. E. Humphrey. *Managing the software process*. Addison Wesley, 1989.

[90] D. H. Hutchens and V. R. Basili. System structure analysis: clustering with data bindings. *IEEE Transactions on Software Engineering*, SE-11(8):749–757, Aug. 1985.

[91] IEEE. Software engineeing standards. Technical report, 1987.

[92] IEEE. IEEE software engineeing standards collection, 1994 edition. Technical report, 1994.

[93] IEEE. IEEE recommended practice for architectural description of software-intensive systems. Technical Report 1471-2000, 2000.

[94] International Standards Organization. Software engineering—product quality. part 1: Quality model. Technical Report ISO9126-1, 2001.

[95] I. Jacobson. *Object-oriented Software Engineering—A Use Case Driven Approach*. Addison Wesley Publishing Co., 1992.

[96] P. Jalote. *CMM in Practice—Processes for Executing Software Projects at Infosys*. Addison-Wesley, 1999.

[97] P. Jalote. *Software Project Management in Practice.* Addison-Wesley, 2002.

[98] P. Jalote and M. Haragopal. Overcoming the nah syndrome for inspection deployment. In *Proc. 20th Intl. Conf. On Software Engg.*, pages 371–378, Kyoto, Japan, 1998.

[99] P. Jalote, A. Palit, and P. Kurien. The timeboxing process model for iterative software development. In *Advances in Computers, Vol. 62*, pages 67–103. Academic Press, 2004.

[100] P. Jalote, A. Palit, P. Kurien, and V. T. Peethamber. Timeboxing: A process model for iterative software development. *The Journal of Systems and Software*, 70:117–127.

[101] P. Jalote and A. Saxena. Optimum control limits for employing statistical process control in software processes. *IEEE Transactions on Software Engineering*, 28(12):1126–1134, Dec 2002.

[102] P. Jalote and B. Vishal. Optimal resource allocation for the quality control process. In *Proceedings, Int. Symp. on Sw Reliability (ISSRE-2003)*, Denver, Colorado, 2003.

[103] R. E. Johnson and B. Foote. Designing reusable classes. *Journal of Object Oriented Programming*, 1(2):22–25, 1988.

[104] S.H. Kan. *Metrics and Models in Software Quality Engineering.* Addison Wesley, 1995.

[105] R. Kazman, M. Klein, M. Barbacci, T. Longstaff, H. Lipson, and J. Carriere. The architecture tradeoff analysis method. In *Proceedings, IEEE International Conference on Engineering of Complex Computer Systems (ICECCS)*, pages 68–78, Aug 1998.

[106] C. F. Kemerer. An empirical validation of software cost estimation models. *CACM*, 30(5):416–429, May 1987.

[107] T. Korson and J. D. Gregor. Understanding object-oriented: A unifying paradigm. *Commn. of the ACM*, 33(9):40–60, Sept. 1990.

[108] P. Kruchten. *The Rational Unified Process—An Introduction.* Addison-Wesley, 2000.

[109] J. W. Laski and B. Korel. A data flow oriented program testing strategy. *IEEE Transactions on Software Engineering*, 9(3):347–354, May 1983.

[110] H. Lichter, M. S. Jufschmidt, and H. Zullighoven. Prototyping in industrial software projects—bridging the gap between theory and practice. *IEEE Transactions on Software Engineering*, 20(11):825–832, Nov. 1994.

[111] W. Lie and S. Henry. Object-oriented metrics that predict maintainability. *Journal of Systems and Software*, 23(2):111–122, 1993.

[112] B. Liskov. Data abstraction and hierarchy. *SIGPLAN Notices*, 23(5), May 1988.

[113] G. C. Low and D. R. Jeffery. Function points in the estimation and evaluation of the software process. *IEEE Transactions on Software Engineering*, 16(1):64–71, Jan. 1990.

[114] M. Mantei. The effect of programming team structure on programming tasks. *Communications of the ACM*, 24(3), March 1981.

[115] A. P. Mathur. Mutation testing. In *Encyclopedia of Software Engineering*, pages 707–713. John Wiley, 1994.

[116] T. J. McCabe. A complexity measure. *IEEE Transactions on Software*, SE-2(4):308–320, Dec. 1976.

[117] M. Mock. Dynamic analysis: bottom-up. In *WODA 2003: ICSE Workshop on Dynamic Analysis*, Portland, OR, May 2003.

[118] D. E. Monarchi and G. I. Puhr. A research topology for object-oriented analysis and design. *Communications of the ACM*, 35(9):35–47, Sept. 1992.

[119] D.C. Montgomery. *Introduction to Statistical Quality Control, Third Edition*. John Wiley and Sons, 1996.

[120] J. D. Musa, A. Iannino, and K. Okumoto. *Software reliability—measurement, prediction, application*. McGraw Hill Book Company, 1987.

[121] G. Myers. *The art of software testing*. Wiley-Interscience, New York, 1979.

[122] P. G. Neumann. Risks to the public in computers and related systems. *Software engineering notes*, 13(2):5–18, April 1988.

[123] J. Offutt, S. Liu, A. Abdurazik, and P. Ammann. Generating test data from state-based specifications. *The Journal of Software Testing, Verification, and Reliability*, 13(1):25–53, March 2003.

[124] M. Page-Jones. *Fundamentals of Object-Oriented Design in UML*. Addison-Wesley, 1999.

[125] M.S. Phadke. Planning efficient software tests. *Crosstalk*, Oct 1997.

[126] L. H. Putnam. A general empirical solution to the macro software sizing and estimation problem. *IEEE Transactions on Software Engineering*, pages 345–361, July 1978.

[127] L. H. Putnam and W. Myers. *Industrial Strength Software: Effective Management Using Measurement*. IEEE Computer Society Press, 1997.

[128] R. Radice et al. A programming process architecture. *IBM Systems Journal*, 24(2), 1985.

[129] S. Rapps and E. J. Weyuker. Selecting software test data using data flow information. *IEEE Transactions on Software Engineering*, 11(4):367–375, Apr. 1985.

[130] D. T. Ross. Structured analysis: A language for communicating ideas. *IEEE Transactions on Software Engineering*, 3(1):16–34, Jan. 1977.

[131] J. Rothfeder. Its late, costly, incompetent—but try firing a computer system. In B. W. Boehm, editor, *Tutorial: Software Risk Management*, pages 63–64. IEEE Computer Society, 1989.

[132] W. W. Royce. Managing the development of large software systems. In *Proc. 9th Int. Conf. on Software Engineering (ICSE-9); originally in IEEE Wescon, Aug 1970*, pages 328–338. IEEE, 1987.

[133] J. Rumbaugh et al. *Object-Oriented Modeling and Design*. Prentice Hall, Englewood Cliffs, NJ, 1991.

[134] SEI (Software Engineering Institute). *The Capability Maturity Model: Guidelines for Improving the Software Process*. Addison-Wesley, 1995.

[135] M. Shaw and D. Garlan. *Software Architecture: Perspectives on an Emerging Discipline*. Prentice Hall, 1996.

[136] M. D. Smith and D. J. Robson. Object oriented programming: The problems of validation. *Proc. of 6th International IEEE Conference on Software Maintenance*, pages 272–282, Nov. 1990.

[137] M. D. Smith and D. J. Robson. A framework for testing object-oriented programs. *Jounal of Object-Oriented Programming (JOOP)*, pages 45–53, June 1992.

[138] W. P. Stevens, G. J. Myers, and L. Constantine. Structured design. *IBM Systems Journal*, 13(2), 1974.

[139] J.A. Swift. *Introduction to Modern Statistical Quality Control and Management*. St. Lucie Press, Florida, 1995.

[140] K. S. Trivedi. *Probability and statistics with reliability, queuing, and computer science applications, Second Edition*. Wiley-Interscience, New York, 2002.

[141] V. Vagela and P. Jalote. List of common bugs and programming practices to avoid them. Technical report, Indian Institute of Technology Kanpur, www.cse.iitk.ac.in/users/jalote/papers/CommonBugs.pdf, 2004.

[142] C. Watson and C. Felix. A method of programming measurement and estimation. *IBM Systems Journal*, 16(1), Jan. 1977.

[143] G. M. Weinberg and E. L. Schulman. Goals and performance in computer programming. *Human Factors*, 16(1):70–77, 1974.

[144] E. F. Weller. Lessons learned from three years of inspection data. *IEEE Software*, pages 38–53, Sept 1993.

[145] E. J. Weyuker. The evaluation of program based software test data adequacy criteria. *Communications of the ACM*, 31(6):668–675, June 1988.

[146] FE. J. Weyuker. The cost of data flow testing: An empirical study. *IEEE Transactions on Software Engineering*, 16(2):121–128, Feb 1990.

[147] D. Whitgift. *Methods and tools for software configuration management*. John Wiley and Sons, 1991.

[148] N. Wirth. Program development by stepwise refinement. *Communications of the ACM*, 14(4):221–227, April 1971.

[149] M. Woodward, M. Hennell, and D. Hedley. A measure of control flow complexity in program text. *IEEE Transactions on Software Engineering*, SE-5:45–50, Jan. 1979.

[150] Y. Xie and D. Engler. Using redundancies to find errors. *IEEE Transactions on Software Engineering*, 29(10):915–928, Oct 2003.

[151] S. S. Yau and J. S. Collofello. Design stability measures for software maintenance. *IEEE Transactions on Software Engineering*, 11(9):849–856, Sept. 1985.

[152] R. T. Yeh and P. Zave. Specifying software requirements. *Proceedings of the IEEE*, 68(9):1077–1088, Sept. 1980.

[153] B. H. Yin and J. W. Winchester. The establishment and use of measures to evaluate the quality of designs. *Software Engineering Notes*, 3:45–52, 1978.

[154] E. Yourdon and L. Constantine. *Structured design*. Prentice Hall, 1979.

[155] W. M. Zage and D. M. Zage. Evaluating design metrics on large-scale software. *IEEE Software*, pages 75–81, July 1993.

Index

of words are in each line. The following program has been written for this text formatter [73]:

```
alarm := false;
bufpos := 0;
fill := 0;
repeat
    inchar(c);
    if (c = BL) or (c = NL) or (c = EOF)
    then
        if bufpos != 0
        then begin
            if (fill + bufpos < MAXPOS) and (fill != 0)
            then begin
                outchar(BL);
                fill := fill + 1; end
            else begin
                outchar(NL);
                fill := 0; end;
            for k:=1 to bufpos do
                outchar(buffer[k]);
            fill := fill + bufpos;
            bufpos := 0; end
    else
        if bufpos = MAXPOS
        then alarm := true
        else begin
            bufpos := bufpos + 1;
            buffer[bufpos] := c; end
until alarm or (c = EOF);
```

For this program, do the following:

(a) Select a set of test cases using the black-box testing approach. Use as many techniques as possible and select test cases for special cases using the "error guessing" method.

(b) Select a set of test cases that will provide 100% branch coverage.

(c) Select a set of test cases that will satisfy the all-defs and the all-uses criteria (except the ones that are not feasible).

(d) Create a few mutants by simple transformations. Then select a set of test cases that will kill these mutants.

(e) Suppose that this program is written as a procedure. Write a driver for testing this procedure with the test cases selected in (a) and (b).

Clearly specify the format of the test cases and how they are used by the driver.

10. Suppose three numbers A, B, and C are given in ascending order representing the lengths of the sides of a triangle. The problem is to determine the type of the triangle (whether it is isosceles, equilateral, right, obtuse, or acute). Consider the following program written for this problem:

```
read(a, b, c);
if (a < b) or (b < c) then
    print("Illegal inputs");
    return;
if (a=b) or (b=c) then
    if (a=b) and (b=c) then print("equilateral triangle")
    else print("isosceles triangle")
else begin
    a := a*a; b := b*b; c := c*c;
    d := b+c;
    if (a = d) then print("right triangle")
    else if (a<d) then print("acute triangle")
    else print("obtuse triangle");
end;
```

For this program, perform the same exercises as in the previous problem.

11. What are the limitations of the reliability model discussed in the chapter for using it for estimating the reliability of a product?

12. Suppose you want to predict the reliability of a product at the time of the release using the model discussed in the chapter. What data will you collect and when for this, and what changes (if any) will you make in your testing?

13. Define some data flow criteria for testing an entire class (i.e., not just for testing the methods independently) (refer to [82]).

14. In your next project, collect the defects in the last stages of testing. Perform the cause-effect analysis for these defects leading to some actions on how you should do things differently in the future for reducing the errors you make.

15. Another method for evaluating software reliability is to use the Mill's seeding approach. In this method some faults are seeded in the program, and reliability is assessed based on how many of these seeded faults are detected during testing. Develop a simple reliability model based on this approach. Define your parameters, and give a formula for estimating the reliability and the number of faults remaining in the system. Also discuss the drawbacks and limitations of this model?

Case Studies

Here we briefly discuss the test plans and strategy for the two case studies. The detailed test case specifications for system testing are available from the Web site.

Test Plan for Case Study 1 (Course Scheduling)

This document describes the plan for testing the course scheduling software. All major testing activities are specified here; additional testing may be scheduled later, if necessary.

1. Test Units

In this project we will perform two levels of testing: unit testing and system testing. Because the system is small, it is felt that there is no need for elaborate integration testing. The basic units to be tested are:

> Modules to input file-1
> Modules to input file-2
> Modules for scheduling

In addition, some other units may be chosen for testing. The testing for these different units will be done independently.

2. Features to be Tested

All the functional features specified in the requirements document will be tested. No testing will be done for the performance, as the response time requirement is quite weak.

3. Approach for Testing

For unit testing, structural testing based on the branch coverage criterion will be used. The goal is to achieve branch coverage of more than 95%. The CCOV coverage analyzer tool will be used to determine the coverage. System testing will be largely functional in nature. The focus is on invalid and valid cases, boundary values, and special cases.

4. Test Deliverables

The following documents are required (besides this test plan):

- Unit test report for each unit

- Test case specification for system testing

- Test report for system testing

- Error report

The test case specification for system testing has to be submitted for review before system testing commences.

5. Test Case Specifications for System Testing

For test case specifications we specify all test cases that are used for system testing. First, the different conditions that need to be tested, along with the test cases used for testing those conditions and the expected outputs are given. Then the data files used for testing are given. The test cases are specified with respect to these data files. The test cases have been selected using the functional approach. The goal is to test the different functional requirements, as specified in the requirements document. Test cases have been selected for both valid and invalid inputs. The entire test case specifications is available from from the Web site.

Case Study 2—PIMS

The test plan for PIMS is similar to the previous one. It also follows a two level testing—unit and then system. Unit testing is performed by the programmers, and no unit test reports are mandated. As the overall plan is the same, we do not discuss it here. We just discuss some aspects of planning for system test cases.

System testing would begin with the development team releasing applications to the test team. The sequence of activities is:

- Development team does a unit testing of the application, fixes identified problems and hands over the environment to the Test team.

- Test team runs some quick checks (e.g., that the system installs, that it can take inputs) and some tests for critical functionality. If 80% of these tests pass, then the application is considered ready for system testing, otherwise it is returned to the developers.

- The test team runs the test cases.